Also by George Howe Colt

The Big House: A Century in the Life of an American Summer Home
November of the Soul: The Enigma of Suicide

BROTHERS

George Howe Colt
On His Brothers and Brothers in History

Scribner
New York   London   Toronto   Sydney   New Delhi

SCRIBNER
A Division of Simon & Schuster, Inc.
1230 Avenue of the Americas
New York, NY 10020

First Scribner hardcover edition November 2012

SCRIBNER and design are registered trademarks of The Gale Group, Inc. used under license by Simon & Schuster, Inc., the publisher of this work.

For information about special discounts for bulk purchases, please contact Simon & Schuster Special Sales at 1-866-506-1949 or business@simonandschuster.com.

The Simon & Schuster Speakers Bureau can bring authors to your live event. For more information or to book an event contact the Simon & Schuster Speakers Bureau at 1-866-248-3049 or visit our website at www.simonspeakers.com.

Designed by Carla Jayne Jones

Manufactured in the United States of America

1   3   5   7   9   10   8   6   4   2

Library of Congress Control Number: 2012027349

ISBN 978-1-4165-4777-8
ISBN 978-1-4516-9766-7 (ebook)

For Harry, Ned, and Mark

Contents

BROTHERS

Chapter One
The Colt Boys

If the handful of black-and-white snapshots that remain from my childhood is any indication, it's a wonder I didn't end up with a permanent crick in my neck from literally and figuratively looking up to my older brother. Harry was born twenty months before me, and I worshiped him with an intensity that must have been both flattering and bewildering to the worshipee. I didn't want to be *like* Harry; I wanted to *be* Harry. I cocked my coonskin cap exactly the way he did when we played Daniel Boone; I made the same *pshew-pshew* sounds he did when I pulled the trigger on my silver plastic six-shooter; I punched the pocket of my baseball glove every time he punched his. When he woke me in the middle of the night one Christmas Eve and invited me downstairs to open presents while our parents slept, I followed. When he said he could help me get rid of my loose tooth, I let him tie it to the playroom doorknob and slam the door. He was my older brother and I would have agreed to anything he proposed; I would have followed him anywhere. And so, one spring evening not long before I turned six, as we lay in our matching twin beds, when Harry suggested that we run away from home, I said yes.

The following morning before dawn, I woke to find him standing next to my bed in his pajamas, clutching to his chest the gray metal strongbox in which he kept his baseball cards. I tiptoed behind him down the back stairs, through the kitchen, and into the garage. Harry opened the front door to the old blue Ford, climbed in, and shimmied over to the driver's seat. I scrambled up next to him. We sat awhile in silence before he unlocked the strongbox and offered me some of the saltines with which he had filled it the night before. (To make room, he had left behind all but his most precious Red Sox cards.) We chewed our crackers and stared through the windshield at the closed garage door. I don't remember what we said, or indeed whether we said anything at all. I don't remember wondering where, if anywhere, we were going, or how far we could get in our pajamas, or what we would eat when the saltines ran out. I certainly didn't ask my brother. Because I believed Harry could do anything, I wouldn't have been surprised if the car had somehow started, the garage door had opened, and we'd sailed off down Village Avenue, our quiet, tree-lined street in suburban Boston, and into the sky.

*   *   *

It never occurred to me to ask my brother *why* we were running away. Ours was not the kind of home from which most people would have thought it necessary, or even advisable, to run away. We lived in a comfy old brown house equipped with a corrugated cardboard fort big enough to stand up in; enough wooden blocks to construct several castles simultaneously; a banister to speed our journey from the second floor to the first; and a bathroom in which every fixture—sink, toilet, and tub—was jet-black, a color scheme so unusual that neighborhood kids were always knocking on our door, asking to use the facilities. We had a backyard big enough for games of catch and a sprinkler to run through on hot summer days. Beyond our fence lay a world that seemed designed for a six-year-old boy: houses close together to maximize candy collection on Halloween; enough kids within shouting distance to field a baseball team; sidewalks that could get our bikes every place worth getting to, their curbs so eroded by generations of Raleighs and Schwinns that we didn't have to dismount when crossing a street; and a huge chestnut tree that provided ammunition for fights, pretend money for card games, and the sheer pleasure of peeling off the rubbery, lime-green skin to uncover the nut within, shiny and polished as a violin.

Best of all, within a stone's throw of our house—if Harry was doing the throwing—there were three places that made our otherwise tame neighborhood seem as thrilling as the wilderness depicted on any explorer's map. Four houses to the east lay the Norfolk County Jail, an ivy-covered granite hulk in which, our mother told us, two prisoners with Italian names I could never remember had been imprisoned before being sent to the electric chair in 1927, an event whose macabre allure still lingered in the air as I hurried past on my way to the library thirty-five years later. (I could never understand why bad guys were always "sent" to the electric chair, which made it sound as if the post office were somehow involved and begged the all-important question of what happened after they reached their destination.) Across the street from the jail lay the graveyard, where we played freeze tag, hide-and-seek, and war, taking care not to step on the bulges in front of the lichen-embossed head-stones, bulges we assumed were the bellies of the dead. A block to the south of us, the tidy lawns gave way to a morass of vines and skunk cabbage we called the swamp, an outpost of botanical anarchy that in well-manicured Dedham seemed as exotic as the Black Lagoon from which the proverbial Creature emerged, and in whose tea-colored water we'd wade in search of smaller but equally slimy creatures. These three land-marks allowed us to believe that we lived in a dangerous world, a world in which an escaped convict, a vengeful ghost, or a hideous monster might appear at any moment. I remember watching *Swiss Family Robinson* and being impressed that the island on which they had shipwrecked somehow encompassed mountains, waterfalls, beaches, caves, lakes, and quicksand (a wealth of natural wonders ecologically unlikely to be found in one place, I later realized). With its prison, its graveyard, and its swamp—which, I felt sure, contained at least a dollop of quicksand—our neighborhood had been no less blessed.

Even without these attractions, I wouldn't have been inclined to run away from home. Dedham was the first place my family had lived long enough to *call* home. Our father was a businessman, and whenever he was promoted, we moved to a new town. (In those days, you went where the company sent you or you wouldn't be with the company for long.) Before Dedham, we had lived in Pittsburgh, El Paso, and Philadelphia—three different places in five years. We had been in Dedham for more than two years, the longest we had ever spent in one place, and I assumed we would be there forever. Dad built us a sandbox and installed a swing set. He and Mum spent Sunday afternoons on their hands and knees, putting in a brick patio. They planted a dogwood tree and a bed of pachysandra. For the first time, our family, too, seemed to be putting down roots.

Nor were our mother and father the type of parents one ran away from. Mum did all the things mothers in the fifties were supposed to do, but she did them a little differently. She made us peanut-butter-and-jelly sandwiches but cut them into triangles and trapezoids we reassembled like puzzle pieces before eating. She read aloud from Mother Goose and Dr. Seuss—and Oscar Wilde. She drew stick figures and animals with us, as well as squiggles we had to turn into pictures. Or she'd draw a face without letting us see it, fold the paper, then pass it to one of us, who'd draw a torso and arms. That person would fold the paper and pass it to the next brother, who would draw the legs. And so on. We'd unfold the paper to find a goofy-looking, cobbled-together character that made us howl with laughter. She sang us songs about fathers buying mockingbirds and children selling shoes to barefooted angels, as well as songs about coal miners striking, southern women done wrong by their men, calves on their way to the slaughterhouse, young lords poisoned by their lovers—songs she'd learned from the copies of *Sing Out!* that lay on the coffee table. When she and Dad went out to dinner parties on Friday nights, she wore muumuus she'd made from Indian-print bedspreads, hoop earrings, scarab bracelets, and scarlet lipstick that made her look like a gypsy. Mum was what the neighbors called "artistic." She painted. She made Christmas ornaments of balsa wood. She played the accordion. She gave guitar lessons to neighborhood teenagers. Sunday-afternoon strollers heard the sounds of "Down in the Valley" and "This Little Light of Mine" wafting from our living room. After one winter snowstorm Mum came out to play with us. By lunchtime she had sculpted a buxom lady so enormous and lifelike it frightened me—surely the first snowwoman our town had ever seen.

Dad was like our friends' fathers, only handsomer, funnier, and more athletic. His arrival home from work was the big event of our day. (We didn't really know what he did when he took the train into Boston each morning—it had something to do with bottled gas—but each spring we swelled with pride when he supplied the tank of helium that enabled the balloons at the school fair to fly.) The moment he came through the door and set down his briefcase, we swarmed him, clamoring to have him squeeze our nonexistent biceps ("Feel my muscle!"), vying for the airplane rides he gave us as he lay on his back and held us aloft on his stockinged feet, pleading for another knock-knock joke. Saturday mornings, we'd pile into the car for errands: the dump, the Esso station, the paper store, and what Dad called the package store—a Massachusetts euphemism that had me imagining shelves of empty brown boxes. (It never failed to surprise me when, at home, Dad would reach into the bag he'd bought there and, like a magician, pull out a frosted bottle of Gilbey's gin and several cartons of Kents.) Fall afternoons, Harry and I sat on either side of Dad in the vast cement horseshoe of Harvard Stadium, cheering the football team I assumed Harry would play for someday. After the final gun, as the sun dipped below the stadium wall, I followed Harry onto the field, where we beseeched the players to sign our programs or give us their sweat-softened chin straps. On Sundays, we helped Dad rake leaves into a pile on the sidewalk, where he'd burn them, one of dozens of piles that smoked like signal fires along the length of Village Avenue.

Dad was a kind of Superman to us, but much cooler than the cape-and-tights-wearing one on TV. Although he couldn't fly, he could pinch out a candle flame with his bare fingers; place a quarter on his bent elbow and, a second later, make it appear in his hand; throw a tennis ball so high we thought it would never come down. In the car, in those pre-seat-belt days, whenever we came to a red light or had to make a sudden stop, he'd reach his arm across the front seat to keep us from pitching forward. No matter how violent the potential crash, we believed his arm would keep us safe. He was always willing to give us piggyback rides, quiz us on our state capitals, take us sledding, tighten our hockey skates, lead a game of crack the whip, have a snowball fight. It seemed that everything important to Harry and me, we learned from Dad: how to ride a bike, how to skate, how to catch a ball. Each evening after work, he'd throw us pop-ups in the backyard. No matter how many times we pleaded for "just one more," Dad would always throw us another until, looking up for the ball, we noticed that the first star had appeared in the sky. Everything Dad owned seemed redolent of the manly, grown-up world to which Harry and I aspired: the monogrammed money clip from which he'd extract a few green bills; the silver Zippo that gave off a pungent whiff of gasoline as he flicked the thumbwheel and lit another Kent; the badger-hair brush he swirled in the foaming wooden tub of Old Spice soap as we watched him shave; the parrot-headed can opener with which he punched two triangles in the top of a can of beer; the Purple Heart he'd won in the war and kept in a cigar box; the frayed black high school letter sweater in which we buried our faces as we threw our arms around him for a hug.

Perhaps because he had the same name—in our extended family he was known as Little Harry or Harry Third—my brother seemed like a pocket-size version of our father. I regarded him with hardly less awe. Like Dad, Harry was smart. He knew the twelve times table. He got all As in school. Like Dad, Harry seemed effortlessly good at sports. He could throw a spiral, pitch a fastball, ride a bike faster than anyone else I knew. In games, Harry was always the first pick, and whichever team picked him usually won. He reminded me of Chip Hilton, the straight-arrow star of the football, basketball, and baseball teams at Valley Falls High in the books by Clair Bee that he and I loved. At recess, I watched as Harry and the older boys played flag football, his plastic belt, with its twin, trailing pennants, looking like some sort of below-the-waist military honor. After school, they played Russian Shmuck, an ersatz football game presumably christened in a spasm of Cold War patriotism, in which one boy ran with the ball while everyone else tried to tackle him. I longed to be as tough as Harry. He and his friends skipped rocks in the street. They lugged shirt-fuls of chestnuts to the graveyard and, crouching behind the headstones, pelted one another with the knobby brown nuts. Harry never cried when Mum dabbed Mercurochrome on his skinned knees. On Saturday mornings, looking like a lumpy knight in his helmet and shoulder pads, he went across town to the field near the Catholic church in East Dedham, where he played tackle football on a real team with real uniforms. I had read about how, in ancient times, an army sent forth its strongest warrior to challenge the enemy's champion. If ever our neighborhood had to send forth a champion to defend us, I knew it would be Harry.

Harry would never have put himself forth for the job. Unlike Dad, who was always making people laugh, Harry was quiet, pensive, vigilant. As a baby he had rarely cried, and when he was a toddler he had been so well-behaved that the elderly woman who babysat him in El Paso said that he was "like the return of the Christ child." In nursery school his teachers wrote to our parents, saying that while Harry was clearly a smart boy, they were concerned that he spoke so little. When I was born, according to Mum, Harry showed no signs of jealousy—nary a tweak, nary a howl-provoking pinch. As I grew, he never lorded it over me that he knew the multiplication tables or that he could hang upside down from the monkey bars. When we played cowboys and Indians, he never made me be the Indian; we were both cowboys. When I began first grade, our parents made it clear to Harry that he was to look out for his little brother. He took his charge to heart. Each morning, we'd ride our bikes the half mile to school together, Harry glancing over his shoulder to make sure I hadn't fallen too far behind. At recess, seeing him across the playground with the older kids, I felt safe. Whenever I walked alone past the jail on my way to the library, I was tempted to run, but with Harry alongside, I dared look over at its arched, Gothic windows, hoping to see—and afraid I'd see—someone looking back at me from behind the iron bars. When he was nine, Harry was named to the Safety Patrol, the highest honor our little four-grade school could bestow. Although I missed riding to school with him—his duties demanded that he get there early—I was recompensed by the pride I felt as I saw him on High Street, the Safety Patrol's glistening white plastic sashes crisscrossing his chest. As he waved me and my friends across the road, I knew not to say hi, knew not to distract him from his lifesaving work, but I didn't need to: everyone knew he was my brother.

It amazed me that this godlike creature deigned to consort with a mere mortal like me. Harry let me watch as he sorted his baseball cards on our bedroom floor. He let me play with the plastic figurine of Willie Mays he'd gotten for Christmas. When he and his friends played baseball in the jailfield, a swatch of weeds that lay in the shadow of the jailhouse wall, he let me tag along. When I called "Wait up," he waited up. If, occasionally, he went off with his friends and it was clear I wasn't to follow, I never once heard him say, "Let's ditch him." When I asked him whether a watermelon would grow inside me if I swallowed a watermelon seed, he told me the truth. At night, in the room we shared above the kitchen, Harry and I whispered across the gulf between our beds. Unlike Harry, I was a garrulous fellow, so it was mostly me asking questions: "Who would you rather be, Alan Shepard or John Glenn?" "Who do you think is better, Eddie Bressoud or Pumpsie Green?" (A moot point, given that the entire Boston Red Sox lineup was prodigiously inept in the early sixties.) "Who do you like more, Tommy or Cubby? . . . Kennedy or Nixon? . . . Spanky or Alfalfa?" Harry's reticence made everything he said all the more valuable; his opinions I took as facts; his answers became the answers I gave my friends when they asked me those same questions. I recently came across my third-grade album, which contained snapshots of my classmates and a section (titled "I LIKE") in which I'd listed my favorite sport (Russian Shmuck), movies (scary), TV shows (*Little Rascals*). Under "My Pal," I had written, in capital letters three times the size of my other answers, HARRY COLT.

I was so preoccupied with my older brother that I sometimes forgot I had a younger brother. Ned was born two years and one day after me. Our mother told us that as the due date approached, the obstetrician offered to induce labor so that we could share a birthday. Mum declined, insisting that she wanted us each to have our own special day to celebrate. When she told me the story, I felt a twinge of relief. I would have been proud to share a birthday with Harry, I realized, but I wasn't sure I wanted to share one with Ned. Indeed, as Ned grew, I took every opportunity to align myself with my older brother and to distance myself from my younger one. I took satisfaction in the fact that I was closer in age—by a mere four months—to Harry than to Ned; that I looked more like dark-haired Harry than like blond-haired Ned; that Harry and I were right-handed but Ned was a lefty. I focused on the things Harry could do, on the things

Ned couldn't. Ned couldn't hang from the monkey bars. He didn't know how to pump. He couldn't ride a bike without training wheels. The only board games he could play were Candy Land and Chutes and Ladders, his only card game was War. He didn't know the capital of North Dakota. He didn't know what seven times twelve equaled. He didn't even go to school. The fact that Ned was too young to do these things—and that I had only recently learned to do them myself—didn't prevent me from scorning him for his ineptitude. Oh, the smug triumph as I trailed in Harry's wake to the jailfield, leaving Ned behind in the sandbox!

There were times, however, when Harry made it clear I wasn't to tag along, times my own friends were busy, times when there was no one to play with but Ned. Much as I hated to admit it, Ned's world, I learned, had its consolations. I began to see the things that Ned *could* do. Ned could spend hours in the sandbox, sculpting mountains, constructing twig houses, laying out pebble lakes, and building sand roadways over which we steered his extensive collection of Matchbox cars. Ned could fluff up the sheets on his bed to create a vast, wrinkled Arctic over which our plastic army men could roam. Under his imaginative eye, a couch became an island, a pillow a pirate ship, the floor a storm-tossed ocean, a table a fort, an Oriental rug a jungle for plastic lions to prowl. (Ned could make the pinkie-size figures in the crèche Mum put out at Christmas come alive for games of cops and robbers: "Cheese it, Mary, it's the fuzz!") Occasionally, when Ned wasn't around, I'd try it myself, but under my gaze, the fluffed-up bedsheets just looked messy; the rug remained a two-dimensional swatch of wool. Ned was the Frank Lloyd Wright of block castles, Lincoln Log cabins, Erector-set towers, and playing-card houses. In winter, Harry's snow forts—thick, icy walls terraced with shelves for spare snowballs—were designed for battle. Form followed function. Ned's creations—elaborate architectural structures with distinct rooms and seating areas—were designed with aesthetics in mind. When a snowball fight broke out, he got creamed.

To Harry, the outdoors was raw material for makeshift baseball diamonds and impromptu football fields; to Ned it was an alluring wilderness filled with extraordinary creatures: lightning bugs he studied in his cupped hands; ladybugs he helped fly away home from his fingertips; fat gray squirrels he tiptoed toward in hopes of taming; miniature toads he scooped up in the backyard, and, unlike me, didn't drop in disgust when they peed. He wasn't afraid to touch the swollen, pink, ribbony worms that surfaced on the lawn after a rain. At the beach, he was less interested in going fishing than in roaming the tide pools, tracking down the crabs and clams we used for bait. I associated Harry with the jailfield, Ned with the swamp. Ducking under vines, stepping over rotting logs, I'd follow along, pretending I was just as interested as he was in finding turtles and polliwogs. One Easter, our mother bought us an incubator, a plastic, domed receptacle that resembled the spaceship in which the infant Superman had flown from Krypton to Kansas. Mr. Romaine, our roly-poly, porkpie-hatted milkman, supplied us with three fertilized eggs, which we nestled carefully in the incubator's bowl. After a few days, Harry and I were satisfied with brief daily checks on our way through the living room; Ned sat there, hour after hour, his face illuminated by the unearthly fluorescent glow of the heat lamp, waiting for the eggs to hatch. They never did. Eventually, we gave up and cracked one open to find a glutinous, feathery soup surrounding an embryonic claw. Ned was crushed.

In some ways I had the best of both worlds: an older brother to look up to, a younger brother to boss around. (I was like the common denominator I learned about when we studied fractions.) There was only one problem—Ned showed no desire to be bossed. When I tried to make him play the bad guy in games of war, when I tried to talk him into trading a Hershey Bar for a Tootsie Pop at Halloween, when I tried to dragoon him into making the Kool-Aid for "our" stand out front, he invariably balked. Although the thought of contradicting my older brother never crossed my mind, my younger brother had no problem contradicting me. Or anyone else, for that matter. The boy who showed infinite patience when building a castle of blocks or stalking a gray squirrel could be remarkably stubborn, and was often sent to his room, where he'd slam the door behind him. When our mother gave guitar lessons on Sunday afternoon, Ned would hear the sound of strumming, rush into the living room, pull on her arm, and plead—"Mummeee, Mummeee"—for her to stop. He rarely took no for an answer. When he was five, he happened to throw a tantrum within range of our grandfather, whose parenting technique, based on the belief that children should be seen and not heard, had been honed in the pre-Spock 1920s. He suggested that Mum put Ned into a cold shower, clothes and all. "That will cool him off," he observed. Indeed, Ned was shocked into momentary silence. But he never forgot the humiliation, and it would be many years before he forgave our mother.

In the early sixties, the world sorted cleanly into good and evil: Americans and Russians, Americans and Germans, cowboys and Indians, cops and robbers. In the books I read and the TV shows I watched, there were heroes and villains and nothing in between: Robin Hood and the Sheriff of Nottingham, Alfalfa and Spike, Rocky and Boris, Bullwinkle and Natasha, Popeye and Bluto, Kennedy and Khrushchev, Superman and Lex Luthor, Fenton Hardy and the swarthy crooks of Bayport, Zorro and an endless supply of chubby, mustachioed Mexicans. On Saturday mornings, after gorging on cartoons, Harry, Ned, and I watched professional wrestling and reveled in its comforting moral divide: Killer Kowalski, the crew-cut villain rumored to have ripped off an opponent's ear with his famous claw hold, versus Bruno Sammartino, the courtly gentleman who, turning away from his opponent to listen politely to the referee, inevitably got a folding chair to the back of the head—no matter how loudly we yelled at him to turn around; Gorilla Monsoon, the pointy-bearded "Manchurian giant" who looked a lot like Fidel Castro, the Cuban dictator we saw on the news, versus Haystack Calhoun, the gentle "man-mountain" who wore overalls, a T-shirt as big as a sheet, and a lucky horseshoe necklace. The sole exception to this black-white dichotomy seemed to be Sacco and Vanzetti, whose names made them sound like tag-team wrestlers and not the Italian anarchists who had languished in the Norfolk County Jail. It was never entirely clear to me whether they were good guys or bad guys.

I had no doubt which kind of guy I wanted to be. Harry was good, and I wanted to be good, too. On TV, when Miss Jean, the disconcertingly pert hostess of *Romper Room*, urged us to be a Do-Bee and not a Don't-Bee (*Do Bee a milk drinker, Don't Bee a milk waster*), I pledged myself to Do-Bee-ism, thinking that if I were good enough, when Miss Jean peered into her Magic Mirror at the end of the show and "saw" some of the children watching at home (*I see Denise . . . I see Jimmy . . .*), she might someday see me. Each month, as I read the latest issue of *Highlights,* I turned first to "Goofus and Gallant," a cartoon in which two curiously named boys reacted differently to the same situation (*Goofus takes the last apple; Gallant shares his orange*). I wanted to be Gallant, the straight-A student who did the dishes without being asked, picked up litter from the sidewalk, and went through life leaving a trail of little old ladies beaming in his wake. I certainly didn't want to be Goofus, the sullen ne'er-do-well who refused to take out the trash, played with matches, and seemed destined to end up, like those Italian anarchists, in the Norfolk County Jail. Although the evidence suggested otherwise—indeed, Gallant's mother and father could often be seen smiling proudly in the background, while Goofus's parents frowned anxiously—I assumed that Goofus and Gallant were brothers. (If so, they would have made ideal subjects for a nature-versus-nurture study.) It was clear that in life, brothers divided into Goofuses and Gallants. Harry, of course, was Gallant. I worried that left me to be Goofus.

And so I tried even harder to be Gallant. In games, I always wanted to be the cowboy, not the Indian; the American, not the German; Robin Hood, not the Sheriff of Nottingham. My children make gagging sounds when I tell them the story of how one day in kindergarten, after the teacher stepped out of the classroom for a moment, admonishing us to "be good," I whispered to the other children, without a scintilla of irony, "Let's be good as *gold.*" (It is a testament to 1950s conformity that my classmates didn't immediately stab me to death with their freshly sharpened Eberhard Faber #2 pencils.) I knew that things would go more smoothly if we behaved, and it was important to me that things go smoothly. I disliked confrontation. I learned that if you were polite to grown-ups, they liked you. And I desperately wanted people to like me. No matter how many times I heard my father say "You can't please all the people all the time," I secretly believed I'd be the exception.

In elementary school I became an even more shameless teacher's pet. It wasn't enough that I knew the answer; I had to be the one to give it, and I had to be first to raise my hand. Before the teacher was halfway through the question, I'd shoot my arm into the air, staking my claim as forcefully as a marine planting the flag at Iwo Jima, waving my hand with a frantic scrubbing motion, fingers splayed to provide an even more visible target, leaning forward so I was as close to the teacher as possible, fanny lifting off my seat, my body on the diagonal, my mouth, fixed in a rictus of need, emitting an occasional sympathy-seeking whimper. I made a point of finishing quizzes and tests first, placing my pencil in its narrow wooden trough and folding my hands on my desk. I lived for spelling bees, when the class lined up in front of the blackboard and one by one, with each mistake, sat back down, until I alone was left standing; for PTA nights, when my parents, after hearing from my teacher how smart I was, would leave a dime in my desk; and for report cards, when with ostentatious humility I'd unfold the mustard-colored paper to find row upon row of carefully inked As like a fleet of sailboats, broken only by a lone C for penmanship. (In my haste to be first, I tended to scribble.) I must have been insufferable.

My brown-nosing wasn't entirely an act. Like Harry, I loved school. Like Harry, I loved reading. Almost every afternoon, I rode my bike down Village Avenue, between the Scylla and Charybdis of the jail and the graveyard, to the library, where I'd borrow seven books, the maximum allowed and the most I could pile in my bike basket without spilling. At home, I'd ferry a glass of Nestlé chocolate milk and a stack of Oreos out to the wooden picnic table in the backyard, and work my way through the cookies, the milk, and the books. Next day, I'd ride down to the library and borrow seven more. I loved books, but I also loved the librarian's nod of approval as she stamped the due dates, the impressed looks I got from grown-ups when I told them what I was reading, the pride on my mother's face when the teacher told her that I was so much further along than the other first-graders that I would skip directly to second grade. I remember the self-satisfaction I felt when I overheard the word *precocious* applied to my name. (And the mortification I felt when, one afternoon in the car with my brothers, I mispronounced the word *Brazil,* rhyming it with hazel, and our babysitter, whom I adored, couldn't stop giggling.) When I was eight, our mother gave us elaborate Christmas presents that she had spent much of the fall making. Ned's was a vast wooden layout for his treasured Matchbox cars, with handpainted streets, scale-model railroad tracks, and mirror lakes. Mine was a massive plywood desk, painted gray. As we entered the living room on Christmas morning and saw the gifts, we immediately knew whose was whose. Ned and I loved our presents; we each got what we wanted. But I also recall the pride I took in knowing our mother had recognized that I was the good student, the worker, the bookish one, and that—however delightful my brother's present might be—Ned was the one who played.

Excelling in school, of course, was one way to get attention. Talking was another. If Harry got attention by virtue of his quiet excellence and Ned by his obstreperousness, I got it by gabbing. My tendency to loquaciousness was reinforced by my size. From kindergarten on, I was the smallest kid in my class, the one school photographers invariably placed in the front row center, fanning my classmates out around me as if I were the hub in a Busby Berkeley extravaganza. After skipping first grade I was, relatively speaking, even smaller, which forced me to depend even more on my mouth. When, in the sixth grade, I finally encountered a classmate shorter than I, a sweet round Argentinian boy we called Pygmy, I was both pleased and dismayed. If I couldn't be big enough to pose a serious threat on the football field, I wanted to be the smallest. It was another way of being noticed.

I also talked a lot because I loved words. Almost as much as I liked playing sports, I liked the vocabulary that came with them. Even before the actual game took place, there were the rhymes we used to choose up sides: the traditional *eeny meeny miny moe*; the slightly more comprehensible *Engine engine number nine, going down Chicago line. If the train goes off the track, do you want your money back?* (I always said yes; I couldn't imagine turning down money, however hypothetical it might be); and the transgressively violent *My mother and your mother were hanging out clothes. My mother socked your mother right in the nose. What color blood came out?* (I always chose an obscure hue—scarlet, maroon, burgundy—to prolong the rhyme and to show off my vocabulary). Then there was the comforting, ambient chatter of the game itself. The way you called *Swing batter swing* at the right moment, with the right inflection, at a volume that didn't call attention to yourself but was nevertheless audible, could almost compensate for lack of actual skill. And if you passed muster on the more elementary exhortations—dropping the *r* with just the right nonchalance on old chestnuts like *Hey battah battah* or *Little peppah, little peppah*—you might graduate to something more provocative, like *We want a pitcher, not a belly itcher,* or the koanlike *We want a pitcher, not a glass of water.* On summer nights, when we played hide-and-seek or kick the can, I thrilled to the polysyllabic wonder of what was surely the most beautiful word in the English language, a word that had the power to summon children from the darkness like bats at dusk: *Oleyoleyincomefree.*

Part of the reason I craved attention was that with three young boys in one house, I harbored the suspicion that there might not be enough to go around and I'd better make sure I got my fair share—or, preferably, a little more. Harry, Ned, and I rarely fought physically, but there seemed to be nothing we didn't contest: who found the most foil-wrapped chocolate eggs in the backyard on Easter; who collected the most Halloween candy; who could make a popsicle last the longest; who got the first look at the Sears Christmas catalogue; who got the Sunday funnies first; who had the best godparents (i.e., whose godparents gave the best presents). Stakes were especially high at the dinner table. Who got the biggest chicken breast? Who got the biggest piece of bacon on his cheese dream? Who got the most cherries in his fruit cocktail? Who got the lamb chop with the marrow—a substance that, according to my mother, would make us as strong as Charles Atlas? Who got the largest slice of pie? (In a vain attempt to forestall quarrels, our mother cut portions so nearly identical it would have taken a micrometer to tell them apart.) Who got praised for turning in a "soldier's plate"? Who ended up holding the biggest end of the wishbone?

Our Holy Grail was the prize at the bottom of the cereal box. In theory, it went to the brother into whose bowl it was poured during the natural order of things—which meant that each of us usually gulped down two helpings, in hopes of eating our way to the prize. In practice, things were more elemental. Ned soon deduced that he could improve his odds by shaking the cereal box upside down before filling his bowl, so the prize might resettle near the top. Whereupon I took to reaching directly into the box, digging down through the sticky layers of Sugar Smacks or Frosted Flakes till my fingers found the plastic geegaw that rested near the bottom. Eventually Ned and I cut to the chase, sneaking into the kitchen to rip open a new box of cereal before we'd finished the old one and fish out the sought-after treasure, which was abandoned as soon as it had been brandished in the losing brother's face.

At the time, I didn't think of our fraternal skirmishing as remarkable. It seemed as inevitable and instinctive as breathing. And if someone had suggested to me that wrestling for the prize at the bottom of the cereal box might have been, as a therapist would suggest to me many years later, a way of vying for the attention of our parents, I would have snorted incredulously. But looking back, I can see that we engaged in a constant jockeying for position in the presence of Mum and Dad. With three of us and two of them, it was like a game of musical chairs in which I worried that I might be the one left standing. If we seemed to vie more openly for the attention of our father—Who got to sit next to him on Saturday morning errands? Who got the longest airplane ride?—it was because Mum, always at home, the constant in our lives, was the less-exotic prize. And yet, deep down, it was Mum's love we longed for. Our father was the battle; our mother was the war. We'd vie to put a finger on the ribbon when she wrapped a present, to sit next to her as she read to us on the couch before bed. And though, like Dad, Mum never showed favoritism, I was alert to the most infinitesimal slight, real or imagined. She taught us a game in which she'd squeeze our hand in time to the unspoken words "DO-YOU-LOVE-ME?" "YES-I-DO," we'd silently squeeze back. "HOW MUCH?" she'd squeeze. And we'd squeeze as hard as we could. Then we'd repeat the game with roles reversed. And whenever I squeezed "How much?" I couldn't help wondering and worrying: Did Mum squeeze Harry's or Ned's hand harder than she squeezed mine?

The notion that my brothers and I were rivals for our parents' affection was reinforced every Sunday morning. When I was six, I joined the choir at the Episcopal church whose spire rose above the graveyard at the end of our street. Harry had joined a few months earlier, and I wanted to follow in his footsteps. At the same time, I took an overweening pride in the fact that I was the youngest boy ever to sing in the St. Paul's choir, even younger than my brother had been when *he* joined. I liked the pay—a dollar or two a month, enough to keep me in red licorice. I liked the starchy smell of the freshly laundered white surplice as I pulled it over my head. I liked the hierarchy of the silver crosses we wore around our necks, the color of the ribbon denoting the length of our servitude. I found the service itself stupefying. I spent much of the sermon writing on the sides of my hymnal, then riffling the pages to create a sort of visual Doppler effect in which the words grew simultaneously larger and fainter. (We were nauseatingly proper vandals; rather than write what our mothers referred to as "swear words," we inscribed the names of the Ivy League schools our fathers had attended.)

The only time I perked up was when the minister talked about brothers. The Bible fairly teemed with brothers (apparently, they had even larger families B.C. than in the baby-booming 1950s) who, from what I gathered, did little else but fight, cheat, and kill each other. I found it shocking that the first fraternal relationship in the Bible—*the very first brothers*, we were led to believe, from *the very first family on earth*—ended in murder. From the facts of the case, I couldn't understand why Cain was the villain. Everything seemed to be going fine in Adam and Eve's household until Cain made God an offering of his crops. Whereupon Abel, in a brazen act of brotherly one-upmanship, brought the Lord the firstborn of his lambs. Cain was understandably upset when, without explanation, God refused his gift and accepted his brother's. (Did God, like me, hate vegetables?) Even as a child, I could see that Cain's anger was misplaced. Cain, however, couldn't take revenge on God, and so—long before Freud identified the psychological parlor trick he called projection—he took revenge on his brother. Abel's murder, while not justifiable, was understandable. God acknowledged as much when, in a rare instance of Old Testament temperance, he punished Cain not with death but with banishment.

God seemed even more cavalier in the case of Jacob and Esau. The elder brother by a matter of seconds, Esau was his father's son, a skillful hunter who trapped game for the family table. Jacob was a mama's boy, hanging out near the tents with Rebekah and the other women. When Rebekah helped Jacob cheat Esau out of his blind father's blessing by wrapping him in animal hides and disguising him as his hirsute brother, both his earthly father (Isaac) and his heavenly father (God) let them get away with it. I was secretly pleased that God, once again, had come down on the side of the younger brother (although, as a middle child, I wasn't sure where this left me), but I couldn't help concluding that there was something unfair about the episode.

Neither God nor Jacob expressed regret for their duplicity, so it didn't surprise me that when Jacob became a father he played favorites, too, giving Joseph an ornamental robe of many colors (the famous "technicolor dreamcoat" that Tim Rice and Andrew Lloyd Webber would one day immortalize), to the dismay of his eleven other sons. Joseph, more adept at prophecy than diplomacy, insisted on making his jealous siblings listen to his vainglorious dreams, in which, to take one example, his brothers' sheaves of wheat were forced to bow down to his. The brothers, who constituted a sort of faceless fraternal mob, began to refer to Joseph as their father's son instead of their brother. Eventually they decided to kill him. At the behest of the eldest brother, however, they contented themselves with tossing him down an empty well, then selling him to passing merchants. Joseph ended up in Egypt, where he made an entire nation jealous by interpreting Pharaoh's dreams.

Listening to these stories, I felt a glimmer of recognition. Rough-and-tumble Esau brought Harry to mind, and I couldn't help wondering whether I—already learning to use words to wheedle my way out of trouble—had something in common with Jacob. Conversely, as I listened to the story of Joseph, I identified with those jealous *older* brothers. And though I doubted that Harry harbored any fratricidal thoughts in his heart, he seemed, like Cain, to be the strong, silent type, while I suspected that, like Abel, I myself was not above some mild duplicity if it meant currying favor among grown-ups and other authoritative types. Even channeled through the rheumy baritone of our pink-faced, silver-haired, clammy-handed minister, the Bible's lessons were unmistakable: brothers compete for the attention of their parents and for the attention of their symbolic parent, God.

But our sibling rivalry was no real rivalry. How could it be? Harry always won. Indeed, in deference to Harry's seniority, size, and general superiority, Ned and I often preemptively conceded, according Harry, as eldest, a sort of droit du seigneur. I didn't resent that he got to take the last bath; that he got to stay up a half-hour later; that he got to sit on Dad's lap and steer the car down the driveway at our grandparents' summer home. It seemed only right that the construction-paper angel he'd made in first grade was always the last ornament to be hung on the Christmas tree, Dad lifting Harry up on his shoulders to settle it on the topmost bough, its halo scraping the living room ceiling. In some ways I liked being second. I liked getting Harry's hand-me-down clothes, his outgrown ice skates, his old bike. They came with his imprimatur. They were pieces of him. I liked that he'd already had my teachers. He could warn me about them, the way a batter coming back to the dugout tells his teammates what the pitcher is throwing. I liked that, having taught Harry, my teachers had high expectations of me. I liked having someone to live up to, and I felt a sense of proprietorship in Harry's achievements. His flawless report cards and his leads in the class plays elevated me by association. In any case, Harry was so superior to Ned and me that it would never have occurred to us to challenge him. The real battle was between Ned and me for what was left after Harry had taken his share. If I couldn't beat Harry, I was all the more determined to beat my friends, my classmates, my younger brother.

And yet it must have been more important to compete with Harry than I realized. When Harry began collecting coins, I began collecting them, too. We scrutinized the dates on every penny, nickel, and dime that came into our hands. Anything worth saving we kept in albums, thick blue cardboard triptychs that unfolded to reveal rows of circles into which coins could be inserted over the appropriate date and place of mint. Around the same time, I discovered the delights of Saturday matinees at the Dedham Community Theatre. At twenty-five cents, however, the price of a ticket was five times my weekly allowance, and I was soon forced to finance my excursions by dipping into my coin collection. At some point, my interest in film exceeded my financial and ethical resources, and when I had plucked my last penny from its circular sanctuary, I began—even now I don't know how I dared—to steal coins from Harry. I started with the newer, less-valuable coins, which let me imagine that my crime was somewhat less reprehensible. When those ran out, I moved back in time, from the 1950s to the 1940s to the 1930s, stealing his collection Mercury dime by Mercury dime, Buffalo nickel by Buffalo nickel, Lincoln penny by Lincoln penny. The further back I went, of course, the more valuable the coins. By the end I was using several dollars' worth to pay for a twenty-five-cent movie. (I left Harry's Indian-head pennies untouched, but only because I worried that the woman at the box office might get suspicious.) I tried to cover my tracks by spreading my crime among different albums and by varying my pattern within each album—taking a coin from the upper right, a coin from the lower left, and so on, in a numismatic version of a barber taking a little off the top. (In the interest of full disclosure, I should add that Harry unwittingly funded not only my budding appreciation for the cinematic arts but my prodigious appetite for Raisinets.)

I justified my crime by telling myself I couldn't help it, but looking back, I wonder whether it wasn't, however unconsciously, a way of showing I could beat my older brother at something, of proving he wasn't as powerful as I thought by besting him in a competition he didn't know he had entered. Or perhaps it was a way of taking some of his power and adding it to mine, the way certain New Guinea tribesmen ate the flesh of their dead ancestors in order to augment their strength. Eventually, however, there were so few coins left that it was impossible not to notice that the once-heavy albums were now as light as comic books. One day Harry opened them and found more empty circles than coins. I was terrified. I tried to blame my crime on Ned, but Mum's gentle questioning soon elicited a full confession. What shocked me was that Harry took it so calmly. He didn't beat me up. He didn't yell at me. He didn't remind me of my crime every day for the next ten years. And that, of course, made him seem all the more admirable. Soon afterward, Harry gave up collecting coins and began to collect stamps, which, thank goodness, were not an acceptable form of currency at the Dedham Community Theatre. I began collecting stamps, too.

Even as I jostled for position with my brothers, I felt an unaccountable surge of pride when the three of us were together in public: getting identical crew cuts every second Saturday at Sergi's barbershop, where I looked in the wall-length mirror and saw us waiting our turn to climb onto the red leather chair; piling on Dad's back and seeing how long we could hold on as we sledded down the Community House hill on our Flexible Flyer; lining up with Mum at nursing homes and singing "Rock My Soul" and "Wade in the Water" to roomfuls of frighteningly ancient men and women; stomping down the sidewalk behind Dad as we chanted his old army marching songs (*Left . . . left . . . I had a good job but I left. Left my wife with eighteen babies on the point of starvation when there wasn't any gingerbread left*). I remember seeing our family Christmas card on a neighbor's mantelpiece, a photo of Harry, Ned, and me posed in front of the living room fireplace in matching outfits. This is how the world sees us, I thought. We were a trio, a team. "The Colt boys," my parents' friends called us. I liked hearing that; it made us sound like a gang of Wild West desperados. Together, my brothers and I constituted an undiluted fraternal concentration in which the whole was greater than the sum of its parts. I sometimes imagined the three of us as tag-team wrestlers, each with a special talent, each of us doing his best in the ring and then, exhausted, stumbling to the ropes and clapping the hand of the next brother, who would take over. With Harry's physical strength, Ned's stubbornness, and my vocabulary, we'd be invincible.

One day when I was seven, Mum and Dad gathered us in the kitchen and announced that we were going to have a baby brother or sister. (I was less interested in the news itself than in Harry's insistence that this new sibling would make its appearance from our mother's belly button.) To make room for the baby, Ned was moved out of the bedroom next to our parents and into the room Harry and I shared; nine-year-old Harry was moved up to the spare room on the third floor. My dismay at losing Harry as a roommate was overshadowed by my awe at his ascension. It seemed an extraordinarily grown-up step to me. He would be alone up there all night. One Saturday, Dad showed Harry how to use the flimsy aluminum fire ladder that lay folded on the floor. Ned and I watched Harry back out the window, his head disappearing as he carefully lowered himself two stories to the ground. We rushed to the window in time to see him looking up from the pachysandra far below.

One winter afternoon, when I returned from school, I was surprised to find Dad at home. He told me to come upstairs. Our mother, looking exhausted, lay in bed; the lump in her arms, she told us, was our baby brother. His name was Mark. "Oh," I said, pausing barely long enough to notice a scraggle of wispy red hair before I rushed off to ride my bike to the library.

My indifference wouldn't last. But Mark's arrival seemed less important than the effect it had on our mother, who no longer had as much time to draw with us or make us jigsaw-puzzle sandwiches. From time to time, she felt so beleaguered that, trying to get what she called "a moment's peace" with her youngest son, she'd lock herself in the bathroom to nurse him, while Harry, Ned, and I pounded on the door, shouting, "Let us in, Mummy! Let us in!" One evening, in a rare moment of tranquility, while Mark lay sleeping in her arms, Mum took my finger and guided it across the top of Mark's head to a silver-dollar-size spot that gave a little, like the rubber surface of Ned's tom-tom. This soft spot, she said, was called a fontanel. I loved the sound of the word. Sometime in the next year, she told me, the bones of Mark's skull would knit together and the fontanel would disappear. For now, like an unexpected patch of thin ice on a winter pond, it made Mark seem strangely vulnerable.

Our new sleeping arrangements didn't last. A few months after Mark was born, our father was promoted to company headquarters in New York City. That summer we loaded up our station wagon and drove down Village Avenue, past the jail, past the graveyard, past the Community House, and got on the highway, heading west.

*   *   *

In the end, Harry and I didn't really run away from home. We sat in the car in the garage. After about twenty minutes, as we finished the last of the saltines, we heard our father in the kitchen. A short time later, the familiar scent of frying bacon seeped into the garage. Harry silently opened the car door and slid out. I followed him inside.

Harry doesn't remember running away. He doubts he would have wanted to run away; he remembers those early years in Dedham as the happiest of his childhood. Indeed, over the following decade, Harry never literally ran away from home, but he gradually pulled away from it. In the process, I couldn't help feeling he was pulling away from me. Perhaps that's why this scene has stayed with me for nearly half a century—because those twenty minutes I spent next to Harry in the car seemed to be the last time for many years that we were truly brothers.

Long after we had grown, my brothers, parents, and I undertook a course of family therapy. During one session, to my surprise—I had always been considered the well-adjusted one, the one who never complained—I found myself talking about my closeness with Harry during those prelapsarian years and wondering what had happened. As Harry described some of the forces that had tugged him away from the family, our father reached into his pocket, pulled out his worn leather wallet, and slipped a photograph from its sleeve. Without saying a word, he unfolded it and held it up. It was an old snapshot, soft and powdery with age. In the photo, I am two, Harry is nearly four; sitting in the sandbox, I'm looking up at him in adoration, he's looking at me with undisguised affection. Dad had kept this photo in his wallet for nearly fifty years. I felt a sort of vindication—here was proof that Harry and I *had* been close, we *had* loved each other! As Dad passed it toward us, the photo, like an ancient artifact that has been dug up and exposed to light for the first time in centuries, split down the middle between Harry and me.

Chapter Two

Good Brother, Bad Brother: Edwin and John Wilkes Booth

In the fall of 1864, with the Civil War well into its fourth year, the attention of most Americans was on Atlanta, where General Sherman, having captured the city, was resting his troops before their march to the sea. The attention of the New York theatrical community, however, was on the Winter Garden, where rehearsals were taking place for a special benefit performance whose proceeds would go toward erecting a statue of Shakespeare in Central Park, the vast public greensward that had opened seven years earlier. The benefit would mark the first time that the celebrated Booth brothers, sons of the late Junius Brutus Booth, would act on the same stage. As the playbill put it, in the overbaked public-relations prose of the time, "The evening will be made memorable by the appearance in the same piece of the three sons of the great Booth, JUNIUS BRUTUS, EDWIN, AND JOHN WILKES, 'FILII PATRI DIGNO DIGNIORES,' Who have come forward with cheerful alacrity to do honor to the immortal bard, from whose works the genius of their father caught its inspiration, and of many of whose greatest creations he was the best and noblest illustrator the stage has ever seen." In a twist that would pique lovers of irony in the years to come, the brothers had chosen to perform *Julius Caesar*.

The playbill listed the brothers in descending order of age. Had they been listed in order of renown, as was usually the practice, Edwin would have come first. At thirty, he was widely acclaimed as the greatest American actor of his day, having eclipsed the legendary Edwin Forrest, for whom he had been named. His twenty-six-year-old brother John, however, was not far behind. John's bombastic, athletic style—it was said that he often slept smothered in raw oysters to soothe the bruises earned in overzealous stage fights—was the antithesis of Edwin's subtle, measured approach. Yet some theater critics, especially in the South, believed that John had surpassed his famous brother. Junius, or June, as his family called him, at forty-two the eldest Booth brother by twelve years, was the least well known, a serviceable but uninspired actor who had made his reputation as a theatrical manager in the West. (A fourth brother, Joseph, had inherited neither the Booth talent nor the inclination for the stage, and worked as a messenger boy.) Although the brothers looked remarkably similar—variations on their father's short stature, tousled black hair, and lustrous brown eyes—they were vastly different in temperament. June, who possessed the stolid, well-fed air of a middle-aged banker, was a cautious, practical businessman rumored never to take a chance on an untried actor. Cast against type, he would play Cassius, of the "lean and hungry look"—his father's role. Edwin was a slender introvert said to suffer stage fright everywhere but on stage. He usually played Cassius, but this time, deferring to his elder brother, took the part of Brutus, the conflicted assassin. John was the darling of the family, a dashing, impetuous bon vivant fond of poetry, pool halls, and brothels. Although his older brothers tut-tutted over John's excesses, they couldn't help being charmed by his boyish enthusiasm. Both June and Edwin considered him their favorite brother. John had shaved his trademark mustache to play the demagogue Mark Antony.

Given the nomadic nature of an actor's life, there were rarely more than two Booth brothers in the same place at the same time. Yet the brothers were loyal and affectionate, if not intimate. June had helped Edwin get his theatrical start in San Francisco; several years later, Edwin had promoted John's career in the East, and recently, after June had made some poor real estate investments, Edwin had paid off his brother's debts and invited him to help manage the Winter Garden. (That this would bring "The Brothers Booth," as Edwin called them, together for the first time in many years had given him the idea for the benefit.) As always when they came to New York, June and John stayed at Edwin's house on East Nineteenth Street, where their mother, Mary Ann, and their spinster sister, Rosalie, also lived.

Yet while the playbill noted the "cheerful alacrity" with which the Booth brothers had volunteered for the benefit, tension was growing between Edwin and John. Like many families, the Booths were divided by the war. Edwin sided with the North. John was passionately, outspokenly, for the South. Although Edwin disliked conflict of any sort, he was fed up with what he called John's "patriotic froth" and tried to reason with his hotheaded younger brother. June, who shared Edwin's pro-Union sympathies, acted as peacemaker, observing that the war was like a family quarrel in which both sides would eventually reconcile. The more desperate the southern cause, however, the more vitriolic John's pronouncements. That summer, the fraternal arguments grew so heated that Edwin forbade the discussion of politics in his home. John, for his part, wrote to their sister Asia, "If it were not for mother I would not enter Edwin's house."

John's support of the Confederacy was far more than mere "froth." Even as they rehearsed the assassination scene in *Julius Caesar*, John was devising his own elaborate plot: to kidnap Abraham Lincoln, smuggle him south of the Mason-Dixon Line, and exchange him for rebel prisoners of war. For several months, he had been pouring his earnings as an actor into horses, rifles, knives, field glasses, handcuffs, and other supplies. (It was a busy summer even for the peripatetic John. As he worked on his plans to kidnap Lincoln, he was also dashing back and forth to western Pennsylvania to oversee his oil-field investments and staying up late at night to write love letters to a sixteen-year-old Boston girl, all the while preparing for *Julius Caesar*.) The fraternal arguments, as well as John's plotting, were temporarily suspended in August when John contracted a severe case of erysipelas, a skin infection that in the nineteenth century could be fatal. When John fainted from the pain, June carried him upstairs to bed. It would be three weeks before John, cared for by his mother and his brothers, recovered.

On the night of November 25, 1864, some two thousand people, paying up to five dollars a ticket, more than six times the usual price, packed the Winter Garden, the largest audience in its fourteen-year history. "The theatre was crowded to suffocation, people standing in every available place," Asia recalled. When the brothers made their entrance, side by side in Caesar's retinue, they were greeted with an ovation that seemed to shake the building. At the end of the first act they stood in front of the curtain, bowing to the audience, to one another, and, finally, to their sixty-two-year-old mother, who beamed down from a private box as the applause swelled, handkerchiefs waved, and shouts of "Bravo" resounded. Asia, listening to people around her compare the brothers, heard someone exclaim "*Our Wilkes* looks like a young god," and turned to see a southerner watching the stage intently. Even the finicky New York critics were impressed. "Brutus was individualized with great force and distinctness," wrote a reviewer for the *Herald*. "Cassius was brought out equally well— and if there was less of real personality given Marc Antony, the fault was rather in the part than in the actor.... He played with a phosphorescent passion and fire, which recalled to old theatregoers the characteristics of the elder Booth." Indeed, some thought that the youngest Booth had outshone his brothers. Asia, who respected Edwin but adored John and may not have been the most objective witness, observed, "Edwin was nervous; he admired Wilkes and thought that he never beheld a being so perfectly handsome. I think he trembled a little for his own laurels."

The evening was a critical, familial, and financial success—it would raise $3,500 for the statue fund—aside from an unsettling incident at the beginning of the second act. Soon after the curtain rose on Edwin Booth, as Brutus, pacing the orchard before dawn, the audience was startled by several firemen who rushed into the Winter Garden lobby shouting "Fire!" People stood in confusion; some scrambled toward the exits. Panic threatened until Edwin walked to the footlights and in a quiet but firm voice announced that there was nothing to fear; the fire, in the hotel next door, was under control. People returned to their seats, the hubbub subsided, and the play went on.

The following morning, over breakfast at Edwin's, the brothers read in the *Herald* that the fire had been one of more than twenty set in Manhattan hotels the previous evening by Confederate saboteurs in "a vast and fiendish plot to burn the city." June said that the arsonists should be hanged in a public square. John defended the fires as a reasonable response to the atrocities committed by Union troops in the Shenandoah Valley. Edwin took this moment to tell his brothers that he had cast his ballot for Lincoln in the recent election—the first time he had ever voted. John, increasingly agitated, told Edwin that he'd regret his vote when Lincoln made the United States a monarchy and had himself crowned king. Edwin told John that he was not welcome in his home if he was going to express such treasonous sentiments.

That afternoon, the brothers parted. Edwin and June headed to the Winter Garden, where Edwin gave the first performance in what became the legendary hundred-night run as Hamlet that would establish him as the country's greatest Shakespearean actor. John returned to Washington, where he took a room in the National Hotel and began to recruit more rebel sympathizers for his plot to kidnap the president. Although the brothers had agreed on a second benefit performance—*Romeo and Juliet*, with John in the title role—scheduled for April 22, 1865, circumstances would conspire to keep that event from taking place.

*　　*　　*

Like many children, I was fascinated by the War Between the States. For my ninth birthday, my parents gave me *The Golden Book of the Civil War*, which I spent much of the next year poring over, its maps of the major battles illustrated with platoons of tiny, meticulously painted soldiers positioned with historical accuracy on olive-green fields. For Christmas I was given a plastic replica of a Civil War cannon whose tennis-ball-size ordnance I fired at Ned's legs. That spring, when we visited our grandparents in Virginia, I spent several weeks of saved allowance on a Union forage cap that I wore as Ned and I reenacted the Civil War in the fields behind our grandparents' house, whose bricks were pocked with real bullet holes made by real Union rifles. Ned, of course, played Johnny Reb to my Billy Yank, for while I secretly admired the South's audacity and was intoxicated by the romantic scent of defeat that even in the 1960s seemed to linger in the sultry air, I was too much the good boy to be anything other than a Union man.

I was fascinated by the Civil War for the same reasons boys are fascinated by any war—my interest in this case no doubt enhanced by my interest in the civil rights struggle unfolding on our television set exactly one hundred years later—but I found something especially intriguing in a conflict so frequently described as pitting "brother against brother" at a time when my own life could have been summarized by the same words. That the phrase was meant not only figuratively but literally seemed incredible to me, for despite my fraternal skirmishes, I found it shocking (and titillating) that brothers from the same family had fought on opposite sides of the war, in some cases in the same battle. The war's association with brothers was reinforced when I read my parents' coffee-table volume about Lincoln and learned that his assassin, the perpetrator of the most reviled act in American history, had an older brother who had become America's most admired actor. How could two brothers grow up in the same family and be so different? Could something like that happen to my brothers and me?

History is full of brothers so different that it seems impossible they could have the same parents. A brief sampling through the ages might include the Arouets (Armand was a sanctimonious, evangelical Catholic; his younger brother François-Marie, better known by his pen name, Voltaire, was a witty, irreverent satirist and a savage critic of the Catholic Church); the Robespierres (Maximilien became the rigid, merciless overlord of the Reign of Terror, known to supporters as the Incorruptible; his younger brother Augustin became a self-indulgent lover of luxury known to friends as Bon Bon); the Melvilles (Gansevoort became a dutiful, responsible lawyer; his younger brother Herman became a world traveler and iconoclastic writer known to his family as "the runaway brother"); the Carters (sober and pious Jimmy became president; his younger brother, Billy, played the court jester and drunken buffoon); and the Newtons (Walter became a street hustler, Melvin a professor of sociology, and the youngest brother, Huey—torn between fraternal poles—a book-loving, poetry-quoting, street-fighting, home-burgling co-founder of the Black Panther Party). Brothers may end up on opposite sides of a moral issue, like John Brown, the cynical, hard-drinking Rhode Island profiteer who became one of the country's wealthiest slave traders, and his idealistic, abstemious younger brother Moses, who became a leading Quaker abolitionist. Brothers not infrequently end up on opposite sides of the law, like Al Capone, who, expelled from school at fourteen for punching a female teacher in the face, became the most powerful gangster in Prohibition-era Chicago, and his eldest brother, Vincenzo, who, running away from his Brooklyn home at sixteen, worked as a circus roustabout, enlisted in the infantry during World War I, served as town marshal and Boy Scout commissioner in Homer, Nebraska, and became a Prohibition enforcement agent responsible for busting up illegal stills.

How can siblings, who share so much genetically and environmentally, be so different? For many years, social scientists assumed that a family affects the children within it almost identically, and that siblings, raised under the same roof by the same parents, tend to be far more similar than not. But over the past three decades, studies of intelligence, personality, interests, attitudes, and psychopathology have concluded that siblings raised in the same family are, in fact, almost as different from each other as unrelated people raised in separate families. The psychologist Sandra Scarr puts it dramatically: "Upper middle-class brothers who attend the same school and whose parents take them to the same plays, sporting events, music lessons, and therapists, and use similar child rearing practices on them are little more similar in personality measures than they are to working class or farm boys, whose lives are totally different." Paradoxically, the longer they live with each other, the more different siblings become.

The answer to sibling difference is, in part, genetic. Biological siblings share, on average, half their genes; if personality traits were entirely genetic, siblings would be 50 percent similar as well as 50 percent different—even before factoring in the effects of being raised in the same family by the same parents. But biological siblings have personality correlations of about 15 percent. (Even identical twins have only about a 50 percent overlap.) Although siblings share about half of each other's genes, not only is the genetic contribution of each parent halved, but the sequence of those shared genes is rearranged through a process called recombination. The behavioral geneticist David Lykken has observed that, genetically speaking, siblings are like people who receive telephone numbers with the same digits arranged in a different sequence. Just as those telephone numbers, when dialed, will result in entirely different connections, genes that have been scrambled will express themselves in widely different personalities.

But this is only part of the puzzle. A growing amount of research suggests that siblings may be influenced most strongly by the things they don't share: birth order, age, friends, teachers, and the vagaries of chance. And they don't even really share the things they appear to have in common—if not identical genes, then seemingly identical parents, homes, and often schools—because each of them perceives those things differently. Psychologists say that the experience of each child within a family is so distinct that each grows up in his own unique "micro-environment." In effect, each sibling grows up in a different family.

* * *

If Edwin and John Wilkes Booth, born less than five years apart, grew up in two essentially different families, it is in large measure because their father, Junius Brutus Booth, lived two essentially different lives. One of those lives he lived on the stage, as the greatest American actor of his day, a man of such prodigious talent that fellow performers were sometimes too moved to deliver their next line, and hostesses besieged him with dinner invitations merely so they could hear his tear-inducing rendition of the Lord's Prayer. ("His genius was to me one of the grandest revelations of my life, a lesson of artistic expression," recalled Walt Whitman, who as a sixteen-year-old saw Booth in *Richard III*.) But Booth, a drunkard judged to be insane by all who knew him, was known no more for his acting than for his erratic behavior, instances of which were legend in the theatrical community: the time, playing Iago, he made his entrance, crossed the stage, walked out the side door, and disappeared for several days; the time he was found naked in a snowstorm at midnight, drunkenly declaiming lines from *King Lear*; the time, playing Hamlet, he deserted Ophelia and scooted up a ladder to the rafters of the theater, where he crowed like a rooster. Not surprisingly, audiences flocked to see "The Mad Tragedian," as he was sometimes billed, never sure whether he would stir them to tears or shock them with a psychotic outburst. (Some suggested that his madness was itself an act designed to sell tickets, but it seems unlikely; at least twice Booth tried to kill himself, and at least twice he tried to kill a fellow actor.) Booth, for whom the line between acting and reality often seemed to blur, blamed his madness on the strain of performing—one reason he urged his children never to go on the stage.

Booth's theory of insanity may have had some truth in it, for he lived a relatively sane second life in a four-room log house in rural Maryland, three miles from his nearest neighbor, twenty-five miles from the nearest theater. Here, Booth created a 150-acre sanctuary, complete with dairy, stables, vineyard, orchard, vegetable garden, swimming pond, and cow-dotted fields, to which he could retreat between professional engagements. He called it the Farm. Here he was known not as The Mad Tragedian but as Farmer Booth, an eccentric but diligent gentleman who subscribed to agricultural journals, hoed his fields barefoot, pioneered the use of animal bones as fertilizer, and drove his milk and eggs to the Baltimore market, where he hawked them in his famously stentorian voice. Here he was a devoted family man to Mary Ann and their ten children (only six of whom would survive childhood), leading them in choruses of "Oats, Peas, Beans, and Barley Grow," reading aloud to them each evening from a library stocked with Milton, Shakespeare, Coleridge, and Keats. Although he occasionally succumbed to the madness his children referred to as "Father's calamity" (he once dug up the body of a daughter who had died of cholera two weeks earlier, believing he might be able to revive her), life on the Farm seemed an idyll, albeit a peculiar one. Booth subscribed to a hodgepodge of beliefs cherry-picked from the Bible, the Koran, and the Talmud; he attended Catholic, Protestant, and Jewish services with equal fervor. (Apparently, he set little stock by the Seventh Commandment; it was common knowledge that Booth was already married when he met Mary Ann, the eighteen-year-old Covent

Garden flower girl with whom he emigrated to America.) Kind, charitable, and, when sane, a firm believer in the sanctity of human life, Booth,
unlike most Marylanders, refused to own slaves, though he compromised
his principles enough to rent them from his neighbors. Like his hero
Pythagoras, he believed that men's souls were reborn into animals' bodies, and thus forbade the eating of meat (at least one newspaper blamed
Booth's insanity on the lack of beef in his diet) or fish (dining out while
on tour, he shouted "Murder!" every time an oyster was cracked open at a
neighboring table), as well as the felling of trees or the picking of flowers.
At their father's insistence, the Booth children weren't permitted to see
doctors; their illnesses were treated with home remedies concocted from
chamomile, sassafras, pennyroyal, and green figs. The boy who grew up to
commit the most infamous murder in American history was raised as a
vegetarian, forbidden to kill even a mouse or to brand a cow for the pain
it would cause the animal.

It is tempting to imagine what might have happened if John Wilkes Booth had been born before Edwin Booth and not the other way
around. If he had, it is a fair bet that Abraham Lincoln would have lived
to serve out his second term. For it would have been John who grew up
on the road with his father, who was forced to fend for himself from
early on, who came of age in free-state California—and Edwin who grew
up coddled by his mother and sister on the family farm in slave-owning
Maryland, encouraged to believe that greatness was his birthright.

Instead, it was Edwin who, when June outgrew the task, was taken
from school at the age of thirteen to barnstorm the country as his father's
dresser: brushing his wigs; applying his makeup; adjusting his robe; keeping track of his swords; putting on his boots; making sure the crumpled-
cloth hump he wore as Richard III was securely fastened; once even
obtaining, when Junius tired of the carved pumpkins or molded dough
supplied to Hamlet by provincial theater managers, a real skull to stand
in for Yorick's. It was Edwin who was charged with keeping his father
sober for the show, sometimes locking him in his hotel room on the day
of a performance, reading aloud or playing the banjo and singing English
ballads as his father paced the floor, and then, after the final curtain, tail-
ing him down to waterfront bars and waiting outside, while his father

sang ribald songs and recited Shakespeare, before helping him back to the hotel. And it was Edwin who, whenever his father was overtaken by shrieking, hallucinating, clothes-rending madness, was expected to lure him back to sanity. Of all the Booths, Edwin alone seemed able to pacify his father. Although his father urged him to become a cabinetmaker (career advice about as effective as a circus ringmaster counseling his son in the front row to become a cobbler), Edwin listened to the play night after night through the keyhole of the dressing room in which he had been left with his schoolbooks, and made his first professional appearance onstage at the age of fifteen, playing Tressel the messenger to his father's Richard III.

In 1852, at the age of eighteen, Edwin squired his father to San Francisco, where June had become a prominent theater manager. His father left for home after three months; Edwin stayed on to make his own name as an actor. When Junius Brutus Booth died of a fever on his way back to the Farm, Edwin blamed himself. Edwin, who had spent most of the last five years on the road, would spend four more years away from home: barnstorming the roughneck towns of Gold Rush California, playing Shakespeare, melodrama, and blackface minstrel shows for hard-bitten but critically demanding prospectors who, if they didn't approve of the way an actor played Desdemona's death scene, might grab Othello from the stage and toss him in a blanket; joining a jury-rigged theatrical tour of Australia that nearly left him stranded in the Sandwich Islands; working his way up the theatrical ladder in a San Francisco only slightly more civilized than Australia. With no one to take care of but himself, Edwin drank heavily (like his father, he was often noticeably drunk on stage), frequented brothels (he contracted a venereal disease that caused him temporary physical discomfort and lifelong guilt), and at least once gambled his way to insolvency (in part because he sent home some of his earnings to pay for his younger brothers' schooling). But older brother June, who had witnessed his father's excesses, took Edwin under his wing, warning him to drink less and work more. And after casting him as Richard III, Macbeth, and Hamlet, June, sensing that Edwin was letting his good reviews go to his head, demoted him for a time to utility roles in comedy, farce, and burlesque. Years later Edwin would recall it as an invaluable lesson, a taste, perhaps, of the parenting he'd given his father but rarely gotten himself. In 1856, when he returned east at the age of twenty-three, Edwin was already being advertised by one hyperbolic promoter as "The Hope of the Living Drama." But his hurly-burly youth had left scars. "Before I was eighteen I was a drunkard, at twenty a libertine. . . ." he wrote a friend. "I grew up in ignorance, allowed by an indulgent mother who knew nothing more than that she loved her child, and a father who, although a good man, seemed to care very little what course I took. I was allowed to roam at large, and at an early age and in a wild and almost barbarous country where boys become old men in vice very speedily." In later years, Edwin often said he had never had a childhood.

If Edwin never had a childhood, Johnny, as he was called by his family, enjoyed a perpetual adolescence, right up to his death at the age of twenty-six. While Edwin was babysitting his father in cities and towns across the country, Johnny was being spoiled by his mother on the Farm. While Edwin grew up in the company of men, traveling by stagecoach on muddy roads, eating and sleeping in flea-ridden beds at theatrical boardinghouses, Johnny spent most of his time with his older sister Asia, a moody, talkative, tomboyish girl who would devote much of her adult life to writing about her father and brothers in an effort to restore the family name. (There were two other Booth children at home: Johnny's older sister Rosalie, a frail, reclusive girl who stayed close to her mother, and his younger brother, Joseph, a morose fellow who was sent away to boarding school.) In *The Unlocked Book*—an affectionate memoir of John written in secret in 1874 but, hatred of her brother still being strong, not published until 1938, fifty years after her death—Asia described the insular world of the Farm, where she and Johnny were, as she put it, "lonely together." Even allowing for sisterly spin, their life sounds like an Arcadian fantasy: walking hand in hand through the woods; playing "Christopher Columbus" by using poles to hop from rock to rock across the brooks that veined the farm; digging for Indian relics; collecting geological specimens that Asia would treasure for the rest of her life; talking for hours by the fireplace; reading Byron and Hawthorne aloud under the cherry tree; playing duets, with Johnny on flute and Asia on piano or guitar; riding horses by moonlight, singing as they rode. While Edwin was mending costumes, running lines, and tracking down his drunken father, Johnny was swimming, climbing trees, and catching (and releasing) butterflies.

Edwin and John were a split of their father not only geographically but temperamentally. If Junius Brutus Booth had been born 150 years later, he would likely have been diagnosed as bipolar. It seemed as if Edwin and John had each inherited a different pole. On the night Edwin was born, there had been a spectacular meteor shower, a sign of good fortune; he had also been born with a caul, a transparent membrane encasing the face, another harbinger of luck. Despite being thus doubly protected, Edwin, who carried his caul in a leather pouch around his neck, always felt a vague sense of doom—"the feeling that evil is hanging over me, that I can't come to good," he told a friend. From childhood, Edwin was shy, somber, introspective, and frequently depressed. He rarely smiled, his laugh was soundless. His natural reserve was reinforced by shame over his illegitimate birth, especially after his father's wife showed up in America and hectored her estranged husband whenever he brought his produce to the Baltimore market. (Although the legal Mrs. Booth eventually agreed to a divorce and, when Edwin was seventeen, his parents married, the shame occasioned by the circumstances of his birth would be lifelong. It would be compounded by other humiliations: his father's public intemperance and insanity, his own youthful indiscretions, and, most painfully, his younger brother's crime.) The boy who spent years as his father's shadow looked something like a shadow himself: a skinny, dark-eyed wraith with an El Greco face and shoulder-length black hair. When he wore his favorite Spanish cape, he resembled a despondent Gypsy. Although Edwin's physical appearance remained preternaturally youthful well into adulthood, even when he was a child his affect was as weary as an old man's—not surprising, perhaps, given that at the age of thirteen he had been saddled with the responsibilities of an adult. It wasn't all acting that enabled him, at twenty-two, to play a convincing Lear.

Johnny reflected his father's manic side. From childhood, he was gregarious, headstrong, unpredictable. On the day Johnny was given his first pair of boots, he ran to the stable and, though he had never ridden before, jumped on a horse and galloped off down the lane, to the delight of his parents. In Asia's telling, the man who killed Lincoln grew up with an optimism that might have made Pollyanna gag. "No setting sun view for me, it is too melancholy; let me see him rise," Johnny told Asia, explaining why he preferred his bedroom facing east. In the woods, he liked to throw himself facedown on the ground, inhaling what he described as the "earth's healthy breath" or nibbling at roots and twigs ("burrowing," he called it). Asia recalled: "Once he burst out with the joyous exclamation, 'Heaven and Earth! how glorious it is to live!'" Whenever Asia was in one of her gloomy moods, her teenaged brother tried to talk her out of it. "Don't let us be sad," he told her. "Life is so short, and the world is so beautiful. Just to *breathe* is delicious." While Edwin liked being alone, Johnny preferred a crowd; he made friends easily and at school became the magnetic center of a circle of boys. Like all the Booths, Johnny had his lugubrious spells, but while Edwin suffered through his with stoic resignation, Johnny fought them off with a determined gaiety. Both Booths had "that touch of 'strangeness,'" the actress Clara Morris would recall. "In Edwin Booth it was a profound melancholy; in John it was an exaggeration of spirit, almost a wildness." Indeed, other than June, John seemed the sanest of the Booth children.

If Edwin grew up expecting doom, Johnny grew up expecting glory. One night, when his mother sat by the hearth nursing her six-month-old and praying to know his future, the dying flames revived and, in rapid succession, formed the shape of an arm, the word *country,* and—the grand finale—all fifteen letters of her son's name. To Mary Ann Booth, the vision suggested not that she possessed a hypertrophic imagination (or an extraordinarily versatile fireplace) but that her third son had been singled out for greatness. The proud mother told the story so often—"a hundred times," according to Asia, who immortalized the incident in an ode entitled "The Mother's Vision"—that it began to take on the aura of manifest destiny in the Booth household.

Whether it was his mother's vision, his optimistic nature, or even his name (Edwin had been named for actor friends of his father, John Wilkes for an eighteenth-century English radical imprisoned for defying the king), Johnny grew up believing he was destined for fame. All the Booth children had been steeped in models of heroism, having been raised by a father, himself named for the founder of the Roman Republic, who declaimed speeches from Shakespeare, read aloud from Plutarch's *Lives,* and decorated his parlor walls with engravings of classical scenes like "Timon of Athens" and "The Roman Matron Showing Her Husband How to Die." But Johnny took these models most to heart. Imitating Agesilaus, a Spartan king known for his frugal lifestyle, Johnny chose for his bed the hardest mattress and straw pillow; he galloped through the forest, tilting at trees, on a horse he'd named for the Roman patriot Cola de Rienzi; he memorized *The Giaour,* Byron's epic poem about a man who risks everything for an act of revenge (years later, he could still recite all 1,300 lines); he devoured the romantic novels of Sir Walter Scott and Edward Bulwer-Lytton. Asia blamed the "unhealthy tales of Bulwer" for feeding to "fever heat . . . that wild ambition born in Wilkes Booth," but she added fuel to the fire. "Seated together in the broad swing under the gum trees and hickories," she recalled, "we would build fantastic temples of fame that were to resound with his name in the days that were coming." At school, Johnny told his friends that he would win undying glory with some extraordinary act.

In much of this, Johnny was no different from most histrionic nineteenth-century boys—he was certainly not the only one to sign his letters to friends "Thine till Death"—but he never outgrew his obsession with fame. Asia wasn't sure whether it would be won on the stage or in politics. To Johnny, it didn't seem to matter *how* he won it, it was the fame itself that counted. But after making his first appearance on the stage at age seventeen, as Richmond in *Richard III,* Johnny rushed home from Baltimore and told Asia that he had found his calling. Sitting in the swing-seat with his sister, he poured out his dreams, saying, recalled Asia, "He could never hope to be as great as father, he never wanted to try to rival Edwin, but he wanted to be loved of the Southern people above all things. He would work to make himself essentially a Southern actor."

There was another factor that made it seem as if Edwin and John had been born into different families: John was his parents' favorite child. This, too, was partly a matter of timing. Two years before John's birth, eleven-year-old Henry Booth, his father's beloved, had died of smallpox. When John was born, the Booth parents transferred their hopes for Henry to their new son. But John's place in their affections was also a matter of temperament. In contrast to cautious June, reclusive Rosalie, reticent Edwin, and prickly Asia, Johnny was easy to love: cheerful, charismatic, exuberant, and, in an extraordinarily good-looking family, handsome to the point of beauty. Such was Johnny's appeal that even after Joseph, a well-behaved but subdued child, was born two years later, Johnny remained the adored baby of the family, the center of attention. Of all the children, Johnny most resembled his high-spirited father in both looks and manner, a fact that surely contributed to his favored status. On the road, Junius relied on Edwin. At home, he all but ignored Edwin and devoted himself to Johnny. As Johnny took center stage, Edwin retreated still further. For Edwin, acting, at least in part, was a way of getting the attention he hadn't gotten as a child; for Johnny, it would be a way of continuing to get the attention he had gotten since birth.

Charmed by his personality and cautious after Henry's death, the Booths didn't have the heart to discipline Johnny, reinforcing a sense of entitlement he would carry to his grave. (Edwin didn't need disciplining; he disciplined himself.) Alone among the Booth children, Johnny dared defy their father's edict against hunting. After Junius Brutus Booth died when Johnny was fourteen, his mother was even less inclined to restrain the child in whom the mercurial spirit of her husband seemed to live on. The adolescent Johnny spent his time playing cards, getting drunk, starting fights, skipping school, pulling pranks. He set off fireworks on a hotel porch, scattering a group of fat-chewing old-timers; he honed his marksmanship on stray cats; he was the architect of a wild drinking party for the school debating club. Home for a visit, June tried to rein in his sixteen-year-old brother as he had reined in Edwin in California, but his mother told him to say nothing that might upset John; she wanted to keep things pleasant while they were together. Two years later, when Edwin returned, he, too, was warned by his mother not to discipline his brother; Johnny would find his own way. But Edwin must have been hurt when, needing some costumes for his upcoming eastern debut, he sorted through his father's theatrical wardrobe, with which he was, of course, intimately familiar, and, finding several that he wanted, was told by his mother he couldn't have them. She was saving them for Johnny. John would inherit his father's entire collection, including the spurs Edwin had worn as Tressel in his first stage appearance—the same spurs that would catch in the Treasury Guard flag, nine years later, when Lincoln's assassin leaped from the president's box at Ford's Theatre.

*   *   *

The notion that parents should treat their children equally is relatively new. In the Bible, favoritism begat favoritism: Abraham favored Isaac, Isaac favored Esau; Rebekah favored Jacob, Jacob favored Joseph ("But when his brothers saw that their father loved him more than all his brothers, they hated him"). Indeed, until well into the twentieth century, Western parents made little attempt to conceal their filial preferences. Thus Louisa Whitman made no secret of her partiality for her second-born, Walt, whose siblings may have been stung but not surprised when, after their mother's death, they came across a scrap of paper on which she had written, not long before the end, "dont mourn for me my beloved sons and daughters. farewell my dear beloved walter."

The Victorian editor and publisher Arthur Waugh had been terrified of his own father, a country doctor known as the Brute, who, to toughen up his timid, asthmatic son, liked to perch him on a tree branch from which he was unable to climb down, then sneak back hours later and fire off a gun inches from his ear. Determined to give his firstborn son the childhood he never had, Arthur took Alec to Shakespeare plays and cricket matches; read aloud each night from Kipling, Tennyson, and Browning; wrote poems to him; and walked hand in hand with him across Hampstead Heath while conducting animated discussions about literature. When Alec went off to his father's old boarding school, 150 miles from home, Arthur wrote him every day, visited him each weekend, and telegraphed his grades and cricket scores to friends and relatives throughout the country. When Alec was kicked out of school for kissing other boys, his father told him he shared his pain, writing, "The nails that pierce the hands of the Son are still driven through the hands of the Father also." All Arthur could talk about was Alec, whom he was convinced would become a great cricket player or a renowned poet. "I have built my earthly hopes on him," he confided to a friend. He said several times that without Alec his life would be over.

Arthur hardly seemed to notice that he had a second son. In later years Evelyn Waugh told friends he had been an unwanted child; indeed, his parents made no secret of the fact that they would have preferred a daughter and had been deeply disappointed when a long, difficult delivery yielded a son. For Evelyn, five years younger than Alec, there were no Shakespeare plays, no cricket matches, no literary give-and-take, and no pet nicknames (although his brother referred to him, early on, as "It"). When eleven-year-old Evelyn asked for a bicycle, Arthur bought one for Alec and gave Evelyn a box of theatrical facepaints instead. When Alec asked for a billiard table, Arthur had it installed in Evelyn's nursery. The banner that greeted Alec on school vacations—WELCOME HOME THE HEIR TO UNDERHILL—was taken down only after Evelyn asked his father, "And when Alec has the house and all that's in it what will be left for me?" Alec attended his father's old boarding school; Evelyn was sent to an inferior institution, which his father rarely visited. At home, conversation revolved around Alec's achievements, and whenever Arthur pointed out Evelyn's shortcomings, he invoked Alec's sterling example. Arthur signed his letters to Alec "Your devotedly loving Daddy," "Ever, Dearest Boy," or "With deep love and unfaltering trust, still and always, your ever devoted and hopeful Daddy." To Evelyn, he simply wrote "Your loving father." Years later, Arthur wrote his first grandchild, Alec's son: "The three great things in my life have been my mother, my wife, and my son—your father. Nothing else has mattered much to me but their love."

It was parents like Arthur Waugh that pediatricians and psychologists had in mind when they began churning out books on child-rearing and behavioral development in which they urged mothers and fathers not to play favorites. Nonetheless, contemporary Arthur Waughs abound. In the 1950s, in one of the first major studies of siblings, the psychologist Helen Koch interviewed 360 five- and six-year-olds, and found that two thirds claimed their mothers showed favoritism. Firstborns were especially likely to report that their mothers paid more attention to their younger siblings. Studies of older children yielded similar results. Looking at it from the parents' point of view, only a third of mothers in a more recent Colorado study reported feeling equal affection for both of their children, and only a third—presumably the same third—said they gave equal attention to both. In most instances, again, it was the younger children who received the lion's share. In an attempt to measure the prevalence of favoritism objectively, the sociologist Katherine Conger interviewed 384 adolescent sibling pairs and their parents once a year for three years, and concluded that 70 percent of fathers and 65 percent of mothers exhibited a preference for one of their children; in this case, however, the favorite was usually the elder child. Favoritism may be in the eye of the beholder. In a survey of thirty elderly mothers and their grown children, 80 percent of the mothers admitted, often reluctantly, that they had a favorite. Eighty percent of their children agreed—but when asked which sibling was the favorite, the majority guessed wrong.

Treating each child according to his or her needs is natural and unavoidable. A restive infant demands more attention than one who sleeps through the night, a rambunctious toddler more than her independent six-year-old brother, a sick child more than a healthy one. "Diverse children have their different natures: some are like flesh which nothing but salt will keep from putrefaction; some again like tender fruits that are best preserved with sugar," wrote the seventeenth-century poet Anne Bradstreet, herself the mother of eight. "Those parents are wise that can fit their nurture according to their nature."

But the line between differential and preferential treatment can be thin. Even the most well-meaning, Spock-indoctrinated parent may be unconsciously drawn to the child who is higher-achieving, less demanding, or more affectionate. The way a parent reacts to a child depends, of course, on that parent's own upbringing and temperament. Like the biblical Jacob, a parent may repeat a pattern of favoritism ingrained in his own family; on the other hand, like Arthur Waugh, whose treatment of his elder son was in part a reaction to his own upbringing at the hands of the Brute, he may reverse it. Like Junius Brutus Booth, parents may be drawn to the child who most resembles them, physically or temperamentally. Like Isaac, who loved Esau "because he ate of his game," they may be drawn to the child with whom they share interests. They may be drawn to a child because of timing. "In one era, the parents may be stressed and unhappy, and a child born at that time may be seen as a burden," writes Stephen Bank, a psychologist who has studied the effects of favoritism, "while in a more felicitous circumstance the same parents may be prepared to give more to a different child." This may depend on whether the pregnancy was wanted or unwanted, planned or unplanned—some 50 percent of all conceptions are unintended—or even on whether the birth was easy or difficult. After the birth of their first child, John Cheever's aging, quarrelsome parents had no desire to have a second, a fact they went out of their way to let him know. "If I hadn't drunk two manhattans one afternoon," his mother told him, "you never would have been conceived." Furthermore, she said, his father had urged her to have an abortion—he had even invited the abortionist to dinner (a scene that would find its way into Cheever's fiction). Although their dinner guest's services were never utilized, Cheever's parents treated their second-born as little more than an appendage to their beloved first (they often referred to John merely as "Brother"), which surely contributed to his lifelong need to be desired. As a friend observed after Cheever's death, "If there's someone who never loved himself, it was John."

In her studies of sibling difference, the psychologist Frances Schachter found that parents almost invariably describe their first- and second-born children as being vastly dissimilar—"as different as day and night." Stephen Bank points out that such pigeonholing can start even before birth: one parent may interpret an unborn child's kicks in the womb as a sign of strength or independence, while another may interpret them as a sign of aggression or anxiety. Often, the firstborn is said to resemble one parent, physically or temperamentally, while the second, almost by default, is said to resemble the other—a dynamic Schacter called "split-parent identification" that is almost certain to divide a family along parental lines. Consider how often parents search their newborn's face and evaluate his every gesture to determine whether he resembles the mother, the father, a grandparent, an uncle. The child who isn't associated with one parent may feel rejected, and compensate by turning to the other. (The Bible doesn't tell us *why* Rebekah favored Jacob. Perhaps it was only to counterbalance Isaac's preference for Esau.) Thus the young Evelyn Waugh said to his mother, "Daddy loves Alec more than me. So do you love me more than Alec?" His mother, not wanting to play favorites—although, in fact, she preferred Alec—told Evelyn she loved them "both the same." This didn't seem fair to Evelyn, who immediately perceived the imbalance. "In which case," he said plaintively, "I am lacking in love."

Anecdotal evidence suggests that favoritism can have enduring consequences. "A man who has been the indisputable favorite of his mother keeps for life the feeling of a conqueror, that confidence of success that often induces real success," wrote Freud, whose parents treated him like a hothouse flower at the expense of his six younger siblings, cultivating a sense of entitlement that he would flex for the rest of his life. (Freud, whose mother called him "My golden Sigi," didn't bother to discuss the effects of favoritism on the nonfavored child.) Benito Mussolini was convinced that being breast-fed by his doting mother, instead of being handed over to a wet nurse like his younger brother, Arnaldo, helped explain why he became Il Duce, while Arnaldo, who introduced himself as "Mussolini the Little," served as his advisor. Alec Waugh, five-foot-five and prematurely bald, strode through life with cock-of-the-walk bravado. In later years, he admitted that being his father's favorite had given him a superiority complex: "I was confident that I was going to make a considerable mark in the world." Evelyn, no shorter and much hairier, grew up fretful and insecure. Freud's disciple Alfred Adler, whose older brother held favored status in the Adler household, would not have been surprised. Comparing children with trees, he wrote: "If one grows faster because it is more favored by the sun and the soil, its development influences the growth of all the others. It overshadows them; its roots stretch out and take away their nourishment. The others are dwarfed and stunted." Children who receive less affection than their siblings are more likely to be anxious, angry, or depressed; to engage in antisocial behavior; to experience feelings of incompetence.

Being the parental favorite, however, may be a mixed blessing. The preferred child may earn the envy or even the enmity of his siblings. He may grow up assuming that the world owes him a living. A Hong Kong study found a higher incidence of low self-esteem and suicidal ideation in adolescents who believed their parents played favorites. Surprisingly, the higher rate held true for both the favored *and* the nonfavored child.

Favoritism, in some cases, may indirectly benefit the less-favored child, whose redoubled efforts to catch a parent's attention may encourage a persistence that serves him well outside the family. (Adler, having pushed even harder to win his parents' approval, became a lifelong striver.) Biographers note that parental disfavor often plays a role in the development of writers and artists, who, feeling relegated to the family perimeter, may develop an outsider's perspective—or may feel pushed into the wider world to find the appreciation they cannot get at home. Alec Waugh, the sun around which his parents revolved, became a mediocre middlebrow novelist. Evelyn, watching from the sidelines, covered up his insecurity by developing an acerbic, satirical tongue, which he trained on his father's sentimental Victorian world to become the voice of youth and change in twentieth-century England. In effect, he usurped his older brother's birthright, becoming the great writer his father believed Alec was born to be.

And yet as Evelyn grew into middle age, he became more and more like the father who had ignored him—an old-fashioned fussbudget, a technophobe, a throwback to the Victorian era he professed to despise. The boy who hated his childhood home turned into an inveterate homebody, filling his modest estate (which he referred to as "Stinkers") with painstakingly selected furniture, books, and paintings. Though he claimed to dislike children, he had seven. Like his father, he played favorites, giving his eldest son the best of the children's bedrooms, calling him (only half-jokingly) "my son and heir," and taking him on trips to London and the south of France. Evelyn showed little interest in his second son, whom he called "dull as ditchwater."

Alec Waugh played no favorites. He treated his three children with equal indifference. If his own father had been suffocatingly close, Alec gave his children space—an ocean's worth. The heir of Underhill spent his adulthood living out of suitcases in hotels, ship's cabins, and gentlemen's clubs around the world. Breezing through two marriages and innumerable affairs, he described parenting as a "civic duty," one he did his best to avoid. For most of his life, he visited his family for only a few weeks a year. At one point, he went six years without seeing his children. When a friend pointed out that his children might never get to know him, Alec suggested that they could read his books. Not long before he died at the age of eighty-three and his ashes were interred in his parents' grave, he wrote of his children, "I hope I have not been a nuisance to them."

*   *   *

John Wilkes Booth had been nine when Edwin first left home to tour with his father. He was eighteen when Edwin returned from San Francisco. Although John admired Edwin, and Edwin, like almost everyone who met John, couldn't help liking his younger brother, they hardly knew each other. But the Booths were a clannish family, bound by their eccentricities and their embarrassment over their father's erratic behavior. As June had helped Edwin, Edwin tried to help John. In 1858, not long after John's debut, Edwin had his brother cast as Richmond to his Richard III, Horatio to his Hamlet, and, eventually, Othello to his Iago. John's early efforts at acting were crude; he lacked confidence, stuttered, and forgot his lines. But Edwin complimented him at every opportunity, covered up his mistakes, arranged the staging so that John was never out of range of the footlights, and gave him more prominent billing than his experience warranted. It was on Edwin's recommendation that John, after three years of stock, was hired for the first time as a leading man. As his brother's reputation grew, Edwin seemed proud that there was more than one famous Booth brother onstage; he considered John's achievements a family triumph. After seeing John star as Pescara in *The Apostate* in Boston in 1863, Edwin wrote gleefully to a friend: "I am happy to state that he is full of the true grit—he has stuff enough in him to make good suits for a dozen such player-folk as we are cursed with; and when time and study round his rough edges he'll bid them all 'stand apart' like 'a bully boy, with a glass eye'; I am delighted with him & feel the name of Booth to be more of a hydra than snakes and things ever was."

It was easier, of course, for Edwin to be happy for John. Edwin was, after all, the acknowledged star in the family. For John, things were more complicated. It must have been difficult to find his niche in a profession that counted his father and older brother among its most celebrated practitioners. Although John had told his schoolmates that *he* was the

Booth who would be remembered, he wanted to make his own mark in the world. When he decided to become an actor, he performed for three years under the stage name J. Wilkes. Once he'd made his reputation, he told a friend, he would take back the family name. But he looked and sounded so much like Edwin that he was often recognized. In 1858, while appearing in Richmond, twenty-year-old John wrote Edwin a chatty, contented letter about his life in the theater. "There is only one objection," he added, "and that is I believe every one knows me already. I have heard my name—Booth—called for, one or two nights, and on account of the *likeness* the papers deigned to mention me." Even after he reclaimed the name Booth, John was irritated at always being linked to more famous family members, as when the playbill for his first Washington appearance announced him to be "SON OF THE GREAT JUNIUS BRUTUS BOOTH AND BROTHER AND ARTISTIC RIVAL OF EDWIN BOOTH." For an 1862 Baltimore run, John had a quote from Richard III printed on his billboards: "I have no brother. I am no brother . . . I AM MYSELF ALONE."

Several biographers have explained Lincoln's assassination as an extreme case of sibling rivalry, suggesting that John was a second-rate thespian who, realizing he'd never eclipse his older brother and inherit the paternal mantle, was driven to seek fame on another stage. Certainly, John was sensitive to his position. A proud man accustomed to getting his way, he may have resented being given direction by Edwin in their early joint appearances. He must have felt patronized when, after one performance, Edwin led him to the footlights and announced to the audience, "I think he has done well. Don't you?" But while John wanted to make it on his own, he also yearned for his older brother's approval. In 1862, when Edwin was touring in England, John sent him his reviews, including one that compared his rendition of Richard III favorably with those of his father and Edwin. And when Edwin suggested that each of the three Booth brothers take a section of the United States for his theatrical territory—Edwin the North, John the South, and June the West—John complained to Asia that Edwin was selfishly trying to keep the sweetest piece of the show business pie for himself. Newspapers played up the competition, but the brothers were mutually supportive. A vain man in most things, John was realistic about his own acting and in awe of Edwin's. If there was a theatrical sibling rivalry, John had no doubt who was the winner. At a rehearsal one day, at the height of John's renown, some actors were discussing well-known Hamlets with him, including his own. "No, oh no!" John interrupted. "There's but one Hamlet to my mind—that's my brother Edwin. You see, between ourselves, he *is* Hamlet—melancholy and all."

As a leading man, however, John was no slouch. His rise from "third walking man" to touring star was meteoric. Within five years of his stage debut he was earning more than $20,000 a year, the equivalent of about $560,000 today. Though John Wilkes Booth is now remembered only as Lincoln's assassin, at the time of his death he was one of the most popular actors in the country, with reviews as glowing as those of any other performer—excepting, perhaps, his brother Edwin's. The *Daily Missouri Democrat* pronounced John "the greatest tragedian in the country," while the *Daily Journal* of Louisville simply called him "a young man of extraordinary genius." Some biographers have suggested that John's fan base was limited to the South, where he was praised as much for his pro-Rebel politics as for his acting, but northerners were no less enthusiastic. "The genius of the Booth family has been bequeathed to this third son," concluded the Detroit *Daily Advertiser*, while the *Philadelphia Press* called the last act of his Richard III "a piece of acting that few actors can rival, and is far above the capacity of Edwin Booth." John was a special favorite in Boston, the cradle of the abolition movement, whose *Transcript* described his achievements as "almost without parallel in the records of the stage." Comparison of the brothers was inevitable. While each reviewer had his preferred Booth, there was general agreement that Edwin was better suited to playing dreamers, deep thinkers, and tortured souls; John to lovers, swashbucklers, and mysterious strangers. According to the *Boston Post*: "Edwin has more poetry, John Wilkes more passion . . . Edwin is more Shakespearean, John Wilkes is more melo-dramatic; and in a word, Edwin is a better Hamlet, John Wilkes a better Richard III." Years later, recalling John's celebrated 1864 Boston run, John T. Ford, owner of the theater in which Lincoln was killed, observed, "Doubtless he would have been the greatest actor of his time if he had lived."

It was difficult to compare the two, in part because their styles were so different. Edwin, who had grown up watching his father on stage, was moving away from the strenuous, scenery-chewing, capital-letter "Acting" that had defined the early-nineteenth-century stage toward a (relatively speaking) more quiet, conversational style—an embryonic version of what, in the twentieth century, would be called "naturalistic" acting. "He was the least extravagant actor imaginable," wrote a biographer. "He seemed most to stir audiences not by the violence of his feelings but by the repression of them."

John kept nothing inside. He was all raw instinct and undisciplined bravado. (Edwin was often asked whether his subtle, nuanced Hamlet was sane or not; when John played Hamlet, he left no doubt that the Danish prince was mad as a hatter.) Although some dismissed John as a "ranter," in the parlance of the times, others found his over-the-top approach galvanic. John Ellsler, a Cleveland actor and theatrical manager who had performed with Junius Brutus Booth, said that "John has more of the old man's power in one performance than Edwin can show in a year. He has the fire, the dash, the touch of *strangeness.*" After a performance in Albany, a group of local spiritualists issued a statement saying that Booth's acting had been so like his father's that the parental spirit must have been hovering onstage above the son. A natural athlete, John threw himself about the stage with abandon. The actress Kate Reignolds recalled that when playing the slain Desdemona to John's Othello, "I used to gather myself together and hold my breath, lest the bang his scimitar gave when he threw himself at me should force me back to life with a shriek." (In contrast, when Edwin played Othello to Ellen Terry's Desdemona, he was chiefly anxious that he not smudge her with his Moorish makeup: "I shall never make you black," he told her. "When I take your hand I shall have a corner of my drapery in my hand. That will protect you.") For *Macbeth*, John had the stage crew build a rock ledge more than ten feet high, from which he could make his entrance with a gasp-inspiring leap. Though an expert swordsman, John fought with such desperate passion that he was badly cut at least three times. (However heavily bleeding, he always finished the battle.) Ellsler recalled of John's Richard III that "his fight with Richmond was a task that many a good swordsman dreaded. John

Wilkes, as Richard, never knew when he was conquered, consequently he was never ready to die, until it was evident to him that his death was necessary to preserve Richmond's life according to the story and the text of the tragedy. In many instances he wore poor Richmond out, and on one occasion Richmond was compelled to whisper, 'For God's sake, John, die! Die! If you don't, I shall.'"

If the brothers' acting styles differed, so too did their motivations. Edwin sought excellence. John wanted renown. Early in his career, when John received several dispiriting reviews, his roommate recalled that rather than studying his lines, he paced the floor of their boardinghouse bedroom, muttering, "I must have fame! Fame!" If Edwin hadn't also been a theater manager, he might have shunned all publicity; he made one impresario take down posters that billed him as "The World's Greatest Actor." Edwin avoided curtain calls whenever possible, stammered when thanking an audience (in a voice barely audible beyond the first few rows), and seemed surprised by their applause. John acted as if the applause was no more than his due. Edwin was a student of the theater; he liked to discuss technique and interpretation with fellow actors, and would stay up long after a show, smoking his pipe, studying his lines, and reading about great thespians of the past. Although John was known for his eagerness to try out unusual approaches and new bits of stage business, he had little patience for hard work, was easily bored, and, used to getting his way, sometimes bridled at being corrected. In retrospect, Asia believed that things had come too easily for John, that he had been spoiled by spending the first few years of his career in the South, where, she wrote, "even his errors were extolled and his successes magnified. The people loved him; he had never known privation or want, was never out of an engagement, while Edwin had had the rough schooling of poverty, hardship in far distant cities, struggles in his professional experience, fiercer struggles with himself. He had gone through the drudgery of his art through the fire of temptation, and he overcame and was victorious."

The brothers' acting styles reflected their personalities. Although he could be merry with his family or a few longtime friends, Edwin was formal and remote with strangers, "sometimes moving in the throng, but never of it," as a theater critic put it. Louisa May Alcott, glimpsing him at a Boston reception, described him in her journal as "a handsome, shy man, glooming in a corner." Embarrassed by his limited schooling, Edwin had an awe of the well-educated that bordered on fear. He never traveled by trolley, worried that someone might recognize him and engage him in conversation. He seemed most relaxed in his letters, filling them with breezy wordplay and atrocious puns for which he immediately apologized. (Always the gentleman, he never wrote "hell" or "damn," always "h__l" and "d__n.") Many people assumed that his favorite role was Hamlet, but in later years he told his daughter how relieved he had been to change the bill after a long run as the prince. Acting offered a respite from being himself. "He wished to forget his own identity, as it were," wrote his daughter. "In *Hamlet* he was less able to achieve this, so closely was it allied with his own temperament and mood." It was because of Edwin that "Booth-like" became a commonly used adjective to describe someone dark, handsome, and brooding; he likely suffered from what would now be called clinical depression. In the first few days after Lincoln's assassination, when it was said that a madman named Booth had killed the president, not a few Americans assumed it was Edwin.

In photos, Edwin looked as if he were retreating, John as if he were about to pounce. A veteran actor compared John with a stallion: "You have seen a high-mettled racer with his sleek skin and eye of unusual brilliancy chafing under a restless impatience to be doing something. It is the only living thing I could liken him to." If Edwin was most comfortable alone in his study, John was most at home at the center of a party, telling stories, playing practical jokes, chatting expansively about politics, literature, war, nature, the theater. He was a familiar sight in Washington's bars, billiard rooms, tenpin alleys, shooting galleries, and brothels—and an expert in all these arenas. As a child, John had been the center of attention on the Farm; as an adult, he was no less eager to see and be seen. "In his leisure he liked to stand in the front of the theater, twirling his mustache and frankly exhibiting himself," a twelve-year-old program boy whom Booth befriended at Ford's Theatre recalled years later. On stage, he performed with his sleeves rolled up so audiences could admire his biceps. Just as his father had impressed dinner party guests with his pull-out-the-stops version of the Lord's Prayer, John drew crowds in saloons and hotel parlors with his dramatic renditions of Poe's "The Raven" or—his favorite—"Beautiful Snow," a maudlin poem about lost innocence that brought even its reciter to tears. After the assassination, when his name was anathema and merely to be found with his carte de visite was to risk arrest, people still spoke of his magnetic charm. Indeed, the lawyer for one of Booth's co-conspirators would use Booth's charisma in his client's defense, suggesting that he was a Svengali who brainwashed his client into cooperation through the sheer force of his personality.

Part of John's appeal was aesthetic. He was commonly described as "the most handsome man in America." Like Edwin, John had wavy black hair, fair skin, an aquiline nose, and unnaturally long eyelashes, but where Edwin had the haunted, epicene look of a doomed poet, John—an inch taller at five-foot-eight, far more muscular (he exercised regularly), and sporting a thick mustache to which he was exceedingly attentive—had a dashing, virile quality that turned writers' prose purple. "Picture to yourself Adonis, with high forehead, ascetic face corrected by rather full lips, sweeping black hair, a figure of perfect youthful proportions and the most wonderful black eyes in the world," wrote a fellow actor. (Those wonderful eyes, after the assassination, would be described by one editorialist as "blazing with hellish malignancy.") John had outgrown his youthful fascination with the Spartan life to become a renowned dandy. Clad in a flowing cape with an astrakhan collar and a slouch hat worn at a rakish angle, his surprisingly delicate hands sheathed in kid gloves, he was instantly recognizable to most passersby. Even those who didn't recognize him usually turned for a second look.

Especially women. From childhood, Booth had been accustomed to the adoration of the female sex, beginning with his mother and his sister Asia. "As the sunflowers turn upon their stalks to follow the beloved sun, so old and young, our faces smiling turned to him," wrote the actress Clara Morris. John was besieged by adoring female fans at stage doors; received a hundred love letters a week from women he'd never met; was propositioned by women of every social station; and, according to the author of *The Matinee Idols,* was the first actor on record to have his clothes shredded by groupies. (One can only imagine the trauma Edwin would have suffered under such close examination.) While there is ample evidence that John was more than willing to meet some of his admirers halfway—his first biographer described him as "one of the world's most successful lovers"—he was not a "seducer," as duplicitous Don Juans were called in his day. Deluged with letters from flirtatious women, he tore out and destroyed the signatures so the writers' reputations could not be compromised, and it was counted in his favor that, as another early biographer put it, "he never knowingly deflowered virgins." At his death, a pocket in his red leatherbound diary contained photographs of five women—four well-known actresses, along with a senator's daughter to whom he was secretly engaged.

Indeed, in most things, John was unfailingly thoughtful. Harry Ford, treasurer of the theater in which Lincoln was shot, recalled him as "one of the simplest, sweetest-dispositioned, and most lovable men he ever knew." Though desperate for fame, when John achieved it he didn't play the prima donna. While Edwin preferred the company of his fellow actors, John idled with the stagehands, gossiping and buying them drinks. "The gentlest man I ever knew...," recalled an actor. "In rehearsal he was always considerate of the other actors, and if he had a suggestion to make, always made it with the utmost courtesy, prefacing it with; 'Now, Mr. ——, don't you think that perhaps this might be a better way to interpret that?'" A friend recalled, "In his ways with his intimates he was as simple and affectionate as a child." John once took up sign language in order to converse with a deaf poetess.

But even as John's theatrical fame grew, he longed for a more tangible form of glory. Edwin's heroes were the great actors of the past, Edmund Kean and Edwin Forrest; the rebel heroes of John's youth, Brutus and William Tell, remained the heroes of his manhood. (After John's death, one of his friends asserted that the actor's oft-proclaimed admiration for Brutus, the tyrant slayer, was the "mainspring of the assassination.") It wasn't the cause that impressed John but the grandness of the gesture. Early in his career, while acting in Richmond, he had impulsively joined a militia bound for Charlestown to guard the abolitionist John Brown as he awaited hanging. Despite their antipodal stances on slavery, Brown became a hero to Booth for daring to take history into his own hands. "John Brown was a man inspired," he told Asia, "the grandest character of this century!" Wanting to be such a hero himself, John tried to pass for heroic. In the matter of John Brown, for instance, he allowed people to believe he had assisted in Brown's capture, although by the time Booth arrived on the scene, the abolitionist had long since been behind bars. When telling a story about himself, John tended to inflate his role, as if he were a character in a Bulwer-Lytton saga. After traveling to an engagement sixty miles by sleigh through a Missouri blizzard, he embellished an already impressive tale by boasting that he had fought off an attack by a pack of wolves. In 1863, after having a fibroid tumor removed from his neck, John asked the doctor to report the injury as a bullet wound. The doctor refused. But whenever John was asked about the scar, he bragged that he had been shot.

Although their personalities and their interests could hardly have been more contrary—it is hard to imagine John sitting still while Edwin smoked a pipe in his study, even harder to imagine Edwin accompanying John to the saloons and shooting galleries of which he was so fond—the Booth brothers shared a deep fraternal devotion. If John was in awe of Edwin's discipline and talent, Edwin would have liked to possess some of John's easy charm. When their work kept them apart, they wrote each other chatty, affectionate letters. When Edwin married in 1860, John was the sole family member present; after the ceremony, held in a clergyman's study in New York City, he impulsively threw his arms around his brother and kissed him. In 1863, after Edwin and his wife had temporarily moved to Dorchester, Massachusetts, for her health, John, appearing for three weeks at a Boston theater, visited almost every day. When she died of pneumonia later that year, John cancelled his performances in Philadelphia, posted "A Card to the Public" in which he wrote that he "felt the necessity imperative upon him to join his afflicted Brother," rushed to Boston to be at Edwin's side for the funeral in Mount Auburn Cemetery, and spent several days helping Edwin pack up his wife's possessions.

*   *   *

In 1874, the Victorian polymath Francis Galton published *English Men of Science: Their Nature and Nurture*. A banker's son whose IQ was later estimated to be 200, Galton would, over the course of his nearly eighty-nine years, explore uncharted regions of southwest Africa, pioneer the use of weather maps, devise a technique for classifying fingerprints, and, shortly before his death, write a utopian novel. But ever since the publication in 1859 of *The Origin of Species,* by his cousin Charles Darwin, Galton's main interest had been heredity. In *English Men of Science,* he reported the results of a questionnaire he had sent to the Fellows of the Royal Society, an association of scientists, in which he asked, among other things, their educational background, their religious beliefs, the circumference of their heads, the color of their hair, the number of siblings in their family, and the order of their birth, in an effort to determine whether their achievements were attributable more to innate intelligence or to environmental circumstances. Although Galton did not reach a definitive conclusion, he remarked, along the way, that a disproportionate number of eminent scientists happened to be firstborn sons. He explained that "elder sons have, on the whole, decided advantages of nurture over the younger sons. They are more likely to become possessed of independent means, and therefore able to follow the pursuits that have most attraction to their tastes; they are treated more as companions by their parents, and have earlier responsibility, both of which would develop independence of character." Galton was himself the youngest of nine children, though he had more than enough money to follow his diverse pursuits. He nevertheless maintained that birth order had a significant effect on sibling difference.

At the time Galton was writing, that notion might have seemed self-evident. After all, primogeniture, the tradition by which a family's entire property is left to the eldest son, had been practiced in England since the arrival of William the Conquerer in 1066. In an effort to make sure the family estate remained intact, the eldest son got the land and the money (and, usually, the girl, in the form of an advantageous marriage), while later-born sons were forced to go off to war, seek their fortunes in the New World, or enter the ministry. This arrangement predictably led to cases in which a dim-witted elder son frittered away the ancestral wealth while his better-qualified younger brother was killed in battle or disappeared in the wilds of Canada. Darwin, himself a second son, commented to his friend Joseph Hooker, "Primogeniture is dreadfully opposed to natural selection; suppose the first-born bull was necessarily made by each farmer the begetter of his stock!" Not surprisingly—America being itself a kind of surrogate younger brother to England—primogeniture was abolished throughout the United States after the Revolution. But a kind of informal primogeniture persisted, in which American parents often invested more heavily in their eldest son, making sure he got an education or offering him first chance at taking over the family business.

Differential treatment of siblings according to birth order has been culturally sanctioned, even institutionalized, for much of recorded history. In biblical times, of course, firstborn sons were entitled to their "birthright": a double portion of the inheritance. A 1974 survey of thirty-nine non-Western societies found that in every culture, firstborns have been accorded greater status and respect than later-borns. In ancient Japan, younger siblings were known as "cold rice," a reference to the tradition of feeding them leftovers after the firstborn had eaten his fill. In China, although brothers inherited equally in their father's estate, Confucian thinkers held that younger brothers should show the same deference to their older brothers that they showed to their father or to the emperor. This philosophy was reflected in Chinese law. Younger brothers who assaulted or killed their older brothers were punished with death by beheading or slicing (a grisly procedure in which the executioner systematically lopped off strips of flesh), while older brothers who assaulted or killed their younger brothers were merely imprisoned or banished. In some cultures, birth order has been literally a matter of life and death. Just as certain species of animals will, in times of stress, kill some of their offspring to ensure the survival of the rest of the litter, parents in traditional societies may, in times of famine or drought, kill the younger of two closely spaced children to ensure that at least one child lives. Such infanticide has been condoned only in the case of the younger sibling, never the elder, who, already past the dangerous first years of life, is considered the better bet for survival. Having outlasted more childhood diseases, older children are more likely to live into adulthood and more likely to reproduce sooner than their younger siblings. Investing in firstborns, therefore, makes evolutionary sense, as the likeliest way to ensure the parents' genetic heritage will endure.

In a 1937 paper, Alfred Adler suggested that birth order has psychological ramifications as well. Observing that "the psychic situation of each child differs because of the order of their birth," Adler declared that the firstborn child, having been "dethroned" by the arrival of a brother or sister, struggles to maintain his dominant status and is likely to become a kind of surrogate parent who cleaves to law and order. The second-born child, said Adler, "behaves as if he were in a race, as if some one were a step or two in front and he had to hurry to get ahead of him. He is under full steam all the time. He trains continually to surpass his older brother and conquer him." Unthreatened by the possibility of dethronement, the last-born tends to be spoiled; overshadowed by elder siblings, however, he may develop an inferiority complex. In keeping with the truism that psychologists tend to devise theories that reflect their personal circumstances, Adler was a second-born who struggled all his life to surpass his elder brother. Even at the height of his success, when he was recognized as one of the foremost psychological theorists of the twentieth century, the otherwise affable Adler remained envious, referring to his brother, a provincial businessman, as "a good industrious fellow [who] was always ahead of me—is *still* ahead of me!"

Subsequent research has refined and expanded on Adler's observations. Born into a hothouse environment in which they enjoy undivided parental attention, firstborns tend to be precocious achievers. They walk and talk earlier than later-borns. They have higher IQs—three points higher, on average, than that of their next eldest sibling, according to a 2007 Norwegian study of more than 240,000 young men. They have been described as assertive, ambitious, conscientious, responsible, organized, and self-reliant. The only children to have known the privileges of a sibling-free state, firstborns zealously defend their territory against encroachment, trying to maintain their alpha sibling status. Hence, they are more likely to be conservative, to identify with their parents and other authority figures, to support the status quo. Leaders in their own families, they often become leaders in the outside world. Not only scientists (Victorian and otherwise) but American presidents, British prime ministers, members of Congress, Rhodes scholars, Ivy League students, Nobel Prize winners, MBAs, CEOs, surgeons, pilots, and professors are more likely to be firstborns. Of the first twenty-three American astronauts in space, twenty-one were firstborns and the other two were only children—only children being considered by birth-order theorists to be a kind of über-eldest.

Being the eldest can be a burden as well as a privilege. First-time parents tend to be anxious and may transmit that anxiety to their child—part of the reason firstborns are also characterized as defensive and neurotic. Parents are more likely to project their dreams and ambitions onto their eldest, who is liable to work especially hard to live up to them. "You come into life with advantages which will disgrace you if your success is mediocre," wrote John Adams, himself the eldest of three sons, to his namesake, John Quincy, a twenty-six-year-old lawyer at the time. "If you do not rise to the head not only of your profession, but of your country, it will be owing to your own *Laziness, Slovenliness,* and *Obstinacy.*" Many sons might have withered under such pressure, but though John Quincy, a brilliant perfectionist who suffered from depression, didn't rise to the top of the legal profession, he did rise to the top of his country, becoming its sixth president. His two younger brothers, of whom his parents expected far less, also became lawyers, but, undone by alcohol, sank to the bottom of their profession.

Firstborn sons are encouraged to be role models. "You know I'm the oldest of my family, and I've got to be the example for a lot of brothers and sisters," young Joe Kennedy explained—bragged?—to a friend. They are expected to act as substitute parents. "You must not reckon yourself only their brother," the Prince of Wales told the ten-year-old future King George III in 1749, "but I hope you will be a kind father to them." (George tried, but his eight siblings, an unusually profligate and promiscuous lot, proved to be no less difficult to control than the thirteen colonies.) They are expected to be babysitters, nursemaids, and nannies. "In those days my mother was given to the exasperating and mysterious habit of having babies," wrote James Baldwin, the eldest of nine children in an impoverished Harlem household. "As they were born, I took them over with one hand and held a book with the other." Benjamin Spock, who grew up feeding, changing, and rocking to sleep his five younger siblings, would, as the author of best-selling baby-care books, become pediatrician-parent to a nation. They serve as mentors. The young A. E. Housman encouraged his six siblings to write poetry, taught them the names of trees, and demonstrated the movements of the heavenly bodies by arranging them on the lawn and setting them in orbit. (With characteristic modesty, he cast himself as the moon and not as the sun around which his brothers and sisters revolved.) When Geoffrey and Tobias Wolff spent the summer of 1961 together before Tobias left for boarding school in the fall, Geoffrey, a recent Princeton graduate, took it on himself to prepare his younger brother. He corrected his pronunciation, showed him how to dress like a preppie, and gave him a customized tutorial in English literature by assigning him a book every day and an essay every week. "I was a tin-pot despot," he recalled. For Tobias, who, like his brother, would become a writer, the lessons were life-changing: "Ever since I was eleven or twelve I'd written tales of mystery and horror and adventure, and had notions of being an 'author,' but after that summer I never really wanted to be anything else."

Stanley ("Bunny") White was, according to his younger brother Elwyn, a born teacher who "imparted information as casually as a tree drops its leaves in the fall." Stanley would become a professor of landscape architecture; Elwyn (E. B.) White would become a writer for *The New Yorker*.

> He taught me the harmonic circle on the pianoforte. He gave me haphazard lessons in the laws of physics: centrifugal force, momentum, inertia, gravity, surface tension, and illustrated everything in a clowning way. He taught me to paddle a canoe so that it would proceed on a straight course instead of a series of zigzags. He showed me how to hold the scissors for trimming the fingernails of my right hand. He showed me how to handle a jacknife without cutting myself. Hardly a day passes in my life without my performing some act that reminds me of something I learned from Bunny.

Henry Kissinger's pedagogical approach was more forceful. Kissinger, whose family fled Germany three months before Kristallnacht and eventually settled in the United States, was drafted shortly after turning nineteen. As he finished basic training, he passed along what he'd learned in a letter to his younger brother, Walter, soon to enter the service himself.

> Always stand in the middle because details are always picked from the end. Always remain inconspicuous because as long as they don't know you, they can't pick on you. . . . Don't become too friendly with the scum you invariably meet there. Don't gamble! There are always a few professional crooks in the crowd and they skin you alive. Don't lend out money. It will be no good to you. You will have a hard time getting your money back and you will lose your friends to the bargain. Don't go to a whore-house. I like a woman as you do. But I wouldn't think of touching those filthy, syphilis-infected camp followers.

Henry closed on a softer note: "You and I sometimes didn't get along so well, but I guess you knew, as I did, that in the 'clutch' we could count on each other. We are in the clutch now."

The line between teacher and boss—and between boss and bully—can be thin, and depends, no doubt, on one's point of view. (Perhaps only a younger brother can fully appreciate the chilling catchphrase in George Orwell's *1984*: "Big Brother Is Watching You.") In 1718, twelve-year-old Benjamin Franklin, the eleventh of thirteen children, was apprenticed to his twenty-one-year-old brother James, printer and publisher of the first independent newspaper in the colonies. The elder Franklin was a stern taskmaster, and "the blows his passion too often urged him to bestow upon me" led the younger Franklin, at age seventeen, four years before his term of indenture would expire, to run away to Philadelphia. (Later, Franklin would allow that his brother had taught him more than typesetting. "I fancy this harsh and tyrannical treatment of me might be a means of impressing me with that aversion to arbitrary power that has stuck to me through my whole life," he wrote archly in the *Autobiography*.) At Anthony Trollope's boarding school, older brothers were responsible not only for their younger brother's academic performance but for their discipline. "The result was that, as a part of his daily exercise, he thrashed me with a big stick," Trollope recalled of his brother Thomas. (Perhaps Trollope was fortunate. Like most older brothers, Thomas beat up his younger brother for insubordination. Antoine de Saint-Exupéry beat up *his* younger brother for refusing to listen to him recite his poetry.) An elder brother's domineering doesn't always take physical form. When young Lyndon Johnson found out that his worshipful nine-year-old brother, Sam, had managed to save $11.20 doing odd jobs in town, Lyndon, in an early version of the manipulative tactics he would perfect as a politician, suggested they "go partners" and use Sam's money to buy a bicycle "together." Sam was thrilled. Lyndon chose the bike, which was just the right size for the gangly older brother but useless to Sam, whose feet couldn't reach the pedals.

Like the biblical Jacob, the second-born child, unable to compete physically with his larger, stronger brother, learns to work things out with words. Second-borns tend to be mediators, compromisers, peacemakers. They are often described as cooperative, sociable, empathetic, flexible, agreeable. Second-borns may also become fiercely competitive as they struggle to keep pace with their older siblings. (I remember identifying with the Avis Rent a Car ads, ubiquitous when I was a boy, whose slogan promised: "We're Number Two. We try harder.") Yet the second-born sibling may feel that no matter what he does, his older brother has done it before him. Henry James wrote that his brother William "had gained such an advance of me in his sixteen months' experience of the world before mine began that I never for all the time of childhood and youth in the least caught up with him or overtook him." The second-born's sense of being second best may be reinforced by parents (the Duchess of Marlborough famously referred to her two sons as "the heir and the spare") or by peers (the English actor Rupert Everett's boarding-school classmates dubbed him "Everett Two," his older brother, of course, being "Everett One"). An elder brother's shadow can loom especially large when that brother is famous. The renowned nineteenth-century animal behaviorist Frédéric Cuvier habitually deferred to his older brother, an even more renowned naturalist; when he died, his tombstone read, "Frédéric Cuvier, brother of Georges Cuvier."

The second-born child may get less attention. He may also get less pressure. With Joe Kennedy Sr. grooming Joe Jr. for the presidency, Jack had more freedom to chart his own path. "I believe that Jack was very glad Joe had taken on the obligation of his father's ambition," one of Jack's Harvard roommates recalled. "He felt that Joe, as the number-one son, had to face a lot, as it worked out, that he would just as soon avoid. The situation gave him a certain independence that he valued." As a perk of primogeniture, being fitted for orthodontia may not be in the same league as being groomed for the presidency, but when his older brother got braces and he didn't, Arthur Miller saw a (nonmetallic) silver lining. "My teeth were no less prognathous, but I was not the eldest son and to my great relief even then was not regarded as worth the money," wrote Miller in his memoir, *Timebends*. "If this put me down, it also freed me from Kermit's weighty responsibilities, which I had much respect for but no desire to share." For Kermit, those responsibilities would include trying to rescue their father's failing coat-manufacturing business during the Depression. Arthur, free to pursue his interests, became a playwright and distilled the family dynamics into *Death of a Salesman*. "As the eldest son he had all the responsibility, and I had all the fun," noted Miller. All five DiMaggio brothers grew up playing baseball in the sandlots of San Francisco—indeed, the second son, Mike, was reckoned to be the hardest hitter in the family. But their father, a Sicilian immigrant, said that baseball was a child's game and insisted his sons work on the family fishing boat. Tom and Mike dutifully quit school by the eighth grade to join their father. The third son, Vince, however, fought bitterly with his father and left home to become a baseball player. In doing so, he cleared a path for his younger brothers. When the father tried to make his fourth son, Joe, a shy, self-conscious fellow two years younger than Vince, work on the fishing boat, his wife told him to let Joe alone. Vince, Joe, and Dom would all go on to long careers in professional baseball. (Tom eventually quit fishing to manage a restaurant for his brother Joe; Mike continued to fish and drowned at the age of forty-four.)

With less time and energy to spare, parents tend to be more relaxed and less strict with later-borns, who, in turn, tend to be more relaxed and less hidebound than firstborns. A friend of mine still recalls the resentment he felt when his mother criticized him for getting an A– on a fourth-grade paper, while cooing over his younger brother, a less conscientious student, for getting a C. (That same friend remembers how unfair it seemed that when his father sat him down for a facts-of-life talk in the sixth grade, he invited his fourth-grade brother to attend—enabling his brother to get possession of the facts at an infuriatingly younger age.) When the Prodigal Son returns home after many years, having squandered his inheritance on prostitutes and wine, his father dresses him in his best robe, gives him a ring, and throws him a party. The older son, working in the fields, hears the celebration and is resentful. "Lo, these many years I have served you, and I never disobeyed your command; yet you never gave me a kid, that I might make merry with my friends," he says to his father. "But when this son of yours came, who has devoured your living with harlots, you killed for him the fatted calf."

If the second-born is a middle child, he may occupy a kind of no-man's-land in the family, getting neither the privileges of the eldest brother nor the attention of the youngest. Like Edwin Booth, he may feel lost in the shuffle, which may explain why middle children are more likely to suffer from low self-esteem and to look outside the family for companionship. With two heroic brothers and four sisters ahead of him, and one sister and a baby brother behind him, Bobby Kennedy had to fight for a toehold in his family. His task was complicated by his temperament; unlike his brothers, he was small, shy, and so sensitive that his grandmother worried he'd become a sissy. "Bobby felt he was weak," said a friend. "He felt he had to toughen himself up and get rid of that vulnerability everyone had remarked on since he was a boy. This was the way for him to get someplace in the family. The drive was incessant, just fierce. He simply remade himself. He got so he could just go through a wall." Despite his diminutive size and limited athletic talent, he fought his way onto the Harvard football team, and played so tenaciously—through a dislocated shoulder and a fractured leg—that the coaches awarded him a varsity letter, something neither of his older brothers had won. Bobby would employ his hard-earned pugnacity as Jack's campaign manager and, later, as his attorney general, doing the political dirty work that allowed his brother to remain above the fray. Bullied political opponents and browbeaten staff members alike would grumble, "Little Brother Is Watching You."

If firstborns often are the achievers and middle children the peacemakers, last-borns are the entertainers and spotlight-seekers. Some of history's greatest satirists—Swift, Voltaire, Franklin, Twain—were born at or near the tail end of large families, and many of their spiritual heirs, twentieth-century comedians like Charlie Chaplin, Will Rogers, Oliver Hardy, Jimmy Durante, Red Skelton, Sid Caesar, Danny Kaye, Jackie Gleason, Art Carney, Mel Brooks, Jim Carrey, Billy Crystal, Eddie Murphy, and Steve Martin, are last-borns. (Stephen Colbert is the eleventh of eleven.) Last-borns are also more likely to be pranksters and risk-takers; they are overrepresented among the ranks of explorers, entrepreneurs, firemen, and fighter pilots. Last-borns are said to be charming, affectionate, spontaneous, mischievous, and—because the baby of the family tends to get infantalized—pampered, temperamental, irresponsible, and manipulative. All these adjectives describe John Wilkes Booth, who, though not a last-born, was treated as if he were.

The last-born of nine, Teddy Kennedy was the family mascot, an object of affection and teasing. He reacted to both by being sunny, cheerful, and eager to please. "If my siblings found themselves in trouble with Dad," he later wrote, "they would sometimes send me into his room ahead of them to 'soften him up' before the reckoning began." Seeing his roly-poly, freckle-faced youngest child, Joe Sr. couldn't help smiling. At the same time, Teddy was so much younger than his brothers—Joe, seventeen years older, and Jack, fifteen years older, were more like fathers to him—that he was often on his own. At dinner, he and his sister Jean ate at a separate little table while the rest of the family gathered at the big table. Because of his family's frequent moves—by age thirteen he had attended ten schools—Teddy learned to make a good impression quickly, to make friends of strangers. This attribute would help him become the most natural politician in the family.

If last-borns can be coddled, they can, like Joseph Booth, also be overlooked. Less may be expected of them. They may not be taken as

James bros.

seriously. "How feeble and diluted, of necessity, must the parental instinct be, trickling down," Alice James observed in her diary, writing about a Victorian family with twenty-five children but perhaps thinking, too, of her own. Henry James Sr. and his wife were so infatuated with their precocious eldest son, William, and their sweet-tempered second-born, Henry, that they paid scant attention to Wilky, a chubby, good-natured boy his father described as "more heart than head," and Bob, an energetic but unpredictable fellow. Much of the younger boys' care, and Alice's as well, was delegated to their aunt Kate. (Bob would look back and say that at times he had felt so peripheral that he assumed he was a foundling.) Henry Sr. believed that his brilliant elder sons would achieve greatness in medicine or science; Wilky and Bob, he told friends, were "destined for commerce." When the Civil War began, the father took pains to keep his elder sons out of the conflict (easy enough, as neither was keen on going into battle); he encouraged his younger sons to fight. Both would have distinguished war careers. Both would leave with scars. Wilky, wounded during the charge at Fort Wagner under Robert Gould Shaw, would limp for the rest of his life, while Bob, who enlisted at the age of sixteen, would return home an eighteen-year-old alcoholic.

After the war, William and Henry shared the third floor of their father's house while Henry wrote and William tried to decide what to do with his life when they weren't taking turns traveling in Europe on their father's dime. Wilky and Bob, kicked from the nest and told to earn a living, ended up as railroad payroll clerks in Milwaukee, Wisconsin. By his mid-thirties, Wilky, the most robust and lighthearted of the brothers in youth, was crippled with rheumatism, Bright's disease, and depression. Both Wilky and Bob had money problems—Wilky was forced to declare bankruptcy—but when Henry Sr. died in 1882, he left Bob a reduced share of the inheritance and omitted Wilky entirely from his will. Wilky succumbed to kidney failure a year later. Bob, who survived a nervous breakdown and several long asylum stays, died, alcoholic and alone, in 1910. It would be two days before his body was discovered.

The further down the birth-order ladder, the less likely a sibling is to be represented in family photo albums, the less likely to get his vaccinations, the less likely to be given the education his older siblings got.

Unless a parent intervenes, it is usually the last-born who gets the smallest piece of chicken on the plate, who gets cast as the robber in games of cops and robbers (last-borns, of course, are more likely to *want* to play the robber), who gets press-ganged into left field in baseball games. Hence Eli Manning was relegated to center in family football, while his older brothers Cooper and Peyton took the glamour positions of quarterback and wide receiver. Hence Christopher Lukas was made to play Hitler and Stalin in his older brother's family theatricals, while the future Pulitzer Prize–winning journalist J. Anthony Lukas took the role of Roosevelt. Last-borns often get the short end of the stick in more serious matters as well. In Muslim "honor killings," in which brothers are expected to kill a sister alleged to have brought disgrace on her family, it is usually the youngest who is chosen to carry out the murder.

Such scapegoating may explain why so many fairy tales revolve around youngest sons outwitting their elder brothers. The plot usually involves a father who sends his sons out into the world on a seemingly impossible task, saying that whoever succeeds will inherit his fortune. The elder brothers tend to be arrogant, selfish, conventional, and a little thick; the youngest, belittled by his siblings as incompetent, turns out to be ethical, courageous, and able to think outside the box. In the end, he outwits his elders, finds the treasure, and marries the princess. An analysis of 112 Grimm's fairy tales found that in those involving three children, the youngest "won" 92 percent of the time. One suspects that a disproportionate number of the country folk whose stories were collected by the Brothers Grimm may have been youngest sons.

Not all eldest brothers, of course, are responsible and high-achieving. And youngest brothers can be conscientious, neurotic, and humorless. Yet birth order seems imprinted on our consciousness, and threats to the hierarchy can be disorienting. After his mother's death, Philip Roth urged his father to leave his inheritance to Philip's older brother, who had greater need of it. Several years later, when his dying father told him he had followed his advice, Roth was unexpectedly upset. "Didn't I think I deserved it? . . ." he wrote in *Patrimony*. "Was I a younger brother who suddenly had become unable to assert his claim against the seniority of someone who had been there first? Or, to the contrary, was I a younger brother who felt that he had encroached too much upon an older brother's prerogatives already?" Leonard Nimoy, best known for playing Mr. Spock on TV's *Star Trek*, was more comfortable as a supporting actor, he said, because as a second son he had learned "not to upstage" his older brother. When birth-order roles are circumvented or reversed, it can seem unnatural. In the *Godfather* movies, after his eldest son is murdered, Don Corleone taps his youngest son, Michael, to be head of the family, passing over Fredo, the marrowless middle brother. Humiliated, Fredo betrays Michael to another Mafia family. Michael confronts his older brother:

"I've always taken care of you, Fredo," he says.

Fredo looks at Michael incredulously. "Taken care of me? You're my kid brother! *You* take care of *me*? You ever think about that? You ever once think about that? Send Fredo off to do this, send Fredo off to do that. Let Fredo take care of some Mickey Mouse nightclub somewhere! Send Fredo off to pick somebody up at the airport! I'm your older brother, Mike, and I was stepped over."

Subconsciously, we are ambivalent about eclipsing our older brothers. We spend a lifetime competing with them, but part of us wants them to remain supreme. Even in old age, the eldest will still be the eldest, the youngest the youngest. Not long after William's death in 1910, Henry James wrote a friend, "I sit heavily stricken and in darkness—for from far back in dimmest childhood he had been my ideal Elder Brother, and I still, through all the years, saw in him, even as a small timorous boy yet, my protector, my backer, my authority and my pride."

In the late 1970s, the psychologist Frances Schachter proposed that siblings, taking into account innate strengths and weaknesses, develop different or contrasting identities in order to minimize rivalry. "Sibling deidentification," as she called it, is especially pronounced when siblings are of the same gender, close in age, or both. According to Schachter, we shape our personalities in reaction to our siblings; like protean jigsaw pieces, we smooth off sharp corners and develop new bumps as we find our places in the family puzzle. Thus, when Joe Kennedy became the family's ambitious, conscientious, responsible son, his younger brother Jack became its underachieving iconoclast. At Choate, Joe was a top student, eager to achieve even in subjects he didn't like. Jack worked only in subjects that interested him, like English and history, and settled into the lower half of his class without a fuss. Joe played varsity football and hockey, edited the yearbook, and tried to set an example for the entire school, as he had for his eight younger siblings. Jack was habitually late to class, dressed carelessly, left his clothes on the floor, and devoted his energy to girls and practical jokes. "Psychologically I was enormously interested," Choate's headmaster recalled. "I couldn't see how two boys from the same family could be so different." After nearly expelling Jack for his part in a prank, the headmaster sent him to a Columbia University psychologist. "A good deal of his trouble is due to comparison with an older brother," wrote Dr. Prescott Lecky, after interviewing Jack. "He remarked, 'My brother is the efficient one in the family, and I am the boy that doesn't get things done. If my brother were not so efficient, it would be easier for me to be efficient. He does it so much better than I do.'" Commented Lecky, "Jack is apparently avoiding comparison and withdraws from the race, so to speak, in order to convince himself that he is not trying." (Underneath Jack's feigned indifference, of course, lay a fierce determination to eclipse his older brother. Eventually, he would.)

Following an older brother who excelled in the classroom and on the basketball court, the Pittsburgh teenager Robby Wideman turned to a life on the streets. Years later, after John Edgar Wideman had become a Rhodes scholar, an English professor, and a prizewinning novelist, Robby, in prison for armed robbery and being an accessory to murder, explained himself to his older brother in what, as psychologist David C. Rowe has pointed out, could stand as a textbook description of sibling deidentification: "See, it was a question of being somebody. Being my own person. Like youns had sports and good grades sewed up. Wasn't nothing I could do in school or sports that youns hadn't done already. . . . Had to figure out a new territory. I had to be a rebel."

In the symbiotic dance of deidentification, the roles siblings try on can easily calcify into stereotypes: the family scholar, the family jock, the family rebel. Asked about his siblings, a young friend of mine, the middle of three brothers, says reflexively: "My older brother's the screwup, my younger brother's the golden boy, I'm the creative one." Parents may reinforce these roles. Neither Kennedy parent thought Jack was in the same league as their beloved Joe, and made no secret of it. In third grade, when Jack was found to have a higher IQ than Joe, Rose contacted the school and insisted that the teacher must have been wrong. (She wasn't.) Sibling deidentification helps explain the pernicious process by which boys often get pigeonholed as the "good" brother or the "bad" brother—the dichotomy of which Cain and Abel were the prototype, and the basis of innumerable myths, novels, and Hollywood melodramas—and why it so often seems that the better the "good" brother becomes, the worse the "bad" brother gets. The more heroic the deeds performed by the polar explorer Ernest Shackleton, the more ambitious the scams perpetrated by his con artist younger brother, Frank. The more sanctimonious President Jimmy Carter's behavior, the more outrageous his hard-drinking younger brother Billy's. Such polarization may be possible because, at bottom, "good" and "bad" brothers aren't so different after all—a point chillingly made in Sam Shepard's play *True West,* in which a mild-mannered, well-to-do screenwriter and his bullying, thieving, ne'er-do-well older brother essentially switch identities by the time the curtain falls.

The psychologist Frank Sulloway likens sibling deidentification to a kind of natural selection at warp speed. Like Darwin's finches, which solved the problem of competing for food in the Galápagos Islands by evolving into different groups, each adapted for a different source of food, children compete within the ecosystem of the family for another form of vital nourishment—the attention of their parents—by developing their own niches. In *Born to Rebel,* Sulloway used this theory to suggest that birth order was linked to the capacity for creative thinking. Analyzing the lives of some six thousand scientists, inventors, and revolutionaries, he concluded that throughout history, innovators and radical thinkers were more likely to be later-born children. Firstborns, he said, naturally identify with power and authority. They tend to conform. Sulloway, the third of four brothers, maintained that later-borns, in an effort to find an unoccupied family niche, are more likely to take risks, experiment, and explore, both geographically and intellectually. Assembling data on 3,890 scientists who took sides on twenty-eight different scientific innovations of their day—the Copernican revolution, Newtonian physics, Einstein's theories of relativity, and so on—Sulloway found later-borns twice as likely as firstborns to support the innovations. The Protestant Reformation and the French Revolution, too, says Sulloway, were driven largely by later-borns. ("Sibling strife, not class conflict, lay at the heart of the Terror.") Not surprisingly, later-borns were almost five times more likely than firstborns to endorse the theory of natural selection.

Sibling niches may be psychological; they may also be vocational. "It is highly expedient that brothers should not seek to acquire honors or power in the same field, but in quite different fields ..." wrote Plutarch in *De Fraterno Amore*. "For brothers to seek eminence or repute from the same art or faculty is precisely the same as for both to fall in love with one woman and each seek to outstrip the other in her esteem." Encouraged to become artists by their widowed mother, who moved them to Paris for twelve years, the eldest brother, William Morris Hunt, became one of nineteenth-century America's greatest painters; the second-born, Richard Morris Hunt, one of its first and most celebrated architects; and the fourth-born, Leavitt, a noted photographer. (The third-born, Jonathan, took the revolutionary step of becoming a doctor.) Even when brothers end up in the same profession, they usually pursue different subspecialties. The Booths were theater folk, but June was a producer, Edwin a tragedian, John an ingenue. (Joseph, the youngest brother, who did his best work in the theater when he served as a ticket taker at the age of eighteen, delivered messages for Wells Fargo and dabbled in real estate before earning his medical degree at the age of forty-nine. Suffering from spells of what he called "melancholy insanity," he would work sporadically as a doctor until his death in 1902.)

Niches may be geographical. According to Roman mythology, after overthrowing Saturn his rivalrous sons divided up his dominions: Jupiter took the heavens, Neptune the ocean, and Pluto the underworld. It wasn't just love of Michelangelo that induced second-born Henry James to spend most of his life in Europe, ceding the United States to his formidable older brother, William. Although they were, in their way, as close as two brothers can be, writing each other long, affectionate letters, and paying each other occasional transatlantic visits (which left both exhausted), they got along better with an ocean between them. (One is struck by how often one James was leaving a continent just as the other James was arriving: fraternal ships passing in the night.) The Emanuel brothers of Chicago didn't deem it necessary to scatter quite so far. Bright, ambitious, and savagely competitive, the three brothers found their familial niches early on. Ezekiel, the eldest, an A+ student, was the brain; Rahm, the middle child, who mediated his brothers' fights, was the politician; Ariel, the youngest, who was both hyperactive and dyslexic, was the jock. The brothers were close, but so rivalrous that they instinctively gravitated to widely disparate careers in distant cities. "We couldn't possibly be within a thousand miles of each other, because the force fields just wouldn't let it happen," Zeke, an oncologist who heads the bioethics department at the National Institutes of Health in Washington, told *The New Yorker*. Rahm became a politician in Chicago, Ari a Hollywood agent. (The brothers suspended their fraternal diaspora for a few years when Rahm came to Washington as chief of staff for President Obama and hired Zeke as a health policy advisor.) All three brothers talk often by phone.

* * *

When Edwin suggested that each Booth brother adopt a section of the United States as his theatrical niche, he characterized it as a way to maximize profits. Privately, he considered it even more desirable as a way to minimize friction with John as their positions on the war grew increasingly polarized. Edwin, who had spent much of his life in the West and Northeast, and whose friends were northerners, naturally sided with the Union. John had grown up in Maryland, where slavery seemed to be the status quo everywhere but on the Booth farm; where, during his two years at military school, he was friends with the sons of some of the South's most prominent slave-owning families; and where, in the 1860 election, only one in every forty votes was cast for Lincoln. John was passionately, virulently for the South. But the brothers' allegiances weren't just a matter of geography. Temperamentally, the restrained, circumspect elder brother was a northerner, and the impetuous, feather-ruffling, rebellion-loving younger brother a southerner. Unlike Edwin, John had a southern gentleman's patrician sense of social order, reinforced by the sense of entitlement he enjoyed as the family favorite. As a young man he had been an enthusiastic member of the anti-immigrant Know-Nothing party. Under Junius Brutus Booth, it had been the custom for the family to dine with the hired hands at harvest, but when John ran the farm after his father's death, he refused to allow his mother and sisters to sit down with the help, lest their delicate sensibilities be offended.

When the war began, John's mother, terrified of losing her favorite son, made him promise he wouldn't join the rebel army. Whether John had intended to enlist cannot be known, but Edwin, who repeatedly asserted that he wasn't "political," clearly had no intention of giving up the stage for the battlefield. "If it were not for the fear of doing my country more harm than good, I'd be a soldier, too; a coward always has an 'if' to slink behind, you know," he wrote a friend. "Those cursed bullets are awkward things, and very uncivil at times; and as for a bayonet charge, I don't hesitate to avow my readiness to 'scoot' if there is a chance. Bull Run would be nothing to the run I'd make of it." And so the brothers waged the Civil War over the breakfast table at Edwin's house. Any rivalry they may have felt over their theatrical careers found expression in those heated arguments. June and Edwin tried to dissuade John from his position, but even as a schoolboy John had never let go of a political debate until he had exhausted his adversary into submission. June would hear him out, but Edwin was dismissive of John's "patriotic froth"; John, who wanted to be taken seriously by his older brother, felt patronized.

In 1863 John was arrested and briefly detained in St. Louis for saying he wished "the whole damn government would go to hell." That same year he throttled Asia's husband when he spoke slightingly of Jefferson Davis. Such outbursts, reported in the paper and repeated in backstage gossip, were mortifying for the thin-skinned Edwin. Yet even as he railed against the North, John remained devoted to his brothers. In July 1863, he happened to be staying at Edwin's during the New York draft riots, in which white thugs roamed the city killing black men, women, and children. When a wounded northern officer, a friend of Edwin's, came to the house to convalesce, John helped carry him to an upstairs bedroom, dress his wound, and nurse him in shifts. "Imagine me helping that wounded soldier with my rebel sinews!" he later told Asia. What John didn't tell his sister was that he had also helped hide the wounded Yankee's black servant in the basement, feeding him for four days while mobs surged through the streets. Throughout the war years, in letters to mutual friends, John always sent his love to Edwin.

John's theatrical fame was a point of pride for the South, whose reviewers repeatedly asserted John's superiority to Edwin; if the South was losing the war of brother against brother, it would, at least, claim victory in one fraternal battle. But John found it increasingly shameful to be playing the hero on stage while, fifty miles from the theater, fellow southerners were fighting and dying in earnest. In 1864, he began turning down roles in order to work sub rosa for the rebel cause: buying black market quinine from northern hospitals, then smuggling it in his horse's collar through the northern lines to beleaguered Confederate troops. He hinted to Asia that he was also passing intelligence to the South, but given his penchant for tall tales, the extent of his involvement may never be known. John's behind-the-scenes role wasn't enough for him. He wanted to do something more visible. Kidnapping the president would not only be a dramatic expression of his political beliefs, it would catapult him, he believed, into the company of Brutus and William Tell, fulfilling his mother's early vision and winning him the "undying fame" he had always sought.

A month after their breakfast-table quarrel, John spent Christmas, as always, at Edwin's. There was a coolness between them. A few weeks later, in a letter to June, John wrote, "But dear brother, you must not think me childish when I say that the *old feeling* roused by our loving brother has not yet died out. I am sure *he thinks I live upon him.*" Nevertheless, he stayed with Edwin several more times that winter, and there is evidence that he was in the audience at the Winter Garden on March 22 to see the last of his brother's record hundred nights as Hamlet. (On that visit, he also availed himself of the services of a bootmaker and a brothel.)

All his life, John had been an optimist, but in the late winter and early spring of 1865, as it became clear the South would lose the war, he grew increasingly cynical, irritable, and combative. After his kidnapping plan fizzled when the president failed to appear along the anticipated route, his tirades against Lincoln became even more reckless. Rather than the heroic figure he had dreamed of becoming, John was now seen as a blowhard. He drank heavily, sometimes downing a quart of brandy within a few hours. He seemed to be coming to a boil. In February, his mother, worried that he might do something rash, dispatched June to Washington in an unsuccessful attempt to persuade John to come home. On April 12, June wrote John, once again urging him to have nothing to do with the rebellion, reminding him that they would see each other in New York on April 22 for the benefit performance of *Romeo and Juliet*.

It is not clear exactly when John decided to assassinate Lincoln. Asia thinks that when Richmond fell on April 3, something in her brother snapped. A few days later, when he traveled to Boston, he may have known. There, after dazzling a crowd at a shooting gallery with an impromptu demonstration of trick shots, he visited Edwin in his dressing room at the Boston Theatre, where he was rehearsing *Hamlet*. Edwin expressed satisfaction that Richmond had fallen at last, but John uncharacteristically didn't rise to the bait. "Good-bye, Ned," he said. "You and I could never agree on that question. I could never argue with you."

A week later, on the night of April 14, while Edwin was onstage at the Boston Theatre playing the villain in the popular melodrama *The Iron Chest*, John entered Lincoln's box at Ford's Theatre, held his single-shot Philadelphia Derringer pistol two and a half feet from the back of the president's head, and pulled the trigger.

*   *   *

Francis Galton may have championed the importance of heredity in shaping one's life, but he also noted that "the whimsical effects of chance" often play a vital role. Siblings may share family milestones—a move, parental job loss, parental depression, the illness or death of a parent—but they may experience them very differently, according to personality or developmental stage. In 1824, when John Dickens was hauled away to the Marshalsea debtors' prison, his eldest son, Charles, was an impressionable twelve-year-old working in a blacking factory, while his younger sons were not quite two and four—too young to feel the disgrace that would fuel Charles's determination never to end up like his improvident father. In 1855, when Henry James Sr. took his family to Europe for three years, twelve-year-old Henry Jr. was introduced to some of the themes that would preoccupy him for most of his writing life, as well as to the places in which he would spend much of that life, while thirteen-year-old William was confirmed in his suspicion that he belonged on the American side of the Atlantic.

For John Adams's three sons, timing was everything. In 1778, when Adams was appointed by Congress to argue the American cause in Europe, he took along ten-year-old John Quincy. Too young for the journey, seven-year-old Charles and five-year-old Thomas remained with their mother, Abigail, on the family farm. John Quincy would spend seven years abroad with his father, traveling from capital to capital; hobnobbing with Jefferson, Franklin, Lafayette, and a host of European artists and intellectuals; serving, at the age of fourteen, as secretary to the American envoy in St. Petersburg; acting as his father's personal secretary in Paris; taking five-mile walks each morning before work with his father, who was grooming the child he called "the joy of my heart" for greatness. Meanwhile, his younger brothers worked at their lessons, did their chores, and submitted to their domineering mother. When Abigail joined her husband and eldest son in Europe, leaving her younger sons in her sister's care, Charles and Thomas went entirely parentless for two years.

Given such curricula vitae, it was, perhaps, not surprising that John Quincy Adams became, among other things, minister to the Netherlands, United States senator, Harvard professor, minister to Great Britain, secretary of state, and president. Or that genial but feckless Charles spent more time drinking than studying at college (he was one of several students reprimanded for running naked through Harvard Yard), struggled to establish a law practice, squandered the $2,000 his older brother left him in trust, abandoned his wife and two small daughters, and died, alcoholic and broke, at the age of thirty. Or that Thomas, unable to sustain a legal practice, served a year in the state legislature before quitting abruptly to become a drinker and gambler who failed to provide for his wife and seven children. Described by a nephew as "one of the most unpleasant characters in this world," Thomas died, also alcoholic and broke, at the age of fifty-nine.

The pattern would repeat itself in the next generation. In 1809, John Quincy Adams was appointed minister to Russia. He brought along his wife, Louisa, as well as his son Charles, who, at the age of two, was too *young* to be left behind. He entrusted eight-year-old George and six-year-old John to the care of an aunt and uncle. John Quincy spent a good part of each day with his youngest son, reading to him, tutoring him, taking him for long walks, as his father had done with him. He raised his elder sons by mail. (When the family was reunited after six years, John Quincy didn't recognize fourteen-year-old George.) The results were predictable. Charles, who had received the full force of parental attention, compiled a career that, while hardly as spectacular as his father's, was nevertheless impressive: wealthy attorney, influential political pamphleteer, doting husband, conscientious father of seven, respected congressman, indispensable minister to Great Britain during the Civil War. The eldest son, George, graduated in the middle of his Harvard class, abandoned his legal studies, and was such an indolent and irresponsible fellow that he was placed under his grandfather Adams's supervision on the family farm. After his grandfather's death, George boarded with relatives and disgraced himself by impregnating a young serving girl. Summoned to Washington by his father, twenty-eight-year-old George leaped overboard from the steamship to his death. The second son fared little better. One of thirty-nine students to be expelled from Harvard for taking part in a student riot, John Adams II appeared to be uninterested in the law—or, for that matter, in any other profession. His exasperated father hired him as his private secretary. But John became an obese, disorderly alcoholic who couldn't take care of himself or his wife and children. In 1834, he fell into a coma and died at thirty-one.

Events experienced by only one sibling may have life-changing consequences. Numerous biographers have suggested that Teddy Roosevelt's hell-bent-for-leather personality was forged in large part by his having had to work so hard to overcome a frail, asthmatic constitution. His charming younger brother Elliott also faced health difficulties—a series of inexplicable seizures—but seemed less able to cope with adversity. He became a feckless, philandering alcoholic who jumped out a window to his death at the age of thirty-four. After the United States entered World War II, Prescott Bush Jr. dropped out of Yale to enlist in the army but was rejected because of near-blindness in one eye. His younger brother, George, enlisted in the navy on the day he turned eighteen, and his heroics as a pilot in the South Pacific jump-started a career that led to the presidency. Prescott would work as an insurance broker, raise money for his younger brother's political campaigns, and serve as town meeting representative in Greenwich, Connecticut. On the other hand, J. R. Ackerley and his older brother, Peter, were both sent to the front during World War I. The younger brother was shot in the buttocks and lived to write about it. The elder was decapitated by a cannon shell two months before the Armistice.

Consider the Darwins. Brilliant, hardworking Erasmus was the pride of the family. Charles, four years younger, a self-absorbed, unfocused boy, was a disappointment. "You care for nothing but shooting, dogs, and rat-catching," his father wrote Charles when he was fifteen, "and you will be a disgrace to yourself and all your family." Charles followed his older brother into medical training, but while Erasmus seemed headed for a distinguished career as a doctor, Charles judged most of the lectures to be "stupid" or "incredibly dull," discovered that the sight of blood made him queasy, and dropped out after two years. He was slightly more successful at the study of divinity, but devoted less time to reading scripture than to collecting beetles, gunning down grouse, gambling, and drinking.

Circumstances would reverse the brothers' career arcs. In 1829, poor health forced Erasmus to give up medicine at the age of twenty-four. He spent his remaining fifty-two years as a melancholy, opium-eating London bachelor who exercised his considerable intellect at literary soirées and the occasional séance. In 1831, twenty-two-year-old Charles decided to apply for the position of naturalist on a ship heading for South America. His father, who wished his son to become a clergyman, refused to fund his passage. But Darwin's uncle, having offered to drive Charles home to Shrewsbury, convinced his father to allow Charles to accept the post. Even then, the position was not assured. The *Beagle*'s captain was a disciple of Johann Kaspar Lavater, the eighteenth-century Swiss physiognomist who believed a man's character could be read in his facial features, and, as Darwin recalled, "he doubted whether anyone with my nose could possess sufficient energy and determination for the voyage." The captain evidently overcame his doubts, and the *Beagle,* with Darwin aboard, set sail. The ne'er-do-well younger brother would go on to become the most influential scientist of the nineteenth century, an outcome that depended, as he would marvel in his autobiography, on "so small a circumstance as my uncle offering to drive me 30 miles to Shrewsbury, which few uncles would have done, and on such a trifle as the shape of my nose."

*   *   *

If John Wilkes Booth had succeeded in his original plot to kidnap Lincoln—*before* the war had ended—he might have been hailed as a hero, at least in the South. Now, on the run through the forests and swamps of Maryland and northern Virginia after killing Lincoln—cold, wet, hungry, feverish, broken-legged—John still believed that his act would win him a place among his pantheon of heroes. Indeed, he seemed less concerned about getting food and medical care than about reading reviews of his deed. He was devastated to find his act reviled throughout the United States. His hometown paper, the *Baltimore Clipper,* called it "cowardly and vile," and even Jefferson Davis described it as "a blot on American civilization." This was a crushing blow. "I am here in despair," John wrote in his daybook. "And why? For doing what Brutus was honored for, what made Tell a Hero. And yet I for striking down a greater tyrant than they ever knew am looked upon as a common cutthroat." (He would have been comforted to know that after his death, an anonymous poem circulated through the South memorializing Booth as "Our Brutus.")

Even in such dire circumstances, John played to the audience: quoting *Macbeth* in a proud note to a man who had begrudged him shelter; impressing three ex-Confederate soldiers with his composure; beguiling a farmer's children with his pocket compass and tall tales. Thomas Jones, a farmer and rebel sympathizer who brought him meals and newspapers, couldn't help noting that "though he was exceedingly pale and his features bore the evident traces of suffering, I have seldom, if ever, seen a more strikingly handsome man." (This without his trademark mustache, which John had shaved off during his escape in a rare concession to prudence.) The twenty-nine Union soldiers who finally cornered him in a tobacco barn remarked on his bravado as he challenged them to fight in what one of them described as a "full, clear, ringing voice, a voice that smacked of the stage." ("Well, my brave boys, prepare me a stretcher, and place another stain on our glorious banner," he sang out.) Even after the barn had been set aflame and John, looking so much like Edwin that one officer was momentarily worried they'd "made a mistake," had been dragged out, mortally injured by a soldier's bullet, he played his part to the end. (As he lay dying, the farmer's wife who had tended to his wounds secretly snipped off a lock of his hair for a memento.) Throat swollen, lips purple, slowly suffocating, barely able to speak—the bullet had severed his spinal cord—he managed to whisper, "Tell my mother that I did it for my country, that I die for my country." And yet one wonders whether in the end he may have realized the futility of his act, whether he may have been referring to more than just his hands when, not long before he stopped breathing, he asked a soldier to lift his paralyzed arms and, looking at them, gasped, "Useless, useless!"

Although many people refused to believe that the charismatic John Wilkes Booth could be the assassin, the moment Edwin Booth learned of the president's death—and read in the newspaper of the brandished dagger, the cry "*Sic semper tyrannis!*," the leap to the stage—he recognized his brother's histrionic touch. He later told his actor friend Joseph Jefferson, "It was just as if I had been struck on the head by a hammer." For weeks, Edwin sat in silence in his New York City apartment. Worried that he might turn to drink, go mad, or even commit suicide, friends took turns sleeping in his room. He received letters saying that he would be killed, that his house would be burned down. (Although June was imprisoned for eight weeks on suspicion that he might have known of the plot— he hadn't—and Joseph was arrested and briefly detained, Edwin, at the request of influential friends, was merely placed under a kind of house arrest.) He did what he could to distance himself from his brother's act. A few days after the assassination, Edwin took out an advertisement in the newspapers in which he spoke of his family's "abhorrence and detestation for this foul and most atrocious of crimes." No one knows whether John saw it. And he did his best to distance himself from the man described in the newspapers as a "Savage Beast" and a "Monster." Writing to Asia during the twelve days John was on the run, Edwin advised, "Think no more of him as your brother; he is dead to us now, as he soon must be to all the world, but imagine the boy you loved to be in that better part of his spirit, in another world." Called to testify in the trial of John's co-conspirators, Edwin, who had spent much of the previous summer with John, had hosted him the previous Christmas, and had received him in Boston two weeks before the assassination, told the lawyer that he "knew less of his brother probably than anyone" and had had nothing to do with him for years.

Month after month, like a wounded animal in its den, Edwin stayed in his study, "chewing my heart in solitude," as he put it, venturing outside only after dark and in the company of a friend, even then disguising himself, and keeping to the shadows for fear of what people might do to him. His fiancée, whom he had met a year after the loss of his beloved wife, broke off their engagement; her father made her promise never to marry into the family of Lincoln's assassin, never to bear children with the name of Booth. (Edwin eventually married another woman, but his wife went mad after the death of their newborn child and was shuttled in and out of institutions until her own death. He spent hours rocking her in his arms as she sobbed; it seemed, perhaps, a kind of penance. Or perhaps he did for her what he wished—but never would have allowed—someone to do for him.)

Believing his career was over, Edwin vowed never to return to the stage. But within a year of the assassination, needing money to pay off family debts, he appeared at the Winter Garden as Hamlet. "The blood of our martyred President is not yet dry in the memory of the people, and the very name of the assassin is appalling to the public mind; still a Booth is advertised to appear before a New York audience!" wrote the *Herald*, suggesting that Brutus, Caesar's assassin, would be "the most suitable character" for Edwin to play. There were rumors that he would be shot, but when the curtain rose on scene two to reveal him sitting in a chair, head bowed, the audience rose to its feet, flung bouquets, and sent wave after wave of applause toward the stage. Edwin would perform for another quarter-century, but he would always wonder whether the crowds came to see "The Hope of the Living Drama" or the brother of the man who had shot Lincoln. He rarely took curtain calls, ordering the houselights up as soon as the play ended. In 1876, he toured the South for the first time since Lincoln's death. He was gratified by his warm reception, but people were so eager to touch the brother of John Wilkes Booth that Edwin persuaded his manager to hire a member of the company to impersonate him whenever their railway car stopped at stations along the route. Just as John, early in his career, had resented being known as Edwin's brother, now Edwin resented being known as John's brother. Seeking fame for himself, John had inadvertently made Edwin even more famous.

Over the decades Edwin played nearly every city in the United States except Washington, which, even when he was asked to perform there by President Chester Arthur, he refused to set foot in or pass through. For the rest of his life, he did his best to repress the events of April 14, 1865. He couldn't bear seeing a photo or drawing of Lincoln. He quietly reimbursed the Virginia farmer whose tobacco barn had been burned down during his brother's capture, writing, "Your family will always have our warmest thanks for your kindness to him whose madness wrought so much ill to us." Edwin forbade his family to touch the funds John had left in a Montreal bank. He wrote to the government for years in an attempt to recover his brother's remains; when he finally succeeded, he could not bring himself to be in the room when his brother's body was identified, though he was present in Baltimore's Greenmount Cemetery when John was buried in the family plot. In 1869, perhaps hoping to associate the family name with a theater other than Ford's, Edwin built the Booth Theatre, an ornate, five-story theatrical temple that cost more than $1 million, in New York City. Edwin lived in an apartment above the stage. One night at three a.m. he told his longtime attendant, Garrie Davidson, to accompany him to the furnace room. There Davidson saw a trunk bound with ropes. Edwin asked him to fetch an axe, cut the ropes, and open the trunk. Inside lay a trove of theatrical costumes and props. Davidson realized immediately to whom they had belonged. One by one, Edwin drew out the wigs, togas, swords, jewelry, belts, jerkins, leggings, and boots his brother had worn to play Romeo, Mark Antony, Shylock, and Othello. He held them up for a moment and then handed them to Davidson, who fed them to the furnace. Many of them, of course, had originally belonged to Edwin's father, including the bejeweled velvet shirt and fur-trimmed cloak Junius Brutus Booth had worn in *Richard III* on the night Edwin had first appeared on stage. There were photographs, too, and sheaves of letters. When the trunk was empty, Edwin told Davidson to chop it up. They threw the wood and the ropes into the furnace, and watched until everything had burned.

The actor whose most famous role was that of a man haunted by the ghost of his father was in life now haunted by the ghost of his brother. Edwin had always been taciturn; after April 1865, he retreated still further into himself. As he aged, he was said to sit up through the nights (he called them his "vulture hours"), smoking his pipe till dawn, reading the memoirs of actors and contemplating their portraits and death masks, which decorated his walls. In his summer home he dozed for hours in the porch hammock, its canvas sides drawn up to make a womblike cocoon. Although John was always just below the surface of his thoughts, Edwin went nearly thirty years without uttering his name. Whenever he was asked how many brothers and sisters he had, he included those who had died in childhood, but omitted John. One night, near the end of his life, reminiscing about his youth at a postperformance Christmas Eve party in his rooms in Boston, Edwin slipped. "Yes, my brother John and I . . ." The room fell silent. "Yes, my unfortunate brother, John . . ." Edwin continued. He began to weep. Then he pulled himself together. "Come, come, I have displaced the mirth," he said. "Let us drink to a Merry Christmas."

In 1889, Edwin founded the Players Club, a gathering place for actors on Gramercy Park South, where he lived in two rooms upstairs. Four years later, when he suffered a massive stroke and died at the age of fifty-nine, there was a portrait of John on his bedside table.

Chapter Three
The Fallout Shelter

A few years ago, Dad told me, in passing, that we probably never would have moved from Dedham had Dad's boss not invited him and Mum out for dinner in Boston one evening in the fall of 1961. Afterward, they repaired to the Ritz-Carlton for drinks. At some point, Jack Lemmon, whom Dad had known casually at Harvard, walked into the bar. Lemmon recognized Dad and came over to say hi. Dad invited him to sit down. Lemmon had already won an Academy Award for *Mister Roberts* and had recently starred in *The Apartment.* Dad's boss and his wife were impressed. They were even more impressed when Lemmon's friend Shelley Winters walked into the bar and joined them. The six of them drank and talked for several hours. Not long after that evening, Dad's boss recommended him for a promotion to company headquarters in Manhattan, and we were on our way to Darien, Connecticut. "We thought we had arrived," Dad said with a rueful laugh.

* * *

When I was a child, it never occurred to me that Harry, Ned, and I, appearing within a span of four years, hadn't surfaced into the same family, into the care of the same, unchanging parents. Looking back, of course, I can see that despite our chronological proximity, we were born in three different cities, three different stages of our parents' relationship, three slightly but recognizably different situations. Yet Harry, Ned, and I grew up with the same familial reference points, the same cultural vocabulary. Even when I was young I could see that Mark, born six years after Ned, was growing up not only in a different place, but in a different time and, in essence, a different family.

Darien, a leafy suburb thirty-five miles from Manhattan, looked a lot like Dedham, except that its houses were larger, its lawns more crew-cut, its automobiles newer and more freshly washed. And yet as we settled into a white clapboard house across the street from a river that glittered through a row of towering maple trees, it seemed as if we had, without realizing it, strayed across an unmarked border into another country. Darien, the real estate agent had proudly informed my father, possessed the second-highest per capita income in the United States—news that in puritan Boston would have been a source of embarrassment, not a marketing tool. It strikes me as ridiculous now, but I remember watching *The Beverly Hillbillies* on television and feeling a twinge of identification with the Clampetts, who had relocated from the hollows of the Ozarks to the gated estates of Los Angeles. The Clampetts, however, were blissfully oblivious to their outsider status, whereas the Colts were exquisitely self-conscious. The distinctions may have been subtle, but my brothers and I felt them keenly. Our neighbors drove Country Squires, the sleek Ford station wagons with fake wood paneling, next to which our blue 1956 Parklane seemed as bulky and plodding as a prairie schooner. At Halloween, in Dedham we had been content with a single Dum Dum or two penny-size Tootsie Rolls carefully counted out and dropped into our bags; in Darien, we were invited to reach into enormous ceramic bowls filled with 5th Avenues and Baby Ruths—the large, five-cent variety— and remove candy by the fistful. In Dedham, we had taken our trash to the town dump, vast mountains of refuse over which we followed our mother on occasional foraging parties in search of useable bric-a-brac; in Darien, my brothers and I watched from a safe distance as our father slung our garbage bags into the flaming maw of the incinerator, into which they vanished without a trace, making it seem as if we were getting rid of incriminating evidence. In Dedham, on hot summer days, we'd run through sprinklers; in Darien, Ned and I, exploring our new backyard on the sweltering afternoon of our arrival, peered over the back fence and were presented with a sight that was, in its way, as silence-inducing as that first glimpse of the Pacific may have been to Cortez in *his* Darien—a plump young girl lolling on an inflatable raft in the Windex-colored water of a swimming pool.

Harry, Ned, and I had appeared during the Eisenhower years, when the country (or at least its upper-middle-class citizens) wallowed in postwar abundance. Magazine advertisements touted bulging refrigerators, gleaming washing machines, finned cars as big as tanks. At times the country itself seemed like an advertisement: In the press, the words "United States of America" were invariably followed by "the richest and most powerful nation in the history of the world." Our capabilities were, apparently, unlimited. Every day, it seemed some American was going faster, higher, farther: a college student ran an unbelievable 9.1 in the hundred-yard dash to become the world's fastest human; a test pilot flew his jet at a celestial altitude of sixty-six miles; an unemployed salesman drove a souped-up car 407 mph across the Utah desert. We'd gather around our old Zenith black-and-white TV and, chanting "three . . . two . . . one . . . *blast off,*" watch another rocket lift off the pad at Cape Canaveral, disappear in a whorl of fire and smoke, then rise majestically above it. We'd witnessed this scene so often over the previous two years, with heroes whose names were as familiar to me as the names of Red Sox players, that orbiting the earth eventually seemed no more extraordinary than sending my Duncan Imperial yo-yo "around the world."

By the time we arrived in Darien, fault lines in the country's self-possession had begun to show. In September, a month after we moved in, we listened to the Liston-Patterson fight on the radio. We weren't boxing fans, but we had been caught up in a morality play in which the sour, menacing ex-con and the deferential, polite gentleman seemed to represent the two different faces of an America we saw only in the pages of the newspaper and on the TV screen. And so we felt a little stunned and uneasy when, with the relentlessness of a schoolyard bully, Liston hammered Patterson to the canvas in the first round. Over the following year, a succession of front-page images insisted that all was not right:

Buddhist monks in South Vietnam engulfed in flames; Negroes (as the newspapers called them) flattened by fire hoses in distant southern cities; Gordon Cooper's Project Mercury capsule losing contact with ground control and orbiting for thirty-four hours before splashing down in the South Pacific. One fall day, my fifth-grade class was reading in the school library when, clapping her hands to pull us away from *Homer Price,* the librarian, voice trembling, told us that President Kennedy had been shot, news so farfetched that a friend and I broke into giggles. (Already, I was the kind of boy who needed to fill awkward silences.) In Darien, which seemed the apotheosis of the perfection toward which the fifties aspired, these events seemed unimaginable, almost impossible—what would, a few years later, be called surreal.

In my own family, too, there were fault lines, which we tried to cover up the way we covered up the rotting floorboards under the rubber mat in our car. Dad's new job seemed to take more out of him, as he tried to work his way up what he called "the corporate ladder." (I imagined a horde of men in suits clinging to a wooden ladder like the one Dad propped against the roof to clean the gutters each November.) He was on the road two weeks a month, and when he took the commuter train into "the city," he came home too late and too tired to play catch. Occasionally, he exuded a faint whiff of what at the time I assumed was a new kind of aftershave, but eventually realized was bourbon. Every Saturday morning, however, he was ours again, wearing his customary weekend attire of frayed high school letter sweater, paint-spattered khakis, and canvas sneakers—frying bacon, joking, tickling, swinging us up to his shoulders. Saturday was allowance day. After breakfast, we three older brothers piled into the car for errands—the incinerator, the hardware store, the liquor store—ending up at Darien News, where, fingering the coins in our pockets, we separated: Harry to the boxes of Topps baseball cards; Ned to the rows of candy bars; I to the comic book rack, which I spun slowly, deciding whether to spring for a *Classics Illustrated,* whose cartoon versions of *A Tale of Two Cities* and *The Count of Monte Cristo* cost three cents more than my usual twelve-cent *Superman.*

But in Darien, even our Saturday-morning errands weren't quite the same. One day, I don't remember why, we gave a ride to someone from

Dad's office, along with his two daughters. The father, a well-built man in a button-down shirt, sharply creased gray flannel slacks, and black hair Vitalised and combed so that every toothmark was visible, sat in front with Dad. Even from where I sat in the way back, I could tell that something wasn't quite right, that Dad, who got along with everyone, was, for some reason, a little nervous. So was I. The man's pretty blond daughters were sitting with my brothers and me in the cargo area among the pine needles, grass clippings, and scraps of newspaper. At ten, being in such close proximity to the opposite sex thrilled and terrified me into uncharacteristic silence. Saturday-morning errands, however, were the highlight of our week; I felt we were sharing the best part of our family with these girls, and I assumed they were impressed. And so I cringed with shame when the younger of the two girls, the one about my age, taking in the mess that was so comfortably familiar to me and exchanging glances with her sister, pinched her pale, stomach-churningly cute nose and squealed, "Pee-yew, it *smells* back here." I looked at Harry, but he was studying something in the window, his face red.

Like many women at that time, our mother was beginning to feel restive. Part of her remained a devoted fifties wife. She drank Metrecal to keep her figure in shape, took fashion hints from the pages of *Woman's Day*, wore her mother's old pearls and fox furs to company cocktail parties, and hosted dinners for "people from the office" Dad needed to impress. Harry, Ned, and I loved watching Mum prepare for a party: making her famous grapes-rolled-in-sour-cream-and-brown-sugar dessert, setting out crystal ashtrays the size of frying pans, stacking Kents in the sterling silver cigarette box inscribed with the names of the ushers at our parents' wedding. Later, we sat on the staircase and watched through the posts of the banister as Dad, cigarette bobbing like a miniature fishing pole from a corner of his mouth, waded into the crowd, brandishing a silver martini shaker, while Mum, looking glamorous in her blue-flowered muumuu, passed a tray of cheese and crackers. As the evening wore on, the party grew increasingly boisterous, and long after Mum shooed us off to bed, our sleep was occasionally interrupted by a shrill burst of laughter. In the morning, as we ate the leftover grapes, our heavy-lidded parents went around the house with a grocery bag, emptying the overflowing ashtrays in silence.

When *The Feminine Mystique* was published the spring after we arrived, Mum devoured it as if she were starving. (Years later she told me that some of her neighbors read it on the sly; others refused to open it, worried that it might shake up their marriages beyond repair.) Gradually, as Dad clung to the well-ordered fifties, Mum reached toward the first stirrings of the sixties. In the guitar lessons she gave to neighborhood teenagers, the repertoire modulated from "Stewball" and "Michael, Row the Boat Ashore" to "If I Had a Hammer," "Universal Soldier," and "Blowin' in the Wind," which had come out that May on an album by a growly-voiced twenty-two-year-old named Bob Dylan that Mum played over and over on the record player in the dining room. I looked over her shoulder as—between loads of laundry—she followed the civil rights struggle in its two-steps-forward one-step-back progress in the news. She yearned to be out marching, but didn't dare stop cooking. There were no black children in our school and, as far as I knew, no black families in our town. The only black person I had ever seen in "real life," as my brothers and I referred to anything that didn't take place on the television screen, was Mattie, the woman who came every other Thursday to clean our house, and with whom Mum spent a good part of those days sitting at the kitchen table, drinking coffee and sharing confidences. Sometimes, Mum drove Mattie home to Norwalk, Mark on the seat between them, Ned and I in the back, peering out the window at what we called the "bad part of town," mentally dividing the faces of the men we passed into Pattersons and Listons.

Exhausted by the demands of tending to four children, dependent on the diet pills she and everyone she knew seemed to be taking, feeling out of place in a town whose social center was a country club we couldn't afford to join even had we been asked, Mum began to chafe. She recently told me she felt as if she were being "pulled in half." She'd disappear into the cellar for hours each day to paint pictures of lute players performing in empty, moonlit rooms; lone seagulls wafting into the wide blue yonder; sad-eyed people reaching toward the sky. When she took out books from the library, she'd slide the borrower's card from its manila pocket and, thinking she might have something in common with the people on the list, daydream about calling them up and making friends. One Sunday, Mattie invited us to her church, and as Mum listened to the joyous, unrestrained gospel singing, she began to weep.

In Dedham, I had wanted so much to be like my older brother that it never occurred to me we might be different. In Darien, under my very nose, Harry seemed to be transforming as suddenly and swiftly as one of those moonstruck horror-movie monsters I watched each Friday night on *Chiller Theatre*. He shot up several inches; his voice grew scratchy and low; his legs and armpits sprouted hair; his biceps became visible to the naked eye. He took showers, not baths. He spent an inordinate amount of time behind a closed bathroom door, consulting an array of jars and tubes whose names I knew from TV: Stridex Medicated Pads, gauzy white moons that smudged gray when wiped alongside one's nose; Clearasil, a flesh-colored paste said to "fight" acne, but which left a telltale range of chalky, beige, miniature volcanos on one's face; pHisoHex, a goopy soap that came in a green plastic bottle and was so expensive only Harry was allowed to use it; Groom & Clean, a translucent gel said to prevent "greasy build-up," but which left one's hair looking as if it were covered in Saran Wrap. I didn't understand Harry's metamorphosis. Health classes wouldn't begin until high school, and I had never heard the word *puberty*. All I knew was that I no longer looked like my older brother.

Against the unfamiliar background of Darien, I began to recognize other differences, differences I hadn't noticed in Dedham. We both played baseball, but Harry batted righty while I batted lefty. We both loved reading, but Harry preferred the Hardy Boys, while I liked biographies and fairy tales. We both loved Swanson TV dinners, but Harry always chose Loin of Pork while I chose Salisbury Steak. Harry liked his sandwiches cut into rectangles; I preferred triangles. Harry liked lima beans; I hated them. Harry's favorite color was blue; mine was green. Other differences were less obvious: Harry seemed impervious to what others thought of him; I cared deeply about the impression I made. Harry was reticent and secretive; I was gregarious and indiscreet, eager to hear others' secrets and quick to share my own. Harry kept his bedroom door closed; I kept mine open, hoping someone would notice me and come in.

Why should these differences have surprised me? Most of the brothers I knew seemed physical and temperamental opposites. Dad was a skinny, sociable jokester, his younger brother a solid, serious bear of a man, so physically imposing that whenever I pinned Ned to the ground and forced him to utter the universally accepted plea for surrender, it seemed absurd that the word should be *uncle*. Our grandfather was a tall, sardonic, dignified pessimist who buried himself in books and crossword puzzles, his younger brother an ebullient, roly-poly optimist fond of declaiming the Declaration of Independence at his Fourth of July parties. In Dedham, the Clark brothers had lived just down the street: Stephen, the eldest, was responsible, high-achieving, statesmanlike; Johnny, the middle child, used his offbeat sense of humor to keep the fraternal peace; and Timmy, the youngest, could be found at the center of every playground dispute. The brothers I read about in books, too, always seemed so different I could hardly believe they were part of the same family: the Hardys (cautious Frank, headstrong Joe); the Hollisters (dependable Pete, rambunctious Ricky); the Sawyers (mischievous Tom, goody-goody Sid).

Harry no longer seemed part of my world; he seemed to belong to another, wider one. We didn't ride bikes to school together anymore. We waited for the bus in front of our house, but when we climbed aboard, Harry pushed ahead to sit in the back with kids his own age. Our new school was much larger. At recess I occasionally glimpsed my brother across the playground in a cloud of sixth-graders; on the rare occasions we passed in the halls, I knew from the look on his face not to say anything. (It felt like one of those movies in which the captured soldier has to pretend he doesn't recognize his old friend, the undercover spy, or he'll blow his buddy's cover and they'll both be killed.) When Harry started junior high and rode an earlier bus to an even larger school across town, I wouldn't see him at all until late afternoon, when he'd shinny up the rope ladder to Jeff Gegenheimer's tree house, pull the rope up behind him, and shut the trapdoor. Not that I dared follow him.

Even when he was home, it was as if he had shut a trapdoor and pulled up the rope. At supper, he asked to be excused as soon as he'd eaten dessert, and disappeared into his room. (Mum and Dad had converted the den into a bedroom, and so he was alone on the first floor while the rest of the family slept upstairs.) From behind closed doors we'd hear him playing the first album he bought, the Beach Boys' *Surfin' USA,* again and again. He came along on Saturday-morning errands less frequently. One Halloween, trick-or-treating along our usual route, a friend and I cut through the woods behind his house to try another neighborhood, and saw hundreds of teenagers milling around on the road, beer cans and bottles in their hands. What were they doing? Why weren't they wearing costumes? Was Harry somewhere among them? As my friend and I crouched behind the trees, I searched for my brother's face. But it was dark, the crowd was large, and at bottom I didn't really want to know.

In Dedham, Harry and I had never fought, but in Darien, our unhappiness rubbed off on each other. It was a matchup as one-sided as Liston versus Patterson. Harry's ostensibly playful shoulder punches stung for minutes; his double chicken-wing could immobilize me as completely as a set of Pilgrim stocks; the mere brandishing of a noogie-ready knuckle was enough to send me running. On the rare occasions I dared resist, he'd methodically, carefully, almost tenderly pin me on my back, sitting on my chest, the knobs of his knees grinding into the place where my biceps would have been if I'd had any. After writhing halfheartedly for a moment or arching my spine in a pro forma attempt to buck him off, I'd lie still, knowing that the sooner I acquiesced, the sooner he'd release me. Sometimes, irritated by my passivity, he'd purse his lips to produce a pearl of saliva. Carefully lowering it on an ever-lengthening, ever-thinning strand, he'd dangle it above my face, seeing how low he could let it go before yoyoing it up at the last moment. Sometimes he failed to retract it in time. When that happened, he'd let me up right away. "Sorry. That was an accident," he'd say as I ran into the house calling for our mother.

Galled by Harry's invincibility, I enlisted my friend to the cause. We challenged Harry to a fight. With these odds—two against one—I was sure I could finally beat my brother. We arranged to meet in the backyard one afternoon after school. Underneath the spreading branches of the maple tree, my friend and I circled my brother warily. Harry looked dismayingly relaxed, his elbows slightly bent like a gunslinger's, his face wearing a small, even smile that unnerved me. Not surprisingly (I was a chicken at heart, and, after all, I knew my brother), my friend made the first move, rushing toward Harry in an all-out kamikaze attack. With the grace of a matador, Harry stepped aside, grabbed my friend's arm, twisted it behind his back, and immobilized him in a hammerlock. Harry eyed me. "If you come any closer," he said quietly, "I'll break his arm." Whether he would have done so or not, I'll never know, but I was sad to realize I couldn't be sure. Choked with rage and admiration, I came no closer.

Looking back, I can see that much of Harry's withdrawal, inexplicable as it seemed to me at the time, was part and parcel of becoming a teenager. (Even drool, I have learned, is a standard weapon in the adolescent fraternal arsenal.) But in Darien, I began to think that although I was closer in age to Harry, I might have more in common with Ned. In Dedham I had shared a bedroom with Harry; in Darien I shared one with Ned. Ned didn't like playing sports as much as Harry and I did. He didn't even collect baseball cards. But he liked to do stuff I never got to do with Harry. We'd build block forts and painstakingly position our army men in massive battles, Ned lying on the floor to get a soldier's-eye view. We'd discuss the relative merits of Matchbox cars and Corgis (slightly larger vehicles with "torsion-bar suspension," a phrase we loved to repeat and pretend we knew what it meant). We stood over the toilet bowl, and, in that universal expression of boyhood fellow feeling known as "crossing swords," aimed our arcs of pee so they'd intersect. With Harry, I had to be on guard; with Ned, I could relax. I feared Harry's judgment; I didn't worry what Ned thought of me. With Harry, I tried to act older than I was; with Ned, I could regress. Playing cards with Harry, I'd play Pounce; with Ned, I'd play War. Harry's jokes often carried a sting. "You belong on the stage," he'd comment admiringly after I'd said something I thought was witty, ". . . that leaves in ten minutes." Or "You're funny . . . but looks aren't everything." These jokes, which Harry had learned in school, were repeated, no doubt, in homes all across town, but because they came from my older brother, I took them to heart. Ned and I often communicated in a kind of gibberish: making up songs and singing them over and over; savoring exotic words like *hors d'oeuvres*; repeating ordinary words like *room* or *water* until they lost all meaning; inventing our own nonsense words, like *oolees* and *looties*, and chanting them until Harry threatened to "beat us to a bloody pulp."

At the same time, Ned was the brother with whom I fought the most furiously and with the least provocation. No matter how engrossed we became in singing a new song, or in maneuvering army men across the rug, or in playing a game of I Doubt It, we'd always end up fighting. We couldn't help it; we had to destroy the fort, scatter the cards. Perhaps it was inevitable: Harry took out his frustration on me, I took out mine on Ned. Ned, however, had no brother on whom to continue this domino effect, Mark being too young to pick on. And so Ned fought back. Each of us was constitutionally unable to let the other have the last word, the last pinch, the last cookie. At times, our communication seemed to consist only of time-honored preadolescent provocations like "Got you last," "I know you are but what am I?" "Takes one to know one," "Same to you and many more, no backs," and "Whatever you say bounces off me and sticks to you." Ned's face was so angelic, his delivery so deadpan, that even on the umpteenth repetition, I still blundered into his traps. "You know what?" he'd say. "What?" I'd ask. "That's what," he'd reply. On car trips, Ned was a genius at finding ways to poke me without our mother catching him in the act. When I'd point out that Ned had "started it" (I was a congenital tattletale), Mum would invariably punish us both, saying, "It takes two to tango."

Although I was marginally bigger and stronger—given how small and spindly we both were, this is like saying that a salamander is bigger and stronger than a newt—Ned carried into battle an inner fury that was impressive and, occasionally, frightening. (He claims to have chased me around the kitchen with a carving knife. Happily, I have repressed this memory.) Just as Harry pinned me, I'd pin Ned, my knees on his bony arms as he sputtered and squirmed and finally, with a sob, said *uncle*. Unlike me, Ned never gave up. The moment I rolled off, he'd be up again, swinging wildly, shouting insults through his tears. I'd pin him down anew and he'd promise—cross his heart, hope to die—not to fight again. The instant I let him up, he'd attack. The cycle repeated itself until, exhausted, I'd trudge up to our room and close the door, at which point Ned, with a stubbornness I found admirable, would proclaim victory to the empty living room. Recently, I saw the movie *Cool Hand Luke*. There is a scene in which the title character, played by Paul Newman, is forced to fight the beefy inmate ringleader. No matter how many times Luke is knocked down, no matter how bloody he becomes, he keeps getting up, until the bully, shrugging, finally walks away, leaving Luke staggering around the prison yard, throwing punches at the air. I thought of Ned.

Fighting, of course, was one way for Ned to be noticed, to clear some elbow room in a crowded family. Another way was to take risks. Of the four of us, Ned was the one to walk out first and farthest on the newly frozen pond, the one to sail closest to the rocky shore. If you dared Ned to do something, you knew he'd do it: ring the neighbor's doorbell and run, light the firecracker, swallow the milk shake with the phlegm in it. You had to say the word *chicken* only once, or even venture a tentative clucking sound, and he was at your throat. In Hearts, while I tried to get rid of the Queen of Spades as quickly as possible, and Harry played whatever the situation called for in order to win, Ned would invariably, recklessly, try to shoot the moon. In Risk, Ned would attack no matter how numerous the enemy. In Monopoly, he was always ready to make a deal. (He liked to hide a cache of $500 bills behind his back. Just when we thought he was broke, he'd produce them with a flourish, saying "Hmmm, what have we here, what have we here? . . . Just saving up for a rainy day.") In Red Light Green Light, Ned would always try for too much and get sent back to the start, while my cautious step or two would carry me to victory. I was frightened of Harry, but Ned certainly wasn't frightened of me. He didn't seem frightened of anyone. Not even our older brother. Harry hated the sight of blood, and when Ned got a bloody nose, he'd smear some on his finger and chase Harry around the living room, Harry fleeing like Superman from Kryptonite.

As one who liked to play it safe, I secretly admired Ned's daring. I'd do things with Ned I'd never risk on my own. One late-winter afternoon, we were playing by the Five Mile River, using sticks to prod the huge cakes of ice that drifted by on their way to Long Island Sound. It was

Ned, I'm sure, who suggested we board a floe, and I, waiting until he had stepped onto one of the icebergs, who gingerly followed; Ned who then stepped across a thick ribbon of ink-black water to another floe, and then another, until we were several yards from shore, balanced uneasily on a car-size cake of ice, slowly drifting toward the point where the river emptied into the Sound. It was the kind of adventure I was always reading about in books. But I wasn't exhilarated, I was scared. And just as I'm sure it was Ned who got us out there, I'm sure it was I who insisted, at a certain point, that we had gone far enough and headed in, and Ned, only because I threatened to tell on him, who followed me reluctantly, floe by floe, back to shore.

Ned may have taken risks because he felt fearful in other areas. He was struggling in school. Most mornings for the first several months, he complained of a stomachache, and while Harry and I rode the bus, Mum drove him in later. In the hallways, just as Harry had ignored me, I wouldn't acknowledge Ned, not when my own position among my classmates was so tenuous. Ned, whose need for our mother seemed the greatest, fought with her the most. (In a way, we were lucky; Ned served as a lightning rod that diverted Mum's attention from the rest of us.) While Harry's battles with her were lengthy sieges, full of reproachful silences and closed doors, Ned's were tearful, high-decibel duets, operatic in scope and volume, often ending in a spanking. One evening, Ned refused to finish the pool of burned creamed corn on his dinner plate. Mum told him he couldn't leave the table till he ate it. Harry and I finished our meals, ate our desserts, ferried our plates to the sink, and went off to do our homework, leaving Ned staring at the yellow puddle on his plate as Mum cleaned the kitchen around him. Half an hour later, I invented an errand to take me through the kitchen. Ned was still there. He was still there when I went to bed. The following day Harry said that at nine thirty, Mum had come downstairs and told Ned, sitting at the table, creamed corn untouched, to go to bed. Not long afterward, Mum announced that each of us was allowed to choose three foods we could refuse to eat.

Every few weeks, we'd hear Ned dragging a suitcase down the stairs. "I'm running away," he'd declare. When he got no answer, he'd say it again, in a slightly louder voice, as if speaking to the hard of hearing. "Are you sure you want to?" Mum might respond, looking up from her book. A long silence. "I'm really going—*right now*," the voice would insist, a little smaller, a little less certain. "All right," Mum would say. "Good luck." Another long silence. "Send us a postcard," I might call after him, cruelly. We'd return to our books, to our homework. Once or twice Ned went so far as to open the front door. Eventually, we'd hear him dragging the suitcase back upstairs. Nothing more would be said about it. I always wondered what he'd packed in that suitcase, or whether he'd packed anything at all.

During those querulous years with my brothers, in which it seemed the only intimacy we shared was when, figuratively and sometimes literally, we had our hands around each other's throats, I longed for the kind of brotherhood I read about in books: King Arthur's knights swearing oaths and trotting off in search of dragons; Howard Pyle's pirates divvying up plunder from yet another captured galleon; Robin Hood's Merry Men roaming the forest, shooting arrows, feasting on venison, and generally engaging in what was then called knavery or derring-do but centuries later would be called male bonding. Even in the books, the ersatz brothers always seemed more brotherly than the real thing. How much more gallant were Peter Pan's Lost Boys, who lived in a hollow tree and battled Captain Hook, than the hopelessly square biological brothers Michael and John, who, even after being exposed to the rough-and-tumble paradise of Neverland, chose to return to the saccharine purgatory of their London nursery? How much more chummy was Tom Sawyer's frog-catching, rat-trapping, cat-swinging buddy Huck Finn than his simpering, tattletale, flesh-and-blood half-brother Sid?

In Darien, I found my Huck in Billy, the boy who had teamed up with me in my would-be conquest of Harry. A freckle-faced, pumpkin-haired fellow who lived in a ranch house on a cul-de-sac just beyond our back fence, Billy was my first real best friend. Like me, he was one of four brothers. Billy and I played every day after school and on weekends from the moment my mother allowed me to race up the path to his house, where his mother, still in her nightgown, was smoking her first cigarette of the day as she set out cereal boxes for her sons while their father slept off the previous night's dinner party. ("Why doesn't that boy ever spend time at his own house?" I once heard her say to her husband.) Like Harry, Billy loved sports, but he wasn't a dishearteningly better athlete than I. Like Ned, he thought up cool games, but not every game ended in a fight. We played Russian Fumble, an offshoot of Russian Shmuck, whose rules evolved as we went along; we refought World War II in the woods behind his house, taking turns being "the dirty Krauts," as they were referred to in the movies we loved; we watched New York Giants football each Sunday afternoon on TV; we drew battle scenes, Rat Finks, and Alfred E. Neumans on manila paper in school whenever the teacher's back was turned. We got into trouble together, we stood up for each other, and if one of us was made to stay after school, the other stayed, too. Why couldn't my real brothers be like Billy? Why couldn't Billy be one of my real brothers? (I overlooked the fact that Billy fought just as furiously with *his* brothers as I did with mine.)

One afternoon when I was eleven, a pack of kids gathered to play tag in a neighbor's yard. I got there late. When I arrived, I realized that I had walked in on an argument between Billy and Ned, something about a missing wallet of Billy's, I believe. My brother and my best friend began to shove each other in an experimental way that suggested neither of them really wanted to fight but neither of them wanted to back down. I'm sure my motives were not entirely pure. Perhaps I worried that my own status would suffer if my brother lost the fight. Perhaps I was angry at Billy because I felt a kind of sibling rivalry with him, too. Perhaps I was stirred to action because the beauteous Cobb sisters—who, I was even then aware, seemed more intrigued by my blond-haired brother than by me—were in attendance. But though I had fought Ned hundreds of times; though I must have put Ned down in front of Billy hundreds of times; though I had constantly compared Ned, however unconsciously, with Billy, and found Ned wanting—nonetheless I suddenly found myself stepping in front of Ned to face Billy.

The fight didn't last long and no one was hurt. I don't recall who won, but I was, at heart, a coward, quick to call others chicken because I suspected I was one myself. I'm sure I extricated myself at the earliest remotely honorable opportunity, and retreated, panting, with a covering fire of muttered insults. My intervention didn't change anything between Ned and me. By dinnertime we were back fighting each other over some minuscule, long-forgotten matter. And the next day Billy—bless his heart—and I were back playing Russian Fumble and poring over *Famous Monsters of Filmland*. I haven't been in a fight (such as it was) in the forty-six years since that afternoon. Yet even at the time, I recall that it wasn't really a choice. Billy was my friend, but Ned was my brother.

I told myself that I was happy, but the evidence contradicted me. The straight As I'd received in Dedham plummeted to Bs and Cs in Darien. The word *underachiever* was brandished in parent-teacher conferences. I mouthed off in class, and more and more often found myself clapping erasers in detention while the other boys and girls slung their book bags over their shoulders and rushed out into the green afternoon. Darien had a library, but I don't remember using it. I had given up books in favor of *MAD* magazine, which, with its nose-thumbing at the status quo, served the kind of liberating function for me that *The Feminine Mystique* served for my mother. I went on a small-scale crime spree: matter-of-factly stealing dimes from my mother's purse, pilfering monster magazines from a classmate's desk, swiping Nestlé Crunch bars from Arnold's, the variety store to which we rode our bikes after school. I was the pettiest of thieves—my biggest heist involved a jelly doughnut, which, under its glass dome, seemed as desirable and inaccessible as the Hope Diamond—and I would never have dared blossom into a full-fledged "juvenile delinquent," in the phrase that horrified parents and titillated kids. I suspect that even at the time I knew my thefts weren't only about the candy. I'm sure, too, that at some level I wanted to be caught. Certainly Mr. Arnold, a balding, bespectacled gentleman shaped, as I recall, something like a jelly doughnut himself, must have detected my crime—the confectioner's sugar on my fingers was a damning clue—but he kept his silence.

At bottom, I still wanted to be a good boy, still wanted to smooth things over, still wanted to fill the silences at the dinner table. But I couldn't help myself. Once, after having my mouth washed out with soap again for sassing my mother, I raced up to my room and, in a clear illustration of Freud's theory that depression is anger turned inward, stomped on all the toy soldiers I'd amassed over several Christmases and birthdays, snapping off their bases so they could no longer stand. *That* would show her. Another time, after I'd spoken rudely to her in the cellar, Mum, furious less at my rudeness than at my importing it into the one place she called her own, smacked me hard on the back of my legs. I stamped upstairs. In the family room, I passed an oil painting Mum had recently finished: a woman leaning out a window, an elbow on the sill, a look of bone-deep sadness on her face. Mum had worked on it for months; it was one of the most delicate and technically accomplished paintings she'd ever done. Quivering with self-righteous rage, I placed my thumb on the woman's still-wet nose and twisted it, rendering her faceless.

When I came downstairs the following morning, I was relieved that Mum wasn't angry. But even the most energetic spanking would have been less painful than the look of weary disappointment on her face as she turned away from me, a look I realized was rather like that of the woman in the painting.

My brothers and I were so involved in our own troubles that none of us had time for Mark, who, in memory, I see only through the mesh squares of his playpen as he held on to the red plastic rail and watched us pass through the living room on our way to someplace else. (Occasionally Ned and I might pause to test out new nonsense words, circling the playpen like children at the zoo, repeating *looties* or *oolees*—the winner being the one whose word elicited the biggest reaction from our baby brother. Mark's face would light up; he'd grip the rail tighter and bounce on his toes.) It surprises and shames me that I can't remember his first step, his first word, his favorite toy. Instead I remember the afternoon he fell on the flagstone patio, after which his baby teeth turned pewter-gray. I remember the afternoon when, sitting alone in the driveway, he was bitten on the head by a neighbor's dog. I remember his lone playmate, the skinny older girl next door with a worm-colored scar on her throat where, my mother told us, doctors had once cut a hole to help her breathe. She bossed Mark around; grateful for the attention, Mark did her bidding. And I remember the afternoon in the car, as we drove through town on some dreary errand, in those precarseat days, when Mark, a toddler at the time, slipped off the seat and began falling through the rusted floor of the Parklane before Mum reached over and pulled him back from the gray asphalt that rushed past below.

Looking back, I wonder why my brothers and I didn't close ranks. Why didn't we watch out for one another? We were, I suppose, too busy fending for ourselves, struggling to fit into a new town, to make friends in a new school. We weren't in a position to help, even if we had known how to ask for help or how to accept it if it were offered.

There were pleasant brotherly times, I'm sure, but I recall them only in general terms: reading the backs of cereal boxes at the breakfast table and wondering what riboflavin was; trading candy on our way home from the News store on Saturday mornings; jumping in the pile of leaves we'd help Dad rake on Sunday afternoons; basking in the eye of the storm as our car inched forward on the chain belt through the car wash, soapsuds swirling on the windows all around us; racing to the front door to meet Dad as he returned from a business trip and produced, from his worn leather briefcase, a miniature cardboard suitcase filled with Howard Johnson lollipops. The few specific memories I have of brotherly bonding during those years are unsettling: chewing popovers in the dining room of the Harvard Club as our parents argued their way into silence on a long-awaited family trip to Manhattan; getting pinworms and lining up by age for scalding showers (Dad manning the faucets and handing us towels, Mum boiling our quarantined underwear in the spaghetti pot); watching a snake die as it choked to death on a too-fat toad on the floor of the garage one summer afternoon; sitting up with Mum after she got a chilling anonymous phone call in the middle of the night when Dad was out of town; watching President Kennedy's funeral on TV, disturbed less by the death than by the riderless horse as it pranced nervously down Pennsylvania Avenue, empty boots facing backward in the stirrups. I don't remember us ever gathering in what the real estate agent had called "the family room." I remember us in our own worlds: Harry in his room, listening to his records; me in the family room, reading the *World Book Encyclopedia*; Ned on the floor of our bedroom, setting up his soldiers; Mark in his playpen, watching. We were engaging in what, years later when I had children of my own, I would learn was called parallel play.

I recall poring over a photograph in *Life* magazine of a family posed in its fallout shelter. The Cold War was at its height, people talked about what would happen if the Russians "dropped the Bomb," and when the alarm sounded in school, we'd stop reciting our times tables to crouch beneath our desks (sneaking peaks at the girls' flowered cotton underwear as their skirts scrunched up), so we'd be prepared in case the Russians decided to drop the "Big One" on Darien—which, to my impressionable mind, seemed entirely likely, Darien possessing, after all, the number two per capita income in the entire *country*. (Mum, asserting that anyone within a two-hundred-mile radius of the target was a goner anyway, said that if the Bomb was coming she wanted to be standing on the bull's-eye, ready to catch it. I pictured her in our backyard, peering into the sky, settling under some distant, plummeting object, like Mickey Mantle under a fly ball.) The *Life* photograph made the fallout shelter seem cozy. The crew-cut father held a collapsible shovel; the mother, an indulgent smile on her Donna Reed face, sat at a foldout table in front of a wall of canned food; the son knelt on the carpeted floor behind a transistor radio and a flashlight; the elder daughter perched on a folding chair, a pile of blankets in her lap; her sister sat cross-legged on the floor, one hand on a stack of board games and books. They looked as if they were posing for their family Christmas card. If only *my* family had a fallout shelter, I thought. I imagined the sirens sounding, Dad herding us into the backyard through a door in the ground, down to a silent, windowless world, in which we'd eat Dinty Moore beef stew from a can, play Parcheesi, and, when the lights were out, talk quietly until we fell asleep. Let the Bomb fall—we'd be a family again.

There was one place Harry, Ned, and I came together peaceably: a small, windowless second-floor alcove furnished with a legless sofa and a black-and-white Zenith television set the size of a toaster. (We may have been the only children in Darien who had to watch *Walt Disney's Wonderful World of Color* in black and white.) Here, in a setting as spare and purposeful as a chapel, we sat side by side, hour after hour, in silent devotion. Although our mother referred to television as "the boob tube," whenever she was fed up with our fighting we'd hear her yell from the kitchen, "GO WATCH TV!" Ned and I, in particular, spent so much time "glued to the set," as Mum put it, that we might as well have run an intravenous line from the TV into our forearms, through which we could absorb even more directly the strange allure of Barbara Feldon's cross-eyed smile in *Get Smart*; the waterfall rustle as the tiles revolved on the *Jeopardy!* game board; the manic ardor with which contestants careered shopping carts down grocery store aisles toward the canned hams on *Supermarket Sweep*. Indeed, much of my conversation with Ned was adopted wholesale from television commercials. "It's chewy, Louie," I'd opine at the dinner table. "It's dandy candy," Ned would respond. Or Ned, arranging plastic animals on the bedroom floor, might announce, apropos of nothing, "Charlie says, 'Love my Good and Plenty,' and I'd answer, "Charlie says, 'Really rings the bell!'" as automatically as—and far more devoutly than—I answered the minister's "The Lord be with you" with "And with thy spirit." (Even now, nearly a half-century later, long after we've forgotten what exactly happened in 1066 or how to calculate the area of a triangle, Ned and I, while doing the dishes or walking on the beach, are liable to break out, to my children's bewilderment, in a spirited a capella rendition of "Honeycomb, Texas treat Post Honeycomb for your own." Indeed, the advertising encomia of the sixties seem so firmly imprinted on my frontal cortex I suspect that when I'm on my deathbed, children and grandchildren gathered around to hear my last words, the only thing I'll be able to remember is "When *your* cat alarm sounds, send for Little Friskies.")

Although we'd watch just about anything, we were drawn to shows about happy families (and in those days, all television families were happy), especially to those, like the Cleavers and the Douglases, that revolved around sons. In television families, brothers might clash—never physically, of course—but they always ended up reconciling, and I'd melt a little as Wally Cleaver, for whom Harry was such a dead ringer that our mother sometimes called him Wally, ruffled the Beave's hair, or Chip Douglas shot gullible, buck-toothed Ernie an exasperated but affectionate glance. This was how brothers were supposed to be—high-spirited and competitive but supportive and loving—and I assumed that every set of brothers in the world was like that, except us. The TV brothers we most resembled, however, were the Three Stooges, who seemed unable to go more than a few seconds without pulling one another's hair or poking one another in the eye. Though I would never have dared tell him this, Harry reminded me of Moe, the eldest brother—omnipotent, unpredictable, and capable, it seemed, of sudden acts of violence. (I grew up with the irrational fear that someday Harry might put my head in the vise on the cellar worktable and turn the crank.) Ned was Curly, the attention-getter, the mischief-maker, the clown who absorbed the most punishment but possessed a certain creative genius. I reluctantly admitted to myself that I was Larry, the bland, frizzy-haired milquetoast. A few years later, a fourth Stooge appeared. Like Mark, Shemp seemed an afterthought, an add-on. We were surprised to learn that Shemp was, in real life, Moe and Curly's *older* brother. Larry, in fact, was the outsider. We laughed at these grown-ups who acted even more like children than we did, but the Stooges' perpetual distress hit uncomfortably close to home. It horrified me to think that when we were fifty and balding, Harry, Ned, and I might still be bopping one another over the head and giving one another noogies.

The apotheosis of fraternal perfection appeared on Sunday night at nine, when an old-fashioned map of Nevada appeared on the screen, a fire burning outward from its center; a rat-a-tat guitar strum sounded (Harry shushing Ned and me as we sang, with more pure joy than we brought to any other brotherly activity, "*Bun-un-un-un-un-un-un-nuh-nuh-nuh-nuh-nuh-nuh-NAN-za!*"); and the Cartwrights galloped toward us. Harry, of course, was Adam, the eldest brother, a lean, laconic, sideburned fellow who dressed in black from his hat to his boots and hovered around the edges of the family adventures. (Indeed, after a few years, at the same time Harry was pulling away from our family, Adam disappeared without explanation. At the time, I wondered whether the responsibilities of being the eldest brother had overwhelmed him. The real reason, I learned eventually, was that, in a sign of the changing times, the actor playing Adam had decided the show was misogynistic and racist.) I longed to be Little Joe, the handsome, insouciant, shaggy-haired youngest Cartwright, but even then I knew the role belonged to angel-faced, devil-may-care Ned. Which left, by default, the gentle man-mountain of a middle child, Hoss, to whom I was no fit in strength or size (I might well have been able to fold myself underneath his ten-gallon hat), but with whom I shared a certain eagerness to please and a desire to make peace. Like the Cleavers and the Douglases, the Cartwright brothers might quarrel among themselves, but they always rode to one another's rescue against the outside world, pooling their strengths—Adam's brain (he had been to college back east), Hoss's muscle, Little Joe's daring—to make an invincible fraternal team. You never saw Adam sitting on Hoss, pinning his arms to the ground, drooling on his face. You never saw Hoss and Little Joe rolling around on the floor, shouting "Got you last." Yes, they might have brief spats over an impetuous remark by Little Joe or a well-intentioned blunder by Hoss, but they would eventually settle them, giving each other sheepish, forgiving grins and playfully punching each other's shoulders before gathering for a nourishing meal cooked by their Chinese housekeeper, Hop Sing. (Many of the TV families we watched were motherless, unless you counted surrogates like Hop Sing or Uncle Charlie on *My Three Sons*, both of whom seemed always to be emerging from the kitchen, wearing aprons and irritated frowns, to the fond teasing of the ersatz sons they served.) As the Cartwright brothers moved across the flickering TV screen, the Colt brothers sat side by side by side on the couch, closer than we'd ever wittingly allow ourselves to be anywhere beyond this alcove without pinching each other, staring straight ahead.

We spent three years in Darien. One day Mum gathered us in the kitchen and said that Dad had taken a new job, and we'd be moving back to

Dedham. It wouldn't be until years later that I learned that Dad had been passed over for promotion. The well-dressed man whose daughters had disliked the smell of our car got the job instead, and was eventually named president, leaving my father stuck on a middle rung of the corporate ladder, with no real future in the company. One August morning we packed up the Parklane and followed the moving van out of Darien.

*   *   *

Two decades later, driving with a friend from New York to Boston, I decided on a whim to turn off at the exit for Darien. The ramp from I-95 delivered us into a hushed, wooded world. We drove past Darien News, where the heraldic wooden pediment still arched over the mullioned glass doors, past the Sport Shop, where the manifestly Caucasian mannequins in the display windows still wore Top-Siders and khakis; past the train station, where the late-model cars in serried ranks awaited their owners' return from the city. We drove past the elementary school, past the street that led to my old friend Billy's house, down Five Mile River Road, the setting sun gilding the river, the automatic sprinklers anointing the newly mowed lawns whose thick green swaths lay as crisp and straight as the stripes on an American flag. At the time, I was living in Manhattan, the city to which my father had journeyed each morning, and I was shocked at how little Darien had changed, and how beautiful it was. How could we have been so unhappy in this place?

It was evening by the time we got to my old house. There it was: the black shutters against the white clapboard, the mailbox where the school bus had picked us up, the tree under which Harry and I had fought, the patio on which Mark had fallen. There were no cars in the driveway. Emboldened, my friend and I pulled over, got out, and walked cautiously into the backyard. I wanted to show her the neighbor's pool, the path to Billy's house through the woods, the garage where my brothers and I had seen the snake swallow the toad. I wanted to show myself how far I'd traveled from this place. Suddenly the porch light came on. The screen door opened. "Who's there?" a man's voice called. "Is anyone there?" We ducked behind the forsythia bushes along the far edge of the property. "Is anyone there?" the man repeated, stepping out onto the flagstone terrace, peering into the darkness. "Is anyone there?" I was twenty-eight years old, but I was a child again and I didn't say a word.

Chapter Four

Brother Against Brother: John and Will Kellogg

Any out-of-towners who happened to wander into the Calhoun County Courthouse in southern Michigan in the spring of 1917 must have found it hard to believe that the plaintiff and the defendant in *Kellogg v. Kellogg* were brothers. At first glance, it was hard to believe that they were even related.

The plaintiff, John Harvey Kellogg, the man everyone called the Doctor, was the flamboyant founder and director of the Battle Creek Sanitarium, a combination spa, hospital, and chautauqua where the well-heeled came to see and be seen as they followed a customized regimen of rest, exercise, and diet. A short, plump sixty-five-year-old banty rooster of a man, the Doctor dressed all in white, from his fedora and tie to his spats and high-button shoes. He said he wore white to allow more of the health-giving rays of the sun to reach his body, but he clearly didn't mind that his sartorial preference helped him stand out in a crowd. He looked more like a man being honored at his own birthday party than a man suing his brother.

The only person in the courtroom the ebullient Doctor didn't try to charm was the defendant. Fifty-seven-year-old Will Kellogg—he was known as W.K., but only the rare few to whom he had given permission dared call him that to his face—was the founder and president of the Toasted Corn Flake Company, the rapidly growing business that would one day be known as Kellogg's. The Corn Flake King, as he was dubbed by the press, was a bald, beady-eyed, moon-faced man who wore a rumpled suit, Coke-bottle glasses, and the dour expression of a snapping turtle. Though he was eight years younger than his brother, his phlegmatic affect made him seem eight years older. Few words escaped his pursed lips, but those that did were incisive. During a recess after W.K. had testified, one of the Doctor's lawyers was heard to say, "Don't ask him anything else. He is too smart."

In the courtroom, the brothers ignored each other with the pointedness of a divorced couple. Indeed, for most of the previous decade, the Doctor and W.K. had communicated almost entirely in lawsuits, in a forensic rondo that made *Kellogg v. Kellogg* seem as arcane and attenuated as *Jarndyce v. Jarndyce*. And yet, in its essentials, the case boiled down to one simple question: which brother had the right to the family name. As in any sibling rivalry, of course, the roots of the conflict went deep.

*　　*　　*

If Sigmund Freud had been an only child, *rivalry* might not be the first word we think of when we hear the word *sibling*. Freud, however, was the eldest of eight children. Seventeen months after his birth, his brother Julius was born, and his mother's attention turned to the new arrival. Looking back on that time, Freud recalled the "genuine childish jealousy" he felt toward his brother and his desire that the tiny, mewling lump would disappear. When he got his wish—Julius died of an intestinal infection at seven months—Freud felt a "germ of self-reproach" that festered, he would tell Wilhelm Fleiss, throughout his life. His brother's death, Freud suggested, left him with a lifelong need for a "hated enemy" and contributed to "what is neurotic, but also what is intense, in all my friendships." (As an adult, Freud was renowned for treating his peers and protégés as surrogate younger brothers who sought to usurp him. If any of them questioned the Freudian party line or tried to emerge as psychiatrists in their own right, Freud cast them out of his circle, figuratively killing them before they killed him.) Freud's second chance at being an only child was brief; within a year of Julius's death, Anna was born, and by the time he was ten years old there were five more little Freuds clamoring for his parents' attention. Freud did his best to ignore them. In his brief autobiography, his siblings are not mentioned.

Freud's experience with his brothers and sisters would provide grist for his characterization of siblings as rivals locked in combat for their parents' affection, who would gladly be rid of one another if they could. "A small child does not necessarily love his brothers and sisters; often he obviously does not," he wrote. "There is no doubt that he hates them as his competitors, and it is a familiar fact that this attitude often persists for long years, till maturity is reached or even later, without interruption."

Despite his strong views on sibling conflict, Freud believed the Oedipal bond to be paramount in the development of the personality and dismissed the sibling relationship as relatively unimportant. The term *sibling rivalry,* in fact, would not be coined until 1933, six years before Freud's death, when the child psychiatrist David Levy gave his patients celluloid dolls that represented their parents and younger siblings. When he asked them what they felt when they saw the baby brother or sister doll nursing at its mother's breast, there ensued scenes of sibling carnage to rival anything in the Old Testament. Among the responses listed by Levy: "dropping," "shooting," "throwing," "slapping," "hitting with stick," "hitting against floor," "hammering," "crushing with truck," "crushing with feet," "crushing with fingers," "tearing apart," "twisting the body," "scattering parts," "biting," "piercing (with screw driver)." So many celluloid dolls were destroyed that Levy had to switch temporarily to dolls made of clay. Levy, who would repeat his experiments among the Kekchi Indians of Guatemala with similarly gruesome results, concluded that regardless of age, gender, birth order, or cultural background, sibling rivalry is a fact of family life. (The word *rival* is derived from the Latin *rivalis,* which means "having rights to the same stream." In pre-Christian times, rivals were people or tribes who fought over water from the same river. "In our terms," the psychoanalyst Peter Neubauer has observed, "the river is the mother who supplies our basic needs, and the children compete for access to her.")

Sibling rivalry is difficult to quantify, but research suggests that it is all but inevitable. Indeed, it has been said that the only way to avoid it is to have a single child. Using hidden microphones, a University of Illinois psychologist found that the average pair of siblings between the ages of three and seven engages in an extended squabble every seventeen minutes. That figure seems low, if my own childhood is any indication, but with four boys, the Colt family may have been especially fertile ground for conflict. In fact, siblings who have a brother tend to be more competitive than those with a sister; of the three sibling combinations, brother/brother pairs are the most rivalrous, sister/sister the least. The closer in age, the greater the rivalry's intensity, just as seeds planted close together may suffer in their competition for the sun's attention. Sibling rivalry may be especially fierce when the age difference is less than three years. If six or more years separate a sibling pair, psychologists say, the relationship may be more paternal than fraternal. (The only sibling with whom Freud got along reasonably well was his youngest brother, Alexander, ten years his junior, who posed no threat to his authority. Whenever Freud went to the baths as a young adult, he made the worshipful Alex carry his bags.) There are exceptions, of course. John Kellogg was eight years older than his brother Will, but their rivalry would become only slightly less ferocious than Cain and Abel's. The age gap may explain why it took so long to boil over.

*   *   *

Growing up in Battle Creek, Michigan, not long after the Civil War, John and Will Kellogg seemed unlikely rivals. Of the fourteen children born to John Preston Kellogg, a devout Seventh-Day Adventist who owned a small broom factory, John Harvey, the tenth child, was the most promising. Although he was a small, delicate, tubercular boy, the runt of a large litter, John made up for his frailty with Napoleonic assertiveness. He was outgoing, headstrong, and ambitious. He was also unusual. While his brothers dug tunnels in the yard, waded in the Kalamazoo River, and smoked clover behind the barn, John played the piano and the violin, wrote poetry, and made up stories in which he cast himself as the hero who made miraculous escapes from ferocious wild beasts. He considered games, even the chess his father tried to teach him, a waste of time. John didn't attend school until he was nine—as Adventists, his parents believed the end of the world was so close at hand that formal education was irrelevant—and he left after two years to work ten-hour shifts in his father's factory, sorting broomcorn for two dollars a day. John educated himself. He soon exhausted his parents' meager collection of books and began borrowing from neighbors. He spent his first paycheck on a four-volume set of Farr's *Ancient History* and went on to assemble a modest private library of his own: books on botany, astronomy, German grammar, and shorthand, as well as a dictionary. (Words fascinated him; as an adult, he'd carry a vest-pocket dictionary to peruse in his spare moments.) When his father named his company J. P. Kellogg and Son, John was the Son he had in mind. But though John didn't know what he wanted to do with his life—he talked of becoming a teacher—he clearly dreamed of more than making brooms.

The twelfth Kellogg child was decidedly unpromising. Will was a cautious, deliberate, taciturn boy whose teacher at the Adventist school he attended through the fifth grade assumed he was "dimwitted," in part because he couldn't read the words on the blackboard. (It wasn't until Will was twenty that he realized he needed glasses.) Will wasn't much to look at either: jug-eared, thin-lipped, and so poker-faced that when he and his classmates played a prank, the teacher never suspected Will. But he was a plugger. At the age of seven, he was working as a stock boy at his father's factory after school and on Sundays. On summer mornings, he uprooted, bunched, and washed vegetables for the local market. The summer he was nine, he pulled and topped 350 bushels of Bermuda onions. Years later, he'd proudly recall that he was paying for his own clothes at ten and supporting himself at fourteen. There was little time for fun, though if his work at the factory was finished and the cows were milked, his father might let him walk to the station and watch the Michigan Central trains come in. Later in life Will would observe wistfully, "I never learned to play." He felt especially self-conscious and inadequate next to his cocksure older brother, who rarely let Will forget the eight years that lay between them. John made Will shine his shoes. He made Will mind his manners. If Will complained, John gave him a whipping. Asked for childhood memories of his brother, an elderly Will Kellogg recalled frigid Michigan nights: "I have vivid recollections of John Harvey warming his cold feet by placing same on my back, not conducive to my sleeping well."

The Kelloggs weren't the only ones who considered John promising. The family shared a pew at the Battle Creek Tabernacle with Elder James White and his wife, Ellen, the prophet who, as a reclusive seventeen-year-old hatter's daughter from Maine, had had a vision in which 144,000 harp-playing saints sat down to a supper of fruits, nuts, and manna at a solid silver table presided over by Jesus. White's lavish revelation won her a leading role in the Seventh-Day Adventist church, whose members believed that the second coming was imminent and that a proper diet was a vital part of preparing for that happy day. Impressed by twelve-year-old John Kellogg, the Whites invited him to learn the printer's trade at the Adventist publishing plant, where John advanced rapidly from errand boy to apprentice typesetter to proofreader. At sixteen, he was editing the *Advent Review and Sabbath Herald*. As he worked on various Adventist publications, John was intrigued by the church's minimalist approach to nutrition. Although one of his favorite foods was oxtail, he decided to become a vegetarian, in part because, at five feet two and a half, he thought it might help him grow a few inches. (It didn't.) John became the Whites' protégé, living with them for months at a time, helping Pastor White with his writing. Years later, Ellen White would observe that her husband had been more of a father to John Kellogg than to his own sons.

The Whites had bigger things in mind for John than setting type. In 1866, acting on another of Ellen White's visions, the Adventists had opened a small medical boardinghouse where ailing guests convalesced on a regime of rest, exercise, and hydrotherapy along with a diet of fruits, vegetables, Graham bread, and water. But the Western Health Reform Institute, as it was called, didn't attract many customers, and the Whites decided they needed a first-rate physician to distinguish it from the other spas and water-cure establishments that were sprouting across the country. They tried out the eldest Kellogg son, Merritt, but he lacked spark. Their printer's devil had spark aplenty. The Whites sent John east, where he graduated from Bellevue Hospital Medical College in 1875. The following year, they made him physician-in-chief of the faltering institute. The twelve patients who remained may have mistaken the diminutive twenty-four-year-old for a student, not the physician-in-charge, but John had the ambition, versatility, and pizzazz of a one-man band. He gave the place a spiffier name, the Battle Creek Sanitarium, and added a barrage of new treatments, including massage, calisthenics, electrical stimulation, deep breathing exercises, and surgery. He led sing-alongs and played his violin. He wrote pamphlets and magazine articles describing his work. Within two years, business at the San, as people called it, was so good that John tore down the old farmhouse and built a five-story, mansard-roofed Victorian pile big enough for two hundred patients—the largest building in Battle Creek.

Will was also singled out by the Whites, but for a less-exalted position. While John was dissecting cadavers in New York City, fourteen-year-old Will was driving a horse and cart across southern Michigan, peddling his father's brooms. Though painfully shy, Will was a determined salesman who rarely took no for an answer. For a time, he worked at his half-brother Albert's broom factory in Kalamazoo, but when the company failed and Albert was unable to pay his employees, Will moved his trunk onto the front porch of his brother's home, sat down on it, and announced that he wouldn't budge until he got his salary. (He didn't have to wait long.) When Will's father broke his hip, he put Will in charge of the family business. He did so well that two years later, when the Whites needed someone to manage a struggling Adventist broom factory in Dallas, they sent Will. Supervising sixty men a thousand miles from home was a challenge for a shy nineteen-year-old, but Will turned the company around within a year. Back in Battle Creek, he took a course in bookkeeping at the local business college and prepared to marry his longtime girlfriend, a timid grocer's daughter he called Puss. Will seemed destined to spend his life making brooms. Then, in April 1880, John Harvey Kellogg asked his younger brother to come work for him at the San.

*   *   *

In an essay about sibling rivalry, Anna Quindlen described the moment her toddler son realized that he was no longer the only child in the family.

> I think it began with Quin one day when the younger one needed me more and I turned to him and said, "You know, Quin, I'm Christopher's mommy, too." The look that passed over his face was the one I imagine usually accompanies the discovery of a dead body in the den: shock, denial, horror. "And Daddy is Christopher's daddy?" he gasped. When I confirmed this he began to cry, wet, sad sobbing.

Quin's response to the phenomenon Freud called displacement was relatively mild. In *Mail Harry to the Moon!*, a children's book by Robie H. Harris, Harry's older brother variously demands that his new sibling be thrown in the trash, flushed down the toilet, given to the zoo, put back inside Mommy, and mailed to the moon. (The author wrote the book after overhearing a four-year-old ask a family friend to take his baby brother with her when she went back to Chicago.) My cousin told me of a friend who found his toddler son standing at his newborn brother's bassinet, his hand hovering above the infant's face, "two fingers locked in a cute little Max Schreck Nosferatu claw." Asked what he was doing to his baby brother, he replied, "I'm *scrambling* him."

Such comments make delightful parental anecdotes, but they are raw expressions of anxiety that constitute the opening salvos in what may be a lifetime of competition. Parental affection is, of course, the Holy Grail, but, like the spirit said to be contained in a primitive talisman, it can be encapsulated in a popsicle, a plastic soldier, or a cloud. (The poet A. E. Housman and his siblings used to sit at the nursery window and argue over which cloud belonged to whom.) The father of two boys told me that whenever the younger brother walked into the playroom, the older brother would immediately sweep all the toys toward a corner, covering them with his arms. Frozen in this position, eyeing his brother warily, he couldn't play with the toys, but, more important, his brother couldn't either. (His preemptive strike, of course, made the toys even more desirable, and the younger brother even more covetous.) Sibling rivalry, however, is rarely rational. A friend of mine gave his elder son a bike with a kickstand for his seventh birthday, whereupon the birthday boy's three-year-old brother threw a tantrum until he was promised a kickstand, too—for his tricycle. My friend's three-year-old would have sympathized with the four-year-old described by Alfred Adler who, weeping in frustration, cried out, "I am so unhappy because I can never be as old as my brother."

A disproportionate number of brotherly quarrels center around food—a relatively literal stand-in for parental nourishment. When seven-year-old Samuel Taylor Coleridge asked his mother to slice him some cheese for toasting, his older brother Frank, jealous because Sam was his mother's favorite, crept into the kitchen and minced the cheese into pieces so tiny they couldn't be toasted. Sam attacked Frank. Frank pretended to be seriously injured, and when Sam bent over him to see if he was all right, Frank punched him in the face. Sam grabbed a kitchen knife and chased after his brother until their mother walked in. (The rivalry between Frank, an extroverted daredevil fond of playing soldiers and stealing apples, and Sam, a timorous dreamer who spent his time reading, was so fierce that the biographer Richard Holmes suggests that the necessity of separating the boys was one of the reasons their parents dispatched Frank to the navy at the age of twelve.) Competition for food was keen in the down-at-heels Joyce household, according to the biographer Richard Ellmann: "On Pancake Night one pancake was left on the platter, and all four boys—James, Stanislaus, Charles, and George—dove for it. James made off with the prize and ran up and down stairs, protesting to his pursuers that he had already eaten it. At last they were convinced, and he then imperturbably removed the pancake from the pocket where it lay hidden, and ate it up with the air of little Jack Horner." (Such schadenfreude was routine in the Colt kitchen, where it was important not only to get more food than one's brothers but to lord the victory over them, a gambit that, in our family, was known as "rubbing it in." Ned would offer me the rest of his milk shake. Touched by his sudden generosity—how gullible I was!—I'd accept, whereupon he'd ostentatiously drink up all but the dregs before presenting it to me with a triumphant "no backs." Or I'd do the same to him.) A friend of mine who took in two baby squirrels told me that whenever she fed them, one of them would drop his own food to snatch his brother's; it was more important that his brother *not* have food than for him to have food himself. In *Paris Spleen,* his collection of autobiographical prose poems, Baudelaire recalls seeing two beggar brothers fight over a piece of bread he'd given them:

> The cake traveled from hand to hand and changed pockets at every instant, changing, alas! in size as well, and when finally, exhausted and panting and covered with blood, they stopped from the sheer impossibility of going on, no cause for feud remained; the piece of bread had disappeared, and the crumbs, scattered all around, were indistinguishable from the grains of sand with which they were mingled.

Such aggression might not have fazed David and Ida Eisenhower. Believing that competition bred mettle, they encouraged their six sons never to let their playmates—or their brothers—beat them in anything. Growing up in Abilene, Kansas, the Eisenhower brothers vied to see who could run the fastest, jump the highest, do his chores the best, read aloud from the Bible the most accurately, and (perhaps demonstrating that they hadn't fully absorbed what they'd read) fight the hardest. One day, wrestling in the kitchen, the second son, Edgar, sat on the third son, Dwight's, chest. When Dwight refused to give up, Edgar grabbed his brother's hair and began pounding his head against the floor. Terrified, the fifth son, Earl, began to pull Edgar off, but their mother, without budging from the stove, said sharply, "Let them alone."

Two thousand miles east, the Kennedy household was more decorous but no less Darwinian. With nine children born in a span of seventeen years, the family was a veritable petri dish for sibling rivalry, overseen by a father whose competitive zeal was stoked by having grown up Irish-Catholic in anti-Irish Boston. "We want winners," Joseph Kennedy Sr. would say. "We don't want losers around here." There seemed to be no activity in which the children did not compete: swimming, sailing, tennis, touch football, running, chess, Categories, dinner-table current events quizzes, after-dinner word games, math contests, rock-skipping, seashell-floating. The eldest brothers, Joe and Jack, separated by a scant twenty-two months, were the most contentious. "I suppose it was inevitable that they were rivals," their mother reflected. "Joe was much stronger than Jack, and if there was any physical encounter, Joe really whacked him." Scrawny Jack wouldn't back down. One afternoon Joe challenged Jack to a bicycle race. Each pedaled around the block in the opposite direction. As they approached each other halfway, neither boy swerved. They smashed into each other. Joe was unhurt, but Jack's cuts would require twenty-eight stitches.

Fierce fraternal competition is often leavened by equally fierce loyalty, in accordance with the unwritten corollary by which even the most rivalrous brothers will unite against an outside threat. "Me against my brother; my brother and me against my cousin; me, my brother, and my cousin against the stranger" goes an Arabic saying. The Eisenhower brothers may have pounded one another's heads on the floor, but they banded together against all non-Eisenhowers. Jack Kennedy may have striven mightily to beat up his older brother, but when he saw a Choate classmate begin to pass Joe in a Hyannis sailboat race, he gunned his motorboat in front of his friend's vessel, slowing him down so that his brother could win. A middle-aged financial planner, the youngest of three sons, told me that his older brothers used to beat him up on a regular basis. "But if someone looked at me cross-eyed at the bus stop, my older brothers beat *them* up," he said. "Even today, they'll give me more grief than anyone else, but if someone attacks me, I know they'll defend me to the death."

* * *

To understand the feud between John and Will Kellogg, one must understand the institution to which they devoted much of their lives. By 1900, the Battle Creek Sanitarium was the largest and most popular spa in the country, with four hundred guest rooms, two indoor swimming pools, a surgical hospital, a thousand-seat chapel, twenty cottages, a lakeside resort, and 400 acres of farmland. Here, some three thousand patients a year—locals dubbed them "Battle Freaks"—pursued what John Harvey Kellogg called "Biologic Living," described by one San brochure as "daily cold water and air baths, swimming, work in the gymnasium, wearing of light and porous clothing and frequent changes of underwear." It was a little more complicated—and controversial—than that. The Doctor, who had chronic gastrointestinal problems that he blamed on his meat-centric childhood meals, believed that the key to happiness lay in a healthy diet, defined at the San largely by what people couldn't eat: meat ("only proper food for hyenas and turkey buzzards," said the Doctor), tobacco ("destroys the sex glands"), coffee ("cripples the liver"), ice cream ("unnatural"), vinegar ("a poison, not a food"), oysters ("swarming with bacteria"), bouillon ("enough creatin to kill nine guinea pigs"), tea, sugar, cheese, chocolate, alcohol, and spices, to name a few. San cuisine consisted largely of nuts and grains, measured out in precise quantities and sculpted to resemble roasts and steaks. The San offered twenty-six basic diets, but each guest had his or her own customized plan: dangerously thin guests might be fed a half pint of milk every thirty minutes from dawn to dusk; guests with high blood pressure might be prescribed ten to fourteen pounds of grapes—peeled—a day. One guest, for reasons that have been lost to medical science, was instructed to follow a goat around the San pasture, "to take nourishment, kid-like, directly from the source," as Ronald Deutsch delicately put it in his history of American food faddists. Even the healthiest intestine, the Doctor insisted, required regular cleansing, for which he proposed a two-pronged attack: bran, leafy vegetables, and paraffin oil ingested at the north end, water injected at the south. Ever since the Doctor had visited a colony of orangutans in Algeria and noticed that our primate cousins defecate almost continuously, he had maintained that frequent bowel movements were the key to what he called "getting the stomach right." Not all patients had the fortitude for the recommended five enemas a day, a regimen made possible with the help of a high-speed machine capable, according to the proud doctor, of forcing fifteen gallons of water through the intestines in a matter of minutes.

Between meals—and enemas—patients submitted to a bewildering array of massages, exercises, and hydrotherapies, many of them devised by the Doctor, like the sinusoidal bath (patients stuck their hands and feet into electrified buckets of water), the electric light bath (patients sat in wooden cabinets lined with illuminated bulbs), or the salt scrub (patients clung to iron hooks while attendants scoured their bodies with a saline mush). At the end of each day, patients gathered on the roof, where the Doctor led them in a series of elaborate marching patterns to the strains of the San's official song, a pulse-quickening two-step called "The Battle Creek Sanitarium March."

If "Biologic Living" sounded a bit joyless, even masochistic, the San was as much cruise ship as hospital. There were gym classes, cooking classes, folk-dancing classes, greenhouse tours, and Indian-club demonstrations. There were picnics and bird walks in summer, sledding and sleigh rides in winter, and four nonsectarian weekly church services year-round. Guests could browse the gift shop for a postcard of the San, a copy of one of Dr. Kellogg's books, a bottle of acidophilus milk, or the latest issue of the San's in-house newsletter, *The Battle Creek Idea*. They could sit up straight in one of the Doctor's posture-enhancing "physiologic" chairs on the veranda and gaze out at the manicured grounds, through which deer, marmosets, and a tame bear roamed, delighting the senses and reinforcing the willpower of newly converted "grass eaters." After dinner, there were plays, singalongs, and basketball games; speeches and performances by notable guests; and concerts by the Sanitarium Glee Club and the Sanitarium Philharmonic Orchestra.

The Doctor was the wizard behind this vegetarian Oz. He was, in his way, no less a visionary than Ellen White, and his goal was no less ambitious: to change the way Americans ate, breathed, dressed, exercised, and defecated. To that end, he churned out nearly fifty books (*Rational Hydrotherapy*); more than two hundred medical papers ("Surgery of the Ileocecal Valve"); and so many pamphlets for the lay reader ("Nuts May Save the Race") that even the publicity-conscious doctor couldn't keep count. He founded a nursing school, a school of hygiene, a liberal arts college, and a medical school, which, not coincidentally, provided the San with a steady stream of low-paid employees. He helped establish more than thirty San franchises across the country. He gave more than five thousand lectures. He made frequent trips abroad: to examine the latest exercise equipment in Sweden; to study advanced surgical techniques in England; to learn about the bowel-cleansing benefits of yogurt in France. He invented a heated operating table, a vibrating chair that increased blood circulation, an electric belt that massaged the hips, a mechanical exercise horse, a machine that kneaded the abdomen to relieve constipation, a canvas sleeve that brought fresh air into a patient's bedroom at night without chilling the entire room, a tobaccoless Turkish pipe. An ostentatiously prodigious worker, the Doctor rose at four a.m. for an enema, a cold bath, and calisthenics before launching into a twenty-hour workday. He bragged of composing between twenty-five and fifty letters a day (many of them novella-size); of dictating eighteen hours at a stretch (pausing only as one exhausted stenographer gave way to another); of working forty hours straight without nourishment (other than the handful of nuts he hoarded like a squirrel in his coat pocket); of performing as many as twenty-five operations in a day. (Though he made his name promoting fringe medical therapies, the Doctor was an accomplished gastrointestinal surgeon whose precise stitching moved the director of the Johns Hopkins Hospital to remark, "I have never seen such beautiful human needlework.") Fortunately, the Doctor was a skilled multitasker. While taking his morning bath, he listened to staff reports; while dictating, he polished off a few medical journals. Once, on a camel caravan in the Sahara Desert, clad in nothing but a pith helmet and a loincloth, he took advantage of a brief stop at an oasis to dictate an entire issue of *Good Health* magazine.

The Doctor percolated with ideas, but he depended on Will to carry them out. The Doctor was the San's artistic director, Will its stage manager. The Doctor had hired his brother because he needed a hard worker who was not only good with numbers but willing to do what he was told. During his first few months at the San, Will's duties consisted of sawing the lumber to make the crates in which to ship copies of the Doctor's books. For this, his brother paid him six dollars a week—less than Will had earned when he worked in his father's factory at the age of eleven. "Apparently The Doctor was afraid he was not getting full value for the salary he paid me," recalled Will, "for he soon asked me to run the little printing press he was operating . . . then he made me manager of subscriptions and advertising of *Good Health*." (The Doctor liked to point out that he received no salary himself—"not a penny"—but the money he made from the sale of his books alone made him a wealthy man.) To support Puss and their three children, Will took care of a neighbor's horse for an additional three dollars a week, and ran a small chicken-and-egg operation in his backyard. Even so, he went into debt. "I feel kind of blue," he confessed to his diary, four years after going to work for his brother. "Am afraid that I will always be a poor man the way things look now." In another entry he noted, "Puss wanted to go to church but I had no decent shoes to wear."

As the San expanded, Will's duties expanded, too. By the turn of the century, not only was he responsible for billing, pricing, and purchasing, but he managed Modern Medicine Publishing and a half dozen other companies his brother had set up to sell his health foods, surgical devices, and exercise machines. He answered the San's mail—some sixty to a hundred letters a day. He was the unofficial credit manager, a member of the labor committee, a volunteer security guard, and, on occasion, a hospital orderly. Each afternoon, he was besieged by petitioners: wealthy patients requesting extra services; disgruntled employees airing complaints; financially strapped patients seeking discounts on their bills. One evening, Will counted the supplicants who arrived after five o'clock: thirty-three. Whenever an insane patient ran off, it was Will who tracked him down. Whenever a patient died, it was Will who helped the grieving family select a casket and plan the funeral, Will who arranged for the body to leave the San as inconspicuously as possible. (Such occasions were minimized by the Doctor's strict admissions standards: no one contagious; no one on a stretcher; no one, indeed, who looked very sick. His ideal patients were overweight or neurasthenic women and overworked or dyspeptic men.) Whenever the Doctor lectured, it was Will who was responsible for generating the gas for the magic lantern, setting up the screen, operating the machine by his brother's side, and putting everything away afterward. Whenever the Doctor stayed up late conferring with a visitor, it was Will who escorted the guest to the railroad station. On one such occasion, the Doctor's meeting went through the night and into the following morning. "Puss came up to the office about half past seven to see why I didn't come home," Will wrote in his diary. "She was so scairt that she cried."

Will might not have minded serving as his brother's dogsbody had his contributions been acknowledged. It rankled that the Doctor never named him business manager, never, in fact, gave him a title or a job description during his twenty-five years at the San. It rankled that he worked there ten years before his brother allowed him an office—a small, dark room on the first floor—and that he worked for fourteen years before his brother paid him enough to enable him to get out of debt. It rankled that, like the thousand other employees, he was expected to call his brother "Dr. Kellogg." Doctor Kellogg didn't seem to notice that he was humiliating Will. While an orderly administered the Doctor's morning enema, the Doctor, not wanting to waste a second, gave his brother his marching orders for the day. While the Doctor rode his bike around the circular driveway in front of the San for exercise, he made his brother, pen and notebook in hand, trot alongside, taking dictation under the gaze of sun-worshiping guests on the veranda. Occasionally, the Doctor had Will shave him, or shine his shoes, just as he had when he was a boy. Will left home before his three children were up in the morning and returned long after they had gone to bed, rendering him, his daughter said, "a stranger to his family." On the rare occasions Will made it home for dinner, he was exhausted. "I don't want to talk," he'd tell his wife and children. "I've had a long, hard day." He worked Christmas, New Year's, and the Fourth of July. He worked for seven years before his brother allowed him a vacation. One week, he was on duty 120 hours. And so it stung when his brother called him a "loafer," or chewed him out for trying to snatch a meal with his family. Well into his thirties, Will was still being treated as the younger brother on whom the older brother warmed his feet.

The Doctor treated most people that way. He found it nearly impossible to apologize, admit a mistake, or delegate. "He was a czar and a law unto himself, ignoring his associates and subordinates," recalled Will. If another San physician began to develop a following, the Doctor found an excuse to get rid of him. If an employee displeased him, he could be sarcastic; the Doctor performed withering impersonations of his detractors behind their backs. "There is with you a love of supremacy whether you see it or not," observed Ellen White, concerned with the size of her former protégé's ego. The Doctor admitted that he had to "play first chair in the orchestra"—even then, he made it sound more like a boast than an apology—but at the same time he scorned those who, like his brother, conceded him that position.

Some San employees felt the Doctor was especially hard on his brother. They believed that the Doctor's attitude stemmed from his height, which was the only thing about which the otherwise imperturbable man was self-conscious. Although Will was no giant, at five feet seven he was more than four inches taller than his older brother, and the Doctor was envious. On the other hand, Will envied John Harvey for being a doctor. Family members said that Will dreamed of becoming a physician himself, but was so busy supporting his family on the meager salary his brother paid him that he never had the opportunity. "I believe the elder deliberately kept the younger down," recalled a San physician. "As a matter of fact, he never encouraged any Kellogg to study medicine, because he did not want more than one doctor in the family." Observed another San physician: "John Harvey Kellogg and W. K. Kellogg were like two fellows trying to climb up the same ladder at the same time."

The brothers' antipathy was intensified by their differences. The dapper Doctor, whose all-white outfits matched the color of his carefully cropped Van Dyke (in winter, he donned a snow-white overcoat, a snow-white hat, and snow-white gloves), liked to pose for photographers with his pet white cockatoo on his shoulder. A vain man, he often refused to wear the glasses without which he could hardly see. Will wore drab, baggy, inexpensive suits, shiny with wear, in part because he could afford no better, in part because he preferred to be inconspicuous. The Doctor, escorted by a convoy of nurses, seemed to be everywhere at the San, correcting one patient's posture, asking another to stick out her tongue (a furred tongue, he said, was a telltale symptom of a poisoned bowel), passing out apples and pears, fawning over new arrivals. Will worked behind the scenes, a quiet, almost furtive presence. The Doctor expressed himself in hyperbolic verbal torrents. Will spoke slowly and carefully when he spoke at all. The Doctor was a preening, pint-size Barnum with a flair for the dramatic: at Christmas, he donned a Santa suit and ho-ho-ho'd as he handed out healthy snacks to guests; at Thanksgiving, he displayed a live turkey in the dining room in front of a sign that read "A THANKFUL TURKEY" so that guests tucking into their turkey-shaped conglomeration of nuts and grains might be reminded of their virtuous deed; at lectures promoting vegetarianism, the Doctor would toss his pet chimpanzee a steak and the chimp would sneer and toss it back, whereupon the Doctor would toss him a banana and the chimp would devour it. Such showmanship disgusted Will, whose natural reticence had been reinforced by a conservative Adventist upbringing that frowned on self-promotion. "He was an austere man—just like he had swallowed a ramrod," recalled a San physician. The Doctor liked to make an entrance. Whenever a train waited an extra five minutes at the Battle Creek station, chances are it was being held for him: all eyes turned as a chauffeured car roared into the station and disgorged a diminutive figure in white, who strode on board (as convincingly as a portly, five-foot-two-and-a-half man can stride), trailed by a brace of secretaries lugging suitcases full of medical journals and baskets of San health foods to sustain the great man on his journey. Each brother found the other irritating: the Doctor thought Will a plodder, Will thought the Doctor a show-off. The more flamboyant the Doctor became, the more Will withdrew. He seemed determined to be as different as possible from his brother.

Even had their Herculean schedules allowed, the brothers, who lived a few blocks from each other, rarely socialized. The Doctor, something of an intellectual snob, spent his scant spare time hobnobbing with the celebrities who frequented the San. Will, embarrassed at never having gotten beyond the sixth grade, spent his with Puss and their children. The Doctor treated Ella Eaton, the *Good Health* editorial assistant he had married in 1879, more like a business associate than a wife. They spent their honeymoon revising the Doctor's new books, *The Proper Diet of Man* and *Plain Facts About Sexual Life*. The latter title was ironic, for even if the Doctor could have found time for intimacy, he believed that sex bred disease and bragged that he and Ella had never consummated their marriage and never intended to. (Fearful of germs, he tended to shy away from physical contact of any kind.) Over the years, however, the Doctor and his wife took in forty-two abandoned or needy children, at least nine of whom they formally adopted. Convinced that a healthy diet and proper upbringing could trump any hereditary deficits, the Doctor treated his "waifs," as he called them, more like research subjects than beloved sons and daughters. Housed in dormitories on the far side of "The Residence," the Doctor's twenty-room Queen Anne mansion, they were raised and home-schooled by Ella and a cadre of San staffers on a modified Bio-logic Living schedule of vegetarian meals, chores, and calisthenics. "All members of the family should consider it a dishonor to violate any of the health principles which they have been taught," was one of numerous household rules. (In the late 1890s, Ella, who served as San dietician in addition to overseeing the Doctor's phalanx of adoptees, had a nervous breakdown, likely from overwork, and lived as a semi-invalid until her death in 1920.)

Whenever the Doctor patronized him, or overturned one of his orders to the staff, Will fumed. But having spent his childhood in thrall to the brilliant older brother anointed by their parents and church leaders as the chosen one, Will had grown accustomed to living in the shadow. Given his lifelong sense of inferiority and his brother's reputation—at the San, the Doctor was regarded as a genius, and his influence over the staff was, a colleague put it, practically "hypnotic"—Will may have felt that he deserved to be "J.H.'s flunky," as he bitterly referred to himself in his journal. At least for the time being.

* * *

As siblings grow up, move away, and start families of their own, rivalries often lose their intensity, diluted by time, geography, and maturity. They may be camouflaged or expressed more discreetly, in teasing or subtle put-downs that reawaken old resentments. Where once siblings squabbled over who got the biggest drumstick, they may now calculate who has more money, the better job, the healthier marriage, the more successful children. Or the better art collection. (Sterling Clark and his younger brother Ste-phen, heirs to the Singer sewing machine fortune, each spent the first half of the twentieth century striving to amass a finer array of masterpieces than the other.) Or the better book sales. (In 1957, Evelyn Waugh sued a literary critic who had written that his earnings were "dwarfed" by Alec's; Alec was forced to testify in court that his younger brother was, indeed, the more financially successful Waugh.) Or the worse health. (Lifelong hypochondriacs, William and Henry James competed over whose symptoms were the more impressive; at times, their correspondence reads like a hyper-literate version of the Merck Manual.) Or the bigger house. (In 1846, determined to build a home that would outshine those of his two older brothers, Thomas Pugh, a Louisiana sugarcane planter, began construction of the 11,000-square-foot Greek revival mansion that would be known as Queen of the Bayou. Alas, Pugh wouldn't get a chance to gloat; he died in 1852, two years before the last of the house's 600,000 bricks was mortared into place.)

Adult siblings may compete directly for the attention of their aging parents: Who takes better care of them? Who calls them more often? Whose spouse do the parents like best? A parent's death may revive long-dormant rivalries, and the disposition of an inheritance can find middle-aged siblings fighting over a coffeepot as fiercely as they once fought over a childhood toy—representing, as it may seem, a last morsel of parental love. Plutarch tells the story of Charicles and Antiochus, who, dividing up their late father's goods, "would not part until they had split in two a silver cup and torn apart a cloak."

Paul and Robert Moses had always had a contentious relationship, but when their mother died of cancer in 1930, leaving the lion's share of her considerable estate to her younger son, Robert, it created a rift that would never heal. Paul believed that on the night of their mother's death Robert persuaded her to sign a new will, cutting him out of his inheritance. In the years that followed, Paul, a brilliant engineer, also came to believe (apparently with some justification) that Robert, the urban planner responsible for much of modern New York City's infrastructure, was doing everything in his considerable power to keep him from getting a job. Paul fell behind on his income tax payments, slept for a time in a Salvation Army shelter, and grew cadaverous from lack of food. Consumed by hatred for his brother, he talked bitterly about Robert to whoever would listen. Sometimes he'd show up at banquets thrown in honor of his famous brother, standing in the back because he couldn't afford a seat, scowling at the honoree, the only one in the audience not applauding. Paul was determined to be acknowledged by his brother—as he had not been acknowledged by the will. Robert seemed equally determined to deny his brother's existence. He refused to see him or take his phone calls, and when Paul asked for a few family photographs by which to remember their parents, Robert, through an intermediary, said no. Asked about his brother by the press, he declined even to say whether his brother was older or younger. (In the first biography of Robert Moses, Paul wasn't mentioned; it wasn't until Robert Caro published *The Power Broker* in 1974 that some of Robert's friends even knew he had a brother.) In 1962, at the age of seventy-five, Paul Moses, working as a salesman, collapsed while climbing the stairs to his apartment, a single room on the top floor of a five-story walk-up. Told his brother was dying, Robert visited him in the hospital. It was the first time he had seen his brother in twenty years. Paul recovered and Robert got him a job as a glorified errand boy at an engineering firm. But now that he knew his brother wasn't dying, Robert refused to see him again. Five years later, Paul died in poverty at the age of eighty.

Few rivalries are as rancorous as that of the Moses brothers. Yet one third of adults describe their relationship with a sibling as "rivalrous" or "distant." Ralph and Herbert Ellison had been allies throughout their hardscrabble Oklahoma City boyhood. But Herbert, a slow-witted, good-natured fellow who didn't share his older brother's literary ambitions, was part of the provincial life Ralph was desperate to leave behind when he moved to New York City at the age of twenty-three. After Ellison became famous for his novel *Invisible Man*, he wrote to his brother and occasionally sent him money, but kept an embarrassed distance. In 1964, when Ellison traveled to Los Angeles, where Herbert now lived, to deliver a series of lectures at UCLA, it was the first time he had seen his brother in twenty-six years.

Several years ago, I spoke with a friend of mine, a renowned psychologist who had recently celebrated his ninetieth birthday and may have intuited that he had only a few months to live. He was reflecting on his long and distinguished life when I asked him whether he had any siblings. There was a pause, and then this supremely self-assured man began to speak, slowly and sadly. "I'm a success—in my own mind—as a husband," he said. "I had a beautiful wife, physically and emotionally, whom I loved and who loved me. I'm a success as a father. I have four sons whom I adore and who adore me, three physicians and a dentist. But I'm a failure as a sibling. I don't understand how I and my stupid brother, who happens to be a surgeon, never got along. We never fought but it's always been a situation of . . . aridity. It's something I will always regret."

*   *   *

In 1883, a few years after Will came to work for his brother, the Doctor established an experimental kitchen in the basement of the San, where the brothers tried to create palatable recipes from the nuts and grains that dominated the San diet. Over the next twenty years, more than eighty different culinary confections would emerge from the kitchen, bearing such appetite-suppressing names as Bromose (small cakes of nuts and dextrinized starch), Nuttose (a croquette-shaped product that could be flavored to taste like chicken, beef, or veal), Malted Nuts (a peanut and almond vegetable milk), and Caramel Cereal Coffee (a coffee substitute made of bran, molasses, corn, and burnt bread crusts). The brothers followed their customary modus operandi: the Doctor jotted down his ideas and passed them along to Will, who, after his fifteen-hour workday, experimented into the night. "Some of the formulae he worked out, some I did, and he made suggestions and I made suggestions, and I think he took most of the credit for the work I did," Will would testify in court in 1916. "I wrote a great many hundreds of notes for experiments to be conducted, and I have never claimed any glory—the Doctor has claimed that." At one point, Will developed yet another nut-and-grain concoction and took it to his brother for approval. "The Doctor did not compliment me very highly on the product," he recalled. "A week later he introduced the identical same thing, and called it Nuttolene, and said it was a very fine article." By 1897, the Sanitarium Food Company, with Will as manager, offered forty-two different kinds of biscuits, breads, crackers, and ersatz coffees, available by mail order, for those who wished to practice Biologic Living at home.

The Holy Grail of the experimental kitchen was cereal. Ever since his medical school days, when his morning meal usually consisted of two apples and seven crackers, John Harvey Kellogg had wanted to create a nutritious, ready-to eat breakfast food. (He dismissed oatmeal as a "half-cooked, pasty, dyspepsia-producing breakfast mush.") In 1893, he and Will took notice when a Denver lawyer with indigestion and the improbable name of Perky began to make money selling miniature pillows of what he called shredded wheat. Working after hours in the experimental kitchen, the brothers attempted to cook up a cereal of their own. They tried wheat, oats, and corn. They tried boiling, steaming, and baking. They tried mashing the cooked grains through a strainer. They tried rolling them out on a breadboard. They tried feeding them through rollers. Nothing tasted right. Then one night Will came across a batch of cooked wheat he'd accidentally left out for a day or two. He ran the stale mixture through the rollers; it came out in large, thin, well-formed flakes. When baked, they were crisp, crinkly, and tasty. The Doctor wanted to pulverize the flakes, but Will insisted that they be left intact. For once, the Doctor deferred to his younger brother. The Doctor christened the product—the first flaked breakfast cereal—Granose Flakes.

In 1895, the brothers began manufacturing Granose Flakes in a barn behind the San. That first year, despite minimal promotion (the Doctor permitted Will to advertise only in San publications), they sold almost fifty-seven tons. Will knew they could sell much more. He tried to convince his brother to let him advertise nationally, but the Doctor said no. Will pleaded for a catchier slogan than the Doctor's "ready for solution by the digestive juice and for prompt assimilation," but the Doctor was unmoved. In 1900, while the Doctor was away, Will visited several members of the San board of directors and told them that, given the opportunity, the San food business would someday be so large that the sanitarium itself would be a mere "side show." (Even then, the idea of eclipsing his brother seems to have been on Will's mind.) The directors thought Will was getting carried away. But they agreed to let him build a small factory behind the Sanitarium bakery to house the Granose operation. When the Doctor returned from his trip and heard that the factory cost $50,000, he was furious. Saying he had not authorized the project, he insisted that his brother pay for it. ("I guess my father did not like that very well," Will's son would testify in court many years later.) Will, who had to beg friends and relatives for the money, eventually paid off the debt. But he never forgave his brother. And when, a few months later, the Doctor pressed ahead on moving the San's business office, although it would interfere with a longtime employee's wedding plans, Will exploded. During the argument that followed, he quit.

After twenty-one years at the San, Will would not find it easy to cut ties to his brother. On February 18, 1902, six months after he left, the San burned to the ground. Having spent more than half his life there, Will felt a responsibility to help rebuild the place in which he had invested so much. He offered to work without pay for "as long my services were needed." The Doctor put him in charge of financing the new building. Fifteen months after the fire, during which Will had worked eighteen-to-twenty-hour days, a new San rose from the ashes: a six-story, 560-foot long, 1,200-bed Italian Renaissance edifice with mosaic marble floors, a solarium, a roof garden, a gymnasium, and a glass-domed courtyard filled with orchids, orange trees, and twenty-foot banana palms. Somehow, in the excitement, Will forgot that he was quitting.

Indeed, he might never have broken permanently with his brother had it not been for C. W. Post, a thirty-six-year-old inventor, real estate broker, and blanket manufacturer from Fort Worth who had arrived at the San in 1891 with a ten-gallon Stetson, an emaciated frame, and an empty bank account. Though he stayed at the San for nine months and gained almost fifty pounds—his wife sold homemade suspenders door-to-door to keep him there—Post pronounced his treatment a failure. He may not have believed in the San's curative powers, but he believed in its financial possibilities. In 1892, he opened a scaled-down, cut-rate, meat-serving version of the San across town. A few years later, Post—who had spent much of his time at the San sniffing around its experimental kitchen and peppering the staff with technical questions—began to market Postum, a bran-and-molasses coffee substitute that bore more than a passing resemblance to the Doctor's Caramel Cereal Coffee. The Doctor was magnanimous, saying, "The more people there are who make such products, the more there are who are likely to use them. That is the important thing." By 1898, when annual sales of Postum totaled $840,000, the Doctor was less gracious, insinuating that Post was a charlatan and a plagiarist. (That the Texan happened to be a dismayingly tall man, from the Doctor's perspective, cannot have helped matters.) By 1903, when Post's fortune was estimated at $10 million, the Doctor became apoplectic at the mere mention of the man's name.

Will, on the other hand, was envious. Post was doing exactly what Will had urged the Doctor to do: pouring money into advertising and promotion. But Will could only watch as would-be tycoons flocked to Battle Creek in an entrepreneurial hegira as frenzied as the California Gold Rush a half-century earlier—a kind of Michigan Cereal Rush. By 1902, there were thirty-two cereal companies in town. Many of them lured away San employees with the promise of higher salaries. Others copied San products and gave them snappy new names, like Malta-Vita, Malta Pura, Norka Oats, Tryabita, Apetiza, X-Celo Flakes, Cero-Fruito, Grain-O, Malt-Too, Flak-Ota, Cereola, Frumenta, Per-Fo, Force, Vim, Egg-O-See, and Mapl-Flakes. "Battle Creek has twenty-one thousand people," observed a visitor from Chicago, "all of whom are engaged in the manufacture of breakfast foods."

It galled Will to slave sixteen hours a day for meager pay while others made fortunes pirating the San's work. He begged his brother to let him take on their competitors. The Doctor refused. Not only was he parsimonious by nature, he worried that associating his name with commercial advertising would jeopardize his reputation in the medical community. The American Medical Association already looked askance at his fondness for hydrotherapy, vegetarianism, and massage. In any case, he'd rather invent something new than promote something old. The Doctor considered the San's products to be outgrowths of his real work: spreading the Biologic Living gospel. "I am not after the business," he said. "I am after the reform." Will, who was after the business, grew frustrated with his brother. At times they quarreled fiercely; at times they stopped speaking to each other. Hoping, at least, to distinguish the San cereals from their imitators, Will suggested they use *his* name on the packaging, making it clear that Will, not the Doctor, was endorsing the product and thereby protecting the Doctor from accusations of venality. The Doctor gave in. In 1903, these red-inked words began appearing on a few San products: "Beware of imitations. None genuine without this signature. W. K. Kellogg." It was a first step not only in differentiating San products from those of their competitors, but in differentiating Will (or W.K., as he would soon be known to the world) from his brother. There was, it seemed, another Kellogg in Battle Creek.

Most of the new companies peddled wheat flakes. Few made cereals from corn, which was considered a lesser grain—"horse food," some called it. In 1898, the Kellogg brothers had produced a flaked corn cereal, but it lacked flavor. In 1902, they added malt to their flakes, which gave them a richer, nuttier taste. The brothers argued over what to call their new product. Will lobbied for "Kellogg's Toasted Korn Krisp," but the Doctor insisted on "Sanitas Flakes." Once again, the Doctor discouraged promotion, insisting that their mail order sales were perfectly respectable. "I'm not interested in a mail order business," Will told an associate. "I want to sell those corn flakes by the carload." Fed up with his brother, galvanized by Post (who was pushing a flaked corn cereal of his own called Elijah's Manna), Will forged ahead without the Doctor's permission. He sent salesmen door to door with free samples. He advertised in newspapers, put up streetcar signs, and sponsored store window displays. Reasoning that there were more well people in the world than sick people, he marketed corn flakes as something tasty rather than something healthy: "A BREAKFAST TREAT—THAT MAKES YOU EAT"—hardly Madison Avenue–caliber genius, but an improvement on the Doctor's "ready for solution by the digestive juice and for prompt assimilation." In 1905, while the Doctor was on a trip to Europe, Will did the unthinkable—he coated the flakes with sugar. When the doctor returned, he "had a fit," recalled Will's son. But sales soared and the sugar stayed.

The end would come not long afterward, when an insurance executive from St. Louis who had enjoyed Sanitas Flakes as a patient at the San offered to help finance a company devoted solely to corn flakes. Will presented the idea to his brother. The Doctor wasn't interested. Will offered to buy the corn flake rights from his brother. They haggled for six months before the Doctor, still in debt from the fire, settled for $35,000 cash and more than half the new company's stock. In February 1906, Will opened the Battle Creek Toasted Corn Flake Company in a ramshackle, one-story wooden building with a single oven left behind by its previous occupant, a failed cereal start-up named Hygienic Food, erstwhile

purveyor of Mapl-Flakes. Although Will was president and chief executive, the Doctor, as majority stockholder, retained the controlling interest.
Not believing his brother's company would amount to much, the frugal
Doctor distributed chunks of his stock to San physicians in lieu of salary
increases before traveling to Russia to observe the work of a physiologist
named Ivan Pavlov. He returned several months later to find that while
he had been watching dogs salivate, his younger brother had been tracking down and buying up the stock that the Doctor had so cavalierly given
away. Will now had the controlling interest in his own company. On the
eve of his forty-sixth birthday, he was no longer his brother's lackey.

*   *   *

In the animal kingdom, some sibling groups get along famously: wild turkey brothers are lifelong companions, adolescent peregrine falcons teach
each other to hunt. Others turn against each other as they attempt to
establish dominance or compete for food, in scenes that make mealtime
in the Joyce or Coleridge households seem downright tame. The female
blue-footed booby usually lays one egg more than she and her mate can
successfully feed, triggering a round of avian musical chairs in which the
eldest chick in the nest may peck to death the youngest chick in order
to increase its own chances of survival. The blue-footed booby is one of
about two dozen bird species—including the cattle egret, the tawny eagle,
the brown pelican, and the kittiwake—that routinely engage in siblicide.
Among mammals, siblicide is less common, but researchers at the University of California, Berkeley, filming the births of cubs in pens, found that
spotted hyenas routinely attack their younger sibling within minutes of its
birth, sinking their teeth into its shoulder blades and shaking, in order to
decrease the competition for their mother's milk. Sand tiger sharks get a
head start: they devour one another inside their mother's womb until only
one shark is left to be born. Spadefoot tadpoles are more considerate; they
taste other tadpoles before devouring them in order to determine whether
their prospective meal is a relative. If they accidentally swallow a sibling,
they spit it out, but if food is scarce, they become less gastronomically
discriminating and gobble up any passing tadpole, related or not.

Most sibling rivalry in the animal kingdom doesn't end in death, of course. Piglets, for instance, are born with eight temporary "needle" teeth they use to fight for a position nearest the sow's head, where the nipples deliver the most milk. Aggressive piglets thrive; their kinder, gentler siblings, forced to settle for the less productive teats in the rear, may become runts. Evolutionary biologists point out that sibling rivalry in *Homo sapiens* serves a similar function, as an adaptive response to limited resources. Sibling rivalry, they say, is perfectly natural. Indeed, psychologists point out that some sibling rivalry may be healthy. It may teach a child lessons he'll need in the wider world: how to cooperate, negotiate, and compromise; how to manage and resolve frustration. (I doubt it occurred to Ned or me as we squabbled over the marshmallows in a box of Lucky Charms that we were learning conflict-resolution skills.) It may, as the Eisenhower parents hoped, teach toughness. Children who haven't been exposed to the rigors of in-house rivalry may be ill-equipped to fight for a seat on the subway or to win a job in a recession. (In China, critics of the government's one-child-per-family policy complain that the pampered male children that result—known as "little emperors"—have never learned to overcome obstacles or "eat bitterness.") Rivalry may spur a sibling to greater accomplishment in the wider world. If John and Will Kellogg had been only children, the corn flake might never have been invented.

And if George W. Bush had been an only child, he might never have become president. From an early age, George and his younger brother Jeb competed fiercely to prove their worth to the father they idolized. George, seven years older than Jeb, seemed the front-runner. Like his father, he attended Andover and Yale and, after graduation, went to Texas to get into the oil business. Unlike his father, however, he was a C student, an unexceptional athlete, and a disappointing oilman. He was also a joker, a braggart, and a drinker. If George was "the family clown," as his youngest brother, Marvin, described him, Jeb was the family striver. Responsible, articulate, and hardworking, he finished the University of Texas in three years, and, like his father, made Phi Beta Kappa. Jeb was the first son to marry, the first to have children, the first to become wealthy, the first to consider following his father into politics. At six feet four, he was also the tallest, an issue about which George, five inches shorter, was sensitive. At a certain point, it was evident that Jeb had outgrown his older brother in maturity as well, and become his father's heir apparent. ("I want to be able to look my father in the eye and say, 'I continued the legacy,'" Jeb told a reporter.) Sensing his father's disappointment in him, believing both his parents preferred Jeb, George embraced his role as the profane, wise-cracking, hard-drinking, chip-on-the-shoulder rebel. (At a state dinner for Queen Elizabeth II, he introduced himself to the British monarch as "the black sheep of the family.") He was a rebel with a thin skin. Attending a Houston Astros baseball game, George fumed when Jeb and his son were seated in their father's vice-presidential box while he was assigned a seat several rows behind them.

In 1986, at the age of forty, George gave up drinking and became an evangelical Christian. Seven years later, knowing that Jeb was running for governor of Florida, George shocked his family by announcing that he was running for governor of Texas. His mother urged him not to, worried that he'd take the limelight—and the financial contributions—away from Jeb. The brothers' relationship, never close, grew strained as they competed not only against their gubernatorial opponents but, indirectly, against each other. When George won and Jeb lost, the Bush parents couldn't conceal their surprise. "Why do you feel bad about Jeb?" George asked his father, talking on the phone on election night. "Why don't you feel good about me?" By the time Jeb won the Florida governorship in 1998, George was planning to run for the presidency, which he would win only when Jeb swallowed his envy and worked to help George take Jeb's home state. Even then, their mother made a joke of her astonishment that it was George and not Jeb who was running for president.

Growing up in Georgia, Ray Guy used to kick a football with his older brother, who took fiendish joy in booting the ball over Ray's head and making him retrieve it. "When I started, I was just trying to make the ball do what Al did with it," Guy explained. "I'd experiment: how to hold the ball, how to drop it. I had no clue what the hell I was doing. I just knew that one day I was going to kick it over Al's head and make him go chase after it." The younger Guy would become the greatest punter in National Football League history, one of thousands of professional athletes whose skills were honed in backyard games against their siblings. In large families, the competition multiplies exponentially. Growing up on a farm in Alberta, Canada, the seven Sutter brothers competed ferociously in everything from hay baling to bathroom access to pond hockey. "Going out to catch the school bus, we'd have had five fights by the time we'd get to the end of [the] lane," recalls Brian, the second oldest. Six of the seven Sutters would go on to play in the National Hockey League, one of more than 230 sets of brothers to reach the NHL. (The National Football League has had more than 330 sets of brothers, Major League Baseball more than 350.) In 1980, when Brian's St. Louis Blues played Darryl's Chicago Blackhawks, the first of hundreds of NHL games in which Sutters played Sutters, fraternal pride took a backseat to sibling rivalry. "I would have run over him if that's what it had taken for us to win," said Brian. "If anything, I tried harder when he was out there. The last thing any of us wants to do is lose to one of our brothers." Especially if that brother is younger. As Peyton Manning put it, in a radio ad promoting a 2006 football game between the Indianapolis Colts, the team he quarter-backed, and the New York Giants, quarterbacked by his younger brother, Eli, "You're not supposed to lose to your little brother." (He didn't.)

Given that brothers under the age of seven fight every seventeen minutes, it may not be surprising that seven pairs of American brothers have won Olympic medals in wrestling or boxing. In most of these cases, the brothers were each other's first, unofficial opponents. When fifteen-year-old Leon Spinks took up boxing to defend himself against the gangs that roamed his St. Louis housing project, he'd come home from the gym each night and practice on his brother Michael. Three years younger and desperate to emulate his older brother, Michael followed Leon to the gym. "We were like race horses racing each other," said Michael. "Leon never could stand to see me outdo him, especially in boxing. He says he's supposed to set the examples." Both won gold medals at the 1976 Olympics, both became world champions. Jerry Quarry and his younger brother, Mike, literally fought each other for the attention of their father, a hard-luck day laborer and sometime boxer bent on turning his sons into prize-fighters. As they grew, their father, who served as their co-manager, made them spar. Jerry, six years older and twenty-five pounds heavier, always got the better of his little brother, but Mike heeded their father's motto, "There's no quit in a Quarry," and their battles invariably ended in brawls. Unfortunately, the Quarrys, both of whom went on to distinguished ring careers, followed their father's motto too faithfully, boxing long after they should have retired and developing symptoms of pugilistic dementia, in which repeated blows to the head cause the brain to atrophy. Shortly before his death in 1999 at the age of fifty-three, Jerry, by now unable to feed or dress himself, apologized to Mike for hitting him so hard when they were young. Seven years later, Mike would die in an assisted-living facility, unable to walk or talk.

Like the theater managers who played up the rivalry between Edwin and John Wilkes Booth, Harry Houdini understood that fraternal competition could be good for business. A master showman about whom a friend said he "would murder his grandmother for publicity," Houdini staged a mock rivalry with his younger brother, Theo, also a well-known escape artist, in which they traded boasts and accusations in the press to boost ticket sales. Underneath the fake rivalry, however, there lurked a measure of real rivalry, mostly on Harry's side. Theo worshiped his older brother, who had taught him most of his illusions and escapes, and had given him his stage name, "Hardeen." Houdini, for his part, was perfectly happy for Hardeen to do well—as long as he didn't do as well as Houdini. (Houdini was also keenly aware that while he and his wife were unable to have children, his younger, taller, stronger brother had sired two.) When Hardeen took their faux rivalry a little too far, suggesting to an interviewer that his admiration for the legendary Houdini was so great that he might even be willing to hire him as his assistant, an enraged Houdini forgot that the insult was part of the act he himself had invented. "There was nothing synthetic about his anger," Hardeen recalled.

Authentic fraternal anger can be highly profitable. After serving in the German Army during World War I, Rudolf and Adolf Dassler returned to the Bavarian village of Herzogenaurach and started a sports shoe company in the laundry room of their family home. With Rudi overseeing sales and younger brother Adi overseeing design, Gebrüder Dassler flourished. (At the 1936 Olympics, Jesse Owens won four gold medals in Dassler spikes.) The brothers' contrasting personalities, however, caused friction. Adi, a thoughtful, down-to-earth fellow, was happiest tinkering in his leather-littered workshop or taking long runs through the forest. Rudi was subject to mood swings that left him infectiously enthusiastic one minute, brash and bullying the next. Though they built partitions in the house they shared with their parents, their poisonous arguments reverberated throughout all three floors. In 1943, when the Nazis mobilized Rudi but told Adi he was more valuable to them at the Dassler factory making soldiers' boots, Rudi suspected Adi of engineering his removal so he could take control of their company. In 1948, the brothers agreed to split. Rudi moved to the other side of the river that ran through town and started his own shoe company, calling it Puma. Adi renamed his business Adidas. (Herzogenaurach became known as "the town of bent necks," because its citizens—most of whom worked for one brother or the other—were careful to notice what shoes someone wore before starting a conversation.) Engaging in cutthroat competition from their offices a few miles from each other, the brothers made fortunes as their rival companies dominated the sports shoe industry for decades. They never reconciled; when they died, they were buried as far as possible from each other in the town cemetery. Their sons, however, continued the feud, even as the companies they inherited continued to grow.

Brothers don't have to work in the same field to push each other. "I would not have a career without my brother," observed the actor John Malkovich, who used the memory of his daily childhood brawls with his older brother to inspire many of his performances. "He was imitating Danny," Malkovich's mother said of her son's performance in *True West*, Sam Shepard's play about fratricidal brothers. "All that craziness and fighting and destroying everything in sight—that was Danny. I'd stay in the kitchen and hum so I couldn't hear them fighting." (Danny, who woke up his younger brother by sitting on his head and drooling, would channel his aggressiveness into a career as a small-town newspaper publisher.)

According to his biographer James Atlas, Saul Bellow spent a lifetime trying to prove himself to the brothers with whom he shared a bed in childhood. Crude, aggressive boys, Maurice and Sam belittled their sickly, bookish baby brother's literary aspirations. Even after Bellow won the National Book Award in 1953 for *The Adventures of Augie March*, they were dismissive. "It's true that my name won't go down in the *Ency-clopaedia Britannica*, but I have money, and he doesn't," said Maurice, a developer who drove a black Cadillac, brandished a thick roll of bills, and liked to tease Saul by asking him who "Prowst" was. Sam, a nursing-home magnate, pointed out that while Saul's books could be found in the library, he still had to turn to his older brothers for handouts. Bellow, whose fictional portraits of philistine businessmen were inspired by Maurice and Sam, impressed the literary critics, but he couldn't impress his brothers. "A lot of people in my family just think I'm some schmuck with a pen," he told a friend. A few years later, when he was awarded the 1976 Nobel Prize in Literature, Bellow marveled, "All I started out to do was show up my brothers."

*   *   *

Will Kellogg liked to say he was "an old man" when he finally went into business for himself, but like the stone released from a slingshot, whose thrust is directly proportional to the force with which it has been restrained, he quickly made up for lost time. In his first year, he handed out four million free samples, convinced that once people tried his corn flakes, they'd continue to buy them. He spent $30,000—one third of the company's initial working capital—on a single full-page ad in *Ladies' Home Journal*. By the end of 1906, Will was indeed selling corn flakes by the carload: 178,943 cases in that first year alone. The following year, when some stray Independence Day fireworks set off a blaze that demolished his factory, Will had a Chicago architect on site within twelve hours and a new, fireproof plant in full production within six months. In 1907, while the Doctor was abroad, Will, observing that "the word 'Sanitas' partakes too much of a disinfectant," changed the name of his product to Kellogg's Toasted Corn Flakes. His promotion grew ever more aggressive. "Please Stop Eating Toasted Corn Flakes for Thirty Days," one ad implored, explaining that production needed time to catch up with sales. There were baby picture contests; food-show demonstrations; mail-order premiums; sandwich men walking the streets in eight-foot papier-mâché ears of corn; a thirty-inch Tiffany urn for the farmer who grew the best-looking corn; and a girl-next-door type plucked from the stenography pool to represent the company as "The Sweetheart of the Corn." Will may have absorbed more of his brother's Barnumesque flair than he cared to admit. In 1912 he erected an 80-by-106-foot electric billboard—the largest advertising sign in the world—on the roof of the Mecca Building in Times Square. It showed a boy's face. When the words "I WANT KELLOGG'S" appeared, the boy began to cry. When the words "I GOT KELLOGG'S" appeared, the boy smiled. By now Will was running a million-dollar-a-year business. He had come a long way from trotting alongside his brother's bicycle, taking dictation.

The Doctor was infuriated by his brother's success. The way he saw it, he had given Will a job and an identity, and his brother repaid him by becoming a greater traitor than C. W. Post. The Doctor had never brooked challenges to his authority. Now he tried to put his younger brother back in his place. He insisted that Will, as manager of the Sanitas Food Company, was technically still his employee, and was therefore entitled to only one quarter of the $250 monthly salary he received as president of the new company. For nearly a year, the Doctor made Will sign his paychecks over to him, whereupon he returned one fourth of the amount and kept the rest for himself. This bit of petty harrassment triggered an escalating game of sibling Got You Last. Will resigned his position in the Sanitas Food Company. The Doctor resigned as a director of the Toasted Corn Flake Company. Will removed the picture of the Battle Creek Sanitarium from his corn flake packages. The Doctor began printing his cereal boxes with the legend "Sanitas Toasted Wheat Flakes is the only flaked product which has a legitimate pedigree." When rumors circulated that Will's new corn flake company had cheated the Doctor's Sanitas company out of five thousand dollars, Will was convinced that his loose-lipped brother was the source. "For twenty-two and one-half years, I had absolutely lost all my individuality in you," he wrote the Doctor. "I tried to see things with your eyes and do things as you would do them. You know in your heart whether or not I am a rascal. You also know whether or not I would defraud anyone, under any circumstances."

But these were minor skirmishes. The war began in 1908, when the Doctor, claiming he had never liked the name, changed the Sanitas

Nut Food Company to the Kellogg Food Company. Will was outraged. The Doctor had never shown the slightest interest in using the Kellogg name on his products—indeed, he had insisted on *not* using it—until his brother began printing it on his corn flake boxes. The Doctor, said Will, was trying to reap the benefits of the advertising dollars Will had spent to "make the name Kellogg's of some value." The Doctor countered that *he* was the one whose work at the San had made the name Kellogg valuable, and anyone seeing the name on a cereal box would assume that it referred to him. Will called on the Doctor and demanded that he stop using the name Kellogg on his products. The meeting quickly turned acrimonious. "Having been importuned for many hours in a most strenuous manner," the Doctor would later testify, he agreed to stop using the name, "purely as a matter of brotherly regard." (That his brother agreed to pay him $50,000 for the gesture surely didn't hurt.) A few days later, however, when Will's lawyers presented him with a contract to that effect, the Doctor refused to sign. Later still, the Doctor relented and telephoned Will to inform him that, "as an evidence of goodwill," he had decided to drop the name Kellogg from his Toasted Rice Flakes. But the following day, when he learned that Will had enticed away one of his sales managers, the Doctor's goodwill evaporated and he retracted his offer. On August 11, 1910, Will filed suit to keep his brother from using the name Kellogg "either in a corporate name or as a descriptive name of a food." The issue was literal: which brother had the legal right to put the family name on his products? It was also figurative: which brother was the "original and the genuine" Kellogg?

The suit would be settled the following year with an out-of-court compromise in which the Doctor agreed not to use the word *Kellogg* on any flaked cereal food or display it conspicuously on any packaging. The truce lasted a few months. When Will tried to trademark the facsimile of his signature, the Doctor filed suit, triggering another series of legal maneuvers that kept the brothers in and out of court for several more years. The jousting would culminate in what newspapers called "The Battle of Bran." A longtime proselytizer for bran's laxative qualities, the Doctor had for several years been selling a breakfast cereal he called, with his unerring ear for mouth-watering names, Battle Creek Diet System

Sterilized Bran. In 1915, the Doctor changed its name to Kellogg's Sterilized Bran, insisting that the 1911 agreement applied only to flaked cereals. In any case, he argued, the name change wouldn't harm his brother's business, because Will didn't sell any bran products. At the same time, the formerly ad-phobic doctor began advertising Kellogg's Sterilized Bran in national publications. It was a shot across his brother's bow.

Will returned fire. Shortly after the name change, he suddenly discovered that he had a passion for bran. He began manufacturing Kellogg's Toasted Bran Flakes, followed closely by Kellogg's Flaked Bran, then Kellogg's Bran in granular form. Accusing Will of invading the bran market purely from spite, the Doctor sued. Will countersued. The suits came to trial in 1917. After three weeks of testimony, the judge ruled against the Doctor on every major point: Will, he reiterated, was the exclusive owner of the trade name Kellogg. Three years later, the ruling would be upheld unanimously by the Michigan State Supreme Court. Showing his brother a measure of mercy, Will agreed to waive his right to damages as long as the Doctor paid legal costs for both sides—a not insignificant $225,000. When a payment of $78,620.54 came due, Will went out of his way to let the Doctor's friends know that he would insist on collecting every last one of those fifty-four cents. Ten years of legal battles were over, but the brothers' estrangement was complete.

For more than a decade, the Kelloggs had seen each other primarily in court. During that time, the Doctor's other antagonists had left the battlefield. In 1914, C. W. Post, hobbled by a chronic digestive ailment and beset by depression, shot himself in his ailing stomach with a hunting rifle and died at fifty-nine. A year later, eighty-seven-year-old Ellen White (who, rightly suspecting that the San had become more important to her former protégé than the church, had "disfellowshipped" the Doctor in 1907), died in California. As in Hollywood Westerns after the smoke clears, only the Kellogg brothers were left to fight. There were periods of relative calm, ruffled only by minor annoyances, as when mail for one Kellogg was mistakenly delivered to the other. When feeling run-down, Will even checked himself into the San for short stays, though he complained bitterly about the place while he was there. But inevitably, something would come up—one of Will's salesmen would discover one of the Doctor's cereals on a grocery store shelf it wasn't legally allowed to be on—and the injunctions would fly. At times, Will wouldn't talk to his brother on the phone without having his vice-president listen in on an extension. When Will met a man who had recently left his brother's employ, he congratulated him: "Your happiness is just beginning."

Will seemed determined to pay back his brother for his years of abuse. When the Doctor brought out a pulverized zwieback-and-vitamin snack called Pep, and it sold well, a jealous Will did some research and learned that a small candy manufacturer in New York City had already trademarked that name. Will dispatched a Kellogg lawyer to visit the man, one J. W. Surbrug of Surbrug's Nut Products. Surburg told the lawyer that someone named John Kellogg of Battle Creek had recently offered him $5,000 for the name. Surbrug was holding out for $7,500. Will instructed his lawyer to pay the $7,500. Two days later, the Doctor called on the candy manufacturer and was told he had lost out over a mere $2,500 to a lawyer named Clarke. The Doctor was forced to destroy thousands of preprinted Pep cartons. When he found out that it was his brother who had bought the rights from under his nose, he was doubly incensed. The Doctor renamed his snack Zep, but had to abandon his plans when his brother filed suit for trademark infringement. Meanwhile, Will cooked up a granulated cereal, called it Pep, and made another fortune.

The Doctor fought back with the means at his disposal. In 1917, five years after the death of his beloved Puss, at the height of the fraternal lawsuits, Will began showing up at the San to take Carrie Staines, a staff physician, for rides in his car. The Doctor told Staines she'd be fired if she continued to date his brother. Challenged by his brother's opposition, fifty-seven-year-old Will, who had vowed never to remarry ("I made one woman unhappy. Why should I inflict myself upon another?" he said), suddenly proposed. The wedding took place on New Year's Day, 1918. (The Doctor was not invited.) But Will and his bride had little in common except their introversion and their devotion to their work. In the second year of their marriage, Will left his wife at home while he went on a five-month cruise to the Orient with a friend. As time went on, and they led increasingly separate lives, it was hard not to escape the conclusion that even when it came to marriage, Will was motivated by a desire to spite his brother.

Even as they battered each other in court, the Kelloggs goaded each other to greater achievements. The San prospered in the magnificent new building Will's work had made possible, its 1,390 beds filled with movers and shakers, including the novelist Upton Sinclair (whose 1906 exposé of the meatpacking industry, *The Jungle,* had given vegetarianism a boost); the automobile mogul Henry Ford (who brought along his own square dance band); the aviator Amelia Earhart (who took the Doctor for a spin above the San, permitting him a God's-eye view of his creation); the Olympic swimmer and Tarzan impersonator Johnny Weissmuller (who broke one of his records in the San pool, a feat the Doctor attributed to the salubrity of the San cuisine); and the grape juice tycoon Charles Edgar Welch (who liked the San so much he returned thirty-one times). Not every celebrity signed up for the full enema-and-Nuttose regimen, but the Doctor was flexible when it came to the famous, whose photos mingled on his office walls with portraits of Greek philosophers. Given the Doctor's nose for publicity, it was surely no coincidence that the San's 100,000th patient, registered by the Doctor with a maximum of fanfare, happened to be former President William Howard Taft. In 1916, in the midst of the Bran Wars, the Doctor organized a three-day celebration of the San's fiftieth anniversary that culminated in a torchlight parade through the streets of Battle Creek with seven bands, twenty-three floats, a fireworks display, and a keynote address by the San habitué William Jennings Bryan.

In his sixties, the Doctor still put in eighteen-hour days: inventing foods (chocolate-caramel laxatives he called Paramels); bubbling over with ideas (unrealized plans for 800 acres of litchi trees in Battle Creek); and churning out books (*The Itinerary of a Breakfast: A Popular Account of the Travels of a Breakfast Through the Food Tube and of the Ten Gates and Several Stations Through Which It Passes, Also of the Obstacles Which It Sometimes Meets*). A half-century before Jane Fonda popularized workout tapes, the Doctor produced a 78 rpm record of himself leading calisthenics, so that patients could keep up their San-approved exercise at home. He revived the old Battle Creek College and cheered for its football team, which he predicted would be especially successful because of its customized San diet. (The administration dropped the sport after a single season, concluding that football was too violent to be healthy; Battle Creek locals suspected the real reason was that the team lost so many games.) He somehow found time to take up golf, though he played as quickly as possible, trotting from shot to shot. Linking Biologic Living to the increasing interest in eugenics, he created the Race Betterment Foundation and proposed a Eugenics Registry to encourage Americans to consider heredity when choosing a spouse. He founded Three-Quarter-of-a-Century Clubs, whose septuagenarian members pledged: "I hereby promise to do my best to attain the age of one hundred years." The Doctor was determined to reach the century mark himself. He was even more determined to live longer than his brother.

Two miles away, the Corn Flake King, as he was dubbed by the press, focused on one thing: cereal. His office was decorated with a photo of the corn flake milling room at the Battle Creek plant. Like his brother, Will was an indefatigable worker. Unlike his brother, he had an eye for detail and an almost photographic memory. (The Doctor had always assumed that Will would take care of the details for him.) "He never forgot figures and could reel off data and statistics by the page, sales, carloadings, the price of grain," a colleague recalled. Like his brother, Will was whipsmart. Unlike his brother, he was concise; when he asked someone for a minute of his time, he meant sixty seconds, no more. Like his brother, Will was frugal; on factory tours, he pointedly turned off unused lights as he went. Unlike his brother, he didn't hesitate to take financial risks. "Attack boldly. Crack it or quit," he told his executives. "The trouble with you men is that you don't know how to lose money." After the 1929 crash, when most companies were retrenching, Will ordered his executives to double the advertising budget, saying, "This is the time to go out and spend more money." His boldness paid off. By the early 1930s, Kellogg was a $5.7 million company, with plants in Canada and Australia.

Will often said that he was motivated not by money but by competition. Those who knew him had no doubt as to its source. "Dominated as he was by an older brother for many years, Will Kellogg developed what is known today as an inferiority complex," observed a psychologist friend. "In overcompensating for this complex, Mr. Kellogg went to limitless bounds and it is likely that this was the greatest driving force behind the success. He was going to show his brother, himself, and the world that he, too, had superior qualities." (After so many years under the Doctor, Will did not like to be second in anything. On long drives, he'd urge his chauffeur to "open her up to seventy or eighty so that the other cars can't pass us.") Will delighted in proving doubters wrong. When a prominent San administrator sold his Kellogg's stock early on, Will was annoyed. As the stock rose, whenever Will encountered the man, he'd take out his little black book—"Let's see, now," he'd say. "If you had held on to your several hundred shares . . ."—and gleefully calculate how many thousands the disbeliever's stake would now be worth. It was, of course, an act of projection. The man he really wanted to prove wrong was his brother.

*   *   *

Sibling rivalry may push people to greatness; it may also do great damage. In a 2006 study, University of New Hampshire sociologists interviewed more than two thousand children (or their caregivers) between the ages of two and seventeen and found that 35 percent had been "hit or attacked" by a sibling in the previous year. This may not seem surprising, perhaps not even troubling. (In the Eisenhower and Kennedy households, it was business as usual.) Fourteen percent, however, were attacked repeatedly; 5 percent were hit hard enough to sustain cuts, bruises, chipped teeth, or broken bones; and 2 percent were hit with weapons—toys, broom handles, sticks, shovels, rocks, knives. If the attackers had been adults, the authors pointed out, they could have been arrested for assault and battery. Because they were children, however, their behavior could be dismissed as "roughhousing" or "horseplay," with the observation that "boys will be boys." Sibling violence, which tends to taper off as children enter adolescence and turn outside the family for companionship, is found most often in large families composed of closely spaced boys and in families in which parents are physically or emotionally absent.

Although sibling violence among *Homo sapiens* is fairly common, it rarely ends in death. (One is more likely to kill one's child, parent, or spouse than one's brother.) Literature, on the other hand, teems with fratricide and near-fratricide, from the mythical Romulus, who killed his identical twin, Remus, in an argument over where to build the city of Rome (not altogether surprising given that their father was Mars, the god of war), to Claudius, who killed his brother, Hamlet, married his sister-in-law, and became king of Denmark (one of several fratricidal brothers in Shake-speare), to Cal Trask ("sharp and dark and watchful"), who heedlessly drives his straight-arrow twin, Aron ("a boy you like before he speaks and like more afterwards"), to his death in John Steinbeck's *East of Eden.* Steinbeck, who grew up the only boy among three sisters, was inspired to write the novel by his two sons, to whom he would dedicate the book. He was fascinated by how different they were: one troubled and defiant, the other more easygoing and well-mannered. Steinbeck, who had a tendency to view life in dichotomous terms, told a friend that he saw Cain and Abel—whose story he called "the basis of all human neurosis"—in his boys. They were five and three at the time. Both would grow up to serve in Vietnam, become writers, and struggle with addiction. According to the younger brother's wife, *East of Eden* acted as a "self-fulfilling proph-ecy." Whenever the brothers got together, wrote Nancy Steinbeck in *The Other Side of Eden,* they'd drink themselves senseless while engaging in a "primal tug of war" over "who had it worse when they were kids. And who had more delayed stress from Vietnam. And who drank more or fought less with their girlfriends. Even, which one Mother loved more."

John Cheever, whose fiction abounds with rivalrous and fratricidal brothers, had a fraught relationship with his own brother. They were inseparable in youth, when Fred, a bluff, athletic boy almost seven years older, had been, as John told a therapist years later, "mother, father, brother and friend" to him. But their relationship had what Cheever called "an ungainly closeness" (the biographer Blake Bailey suggests it may have been sexually as well as emotionally incestuous), and at twenty-two John left small-town Massachusetts to become a writer in New York. Fred would become the kind of alcoholic, failed businessman about whom Cheever wrote with sorrowful affection in his fiction. If in life Cheever couldn't resolve his feelings for his brother—his journal entries about Fred are a stew of contempt, resentment, and adoration, all of them complicated by the guilt he felt over his own bisexuality—he did his best to rid himself of his brother in his work. In the short story "Goodbye, My Brother," the narrator, irritated with his youngest brother's behavior at a family reunion, impulsively bashes him over the head with a piece of driftwood. In May 1976, as Cheever was finishing the novel *Falconer*, whose main character is a college professor imprisoned for murdering his brother with a fire iron, he visited his ailing brother. "I killed you off in *Falconer*," John told him. "Oh good, Joey, good," Fred, using his brother's family nickname, replied. "You've been trying all these years." A few weeks later, when his flesh-and-blood brother died of a massive heart attack, Cheever felt some relief. As the months went on, however, he felt restless and bereft. His relationship with Fred was, he told his daughter, "the strongest love of my life." Several years before his own death in 1982, talking with his biographer Scott Donaldson, Cheever said, "Some people have parents or children. I had a brother."

Far more common than actual fratricide is the symbolic fratricide in which rivalrous siblings break off contact and become, figuratively, dead to each other, like the Moses brothers, who didn't speak to each other for twenty years, or the Clarks, who didn't speak to each other for thirty-four. Sigmund Freud's grandsons Lucian, the painter, and Clement, the politician and television personality, went more than fifty years without exchanging a word. Some say the Freuds fell out in the 1950s when Lucian asked his younger brother for a loan to pay off a gambling debt. Others date it back to a boyhood race that Clement was about to win when Lucian called out, "Stop, thief!" A passerby detained Clement, and Lucian sprinted past his furious brother to the finish line. Either way, the brothers were famously, nastily, estranged. (Offered a knighthood, Lucian turned it down with the explanation, "My younger brother has one of those. That's all that needs to be said on the matter.") By the time of Clement's death in 2009, Lucian had also stopped speaking to his older brother, Stephen, the owner of a hardware shop, but their estrangement was of shorter duration, lasting a mere decade or so.

Estrangement is harder when siblings live under the same roof. After several years of increasingly volatile arguments, a college student of my acquaintance hasn't spoken to his older brother in five years. "I decided that if he wasn't going to try to get along, I wouldn't either." When he comes home on vacation, they avoid eye contact, refuse to acknowledge each other, and take pains never to be in the same room, which, given that their bedrooms are next to each other, requires careful choreography. If one brother walks into a room and finds the other there, the other brother will leave. "My parents insist that we are brothers and ought to be close," says the student. He agrees. But as the years go by, he can't imagine how they'll repair the rift. At the same time, he can't bear the thought of it continuing into their old age.

As children, Heinrich and Thomas Mann fought so fiercely for their mother's affection that they went a year without speaking to each other, despite sharing a bedroom. But when Thomas decided to become a writer like his older brother, Heinrich encouraged him, commissioning reviews for the literary monthly he edited and inviting him to spend summers with him in Italy, where they wrote together, drank wine together, played dominoes together, and argued about art together. In May 1901, when Thomas, suicidally depressed, asked Heinrich to meet him in Venice, Heinrich came at once and spent much of the rest of the year at his brother's side.

That same year, the publication of *Buddenbrooks* made Thomas famous. Critics began to compare and rank the writer-brothers. The competition kindled in childhood flared anew. In a 1903 review, Thomas criticized "the bellows-type of poetry which has been introduced in recent years from the beautiful land of Italy"; though he didn't name Heinrich, his brother knew to whom he was referring and took offense. When Heinrich repeated some unflattering remarks he'd heard about his brother's work, hypersensitive Thomas was furious. Their rivalry was exacerbated by their differences. Heinrich was a lifelong outsider who felt more at home in Italy and France, and wrote witheringly about his homeland. Thomas, a self-described "good" German, married a millionaire's daughter, built a mansion in Munich and a summerhouse in the Bavarian hills, and settled into the kind of comfortable bourgeois life Heinrich satirized in his fiction. Heinrich felt his brother's work was narcissistic and reactionary;

Thomas felt his brother's work was tasteless and hastily written. (In 1905, after Heinrich's eighth book was published, Thomas wrote in his journal, under the heading "Anti-Heinrich," "I consider it immoral to write one bad book after another out of fear of idleness.") Thomas craved fame and ridiculed his brother's progressive ideals; Heinrich felt it was a writer's duty to speak out against injustice, yet was jealous of his brother's commercial success. Neither approved of the other's wife; each aligned himself with a different sister. "That you turn away from your brother and sister completely makes me *very sad* for you," his mother wrote. "Hold to them, my dear Heinrich, send them now and then a few friendly lines, and do not let them see that you feel less appreciated by the literary world than Thomas is at the moment—or if you do, then that it does not affect you." There were moments of hatchet-burying. In 1906, when one of Thomas's books was savaged by a critic, Heinrich published a spirited defense. "It is like old times: someone attacks me, and my elder brother comes and avenges me," Thomas wrote. That same year, taking notes for a new book, Thomas observed, *"the fraternal problem still preoccupies me."*

The fraternal problem might have resolved had not the First World War intervened. Thomas defended militarism as an essential ingredient in his country's character and called the war, in which thousands were slaughtered each day, a "festive struggle" that would have a "cleansing" effect on the nation. Heinrich, one of the few German intellectuals to oppose the war from the start, was appalled. The brothers refused to see each other, but from their writing desks a mile apart in Munich, they engaged in what their biographer Nigel Hamilton called "an act of mutual literary fratricide." In 1915, Heinrich wrote an essay praising Zola's stand in the Dreyfus case. The essay was an allegory, in which Heinrich identified himself with the "banned and silenced" Zola, and his brother with Zola's nationalist persecutors. Reading the essay, Thomas wrote a friend, "rendered me ill for weeks." He responded with *Reflections of a Non-Political Man*, a 650-page attack clearly aimed at Heinrich. By now, all Germany was aware of the rift between its two best-known writers. In 1917, Heinrich wrote Thomas a letter titled "Attempt at Reconciliation," in which he insisted that he had always tried to defend, support, and understand his brother. Thomas was having none of it. "If you have found me a difficult brother, I naturally have found you even more so . . ." he replied. "Every line of your letter was dictated by moral smugness and self-righteousness. Don't expect me to fall sobbing on your breast." The letter concluded: "Let the tragedy of our brotherhood take its course to the bitter end. . . . Farewell."

*   *   *

When there was nothing left to sue each other over, the Kelloggs found another arena in which to compete: philanthropy. The Doctor put most of his money into ad hoc charitable work. His own home, with its bumper crop of "waifs," was a charitable work in itself, and when he could fit no more children into his house, he established a two-hundred-bed orphanage in Battle Creek and invited its occupants to use the playground and swimming pool at The Residence. In 1893, asking Chicago police to show him the "dirtiest and wickedest" part of the city, he opened a mission on the South Side that provided free medical care, baths, laundry service, San health foods, and San water treatments (which proved to be remarkably effective in sobering up drunkards). Three years later he opened a "Workingmen's Home" that provided room and meatless board for four hundred homeless Chicago men, and instituted a "Life Boat Rescue Service," in which pairs of nurses roamed the streets, trying to persuade prostitutes to find a new line of work. In Battle Creek, he organized "Christian Help Bands," groups of San employees who visited the sick and poor to demonstrate healthy cooking and hygienic housekeeping. All this in addition to a regular slate of individualized giving. In 1895, his biographer Richard Schwarz points out, "while supporting a family of twenty-nine, he also paid the salaries of a Methodist and a Baptist missionary in India, met half of the expenses of ten boys in a mission school, and endowed two charity beds in the Seventh-Day Baptist hospital in Shanghai, a bed in the Adventist medical mission in Mexico, and one in the Battle Creek Sanitarium."

Will scoffed at his brother's scattershot approach, which often left his charitable programs sputtering as his interest turned elsewhere. "My brother is the best disorganizer in the world," observed Will, who applied the same systematic efficiency to philanthropy that he applied to making corn flakes. The Doctor gave away his money as soon as it came in; Will let his money grow and *then* gave it away. Staked over the years to more than $66 million of Will's own funds, the W. K. Kellogg Foundation became one of the largest charitable organizations in the United States. The man who had never learned how to play was determined that others might have that opportunity: he built schools, libraries, parks, playgrounds, swimming pools, gymnasiums, auditoriums, Boy Scout campgrounds, hospitals, bird sanctuaries, and farms. His generosity no doubt came from an innate sympathy for the less fortunate. He often anonymously covered a struggling employee's rent payment or hospital bill, and he made Kellogg's one of the first companies in the United States to institute eight-hour shifts and five-day weeks and provide life insurance, a health plan, and day care. But he also wanted to show that not only could he make more money than his brother, he could give more away. Indeed, the schools and sanctuaries and airports he funded were often named for himself; the man may have been shy, but he wanted to make sure people knew *which* Kellogg had donated them. In the last year of his life, he told his advisors that he wanted to drop his name from the title of the W. K. Kellogg Foundation. When his advisors convinced him that it should retain the Kellogg name, he suggested that they eliminate his initials. "The only way I could stave off this suggestion," recalled the foundation president, "was to tell Mr. Kellogg that to take the initials from the name of the Foundation would be to leave the public in wonderment as to which Kellogg (W.K. or John Harvey) was back of the Foundation."

In all nonfraternal matters, Will preferred anonymity. Though he was now at least as famous as his brother, Will shunned publicity as if it were a toxic gas. He declined honorary degrees, refused to be listed in *Who's Who* (observing that he "preferred to pay for any advertising"), and rarely appeared at public gatherings, especially those designed to honor him. If he couldn't avoid being present, he sat in the back row. He agreed to attend the dedication ceremony for the W. K. Kellogg Auditorium and Junior High School on the condition that the speaker not mention him. When the man couldn't resist thanking him in a single sentence, Will walked out. (The Doctor, by contrast, had been known to walk out in the middle of a medical conference if he felt that not *enough* fuss had been made over him.) When he gave the Youth Building to Battle Creek, Will refused a newspaper's request for a photograph: "Print the Doctor's picture," he snapped. Kellogg employees knew not to gossip about their boss, who often traveled under a pseudonym to avoid being recognized. Asked to prepare a short autobiography, Will came up with a mere sixteen sentences, dismissing his quarter-century at the San in a single, inscrutable, brother-free phrase: "took a job in April, 1880, continued same 25 years."

But Will was haunted by the past, recapitulating his rivalry with his brother in his relationships with the competitors he sued, with the former colleagues he needled, and, most tragically, with the family members he criticized. An insomniac ever since those late nights at the San, Will would lie awake and, in the notebook he kept at his bedside to jot down business ideas, take notes on what he wanted each of his children and grandchildren to accomplish. What he wanted most was for his son Lenn to take over the business someday. Like his father, Lenn was hard-working and ambitious; like his uncle, for whom he worked when he was young, stirring vats of steaming wheat flakes by hand, he was outgoing and creative. In seventeen years with Kellogg's, he would be responsible for more than two hundred patents. But father and son found it no easier to coexist than brother and brother. Like the Doctor, Will rarely handed out compliments and didn't tolerate failure, especially in his own family. (On a grandson's twenty-first birthday, Will sent him a check and a note that ended with the admonition, "A Kellogg should always be successful.") When Will took a five-month trip to the Far East in 1919, he left Lenn in charge; he returned to find the company in financial difficulty. Although the falloff was likely due to the postwar recession, Will blamed his son. The son, no less hard-headed than the father, protested, and they quarreled. Several years later, when Will was in Europe, Lenn, now president of the company, bought an oat-milling plant in Iowa. (As with the Doctor and Will, the trouble always seemed to begin when the boss was away.) The plant ended up losing heavily, and Will was furious. Not long afterward, Lenn divorced his wife to marry a young employee in the Kellogg office. Will, a strict moralist who had always interfered in his children's personal lives, demanded his son's resignation. Although father and son would eventually reconcile, they never worked together again.

Disappointed by his son, Will turned to his grandson, fourteen-year-old John L. Kellogg Jr. He took the boy to the plant and taught him the basics of manufacturing, shipping, and advertising. He made him stand next to him in the company lobby at Christmas, shaking the hand of every employee as he or she left for the holiday. He sent him a list of fifteen "SUGGESTIONS FOR ONE WHO WISHES TO HIT THE TRAIL SUCCESSFULLY, MAKE THE GRADE, PLAY THE GAME, AND WIN." He put him through business college, gave him a five-month round-the-world trip for graduation, and, on his return, appointed him a vice president in the company at $10,000 a year. It proved to be too much too soon for the mercurial young man, who, like his great-uncle, fizzed with ideas and ambition but lacked his grandfather's stick-to-it-iveness. Realizing that he might have brought his grandson along prematurely, Will cut his salary to $40 a week and put him on the road as a salesman. John hated sales and asked to be transferred to the experimental laboratory, where he came up with a process for puffing corn grits. When he tried to sell the rights to his own grandfather, Will was outraged, John resigned from the company, and Will brought an infringement suit against his grandson. Once again, a Kellogg family spat ended in court. "There was great affection between grandfather and grandson," reflected a family friend. "However, there was something about the Kellogg breed . . . apparently there was no organization, house or other thing big enough to hold two male Kelloggs." John moved to Chicago, where he started his own company to manufacture the cheese-coated puffed treats he called Nu-Corn. The following year, when a patent application for his Nu-Corn machine was rejected, the twenty-six-year-old entrepreneur, recently married and with a baby on the way, went to his office on a Sunday and shot himself.

Will went out of his way to help his employees enjoy themselves, but he didn't know how to do so himself. He tried. He traded in his baggy old black suits for bespoke ones. He replaced his modest stucco home with a thirty-room Tudor mansion, complete with seven-car garage, tennis court, croquet pitch, greenhouse, $100,000 lawn sprinkler system, and Dutch windmill. He later added an 800-acre Arabian horse ranch in southern California, a home in Palm Springs, an Italian-style villa on the Gulf Coast of Florida, and an apartment building across the street from the San, from which he could keep an eye on his brother's operation. After all those years minding the San while his brother went abroad, he began traveling: to Alaska, Hawaii, Europe, South America, Africa, Asia, and Australia. And after all that Bromose and Nuttose, he feasted on his forbidden favorites—lobster, chocolate, and oysters—even after he began suffering from gout. A friend invited for lunch recalled Will pointedly remarking that "this was one Kellogg home where they served chicken."

Despite his wealth, Will was no less shy than he had been as a boy. In news photographs taken with Tom Mix, Mary Pickford, and other Hollywood stars who came to his Sunday-afternoon Arabian horse shows, he looks as comfortable as a man submitting to an enema. He could talk with animation about the cereal business, but he fiddled with his watch chain when the conversation turned to anything else. "I would give the world to be able to get along with people as well as you do," he told one of his few close friends. Underneath the forbidding exterior lay the insecure boy who had always felt inadequate next to his charismatic brother. "While Mr. Kellogg would rebuff any effusive thanks for his various generosities, he was a man literally starving to death for appreciation, understanding and compliments," observed a friend. (The friend couldn't have meant "literally" literally; the well-fed Will was as round as a grapefruit.) Although few dared approach the Corn Flake King, he was almost pathetically grateful when anyone did. A secretary who sent him flowers before the start of an ocean voyage was taken aback by the effusiveness of his thanks. A foundation staffer who sent him a birthday cake was touched by his obvious delight. Company executives called him Mr. Kellogg; it was an honor akin to knighthood when he gruffly gave someone permission to call him "W.K." He was formal and self-conscious with his children, hugging them only when he knew no one was watching. "W.K. did not really approve of strong feelings of any kind unless pets were concerned," said a friend. A relative who happened to be a therapist commented, "In all my long practice of psychiatry, I don't know of a more lonely, isolated individual."

For all his ebullience, the Doctor, too, was lonely. He had thousands of acquaintances around the world, many of them famous, but few close friends. His wife died in 1920, and he never remarried. He remained proudly and publicly celibate. He seemed hardly able to keep track of his adopted children; his parenthood had seemed less a labor of love than an experiment in the relative importance of nature and nurture. (When one of his adoptees, despite being raised on the San regime, became a drunkard who tried to blackmail his foster father, the Doctor became an even more fervent proselytizer for eugenics.) Other than his sister Clara, the only sibling with whom he had much contact—albeit antagonistic—was Will.

As the brothers aged and their lawsuits faded into the past, their relationship seemed, at times, almost guardedly cordial. The Doctor addressed an occasional letter to "Dear Brother Will," and signed it, "As ever, your affectionate brother." Will sent the Doctor cucumbers from his garden, and, on another occasion, orchids from his greenhouse. In turn, the Doctor sent Will some iris bulbs he'd transplanted from their ancestral home in western Massachusetts. At one point, Will invited his brother to use his Palm Springs home as a place to work; afterward, the Doctor wrote a thank-you note: "I am starting home tonight, and am writing this note to tell you how much I appreciate your courtesy." Although Will took every opportunity to criticize his brother, he reserved that right for himself. An employee who had heard her boss make numerous derisive remarks about his brother was surprised when, out of the blue, Will said to her, "I never want to hear of you saying anything derogatory about Dr. Kellogg. I don't want anyone around me to talk against my brother."

Pride, however, kept both brothers from reaching out far enough to forgive each other. In the 1930s, when Battle Creek College was struggling, it was said that Will stood ready to give the college a million dollars, but wanted the Doctor to ask him for it. The Doctor didn't; he wouldn't. They did their best to avoid each other, but Battle Creek was a small town, and when they met by accident two or three times a year, they were both on edge. It didn't take much to get them fighting again. Both brothers had the same favorite sister, Clara, who, after her children had grown, moved in with the Doctor and served as his secretary. One year, Will invited her to stay with him at his lakeside estate. Clara enjoyed her visit, but when she wrote a letter to the Doctor in which she mentioned that she missed him, the Doctor, like an aging knight rescuing a damsel who isn't in distress, rushed over to Will's house to fetch his elderly sister.

"She wants to come back," he told his brother curtly.

"She doesn't need to come home," growled Will. "She is well cared for here."

After an extended verbal tug of war, Clara went home with the Doctor.

*   *   *

Twenty years after Jacob hoodwinked Esau out of his birthright, the brothers met again. Hearing that Esau was approaching with an army of four hundred men, Jacob assumed that his brother had come to slay him and all his people. "But Esau ran to meet him, and embraced him, and fell on his neck and kissed him, and they wept."

Rivalry usually mellows with age—even Joseph and his brothers ended up reconciling. Sometimes, however, it takes a glimpse of mortality to bring brothers together. In January 1922, fifty-year-old Heinrich Mann developed peritonitis. The surgery went well, but there were bronchial complications and for several days he lay near death. Terrified he might lose his brother, Thomas sent flowers and a card whose message ended, "Those were difficult days that lie behind us, but now we are over the hill and will get better—together if in your heart you feel as I do." A week later, Heinrich was out of danger, and Thomas came to see him. They hadn't spoken in seven years. A grateful Heinrich told him they should "never lose each other again." Cautiously, they resumed their friendship. In 1927, Thomas refused a place in the Berlin Academy of Arts unless Heinrich was also elected. When Thomas was awarded the 1929 Nobel Prize, Heinrich made a warm congratulatory speech on the radio. Heinrich didn't even seem to mind when, at the ceremony installing him as president of the literature section of the Prussian Academy of the Arts in 1931, the chairman slipped and called him "Thomas." In 1932, after Thomas praised his brother's most recent novel, Heinrich thanked him, writing, "You were always, in every moment of my life, my closest friend, and here again you demonstrate it."

The First World War had cemented their rift; the second solidified their reunion. As Hitler rose to power, Thomas joined Heinrich to become an outspoken opponent of fascism and a supporter of the democratic ideals his brother had long championed. In 1930, Thomas's speech denouncing National Socialism was interrupted by the catcalls of SA men. In 1933, Heinrich's books were burned on Goebbels's orders. A Nazi Party newspaper called Heinrich "national vermin" and suggested he "should have a bomb put under him." Heinrich escaped into France, carrying only an umbrella and a briefcase containing the notes for his next book. Later that year, after delivering a speech deemed insufficiently complimentary to Richard Wagner, Thomas was accused of "intellectual high treason." He eventually fled with his family to the United States. When Heinrich was able to make his way to America in 1940, Thomas, who had arranged his brother's entry visa, was at the dock in New York to meet him.

When they were young writers, Heinrich had looked after Thomas. In the United States, where Thomas was lionized as a giant of twentieth-century literature and Heinrich was all but unknown, Thomas played the paternal role. He got his seventy-year-old brother a job writing screenplays at Warner Brothers and, when that ended, helped support him with monthly checks. After Heinrich's second wife killed herself in 1944, the older brother, lonely and ailing, grew ever more dependent on the younger. When Thomas fell ill with grippe and was taken to Chicago for treatment, Heinrich cabled him: "My beloved brother you must have the strength to live and you will. You are indispensable to your great purposes and to all persons who love you. There is one who would feel vain to continue without you. This is the moment for confessing you my absolute attachment." Yet even in old age, the brothers were concerned with their relative rank in the literary pantheon. In 1950, not long before he died of a brain hemorrhage at the age of seventy-eight, Heinrich told his sister-in-law, "You know, of the two of us, Tommy is the greater, of that I am certain." Six weeks before his own death of lung cancer in 1955, Thomas wrote to a friend, "my basic attitude toward him and his somewhat formidably intellectual work was always that of the little brother looking up at the elder. . . . It was an indescribable shock to me, and seemed like a dream, when shortly before his death Heinrich dedicated one of his books to me with the words: 'To my great brother, who wrote *Doctor Faustus.*' What? How? *He* had always been the great, the big brother. And I puffed out my chest and thought of Goethe's remark about the Germans' silly bickering over who was the greater, he or Schiller: 'They ought to be glad they have two such sons.'"

Rivalry, psychologists point out, can be an expression of intimacy; a fight can, paradoxically, be a way of connecting. One sees this most clearly in childhood, when the fraternal mood can be as changeable as Mark Twain's weather. "Frank had a violent love of beating me," wrote Samuel Taylor Coleridge, "but whenever that was superseded by any humour or circumstance, he was always very fond of me—& used to regard me with a strange mixture of admiration & contempt." In Dylan Thomas's *A Child's Christmas in Wales,* a small boy, watching the snow fall, matter-of-factly observes, "It snowed last year, too. I made a snowman and my brother knocked it down and I knocked my brother down and then we had tea." A friend of mine has thirteen-year-old twins. "They are each other's best friends and worst enemies," he tells me. "They fight over which one gets to go through a doorway first, yet if one gets invited to a birthday party or a sleepover, he won't go without the other." In Eugene O'Neill's *Long Day's Journey into Night,* Jamie Tyrone, after telling his younger brother, Edmund, how jealous of him he has always been, adds, "But don't get the wrong idea, Kid. I love you more than I hate you." The muted rivalry between William and Henry James lasted a lifetime, but they were always each other's best friend and never stopped writing each other long, newsy, affectionate letters, signing them "Bro" or "your brotha." On his deathbed in 1910, William made his wife promise that she would be at his bachelor brother's side when Henry himself approached the end. She was. In December 1915, Alice crossed the wartime Atlantic to nurse seventy-two-year-old Henry through his final months. "He thinks he is in foreign cities, among old friends," she wrote to a friend of Henry's, a few weeks before his death, "and that his brother William, the only one he asks for, will be coming in ere long."

Plutarch, one of three brothers himself, compared the relatives and friends acquired by marriage to tools that can be replaced when lost, "yet the acquisition of another brother is impossible, as is that of a new hand when one has been removed or that of a new eye when one has been knocked out." Even estranged brothers will always be brothers. Indeed, like the "dry alcoholic," who no longer drinks but whose life now revolves around *not* drinking, estranged brothers can be more profoundly connected than brothers who get along but don't really connect. My college acquaintance and his brother may not speak to each other, but as they tiptoe around the house, listening for the other's every step, they are, perhaps, no less entwined than they would be if they were sitting side by side on the couch, talking about their days. "I try to stop thinking about him," the student says. "But it's impossible to stop thinking about him. He's my brother." Thomas Mann peppered his journal with scornful references to the brother he was estranged from and preoccupied with, while thoughts about their conflict filtered into his fiction. "When all is said and done, one ought to treat a rift like ours with respect, one ought not to try and take away its deadly seriousness," he wrote to a friend, on the occasion of Heinrich's fiftieth birthday. "Perhaps separated we are *more* brothers to one another than we would be at the same table, celebrating this occasion."

No matter how rivalrous, no matter how malicious, brothers seem inexorably bound, unable and, perhaps, unwilling, to part, like the legendary German brothers who, fighting over a woman (their old nursemaid, it seems), built neighboring castles along the Rhone so they could keep an eye on each other. Or the Hungarian brothers who, with an entire state to choose from, set up rival restaurants across the street from each other in a tiny Wyoming town. Or the feuding California architects who, asked to design a college classroom building, each designed *half* the building, making sure his floors did not align with his brother's. Yet the architects didn't turn down the commission. They didn't build separate buildings. And the feuding brothers who inherited their ancestral home in a town near ours in western Massachusetts didn't sell it; they divided the house down the middle and, working side by side in silence, created two separate entrances, built two separate staircases, and painted each half of the house a different color. They have lived there, side by side, in silence, ever since. In Athol Fugard's allegorical drama *The Blood Knot*, two South African brothers—one a dark-skinned black, the other light-skinned enough to pass as colored under apartheid's classification system—find that despite their physical differences and their personal antipathy, they cannot escape each other. "You see, we're tied together, Zach," says Morrie, at the end of the play. "It's what they call the blood knot . . . the bond between brothers."

Several years ago, on a cross-country flight, my wife was seated next to two unaccompanied minors, brothers aged seven and ten. "For the entire five-hour trip, they couldn't keep their hands off each other. They were pinching, punching, slapping, pulling hair," recalled Anne. "And yet just as suddenly, they'd be sweetly affectionate." The younger boy clearly revered his older brother. When Anne asked the older brother if he played an instrument, the older brother listed four or five, including the kazoo. "And he's great at all of them," the younger brother volunteered. At one point, the younger brother nestled his head on his brother's lap and the older brother stroked his hair. "It's a very soft pillow," the younger brother murmured. But a moment later, they were trying to demolish each other again. "They couldn't help themselves—it was as if they'd been programmed," Anne told me. "It was love or hate. There seemed to be nothing in between." Anne, who grew up with an older brother with whom she never fought, was astonished that their obvious fondness for each other could not check their casual aggression. "Couldn't you each keep your hands on your side of the armrest and not fight till we land?" she asked. The older brother looked surprised. He turned to Anne and, patiently, as if talking to a child, said, "But that's what brothers do."

*   *   *

The Kelloggs would have one last battle. In 1928, the San expanded again, adding a $4 million, fifteen-story, 265-room tower—the tallest building between Detroit and Chicago. The timing could hardly have been worse.

Planned during the Roaring Twenties, the renovated San opened a year ahead of the Crash. At the height of the 1930 season, some 300 patients were rattling around in a facility designed for 1,300. But the San's problems weren't only financial. New members of the medical team were less willing to adhere to the Doctor's Biologic Living standards. Some smoked on the premises. Some even suggested adding meat to the menu. The Doctor, it seemed, no longer had a "hypnotic" effect on his staff. Indeed, the quintessence of Biologic Living was ailing. He cut his workday to a mere twelve to fifteen hours and began spending his winters in Florida, where, in 1930, he opened the hundred-bed Miami–Battle Creek Sanitarium. The new San thrived, but the Battle Creek flagship went deeper into debt. In 1938, the San underwent bankruptcy reorganization, and the revamped board of directors reduced the aging Doctor to something of a figurehead, denying him even an office in which to see his patients—a humiliation that Will, who had gone officeless at the San for so many years, may have found fitting.

Although the octogenarian doctor was increasingly regarded as a harmless eccentric from another era, he remained indefatigable. He continued his culinary experimentation, no matter the consequences: who but the Doctor could boast of receiving a letter in which a young colleague consoled him, "I'm sorry to learn about the ToFu but I am glad that no one was injured." He continued to stump for the importance of "getting the stomach right," a task he likened to cleaning the Augean stables and to which he personally devoted efforts that can be described only as Herculean. Insisting that with the proper diet and an enema-filled lifestyle, one's bowel movements could smell "as sweet as those of a nursing baby," the Doctor liked to provide visitors with fresh evidence supporting his theory. "He will leave you in the midst of a conversation, go into his little private toilet, come out with a little pot in his hand containing some of his defecation, stick it under your nose, and practically force you to say that it smells very sweet," wrote an elderly friend in 1941. His brother was mortified by such antics. When photos were published of the aged doctor performing calisthenics clad only in a G-string, Will looked into legal measures that might force his brother to wear more clothes. His lawyers told him a lawsuit would be not only unwinnable but likely to bring Will bad publicity.

In 1942, the main San buildings in Michigan were sold to the government for use as a military hospital. After paying off its debt, the San had $725,000 left from the sale. The Doctor herded the remaining patients down the street to one of the few buildings the San still owned. Named superintendent of this skeleton operation, the ever-optimistic Doctor vowed a return to the San's glory days as "a great university of health."

The Doctor's plans would be challenged by a familiar antagonist. When a group of Adventist elders, sensing the Doctor's vulnerability, began organizing an effort to take back control of the San, Will threw his considerable weight behind them. His motivation isn't clear. Perhaps he believed that, having founded the Sanitarium, the Adventists had the right to help decide its future. Perhaps he believed that, having spent a quarter-century at the San, *he* had the right to help decide its future. Or perhaps he just saw one last opportunity to rest *his* cold feet on his brother's back.

On October 3, 1942, Will called on his brother. At ninety, the Doctor, even with an earpiece, had difficulty hearing, and his eyesight was so poor that he barely recognized himself in the photos he autographed for San guests. Eighty-two-year-old Will had been diagnosed with glaucoma five years earlier and was completely blind. He got around with the help of a white cane and a German shepherd. The conversation, which lasted more than five hours, did not go well. Will tried to convince his brother that he was too old to lead the San. If he wasn't willing to relinquish control, then he should at least let his old Adventist colleagues help him. The Doctor rejected his brother's advice. After sixty-six years running the place, he wasn't about to give up the San, especially not to the Adventists. He embarked on a tirade against his old religion. Will cut his brother off and gave him a "tongue-chastisement," as he later called it, the likes of which he had never given anyone "during my rather long life." The Doctor, uncharacteristically, sat still for it, prompting Will to observe: "That the doctor did not resent some of the cutting things I said to him indicated very plainly to me that he, in a way, admitted the truthfulness of my remarks." They discussed the Doctor's health. The Doctor told Will that he was being rejuvenated by a homemade brew of malt honey, vitamins, and minerals that was even helping strengthen the fingernails he compulsively bit. They discussed the war. The Doctor said that the widespread use of tobacco by the army would likely lead to America's defeat. Will later recalled their discussion as "the most rambling conversation I ever had with anybody in my life," and described the Doctor's ideas as "unheard of, unreasonable, and nonsensical." He worried that his aged brother might be losing touch with reality. Their conversation turned to the past. Thirty-six years after Will had left his brother's employ, the wounds were still fresh. Will complained that the Doctor's wee-hour conversations with San visitors had deprived him of many nights of sleep. "I talk too much," the Doctor admitted. "I have to overcome it. I talk too much."

Having failed to convince his brother to give up the San voluntarily, Will tried force. He wrote to members of the Constituency, the governing body responsible for oversight of the San, urging them to attend the upcoming annual meeting and vote an Adventist-approved board of trustees. He pledged $5,000 for transportation, lodging, and food so that members could travel to Battle Creek from as far away as Florida and Oregon for the crucial vote. When the Doctor got wind of his brother's plans, he went on the offensive. He subpoenaed the records of the Seventh-Day Adventists. He dictated sixteen hours at a stretch. He seemed revitalized. But his hopes were dashed at the Constituency meeting on March 31, 1943, when 241 new members recruited with Will's help were deemed eligible to vote, enabling the Adventist forces to elect a new board. The Doctor took out an injunction that prevented the new trustees from convening. He followed up by getting an amended order banning them from interfering with the San. The judge appointed six interim trustees to operate the San until the litigation was resolved. The Kellogg brothers were back in court.

But the Doctor was exhausted. His memory was failing, and an attack of Bell's palsy had left part of his face immobilized. As he awaited the judge's ruling, he stayed in seclusion at The Residence, where he kept abreast of the San by phone, fretting over the patients' comfort, worrying about the new plumbing. He could still rise—briefly—to the occasion. At a photo shoot, the ninety-year-old doctor trotted back and forth across a cinder path, boasting that he could run as long as the photographers' film held out. He proffered a firm forearm. "Feel it—give it a good pinch," he said. "I'm like that all over." But on December 11, an attack of bronchitis developed into pneumonia. On December 14, the Doctor died in his sleep, nine years short of the longed-for century mark. Will sent photos of the grave to the Doctor's friends, a seemingly thoughtful gesture that may also have served as a subtle reminder that he had outlived his brother. Not long afterward, the battle over the San ended in a compromise: the Doctor's associates paid the Adventists $550,000 to relinquish their claim. A scaled-down version of the San remained in operation, but without its Barnum, it was the San in name only.

Three years after his brother's death, eighty-five-year-old Will Kellogg resigned from the Kellogg board of directors, though he continued to keep track of each new advertisement, salary increase, and sales report. Every so often he had his chauffeur drive him to a side street near the Kellogg plant, where he'd roll down the window and listen to the hum of the machines. His second wife had a series of strokes and died in 1948. His son Lenn had a cerebral hemorrhage and died in 1950. His sister Clara died the following year. Although his children and grandchildren would have liked to visit more often, they were afraid to show up at his house without an invitation, and Will wasn't the inviting kind. He spent several Christmases alone with his household staff. He was, perhaps, closest to his nurse, who read aloud to him and listened to him talk about the vicissitudes of his long life.

Will expressed regret several times that he and John Harvey never reconciled. He may have been especially penitent on June 22, 1948, six years after the Doctor's death, when he received a letter from his brother. The Doctor had dictated it not long before he died, but his secretary hadn't sent it, believing that it was demeaning for her boss to write about his failing memory, his difficulty walking, his "doddering," as he called it. Indeed, it would have been the first time the Doctor had allowed himself to show vulnerability to his younger brother. Now eighty-eight-year-old Will listened as an aide read aloud his dead brother's words. The seven-page letter—the Doctor was prolix to the end—was conciliatory, particularly when it touched on their history at the San. "It was the greatest possible misfortune to the work that circumstances arose which led you and me in different channels and separated our interests . . . I am sure that you were right as regards the food business. . . . Your better balanced judgment has doubtless saved you from a vast number of mistakes of the sort I have made and allowed you to achieve magnificent successes for which generations to come will owe you gratitude." Near the end of the letter, the proud old doctor came as close as he could to an apology:

> I am making desperate efforts to get all my affairs into such shape as to preserve as much as possible what good they may represent and to mend as many as possible of the errors I have made. I earnestly desire to make amends for any wrong or injustice of any sort I have done to you and will be glad if you will give me a very definite and frank expression of anything I have said or done which you feel should be justly designated unbrotherly or otherwise open to criticism. . . . I hope that this note may find you more comfortable and that you may have many years left to promote the splendid enterprises that have given the name you bear a place among the notable ones of our time.

Three years later, on October 6, 1951, Will Kellogg died. He was ninety-one. Although he had outlived his brother by eight years, he was three months younger than the Doctor had been when he died. After lying in state in the lobby of the Kellogg Company until workers on every shift had a chance to pay their respects, Will was buried next to his brother. In happier times, Will and the Doctor had put up matching twin monuments on their lots. At some point during their estrangement, however, Will had ordered his monument torn down and replaced by another: a bronze sundial on which a robin tugged a worm out of the earth. Will, it seemed to say, was the proverbial early bird who got the worm—or at least before his brother got it.

Chapter Five

Baseball

One summer afternoon a few years after we moved back to Dedham, my brothers and I were playing baseball in the backyard. Harry was pitching, using a tennis ball instead of a baseball because a tennis ball went a mile when you connected with it and, more important, it hurt a lot less when you got hit by a pitch. Ned was standing over the T-shirt we used for home plate, brandishing Harry's old Pony League bat, a Hillerich & Bradsby 29-ouncer with Bobby Doerr's signature beginning to fade on its barrel. Ned, who didn't play much baseball, was imitating the tics of players he'd seen on television—tapping the plate with his bat, wiggling his fanny as he dug his feet into the grass—to let us know, in case he struck out, that he wasn't taking things too seriously. I was in the outfield, needling Ned with a peppy "swing, batter swing," which, when Ned kept waving unproductively at Harry's pitches, gave way to a plaintive "Come on, just *hit* the ball." Mark, five years old, was standing behind the plate, eagerly retrieving tennis balls as they sailed past Ned toward the garden. It was rare for all four of us to be playing the same game at the same time, rarer still to be playing it without fighting—the peace likely attributable to Mark, in whose worshipful presence we were more apt to behave—and, despite the sweat runneling down my back in the August heat, I felt a lazy, pleasant complacence that was interrupted when Ned swung so hard at a pitch that the bat flew out of his hands and hit Mark in the head, knocking him to the ground. A moment later, Mark's temple oozed with blood.

I don't remember whether anyone said anything. I do remember that even as I stood there, not quite believing what I'd seen, Harry ran to Mark, scooped him up, and, in the curiously high pitch his voice assumes even now at times of surprise or strong emotion, shouted for our mother as he staggered toward the house with Mark—who, in his bewilderment, hadn't yet begun to cry—draped over his arms, the way in war movies soldiers carried their wounded buddies to safety. Ned and I, finally in motion, trotted behind Harry, Ned worrying about Mark but also likely already formulating a defense (*it was an accident, it wasn't my fault, he shouldn't have been standing so close to the plate*), and me watching, relieved I wasn't the one who had hit him, curious whether Ned would be punished, admiring of how oblivious Harry seemed to the blood dripping on his T-shirt, and a little envious of how quickly he had taken charge. As Harry started up the steps to the back door, Mum came out of the house, her quizzical look turning to one of horror when she saw Mark, limp in Harry's arms, carried toward her like an offering. "Take him to the car," she said, then hurried inside to get her purse. Ned and I watched mutely from the driveway as they raced off to the doctor, Harry in the backseat with Mark, who was whimpering by now, across his lap—and even in that moment, I felt a pinch of resentment that Mum had spoken to Harry as if they were alone.

The cut looked much worse than it really was. If Ned had been an inch shorter, or Mark an inch taller, Mark might have lost an eye. As it was, the bat struck the orbital bone over the socket. It took only seven stitches to sew up the wound. (Mark still has an inch-long salmon-colored scar on his temple that turns a shade darker when he laughs.) I remember the incident not so much because of Mark's injury but because it was the moment I began to realize that my brothers and I filled certain roles within our family: Harry quietly taking responsibility, doing what needed to be done; me playing it safe, neither hero nor villain, watching and waiting to see what happened; Ned creating drama, albeit unintentionally, and—though utterly blameless—worrying about being blamed; Mark the innocent victim. I had heard it said that in times of crisis we reveal our true selves. Is this who we really were? I wondered. Is this who we were always going to be? It would be many years later, when the four of us came together after Mark sustained another, far more severe injury, before I understood how confining these roles had been, how firmly I had come to accept them, and how difficult it had been for us to escape them.

* * *

We had returned to the same town, but nothing was quite the same. Although only six blocks from our old home, our new one lay in a transition zone between the charming two-hundred-year-old colonials of our former neighborhood and Route 1, a gauntlet of car dealerships, fast-food outlets, and discount furniture stores that ran through town on its way from Maine to Florida. Our family was in a transition zone as well. Dad's new job—fund-raising for his alma mater—didn't require nearly as much travel and returned him to the social circles in which he felt most comfortable. Once again, there were Harvard football games and weekend trips to the Cape. Mum went to work as an art teacher, enthralling her students with the kind of imaginative projects that had enthralled us when we were children. A few months after we moved into our new house, she began painting the white kitchen walls with lush green jungle foliage. Over the next few years, the jungle would reach up the stairwell, curl around the landing and fill the second floor hall. During that time, Mum, too, began to bloom, with a vitality in direct proportion to the degree to which she had felt repressed. She took painting classes, wrote poetry, composed a folk mass, read underground newspapers, joined the fledgling women's liberation movement, marched against the Vietnam War, and festooned the back of our car with bumper stickers that proclaimed her causes. On the very day that the Harvard administration, of which my father was a part, was trying to formulate a response to students who had occupied University Hall to protest the war, my mother was escorting a group of her students to Boston Common for an antiwar rally.

Our parents were happier, but they were moving in different directions. Mum, who had married at twenty and had three children by the time she was twenty-five, was, to use the vocabulary of the times, finding herself. In the meantime, she resembled less and less the pliant, adoring woman Dad had married. Sometimes Dad would come home from work a little tipsy, long after we'd finished supper. Mum, the plate of food she'd saved him drying out in the oven, would meet him at the door, and though they'd try to argue quietly so that we couldn't hear them, their voices would spike with frustration, drawing me from my room to the second-floor landing, where I'd find Harry standing at the railing, one hand on the banister. We'd listen for a moment before turning, in silence, back to our rooms.

Harry and I never talked about Dad's drinking. In part, this was because he drank no more than most of our friends' fathers, in an era in which one rarely saw a middle-aged man after five o'clock without a cocktail in hand and a glazed look on his face. But we didn't talk much about anything. At home, Harry kept to his bedroom under the third-floor eaves, coming down when dinner was on the table or for an occasional episode of *The Man from U.N.C.L.E.* Sometimes he'd walk to the library and spend the evening browsing the stacks. His room lay directly over mine. At night, lying in bed, waiting for sleep, I'd hear him moving about upstairs and wonder what he was doing. I assumed that it must be something secret and important.

It seemed strange and somewhat perverse that despite my early efforts to emulate my older brother, the more time passed the more different we seemed. Some of that difference was attributable to the vagaries of the pituitary gland. Harry, who occasionally retreated to the basement to lift a set of Joe Weider barbells he'd gotten for his birthday, was sturdy, swarthy, and sufficiently hirsute—he'd begun shaving and had grown an impressive pair of sideburns—that I thought of him as he-man Esau to my feeble Jacob. Not only was I hairless in all the places that mattered, but I was short, skinny, and weak, with wrists as thin as butter knives and arms that wobbled uncontrollably when I tried to hoist Harry's barbells over my head. Harry recently came across a snapshot of us taken when I was in eighth grade. Standing awkwardly against the car, studiously staring away from each other, we looked, he told me, "like representatives of two different species."

Harry and I no longer fought—I wasn't foolish enough to provoke him—but I remained on my guard in his presence. Now, on the rare occasions we threw a ball or got out a board game, there was a ruthlessness in his play that kept me on edge. It seemed desperately important to him that he win. And whether it was baseball, football, Ping-Pong, or Yahtzee, he won. Playing croquet, he sent enemy balls into the bushes even when he was five wickets ahead. Playing Pounce, he wormed his stronger hand inexorably under mine to claim the stack of cards. Playing Risk, he goaded Ned and me into attacking countries in which he had amassed an insurmountable pile of armies. Playing Monopoly, he talked us into deals we knew we shouldn't make but that he'd convince us were for our own good—that, for instance, even though the rent on the B & O railroad was a tiny fraction of the rent on Boardwalk, there was a higher probability of landing on one of the four railroads than on one of the two blue properties; the railroad rent would accumulate over time, and besides, at $200 a house he would probably never have enough money to build on the blues, and it therefore made sense for you to trade him Boardwalk for the B & O—and, because he was giving you such a good deal, you should probably throw in an extra $500. Harry was so persuasive he could make the utilities sound like highly desirable real estate. And he was so insistent that even when you *knew* he was screwing you, you'd make the trade anyway. Because if you didn't, you were subject to a head-shaking "When you end up losing, don't blame me," and, after you lost, "I hate to say I told you so but I told you so." Sometimes, in our desperation, Ned and I would team up against Harry, making sweetheart deals that gave each of us monopolies. This infuriated Harry, but he'd beat us anyway. In the rare instances in which it looked as if Ned or I might win, Harry would reinterpret the rules to his advantage mid-game; if *that* didn't work, he'd accuse us of ganging up on him and threaten to quit. Two-person Monopoly was no fun, so Ned and I would give in, voiding our trade to get him back to the table. At some point, realizing I couldn't beat Harry, I would turn on Ned—I had to beat someone—and as ruthless, in my own ingratiating way, as Harry, systematically attempt to put *him* out of business. Since Mark was too young to play, poor Ned had no one to beat and, recognizing the futility of his position, often ended the game by overturning the board in frustration, sending houses and money and hotels and small silver top hats across the living room rug.

Although I was frustrated by my inability to beat my older brother, I respected him for his determination. I admired how he spent hours alone at the neighborhood tennis court, perfecting his backhand against the bangboard. I admired the fact that Harry, alone among us, possessed what we called "the killer instinct." I took pride in the tennis trophies, inscribed with Harry's initials, that accumulated on the shelves of the glassed-in bookcase in the front hall, next to Dad's. One summer our parents arranged for Harry to take tennis lessons from an older boy down the road. When Harry came home after the first session, he was troubled. It had quickly become apparent that he was a better player than his instructor, so they had just rallied. This went on for a few more "lessons," my parents still paying the boy, although everyone knew who should be paying whom. I felt sorry for the older boy, who must have been embarrassed, but I felt a vicarious triumph: my brother was so good he could beat his teacher.

When we moved back to Dedham, Harry had signed up for Pony League baseball. Twice a week he'd come home from practice after dinner with a dirt-stained uniform and the air of having been in the wider world. One night we went to see him play. The game was in East Dedham, literally on the other side of the tracks that ran through the center of town. The field was mostly dirt, speckled with islands of grass, and surrounded by a chain-link fence, which, in turn, was surrounded by compact two-decker houses. We took our place among the shouting parents. Harry was playing second base. It was some time before he noticed we were there. I expected him to be his usual fierce self, but he looked a little nervous—the way I felt when I played baseball, worried I would let my teammates down, hoping the ball wouldn't be hit toward me. When he came to bat, I assumed he'd hit home runs, like the tennis-ball blasts he walloped over our backyard fence. But he popped up or beat out grounders. He was, I saw, a perfectly decent player, no better and no worse than the others on his team. It was the first time I understood that there were people in the world who might be able to beat my brother. I took no delight in the knowledge. I wanted to beat him, but I didn't want anyone else to beat him. I didn't go back to see him play again. In any case, he quit the team after one season.

It never occurred to me that Harry's aura of invincibility might have come at a price. It never occurred to me that he might have crushed his brothers because he felt crushed himself; that he tried to seem invulnerable at home because he felt so vulnerable beyond it; that he might feel self-conscious or insecure, or any of the things I was just beginning to feel myself; that, as the eldest brother, he might have felt the weight of our family discontent more keenly. I had no idea that he no longer made straight As in school, or, more shockingly, that he no longer seemed to care; that he was alone in his room upstairs not because he was working on some important project but because he was lonely; that his remove was a sign not of sophistication but of depression. I wouldn't know until we were both in our fifties that at one point, alone in the house one summer afternoon, he had stood at his third-floor window and thought about jumping.

Eventually, our parents decided that Harry needed to get away from home—hadn't he already left? I wondered—and our grandparents paid for him to attend our father's old boarding school. "If you want me to go, I'll go," Harry said. Deep down he knew he needed a change. After a subdued two-hour ride, my father pulled up in front of the school. Harry began to sob. Dad wept quietly. Both of them would have been hard-pressed to say why. They sat in the car until their tears subsided. Then, like good WASP men of their era, they shook hands and said good-bye.

A few days after Harry left, I went upstairs. Although I knew he was hundreds of miles from home, I found myself tiptoeing. Most of the third floor was used for storage: the landing stacked with family suitcases and Dad's old army duffel bags, the extra bedroom cluttered with spare bureaus, lamps, and Mum's old paintings. Harry's room, however, was nearly empty. His shelves held few clues to the occupant's identity: a row of old Hardy Boys books, a collection of Sherlock Holmes mysteries, a copy of *Robin Hood* passed down from our grandfather, a few half-filled stamp albums. There were no posters on the walls, no souvenirs on the bureau. There were few signs of life. It was the room of someone who was just passing through. The gray strongbox that had once held baseball cards and saltines stood on the desk. I wondered what was in it now.

From a distance, it seems odd that when we returned to Dedham, each of the four brothers went to a different school: Harry to a local private high school, me to a middle school several towns away, Mark to the progressive elementary school where our mother taught. Ned attended our old public school, which, in our absence, had moved from the cozy, three-story whitewashed colonial to which Harry and I had ridden our bikes to an antiseptic, one-story sprawl amid a cluster of new developments on the edge of town. Ned dreaded school even more than he had in Darien, in large measure because he attracted the attention of the class bully, a well-padded sixth-grader named Ricky Ratters, who lay in wait with his henchmen as Ned arrived each morning, punching him in the shoulder, spitting on his jacket and rubbing it in, calling him (among other things) "Neddie Nudie." Resisting our mother's advice to ignore his tormenters (*It takes two to tango*), Ned fought back, with words and, eventually, with fists. Years later, he would confess how disappointed he had been that his older brothers had never done anything to stop the teasing. Harry recalls that he and I went so far as to discuss roughing up Ricky Ratters on his way home from school, warning him that if he knew what was good for him, he'd leave our brother alone. But it was all talk. (I suspect I was relieved. In Ned's telling, this Ratters fellow sounded pretty dangerous.) Instead, I am ashamed to say that, hearing the unimaginative but irresistibly alliterative nickname the equally alliterative Mr. Ratters had given Ned, I began applying it to him myself.

Ricky Ratters may not have understood it, but part of his grievance against Ned (and, I suspect, part of mine) may have had something to do with Ned's looks. With his wavy, auburn hair, brown eyes, and symmetrical features, Ned resembled the boys we saw modeling khaki pants and plaid shirts in the Sears catalogue. It was Ned the elderly ladies fawned over during our nursing home concerts, Ned to whom our cleaning ladies gave presents at Christmas, Ned at whom girls found themselves staring, even at an age when they didn't know why they wanted to. When Ned was twelve, our grandmother, who had been something of a beauty herself and who prized beauty in others, commissioned a professional photographer to take Ned's portrait. Under strict orders not to bother my brother, I stewed in the house, pretending to read a book as Ned, in a white button-down shirt our mother had ironed for the occasion, posed against the oak tree in our backyard. In the photo, which our grandmother displayed in her dressing room for the rest of her life, Ned wears a small smile that Grandma no doubt found enchanting but that I thought I recognized as the smirk he flashed while getting away with something.

Ned found other ways to get the nourishment he wasn't getting from his brothers. Over the years he had worked his way through the gamut of childhood pets: plastic-bagged goldfish he won at the school fair and tended for a week or two before they died; silver-dollar-size turtles from Woolworth's who rarely budged from under their plastic palm tree on their plastic island in their plastic dish; a series of gerbils and hamsters whose names we could never keep straight, who lent his room a faint sour smell, and whom we'd occasionally encounter AWOL in the hallway. Each time we moved, we left behind a cluster of miniature graves in the backyard, marked with twig crosses or pebble headstones.

But all this was preparation for the day a small brown mutt who hadn't fallen far from beaglehood wandered into our mother's classroom. No one ever said so, but from the moment we took her in, she was Ned's dog. He named her Penny, for her color. (I obstinately preferred to think she'd been named for "Penny Lane," my favorite new Beatles song.) At this time in his life, Ned was a bit of a stray, too, and he and Penny loved each other with a fierceness that betrayed their mutual need. When Ned got home from school he'd curl up around Penny on the living room rug; when Ned watched TV, Penny nosed her way onto his lap; when Ned slept, Penny slept at the foot of his bed. Like Ned, Penny was a risk-taker; her favorite indoor activity was splashing the contents of the trash can, Jackson Pollock–style, across the kitchen floor. Like Ned, Penny craved independence; every so often she dug a hole under the fence and wandered off, an act that galvanized our family, lending us a shared purpose we otherwise lacked. Ned and I would bicycle furiously around the neighborhood, calling her name into the gathering dark. Later, Ned and Mum would pile into the car to continue the search, headlights probing the shadows for that small, familiar shape. We always wondered when we'd get the call that told us Penny had been killed, or when she might roam so far she'd never find her way home. But next morning we'd hear a scratch at the door. We'd let her in and she'd go straight to Ned.

If, in Darien, I had fallen into an interlude of mild rebelliousness, back in Dedham I rededicated myself to the role for which I was temperamentally inclined: the good boy, the conciliator, the equivocator, the filler of silences, the eater of creamed corn. (There was symbiosis at play: as I saw Mum discipline Ned and sensed how unhappy it made them both, I reveled even more in being the good son, and that, in turn, drove Ned to be even more fractious.) My return to goody-goodyhood was reinforced by the school I attended, a gloomy, wood-paneled old place where the staff maintained hegemony with verbal threats, knuckle raps, and, in rare instances, "chinnies," a disciplinary technique in which the teacher pinched the tender flesh under a student's jaw, then wiggled it back and forth until the victim begged for mercy. Modeled on such venerable English institutions as Rugby, my new school more nearly resembled Dotheboys Hall, the ne plus ultra of educational sadism from which Dickens's Nicholas Nickleby rescues the unfortunate Smike. It terrorized me back to my straight-A ways.

At home, I no longer found it difficult to stay on Mum's good side. In the mid-sixties, I entered adolescence and our interests converged. We liked the same music (the Beatles, the Byrds), the same TV shows (*The Smothers Brothers Comedy Hour, Masterpiece Theater*), the same FM radio station (WBCN: *a boss sound in a boss town*), the same sad books (*The Heart Is a Lonely Hunter*; *Black Like Me*; *Tell Me That You Love Me, Junie Moon*). Where once I had devoured the literature of male bonding, I now wanted to read about loners and oddballs in far-off places: Tom Wingfield in the alleyways of St. Louis, David Schearl in the tenements of the Lower East Side, Eugene Gant in the hills of North Carolina. I joined the guitar lessons Mum gave on Sunday afternoons in our dining room. I played in the year-end hootenannies she organized in our back-yard, at which parents sat in folding lawn chairs, sipping lemonade and listening to their children sing about careless love, the sounds of silence, satisfaction. I accompanied her to teach-ins and antiwar rallies. Like her, I started to keep a journal, to write poetry. Mum's father, for whom I had been named, was a writer, and I dreamed of being a writer myself. Mum was gratified to find a kindred spirit in the house, with whom she could harmonize on "Mr. Tambourine Man" or discuss the Chicago Eight. She showed me how to do psychedelic lettering. She knew exactly what to get me for Christmas: The Beatles' White Album, the annotated edition of *The Waste Land*. Three years after she had refused to let me see *Goldfinger* in Darien (too racy), she took me to see *Easy Rider* and *Midnight Cowboy*. If she hadn't been my mother, I would have had to admit that she was pretty far out.

I read Mum's books, listened to her records, and accompanied her to peace demonstrations because I was interested in those things myself. I was also aware that my interest pleased her. Was I motivated by Oedi-pal issues? Sibling rivalry? Both? In any case, as Harry and Ned pulled away from Mum, I moved closer, aligning myself with her to an extent I wouldn't fully realize until I was in my early thirties, when a therapist suggested that my identity had been shaped, in large measure, by the fact that I was one of four boys competing, however unconsciously, for our mother's affection. I dismissed the possibility; the therapist pursued it. "There was no rivalry," I found myself retorting. "She loved me most." What shocked me was not that I said it, but how instinctive it was—and how, even then, so many years later, it was accompanied by a frisson of triumph.

By the time I moved on to high school, the sixties were in full swing. Like my mother, I longed to be a hippie, but she was a little too old and I was a little too young. Attending a private school in an affluent suburb didn't aid my cause, though I consoled myself with the fact that James Taylor had spent a few years at a rival prep school before dropping out. In ninth grade, I glommed on to a small group of would-be hipsters who met in the music room after school, where the smartest boy in the class, a wild-haired kid from Brookline, read aloud from Rimbaud, quoted Lenny Bruce, and played Hendrix and Coltrane on the school record player. Though we didn't understand much of it, we'd nod, chuckle knowingly, and rail against the establishment, by which we had in mind not the military-industrial complex but our headmaster, a hawk-nosed ex–Harvard football player in his seventies. As the year went on, the Brookline boy's hair grew longer, his grades fell, and he left for public school. That summer, he wrote me a scornful eight-page letter, daring me to revolt against my preppie, provincial existence. (A year later I heard he'd gotten heavily into drugs and been hospitalized for depression.)

I would have liked to comply. Yet I wanted to have it both ways. I wanted to be Rimbaud, but I wanted to play varsity soccer. I wanted to dance beneath the diamond sky with one hand waving free, but I didn't want to look like a dork. I wanted to be Goofus *and* Gallant. And so my revolution wasn't very revolutionary. I thumbed my nose at the school's coat-and-tie dress code by wearing my grandfather's old smoking jackets and paisley ties, the thick leather moccasins Harry left behind when he went away to school, and a pair of red-white-and-blue-striped American flag bell-bottoms I bought at the Dedham Mall. For the Wiggins Memorial Essay competition, in which each junior was required to write a short biography of a historical figure whom the late headmaster Charles Wiggins II might have admired, I wrote a windy appreciation of John Lennon and dedicated it to "the man who blew his mind out in a car." I composed a pro–Abbie Hoffman editorial for my history class, but when *Steal This Book* was published I haunted the rack at Lechmere, longing to obey the author's imperative, knowing I wouldn't dare, and finally forking over the $1.95. I scrutinized my mother's copy of *Summerhill,* a book about an English school in which there were no grades, no dress code, and no rules, but I stayed at my stodgy old prep school, making sure to keep up my grades so I could get into a good college. I questioned authority, but I ended my questions with "sir." I heard about Woodstock only after the fact—I'd been away at tennis camp—but even if I'd known about it, my parents would *never* have let me go. Instead, I bought the dove-and-guitar T-shirt and the *Life* commemorative issue and saw the movie the weekend it was released, sitting between Mum and Ned at the Chestnut Hill multiplex.

With Harry away at boarding school, I felt more leeway to be different than I would have otherwise—it's hard to imagine that with my older brother at home I would have dared flash the peace sign and utter the word *groovy* so indiscriminately—but I still went only halfway. (It was, of course, coincidental, but somehow not surprising, that I finally reached puberty only after Harry was gone.) I dreamed of singing in a rock band; instead, I sang Rodgers and Hammerstein in the school musical. I dreamed of drinking absinthe in Montmartre; instead, my friends and I shared cans of Budweiser in the Dedham graveyard. I dreamed of roaming the streets of Greenwich Village; instead I haunted the Plaza, a strip of desultory shops along Route 1, three blocks from our house, where I'd sift through the record bins at Lechmere, sneak peeks at the high school girls outside Friendly's, and check the magazine rack at the Liggett Rexall drugstore for the latest issue of *Rolling Stone*.

I lived for *Rolling Stone*. It was my umbilicus to the real world, its arrival an event so vital to my continued existence that I usually walked down to the drugstore three or four times hoping it had come in, before it actually did. That night, after I'd finished my homework, I'd head upstairs, past the bedroom where Ned communed with Penny, past the den, where Mark and Dad watched a Bruins hockey game, past my parents' bedroom, where my mother graded papers for the English classes she'd added to her teaching load, and, pushing through the strands of yellow-and-black beads I'd hung in my doorway, I'd lie on my bed under my Jefferson Airplane poster and imagine for a few hours that I was part of a world where people ran away to San Francisco, danced un-self-consciously at rock festivals, used the word *reefer* without blushing, and, most important, had sex—or in the strangely dreary way the *Rolling Stone* writers were wont to describe it, "got laid." Then I'd brush my teeth, stack three or four records on the seventy-dollar stereo I'd gotten for Christmas, and listen to Neil Young as I watched the lights of passing cars accelerate across the ceiling until I fell asleep.

*   *   *

Although the Colt brothers seemed to have retreated into separate lives, in the aggregate we constituted a critical mass of overwhelming maleness. The wicker hamper on the landing overflowed with dirty socks. The back hall was a midden of bats, balls, shin pads, and hockey sticks. The TV room in the basement doubled as a knee hockey arena. Certain key areas in the house smelled like feet. No matter how many times our mother cleaned it, the cramped second-floor bathroom we shared with our parents was a mess: the sink streaked with Oldenburgian blobs of toothpaste; the Crest tube capless and squeezed from the middle; the shower curtain bunched and dripping on the wrong side of the tub; the bathtub drain clogged with a medusa of hair; the toilet paper unfurled to its cardboard tube; the toilet seat, despite our mother's pleas, down. (Recently, at my parents' house, my father and I commented on a peculiar smell, and my eighty-one-year-old mother, no less transported than Proust by his madeleine, observed, "You don't know what smell is unless you're a woman with four sons who never lifted the toilet seat before they peed.") Dinnertime was a fraternal free-for-all over who got the biggest piece of chicken on the plate, the last Nilla wafer in the box. Brotherly talk revolved around sports, TV shows, and bodily functions. The amount of intellectual energy devoted to the subject of flatulence was mind-boggling. The simple conversation starter "Who cut one?" could kick off a ten-minute series of ripostes ranging from the elementary "He who smelt it dealt it" to the more linguistically and philosophically subtle "He who revealed it concealed it," with an occasional detour into foreign languages, as in the interrogative *"Qui a coupé le fromage?"* Earnest fraternal colloquies took place on the relationship of volume to smell—whether, in fact, SBDs really *were,* as folk wisdom had it, more mephitic than percussive "rippers." Against this creative barrage, our mother's attempts to persuade us to describe our farting as "dropping a rose" didn't stand a chance.

Poor Mum! At school, her students adored her. Wearing her Indian-print shawl and her bangle earrings, she talked with them about the war, about the new Joni Mitchell album, about their problems with their parents. (Meeting us, her students would gush, "You're so lucky—you have the *coolest* mother!") At home, trying to get dinner on the table after a long day of work, Mum struggled to keep the peace among four restless boys who didn't want to talk about their feelings, who saw her as the force from which they struggled to free themselves. Four decades later, Mum would laugh at the notion that we could have thought her so confident and powerful when, as a young mother of four, she herself had felt "like a deer caught in the headlights." And yet, even though everyone, including me, had always assumed that she had had four children because she kept hoping for a daughter, she told my wife that she had been glad to be the only woman in the family: "That way, I got more of the attention."

Growing up in a house with a 5:1 male-to-female ratio, of course, led to a good deal of confusion about girls. Part of the problem was technical. Neither of our parents had ever talked to us about sex, although Mum had tried. When Harry was fourteen, she attempted to get him to sit still for a facts-of-life chat, but was able to corner him only long enough to say, "Don't *ever* get a girl pregnant" before he fled. (In an illustration of the truism that it's easier to parent other people's children, a few years later my mother would be acclaimed as an extraordinarily sensitive teacher of seventh-grade sex education.) If the Brady Bunch was any indication, one's brothers were a potential source of information. But I didn't dare ask Harry, and, even if I could have suffered the ignominy of consulting a younger brother, I was sure Ned would make merciless fun of me (*Could you kiss her? Could you marry her?*).

At school, rather than risk being branded a "homo" (or, in the more sophisticated but no less odious variation applied to one luckless classmate who wore glasses and couldn't throw a spiral, a *puella*—Latin for "girl"), I pretended I knew what people were talking about. When my Brookline friend played us a recording of Lenny Bruce's "To is a preposition, Come is a verb" monologue, I nodded knowingly; when an eighth-grade classmate placed a spoonful of butterscotch pudding in his mouth, massaged the flesh of his throat between his thumb and forefinger, tilted his head back at an ever-increasing angle and, finally, spat the pudding from between his pursed lips, I howled along with the others at the lunch table; when a friend lent me a copy of *Playboy* and I happened across a (scrupulously nongraphic) photo of a man "going down" on a woman, I assumed he was administering the male-on-female version of a "blow job," gently puffing into her vagina, in a kind of sexual CPR; when I encountered the word *clitoris* in a novel by John Updike, I assumed that it rhymed with the name of the mouthwash—Lavoris—we saw advertised on TV. (Either way, I had no idea what it was or, even after I knew, where to find it or what to do with it.) When a mustard-yellow volume with the dismayingly clinical title *Everything You Always Wanted to Know About Sex—But Were Afraid to Ask* appeared on the bookshelf in my parents' bedroom, I devoured it in brief, furtive study sessions when no one else was at home, one ear listening for footsteps.

But even after I'd learned how the word *clitoris* was pronounced and—at least hypothetically—the general area in which it was located, I had no opportunity to apply that knowledge. I had no idea what girls were like or how to act around them. I sang along with Dylan's "Just Like a Woman" as if I knew what he meant, but I had no clue. Part of that came from growing up surrounded by brothers. I had no sister in whom I could confide, no sister to whose friends I could practice talking. At my all-male school, the only members of the opposite sex we encountered were the librarian, the secretaries, the elderly women who served us lunch, and the school dietitian, who, it was rumored, spiked the shepherd's pie with saltpeter to dampen our libidos—to no apparent effect, given that in the locker room, the entire eighth grade, like soon-to-riot inmates in a prison movie, periodically erupted into feral chants juxtaposing the name of a nearby girls' school with a grunt into which was poured a world of desperate, inchoate longing: *Dana Hall-UNH. Dana Hall-UNH. Dana Hall-UNH.*

At a time when (if *Rolling Stone* was to be believed) everyone in the world under the age of thirty was engaged in a nonstop orgy, my sex life was limited to scrutinizing a friend's Herb Alpert & the Tijuana Brass album cover on which a dark-haired woman was buried up to her ample breasts in an alp of whipped cream; ogling leggy "bachelorettes" perched on stools as they smoothed their miniskirts during episodes of *The Dating*

Game; copying a particularly alluring photograph from the *Sports Illustrated* swimsuit issue into my art class sketch pad, erasing and redrawing the woman's bikini to make it smaller and smaller, in hopes, I suppose, that I could eventually—magically—get a glimpse of what lay beneath. On Saturday trips into Boston with friends, the part I looked forward to most was not Jack's Joke Shop, with its whoopee cushions and puddles of plastic vomit, but the walk from the subway station, which took us along the edge of the Combat Zone (as the city's red-light district was piquantly known), past windowless brick buildings in whose dusty display cases were taped black-and-white publicity shots of outlandishly buxom women wearing cardboard stars on their nipples as they bent over to adjust a stiletto heel. From these clues, I learned that sex, like masturbation (the only carnal activity in which I regularly engaged), was something done quickly, in secret, and with an overwhelming sense of shame.

I was desperate to have a girlfriend, but I was terrified of girls. (It didn't help that I arrived so mortifyingly late to puberty.) I wrote poems in my journal about girls who barely knew I existed. I wrote letters to girls I'd seen from afar, hoping they'd write back, so I'd have tangible evidence that I wasn't a total loser. (If they wrote back at all, it was a gently pitying brush-off I ripped into pieces so small that Ned couldn't possibly reconstitute the evidence of my ignominy). I wasn't picky. When the Beatles' *Revolver* came out, I told myself that *I* would have loved Eleanor Rigby, as long as the face that she kept in a jar by the door wasn't *too* hideous. (In my imagination, of course, Eleanor was one of those librarian types you see only in movies who eventually take off their glasses, unpin their suddenly voluminous hair, and turn into Barbara Stanwyck.) When Tiny Tim, the stringy-haired, beak-nosed, ukulele-playing falsetto crooner, appeared on *The Smothers Brothers* with his fiancée, a surprisingly cute girl he called Miss Vicki, I thought: If only *I'd* met her first. Paging through my *Life* special issue on Woodstock, I kept thinking that if only I'd been *there*, I could have gotten laid. (In the unlikely event that I ever got the chance, I told myself I wouldn't "get laid," I'd *make love*, thereby rendering girls helplessly pliant in the face of my extraordinary sensitivity.) But this was all theoretical. A friend, disgusted by my ineptness, knowing that

I wrote poetry—and with a vehemence fueled, I realize now, by the fact that he was only slightly less inept than I—hissed the cruelest insult he could imagine: "You're going to end up just like *Emily Dickinson*."

My ineptitude was all the more galling when contrasted with Harry's and Ned's seeming expertise. *They* had no need for Dr. Reuben's sex book, I felt sure. In Darien, Harry used to sing a line, over and over, from one of his favorite Herman's Hermits songs: *I'm leaning on the lamp post at the corner of the street in case a certain little lady comes by.* On such slim evidence I'd credited him ever since with a certain savoir faire, picturing him, James Bond–like, in a pool of light on an otherwise dark and empty street, occasionally consulting his watch, looking up with a debonair smile at the sound of footsteps. In Dedham, Harry sang the Yardley Black Label aftershave commercial (*Some guys have it—some guys never will*) into our faces with such intensity I grew up assuming that Harry had it and I never would. (I wasn't certain what "it" was, but I suspected it had something to do with Stridex Medicated Pads.) Harry was so good at everything he did, I assumed he was good at this, too. My suspicions were confirmed when he came home one day with a pack of friends that included a quiet, dark-haired girl whom he matter-of-factly introduced to us—as if bringing home a girl were an everyday occurrence in our house and this weren't, in fact, the very first time—as Fern, a name that not only brought to mind the heroine of *Charlotte's Web,* an early literary crush of mine, but seemed redolent of an earthy sixties sexuality. Harry and his friends stayed only long enough to pick up some of his clothes. We never saw Fern again. But those few minutes of having a girl in the house had lent the air an electric charge.

Ned seemed even more precocious in the ways of the flesh. Back in third grade, at a classmate's party, I followed a crowd of kids out to the garage, where, at the birthday girl's suggestion, they began to play what I recognized with excitement to be a bona fide game of doctor. As our hostess wriggled out of her shorts, I stood in the back, feeling like an anthropologist who has stumbled on a sacred ritual he's heard rumors about but has never quite believed really existed. The spell was broken when I noticed Ned on the far side of the garage, taking in the scene as if it were nothing unusual. Fortunately, we were called inside for cake before I found out whether Ned intended to take a more active role in the proceedings. I myself, of course, would never have dared.

As Ned grew older, he became a natural magnet for the caliber of girls I secretly aspired to but failed to attract. (I knew this because while I was ogling those girls, they were ogling Ned.) In summer, the only time of year when we came in contact with the opposite sex on a regular basis, the prettiest girl on our town beach was clearly smitten with my fourteen-year-old brother. No matter how fast I swam, no matter how wittily I joked, no matter how adroitly I put him down, she had eyes only for Ned. In high school, while I was joining every club imaginable, Ned, two years younger than I, seemed to have far more experience in the only two extra-curricular activities that really mattered: parties and girls.

It never occurred to me that my brothers might have been just as clueless as I—and were working just as hard not to show it. Years later Harry would tell me that Fern was just a friend of a friend, and that he had considered going to Vassar instead of Harvard because it had just gone co-ed and, with only a handful of males there, he'd have a decent chance. Ned would tell me that despite appearances, he, too, had felt awkward and insecure around girls. All three of my brothers would tell me how socially crippling it had been to grow up in a house with all boys. If only we could have confided in one another! But that would have been too mortifying.

As Harry, Ned, and I followed each other into adolescence, the age difference between us and Mark seemed even wider. In some ways Mark was like an only child, but he got none of the perks that come with that distinction. Mum and Dad hadn't had time to keep a baby book to mark his arrival, as they had for the rest of us, and by the time he was born, they had stopped sending out photos of the Colt boys at Christmas. On Christmas Eve, Harry, Ned, and I hung up store-bought stockings of thick, burgundy-colored corduroy, identical save for the rickrack trim with which Mum had customized them; Mark's was a baggy carrot-colored bootie she'd stitched together. No doubt she had tried to make it especially capacious and distinctive, but it looked nothing like its siblings as it dangled next to them from the fireplace mantel. We were too old to be interested in Mark's favorite TV shows, so he'd watch *The Mod Squad* or *The Wild Wild West* with us, or we'd find him in the basement alone, watching reruns of the shows of which we'd watched the originals—*Father Knows Best, Leave it to Beaver, My Three Sons.* By the time Mark came along, Morgan Memorial had already inherited the clothing that had been passed down from Harry to me to Ned. In the fraternal pecking order that had Harry beating me up and me beating Ned up, Mark not only had no one to beat up but was too much younger than Ned to be considered fair game, and thus didn't receive the noogies, punches, and ritual humiliations that were at least a sign of brotherly connection. Consequently, he seemed to lack the protective callus produced by fraternal friction. At the dinner table, a Darwinian free-for-all over food and floor time, Mum would have to call for silence so that shy, soft-spoken Mark, who had been quietly trying to say something, could be heard. "It doesn't matter," he'd say, embarrassed, in the momentary calm before chaos resumed.

If the four Colt brothers had been depicted in one of those children's puzzles in which you're instructed to "find the one that doesn't belong," you'd pick Mark. He was no less handsome, but while Harry, Ned, and I were variations on a theme—tall, brown eyes, brown hair—Mark was compact, with wavy, copper-colored hair, blue eyes, a blur of freckles, and fair skin that burned easily. We wondered where those looks had come from, until we came across a photo of our father's father as a dashing young man. He looked exactly like an older version of Mark.

At school, Mark was a determined worker, but reading didn't come easily and homework was a struggle. (Looking back, I find it hard not to believe that Mark didn't have what, years later, would have been routinely diagnosed as some mild form of ADD. But the psychologist to whom my mother took him for testing in the fourth grade told her that Mark was merely a sensitive, anxious child whose feelings were always close to the surface.) I would learn many years later that, like Ned, Mark had been teased by a few of the elementary school BMOCs. Unlike Ned, Mark lacked the temper that might have driven them off in search of more tractable victims. At sports, Mark was game but undersized—like Ned and me, he was for many years one of the smallest boys in his class—and he hadn't had the benefit of the nightly games of catch that Harry and I had gotten. Although we included Mark in our activities when we could, Harry was away at school, and Ned and I, busy with extracurricular commitments, usually didn't get home till after dark. Mark's most enduring athletic memory from elementary school is of the time when, after sitting on the bench for most of the hockey game, he heard his coach bark "Fourth Line!" and, determined to make the most of his big chance, clambered over the boards. Rather than swiftly skating off as he'd imagined, he stumbled, fell to the ice, and struggled to rise as play swirled on around him, his teammates yelling "Get up! Get up!" Mark, who in the intervening years became a fine athlete, tells the story with a laugh now, but also with an intensity that suggests how humiliating it was at the time. (It didn't help Mark's credibility on the rink when our mother, thinking it would please him, surprised him by painting his hockey gloves with psychedelic flowers.)

What Mark didn't get from his brothers, however, he began to get from his friends, a loyal group drawn by his sweetness and his enthusiasm, with whom he did all the things we used to do: toss a football, sing in the choir, play tag in the graveyard. But if we weren't paying much attention to him, he was clearly paying attention to us. Asked by the psychologist whether he wanted be like his three older brothers, Mark's face lit up: "Oh, *yes*."

Not long ago, Mark told me that when he was young, he thought of his older brothers as gods. If only he had known how mortal we were! Away at school, far from the family, Harry resumed his high-achieving ways: top student, captain of two sports, student council leader. I pored over his school newspapers and yearbooks, secretly proud of his success. When I was a high school junior, my tennis team traveled to Rhode Island to play his. I was low man on our ladder. Although I beat my opponent, I was far more concerned with the match between my brother, the number one player on his team, and our number one, a classmate of mine I'd once overheard referring to me as a doofus. I was pleased when my brother easily beat him. It was as if Harry had dispatched a playground bully on my behalf. (I had a momentary urge to run up to my vanquished class-mate and crow, "My brother kicked your ass!") When I saw Harry, all I could say was "Good match." When he came home for Christmas vaca-tion, quiet and preoccupied, I reverted to a more muted, careful version of myself.

At Harry's graduation, on a sunny June afternoon, we watched as he was awarded prize after prize—so many that the audience began to chuckle when his name was called. On the long ride home, we oohed over his triumphs. Harry was quiet. Halfway through a celebratory dinner, he excused himself from the table and went upstairs.

As we grew older, Ned and I eased into a kind of unacknowledged truce. We attended the same high school now, but other than carpooling to and from campus each day, we had little contact. Looking back, I can see that in my adolescent self-absorption I pulled away from Ned no less com-pletely, and no less inadvertently, than Harry had pulled away from me.

All the while, unbeknown to me, Ned was finding his own niche. As an adolescent less inclined to sports or good grades, areas of expertise to which Harry and I had already staked our claims, he spent much of his time on stage, where, abetted by his voice—in a family of singers, his rich baritone stood out—he flourished, getting from the audience the approval he didn't get at home. His favorite sport was one Harry and I had never tried: rowing. He began to move away from the family, not, like Harry, by going off to boarding school but by spending as much time as he could at our grandparents' house on Cape Cod. He felt far more at home on the water than on land. While Harry and I spent hour after hour on the tennis court, Ned sailed. Back in Dedham, he developed a tight circle of friends with whom he attended rock concerts, went to parties, and got into teenage scrapes. One night, after watching Ned perform in a play, I drove him to a nearby town where a friend of his was throwing a cast party. It was a wilder party than I'd ever been to, with a seemingly unlimited amount of liquor. One of Ned's classmates vomited on the lawn. Another drove down the driveway at forty miles per hour and hit a lamppost, totaling the car. Somebody called the police; Ned and I raced home before they got there. I looked at my brother with new respect.

Senior year, I coached intramural hockey. Though I worried that Ned might challenge my authority, as he did so reflexively at home (I imagined him responding to my Lombardiesque exhortations with *I know you are but what am I?*), I chose him for my team. He worked hard, made not a single caustic remark, and became my most indispensable player. One evening after practice, as I watched him walk away from the rink with his friends, I realized that I had always seen Ned only as the younger brother I had to keep in line. Without my noticing, he had made a life of his own.

I think both Ned and I wanted to be closer but neither of us dared let our guard down. As the older brother, I knew I should be the one to reach out, but I couldn't show weakness to my younger brother, I couldn't give him ammunition. In any case, by then it seemed too late. It was Ned I thought of one Friday night when, watching TV, I stumbled across *What Ever Happened to Baby Jane?*, a melodrama in which Bette Davis and Joan Crawford play murderously rivalrous sisters. In the final scene, Bette learns that her lifelong persecution of Joan has been based on a misunderstanding. She turns to her dying sister, those moony Bette Davis eyes glistening with sadness and wonder. "Oh, if only I'd known," she says tenderly. "All this time, we could have been friends."

One spring afternoon, I was surprised to see our green Ford station wagon barrel up the school driveway. My mother was behind the wheel, distraught. Penny was in the backseat. She had wriggled under the fence, wandered into the road, been struck by a car and killed. My mother had been driving around aimlessly, not knowing what to do, but knowing she had to tell Ned. She searched the campus but couldn't find him. That evening, after school, Ned and I were carpooled home by a friend's mother. As I sat next to him, I burned with my secret. After we were dropped off, Ned opened the gate to the backyard and started toward the house. Even as I called his name, I knew I should let our mother, just inside the door preparing dinner, tell him. But I couldn't stop myself. "There's bad news,"

I said quickly. "Penny was hit by a car. She's dead." Ned whirled around and looked at me. "If you're lying, I'll kill you," he said quietly.

I may have justified my act by telling myself that someone had to prepare Ned before he got home. I may have justified it by telling myself I was taking responsibility, the way Harry had when Mark was hit by the baseball bat. But even as Ned disappeared into the house, I knew I'd told him because I wanted the power; I wanted to be at the officious center of things; I wanted, perhaps, to play a particularly cruel form of Got You Last. The moment confirmed something I'd suspected all along: that no matter how many dishes I washed or how many times I said "sir," I wasn't really a good boy. And I wasn't a good brother.

Chapter Six

Brother's Keeper:
Vincent and Theo van Gogh

One morning in early March of 1886, Theo van Gogh, the twenty-eight-year-old manager of the Montmartre branch of Boussod, Valadon & Co., a leading European art dealership, received a note written in black crayon:

> My dear Theo,
>
> Don't be angry with me for arriving out of the blue. I've given it so much thought and I'm sure we'll gain time this way. Shall be at the Louvre from midday onwards, or earlier if you like.
>
> Please let me know what time you can get to the Salle Carrée. As far as expenses are concerned, I repeat that it won't make much difference. I still have some money left, of course, and I want to talk to you before spending any of it. We'll sort everything out, you'll see.
>
> So come as soon as you can. I shake your hand.
>
> Ever yours,
>
> *Vincent*

Theo must have read the hastily scrawled message with apprehension. Each sentence in the seemingly innocuous note had a subtext. *Don't be angry with me for arriving out of the blue.* Ever since 1880, when Vincent had given up work as an evangelist to become an artist, Theo had periodically suggested that his brother come to Paris, the epicenter of the art world, but Vincent had insisted that he wasn't ready. He had spent most of that time in remote corners of Holland and Belgium, drawing and painting peasants, coal miners, birds' nests, and potatoes. During the last year, however, Vincent had started pestering Theo for the go-ahead; now it was Theo who had been putting Vincent off. Although he was devoted to Vincent, Theo realized that he wasn't quite ready to have his irascible older brother in the same city, much less in the same cramped apartment. It was hard enough getting along with him at a distance. Theo wanted Vincent to wait, at least until June, when he could rent larger quarters. But Vincent was unwilling to postpone his move any longer. Being in Paris, he told Theo, would accelerate his education and give him a better chance of selling his work. *I'm sure we'll gain time this way.* And so Vincent had taken the night train from Antwerp, where he had spent the last three months, to Paris.

As far as expenses are concerned, I repeat that it won't make much difference. For six years, Theo had been his brother's sole support, sending him more than a quarter of his modest salary each month. Theo could ill afford the money—he also supported his widowed mother and two of his sisters—but he knew his brother had nowhere else to turn. Over the years, Vincent had burned his bridges with teachers, friends, and family—everyone except Theo. *I still have some money left, of course, and I want to talk to you before spending any of it.* Vincent, who felt a corrosive shame at being a financial burden to his brother, was attempting to impress Theo with his thriftiness. What he neglected to tell Theo was that he had the money only because he had left Antwerp without paying his bills.

We'll sort everything out, you'll see. Vincent was trying to reassure his younger brother—and perhaps himself, as well. Both brothers suffered from depression, a condition Vincent was convinced ran in the Van Gogh family. But Vincent, despite a life of grinding poverty, had an optimistic, idealistic, almost childlike outlook. Practical, cautious Theo was less hopeful. He was a shy man, eager to please and willing to make accommodations, but his relationship with Vincent had been conducted largely by mail. They hadn't spent more than a weekend or a Christmas vacation in the same house since childhood, and at one point had gone over a year without seeing each other. Theo knew from his parents, with whom Vincent moved in from time to time to save money, how impossible Vincent was to live with. He worried that his quiet, well-ordered life—long days at work, evenings of billiards and conversation at the Holland Club—would be turned upside down. But he knew he had no choice. Theo was his brother's keeper, but no one could keep Vincent; as a former classmate put it, "He did not know what submission was." In the end, it was always Vincent who acted and Theo who sorted everything out. Yet even Theo could not have guessed how difficult the upcoming months would be. Long after both men were dead, Theo's widow would observe, "of all that Theo did for his brother, there was perhaps nothing that entailed a greater sacrifice than his having endured living with him for two years." And yet if Theo had not met Vincent in the Salle Carrée, if he had not put him up—and put up with him—in Paris, there would have been no Arles, no *Sunflowers*, no *Starry Night*.

* * *

It seems ironic that we owe the phrase "brother's keeper" to an incident in which someone *refused* responsibility for his brother. Yet ever since Cain, when asked the whereabouts of the murdered Abel, cried out "Am I my brother's keeper?" the phrase has been shorthand for the assumption that we have a fraternal duty to look after our siblings. That duty may last a lifetime, as it would for Theo van Gogh. It may consist of rising to the occasion during a time of need: John Keats nursing his tubercular younger brother Tom until Tom's death (and, in the process, likely catching the disease that would kill the poet himself three years later); Mathieu Dreyfus petitioning officials, hiring private detectives, and consulting clairvoyants for five years until his younger brother, Alfred, a French army captain falsely convicted of treason, was pardoned; Michael Marrocco leaving his home and job in New York City to live at the Walter Reed Army Medical Center in Washington with his younger brother, Brendan, a twenty-two-year-old infantryman who had lost his arms and legs to a roadside bomb in Iraq in 2009. It may be a short-term intervention: twenty-three-year-old Ronald Herrick donating a kidney to his dying twin, Richard, in the first successful organ transplant, in 1954. It may be a spur-of-the-moment decision: Hector stepping in for feckless Paris to fight Achilles (the classical version of the older brother fighting the playground bully on a younger brother's behalf); the future naturalist John Muir seeing a man stick a needle into his infant brother's arm and, never having heard of vaccinations, biting the doctor on *his* arm.

It may consist of a simple act of kindness. When Booker T. Washington, born into slavery on a Virginia plantation, was a child, his clothing was made from flax, a coarse material that chafed his skin raw. As he recalled in his autobiography:

> I can scarcely imagine any torture, except, perhaps, the pulling of a tooth, that is equal to that caused by putting on a new flax shirt for the first time. It is almost equal to the feeling that one would experience if he had a dozen or more chestnut burrs, or a hundred small pin-points, in contact with his flesh. Even to this day I can recall accurately the tortures that I underwent when putting on one of these garments.... In connection with the flax shirt, my brother John, who is several years older than I am, performed one of the most generous acts that I ever heard of one slave relative doing for another. On several occasions when I was being forced to wear a new flax shirt, he generously agreed to put it on in my stead and wear it for several days, till it was "broken in."

*   *   *

Theo hadn't always been Vincent's keeper. Growing up, it had been Vincent who, in his own quixotic fashion, looked out for his younger brother. That the balance of their relationship would change was, in some measure, due to a third brother neither of them ever met.

On March 30, 1852, Anna van Gogh, a minister's wife in the village of Zundert in the southern Netherlands, gave birth to a stillborn child, a son named Vincent Willem. The parents, who had married late in life, were still mourning the loss when, a year later to the day, a second son was born. They gave him his older brother's name. The second Vincent spent his early years in a house in which his mother was preoccupied with her grief, his father with his congregation. Each Sunday when the boy went to church, he saw his own name on his brother's gravestone. Years afterward Vincent remembered his childhood as "gloomy and cold and sterile," and went on to observe, "The germinating seed must not be exposed to a frosty wind—that was the case with me in the beginning."

But if Vincent would accuse his parents of pushing him away with their rigidity, his parents would accuse Vincent of pushing them away with his erratic behavior. Vincent was an unusually silent, serious child who preferred to be alone, reading books and collecting beetles he pinned in a box lined with white paper and neatly labeled with their Dutch and Latin names. He liked to draw flowers and animals, but disliked the attention his efforts brought him. When he was eight he destroyed a small clay elephant he'd sculpted because his parents made such a fuss over it. When his mother praised his drawing of a cat climbing an apple tree, he ripped it up. "There was something strange about him," recalled a maid who worked for the Van Goghs. "He did not seem like a child and was different from the others. Besides, he had queer manners and was often punished." Theodorus and Anna van Gogh had high expectations of their six children, particularly of their eldest, but the more they tried to steer their son, the more resistant he became. Worried that the rough-edged village children were a bad influence, they sent eleven-year-old Vincent to boarding school nineteen miles away. On visits home, he took long solitary walks across the marshy flats and pine forests outside Zundert, collecting fallen birds' nests, strengthening tree-bound nests he thought might not survive a storm. It would be the paradox of Vincent's life that he longed for family, for friendship, for community, but was temperamentally unable to get along with people.

Born four years after Vincent, Theo gave Vincent a second chance at brotherhood. Living in the shadow of the brother who died, Vincent would forge a lifelong bond with the brother who lived. (A fourth brother, born ten years after Theo, was so much younger that he grew up, in essence, as an only child.) They made an unusual pair. Theo had the blond hair and delicate features of the father for whom he had been named, while Vincent had his mother's copper hair, sturdy build, and homely face. Vincent was a broad-shouldered fellow of great strength and energy; Theo was slender, frail, and frequently ill. Both boys were unusually sensitive, but Vincent could be brusque and quick-tempered, while Theo was always unassuming and agreeable. Their sister Lies noted that Theo had inherited his father's "warm-heartedness"; their sister Anna believed he had been "a friendly soul" from birth. Perhaps in part to compensate for Vincent's obstinacy, Theo rarely gave his parents cause for worry. Pastor van Gogh liked to compare his two elder sons to Jacob and Esau. There was never any doubt which he considered the rough, uncouth Esau, and which the practical, presentable Jacob.

Unlike the biblical brothers, Vincent and Theo got along well. Theo, alone in the family, enjoyed Vincent's company. In later life, his sisters recalled young Vincent as prickly, teasing, and aloof; Theo remembered him as imaginative and clever. Vincent built sandcastles with Theo, took him fishing and ice skating, taught him how to shoot marbles, invented games for him to play, and talked with him into the night in the attic room they shared. His sisters learned to give Vincent a wide berth, but from the beginning, Theo worshiped his older brother. "I adored him more than anything imaginable," Theo recalled. Years later, when Vincent would quarrel bitterly with his father and look back on his early years with resentment, his letters to Theo cited fond memories of their shared childhood: the walks they took, the starlings that perched on the church, the look of the clouds in the blue sky, the road lined with beech trees. Toward the end of his life, when he lay in a hospital in Arles after cutting off part of his ear, and Theo laid his head in sorrow on the pillow beside him, Vincent, recalling the days when they had shared a bed, would whisper: "Just like Zundert."

When Vincent was sixteen, his godfather, Uncle Cent, a well-known art dealer, secured him a job as an apprentice clerk in The Hague with his firm, Goupil. Vincent was a tireless worker who was fascinated by the lithographs and etchings he spent his days packing and unpacking. His parents were heartened when they received a letter from Vincent's boss, telling them that everyone at the gallery liked dealing with Vincent and that he had a bright future in the profession. In August 1872, fifteen-year-old Theo spent two days with his brother in The Hague. One afternoon, they strolled out of town along a canal path to the mill at Rijswijk. There, over glasses of milk, they promised that no matter what happened, ✓ they would stand by each other for the rest of their lives. It was a day both brothers would long remember, and at times of strain in their relationship, each found reason to remind the other of it. A year later, Vincent sent Theo a reproduction of Jan Weissenbruch's painting of the mill, writing, "That Rijswijk road holds memories for me which are perhaps the most beautiful I have."

It seemed inevitable that Theo would follow his older brother into the art business. On January 1, 1873, several months after their walk to the Rijswijk mill, Theo began work in the Brussels branch of Goupil. "I am so glad that we shall both be in the same profession and in the same firm," wrote Vincent from The Hague. "We must be sure to write to each other regularly." They did. None of Theo's letters to Vincent from those early years have survived (though Theo carefully saved his brother's correspondence, Vincent rarely saved Theo's), but Vincent's letters give a heady sense of two young men from the provinces sharing their excitement at their expanding worlds—the epistolary equivalent of wide-eyed college freshmen staying up all night to discuss life's eternal questions. Vincent played the role of mentor, shaping the tastes of his eager acolyte. "Here are the names of a few painters I particularly like," he wrote. "Scheffer, Delaroche, Hébert, Hamon ..." ("A few," to the enthusiastic Vincent, turned out to mean sixty-one.) Vincent's reading lists for Theo were only slightly less extensive: Balzac, Hugo, Dickens, Michelet, Zola, and Harriet Beecher Stowe, among dozens of others. ("With the money I gave you, you must buy Alphonse Karr's *Voyage autour de mon jardin*. Be sure to do that—I want you to read it.") Vincent copied out verses by his favorite Romantic poets; passed along quotations from thinkers he admired; and sent art prints, some of them duplicates of ones he owned so that he and his brother, a hundred miles apart, could gaze at the same pictures on their bedroom walls. He gave Theo encouragement and advice. Indeed, there seemed to be no subject on which the elder brother did not counsel the younger: what to do ("Try to take as many walks as you can and keep your love of nature, for that is the true way to learn to understand art"); what to feel ("*Admire* as much as you can, most people *don't admire enough*"); how to act ("be as patient and kind as you can"); how to lift one's spirits ("I strongly advise you to smoke a pipe; it is a good remedy for the blues"); and how to deal with the opposite sex, a subject about which the advisor himself was clueless but opinionated ("you are quite right about those priggish girls . . . but watch your heart, boy"). Theo soaked up his brother's counsel; he took long walks, he read Michelet, he smoked a pipe.

Their relationship began to shift with an incident that, like a fault line, would expose deeper rifts in Vincent's equilibrium. In 1873, after four years in The Hague, Vincent had been promoted to a position at Goupil's London gallery. (Theo sent him a wreath of oak leaves he'd gathered from the heath near the parsonage to remind Vincent of home.) For almost a year, Vincent nursed a secret infatuation for his landlady's daughter. One afternoon, finding himself alone with her, the awkward twenty-one-year-old declared his love. The shocked young woman told him she was secretly engaged. With characteristic persistence, Vincent hounded the girl, urging her to break off her engagement, to no avail. He came home that summer almost catatonic with depression. Hoping a change of scene might lift his godson's spirits, Uncle Cent arranged for Vincent to work in Goupil's main office in Paris. (Vincent unsuccessfully petitioned his uncle to transfer Theo there to keep him company.) But Vincent was no less morose. At work he argued with his employers and insulted his customers. If a client wanted to buy a painting Vincent considered inferior, he tried to steer him toward work he considered worthy; if a client chose to disregard his advice, Vincent couldn't hide his disgust. When his superiors complained about his sales technique, Vincent insisted he couldn't keep quiet when a customer showed poor taste—didn't they want him to tell the truth? Not surprisingly, two days after his twenty-third birthday, seven years after he first came to Goupil, Vincent was asked to leave the company.

Vincent's intensity had found a new focus. In his letters to Theo, reports on museums were replaced by reports on church services; critiques of paintings by critiques of scripture; swatches of romantic poetry by lyrics to hymns; quotes from Zola and Michelet by quotes from the Old Testament and *The Pilgrim's Progress*. In October 1876, after preaching for the first time, Vincent copied out the entire sermon and sent it to his brother. Any gratification his parents felt when their son turned to religion curdled as Vincent, who never did anything halfway, became increasingly fanatic. He fell asleep each night reading the Bible, he attended as many as seven services each Sunday. One Sunday he threw his monogrammed silver watch into the collection plate, another Sunday his gloves—the initial symptoms of an obsession with sacrifice and suffering that would end with him wearing rags. His advice to Theo turned rigidly pious: go to church as often as possible; learn to distinguish between good and evil; eat only *plain* food; throw out every book but the Bible. "Do not be afraid to sing a hymn in the evening when you are out for a walk and nobody is about," he urged, a suggestion his self-conscious brother was unlikely to follow. It was a measure of Theo's growing confidence that he didn't succumb to his brother's proselytizing; as he watched his brother slip into zealotry, Theo became less enamored of organized religion and eventually renounced the church.

Confused, lonely, and consumed by religious fervor, Vincent bounced from job to job: boarding-school teacher (given the end-of-term task of collecting overdue tuition, Vincent couldn't bring himself to put the squeeze on impoverished families and was dismissed); lay preacher (like his father, he was an awkward speaker and was seldom invited to the pulpit); bookseller's clerk (he spent much of his time translating the Bible into French, German, and English, or making what the boss's son described as "silly pen-and-ink drawings"); theological scholar (he quit less than a year into his studies, insisting one didn't need to know Latin and Greek to relieve human suffering); probationary evangelist (he was so obstinate—asked whether a certain word was dative or accusative, he replied, "I really don't care, sir"—that after his three-month trial period, the mission-school elders refused to appoint him). In December 1878, the evangelical-school dropout went off to serve anyway, "to preach the Gospel to the poor and to all those who needed it," as he put it, in the coal fields of Belgium.

Vincent's parents despaired. Proper Calvinists who had envisioned Vincent as a respectable country minister, they were embarrassed by their brooding, unpredictable son and did their best to keep news of his failures from their neighbors. Vincent's sisters worried that their peculiar brother would ruin their chances for marriage. "His religion makes him absolutely dull and unsociable," one of them wrote. Alone in the family, Theo still believed in his brother, telling his parents that Vincent's quirks were marks of his special character, assuring them that Vincent would eventually find his way. Lies scoffed. "You think that he is something more than an ordinary human being," she wrote Theo, "but I think it would be much better if he thought himself just an ordinary being."

When Theo was a child, his parents had urged him to follow in his older brother's footsteps. Now they were terrified that he might do so. But their conscientious younger son was succeeding in the very job at which Vincent had failed. Within eight months at Goupil, Theo had gone from filling orders in the stockroom to standing in for the manager when he was away on business; after only a year, the sixteen-year-old was given Vincent's old salesman's position at the company's more prestigious branch in The Hague. Vincent's troubles made it even more vital to his parents that Theo do well. "Now the oldest has rocked the boat, we hope all the more that the second will steer a steady course," wrote Pastor van Gogh to Theo. The second, who wrote his parents regularly and sent money home to help pay for his sisters' education, rarely disappointed: "The crowning glory of our old age," his doting parents called him, "our most prized possession." While Vincent was failing theology school, Theo was in Paris working for Goupil at the 1878 Exposition Universelle, where he sold a painting, listened to Edison's phonograph, and met the French president, who stopped by the Goupil booth and asked the young Dutchman a few questions. When, in a rare misstep, Theo took a mistress from an inferior social class (the kind of embarrassing behavior his parents had come to expect from Vincent), his parents pressured him into giving her up. "You shall and must be our joy and honour!" his father reminded him. "We cannot do without it." As if trying to expunge evidence of their elder son's failures, the van Gogh parents saved none of Vincent's letters. They kept every one of Theo's.

Pastor van Gogh and his wife confided their worries about their ne'er-do-well elder son to his prematurely responsible younger brother. In October 1874, when they hadn't heard from Vincent in three weeks, they urged seventeen-year-old Theo to keep writing to him, hoping he would be a steadying influence, and asked him to report back on his brother's state of mind. "I'm afraid that something awful will happen, my dear Theo," wrote his father. "I say this to you as your confidante—if you run across something that might be useful, let us know. I believe there must be some kind of illness, whether physical or mental." At times, Theo and his father sounded like anxious parents fretting over a recalcitrant teenager. In 1877, on the eve of Vincent's departure for Amsterdam to study theology, Pastor van Gogh bought new clothes for his chronically disheveled son. "We have improved his appearance a little bit with the help of the best tailor from Breda," he wrote to Theo, imploring him to perform "another work of mercy" and persuade Vincent to visit "a clever hairdresser" who might be able to tame his unruly orange mop. When Vincent dropped out of the seven-year theology program, his father helped him enroll in evangelical school. But he had little hope that things would improve. "It grieves us so to see that he literally knows no joy of life, but always walks with bent head, whilst we did all in our power to bring him to an honorable position!" he wrote Theo. "It seems as if he deliberately chooses the most difficult path."

Theo found himself in the position of intermediary between the parents he revered and the brother he adored, trying to explain each to the other. His aging parents increasingly relied on him to look after the son to whom they referred as "the lost sheep." Unbeknown to Vincent, Theo began sending sixty francs a month to his parents for them to pass along to his brother. A few years later, when Vincent was considering where to live, his father wrote: "Just write to Theo, and arrange with him what is best, and what will be the cheapest way." As Vincent became ever more estranged from his parents, he became ever more dependent on Theo. Eventually, Theo was Vincent's link to the family he yearned to connect with but with which he couldn't stop quarreling. It was in letters and visits with Theo that Vincent kept the idea of home, family, and childhood alive. Each time he moved—and in his brief adulthood he would move more than two dozen times—Vincent never failed to describe his lodgings to Theo: the view from the window, the postcards (many of them supplied by Theo) he had nailed on the walls. It was as if by describing his rented room to his brother, he might make it a home. Vincent treasured the rare times Theo could get off work long enough to visit him in his far-flung retreats, when they'd take long walks and talk about art and family. As soon as Theo left, Vincent would write him a letter, picking up the thread of their conversation. "What a pleasant day we spent in Amsterdam," he wrote after one 1877 visit. "I stood watching your train until it was out of sight. We are such old friends already." Theo's visits buoyed Vincent as he resumed his solitary life. "I still keep thinking of the day you came to Brussels and of our visit to the museum," he wrote in 1878. "And I often wish you were a bit nearer and that we could be together more often. Do reply soon."

*   *   *

Theo van Gogh was part of a long tradition of brothers stepping in for ailing or absent parents. In 1695, after his mother and father died within a year of each other, twenty-three-year-old Johann Christoph Bach took in his thirteen-year-old brother, Johann Jacob, and his nine-year-old brother, Johann Sebastian. Although his modest income as church organist was hardly enough to provide for his own children, Cristoph not only fed and clothed his younger brothers, but taught Johann Sebastian to play the clavier and introduced him to the works of Pachelbel, under whom Cristoph had studied, and other great composers of the day. He would look after Johann Sebastian until the musical prodigy went away to school shortly before his fourteenth birthday. Nearly a century later, sixteen-year-old Ludwig van Beethoven, the eldest of three brothers, traveled to Vienna in hopes of studying with Mozart. In March 1787, two weeks after he arrived, Beethoven learned that his mother was ill with consumption. He rushed home to Bonn, but his mother died not long thereafter, pushing his father deeper into alcoholism. The adolescent Beethoven spent the next five years at home, taking care of his two younger brothers, helping pay for their upkeep by playing viola in the court orchestra. He would be twenty-one before he was able to get away again; by then, Mozart was dead.

Sydney Chaplin spent much of his childhood in late-Victorian London looking after his half-brother, Charlie, as they were shuttled through workhouses and charity institutions while their mother was intermittently confined to mental asylums. Years later, he would serve as Charlie's business manager. "It has always been my unfortunate predicament or should I say fortunate predicament? to concern myself with your protection," wrote Sydney. "This is the result of my fraternal or rather paternal instinct." In 1942, instructed by his dying father to make sure his frail, artistic younger brother went to college, John Warhola, a machine shop worker, not only helped pay Andy's way through the Carnegie Institute, but after his brother left for New York City and became Andy Warhol, he called him every Sunday until the artist's death in 1987. In 1992, following the deaths of his parents within several months of each other, twenty-one-year-old college student Dave Eggers assumed responsibility for his eight-year-old brother (cooking his meals, taking him to Little League practice, attending parent-teacher conferences), an experience he would recount in *A Heartbreaking Work of Staggering Genius*.

Sometimes a brother must protect a sibling from a parent. When the author Richard Rhodes was ten, his widowed father married a disturbed, sadistic woman who all but starved Richard and his brother, Stanley; permitted them to bathe only once a month; and beat them with belt buckles, broom handles, and stiletto heels, among other weapons. Their cowed father didn't intervene, but twelve-year-old, eighty-pound Stanley protected his younger brother as well as he could: scouring trash cans at drive-ins for half-eaten hamburgers, comforting him after beatings, standing up to their tormentor. When Richard, forbidden to use the bathroom at night, resorted to surreptitiously peeing into a bottle, Stanley smuggled the brimming vessel past their sleeping stepmother to the bathroom each morning and poured its contents into the toilet, muffling the splash with the sound of his own urination. After two years of escalating abuse, Stanley, worried that their stepmother might kill one or both of them, persuaded the police to place the brothers in a boys' home. "Stanley saved us," wrote Rhodes in *A Hole in the World,* his account of the ordeal.

The roles of keeper and kept are not fixed. Following Emancipation in 1863, John Washington, breaker-in of Booker's flax shirts, worked in a coal mine so that his younger brother could attend the Hampton Institute. When Booker graduated, he returned the favor, teaching school to help pay for John to study at Hampton himself. (Years later, as president of the Tuskegee Institute, Booker would employ his brother as superintendent of industries.) In 1968, Chuck Hagel, the future Nebraska senator, and his younger brother, Tom, were on patrol in the Mekong Delta during the Vietnam War when someone in their unit stumbled on a trip wire, setting off mines the enemy had hung in the trees. Seeing that Chuck was bleeding profusely from his chest, Tom, who had taken shrapnel in the arms and shoulders, tore open his brother's shirt and bandaged the wound, saving his life. Less than a month later, the Hagels' armored personnel carrier hit a land mine, triggering a barrage of Vietcong machine-gun fire. Badly burned from the initial blast but knowing the ammunition-laden vehicle would soon ignite, Chuck dragged his unconscious brother from the APC just before it exploded.

With a moody, alcoholic father, a doting but hypochondriacal mother, and a bright but unstable older brother who went off to sea, the young Walt Whitman was more parent than brother to his six younger siblings: teaching them how to spell, helping build a succession of family houses, and paying the lion's share of the family expenses as soon as he was old enough to work. It was "as if he had us in his charge . . . " said his brother George. "He was like us—yet he was different from us, too." Whenever there was a family crisis (and there were many; the Whitmans were a prodigiously troubled brood, touched by alcoholism, insanity, prostitution, and early death), it was to Walt his siblings turned. And though he felt close to only one of them—Jeff, an engineer who shared his love of opera and long walks, was, he said, his one "real brother" and only "understander"—Walt was always willing to foot a bill or extricate someone from a jam. When George's name appeared on the list of casualties after the Battle of Fredericksburg, Walt set out at once for the front, searching camps and hospitals, undergoing "the greatest suffering I ever experienced in my life," until he found his wounded brother. Two years later, when George was starving in a Confederate prison, it was Walt who pushed General Grant to negotiate the special prisoner exchange that freed him. That same year, when the eldest brother, Jesse, turned violent and threatened their mother with a chair, it was Walt who reluctantly had him committed to the Kings County Lunatic Asylum. And it was Walt who provided for Eddy, his epileptic, mentally disabled youngest brother, to whom he would leave the majority of his modest estate.

But in 1873, when fifty-four-year-old Walt was crippled by a stroke and immobilized by depression after the death of his beloved mother, George took Walt and Eddy into his Camden home. A stolid, practical man who worked as an inspector in a pipe foundry, George didn't understand his poetry-writing brother—of *Leaves of Grass,* he commented, "didn't think it worth reading—fingered it a little"—yet for eleven years he looked after Walt, who slept late, cared little for schedules, and could be, said George, "stubborner . . . than a load of bricks." (One can only imagine what George thought when a long-haired, velvet-coated, foppish young man who announced himself as Oscar Wilde showed up at his door to pay homage to Walt.) George and his wife named their first child for Walt, who, after the infant died at eight months, visited his grave every few days. In 1884, when George and his wife moved to a farm, they built a room for Walt, but he preferred the city and stayed in Camden, where, despite a series of strokes, he managed the last eight years of his life on his own. Walt never lost his sense of responsibility for his dwindling family. As he would tell an interviewer, a year before he died, "Tho' always unmarried I have had six children."

* * *

In the summer of 1879, Theo visited Vincent in the Borinage, the coal-mining region of southwest Belgium where Vincent served as a combination preacher-cum-teacher-cum-social-worker-cum-nurse to the miners and their families. (To the shock of the miners' wives, he even helped with the laundry.) In an area of abject poverty, Vincent was determined to be as wretched as his congregation. He abandoned his boardinghouse for a miner's hut; gave up his mattress for a bed of straw; redistributed most of the few shabby clothes he possessed; tore up his own underwear to bandage the miners' wounds; went barefoot even in winter; shared all but a few francs of what little money his father was able to send; lived on dry crusts of bread, frostbitten potatoes, and water; and stopped using soap. (Vincent's masochism may have been inspired by his desire to imitate the early Christian martyrs, but it surely stemmed as much from life-long feelings of unworthiness and, perhaps, an unacknowledged desire to outsacrifice his pastor father.) When the Evangelization Council, which had eventually agreed to sponsor him, accused him of "an excess of zeal bordering on the scandalous" and refused to reappoint him, Vincent continued ministering on his own. Alarmed by Vincent's behavior, his father threatened to have him committed to the asylum at Gheel. As Vincent described it years later: "My father assembled the family council to have me locked up like a madman; thanks to my oldest brother, that good Theodore, they left me alone." In what would become a sure sign of trouble, Vincent's letters to Theo grew less frequent. At night—cold, hungry, and unbearably lonely—Vincent could be heard weeping in his hut.

Vincent had hinted at his spartan life, but Theo was shocked by his brother's condition. The young man who three years ago had strode around London in a top hat—"you cannot be in London without one," he had airily written his mother—was dressed in what looked more like rags than clothes, his once-sturdy frame emaciated, his face as black with coal dust as any miner's. The contrast with his brother could hardly have been greater. Twenty-two-year-old Theo, attired in the black coat, vest, and tie of a respectable young businessman, had just been promoted to the Goupil office in Paris. Theo was on his way up in the world; Vincent seemed close to the bottom. As the brothers walked past slag heaps, dung hills, and abandoned mineshafts, Theo, who had been commissioned by his father to talk sense into his older brother, reminded Vincent of the walk they had taken seven years earlier to the mill at Rijswijk, when Vincent had been a promising young art dealer and Theo his eager disciple. Vincent had changed, Theo said. He talked about the pain Vincent's behavior was causing the family. He urged Vincent to try harder to get along with their aging father. Even Theo couldn't understand why Vincent was living like this. Wouldn't it be better, he suggested, to learn a trade—to become a printer, carpenter, baker, barber, or librarian—than to be an "idler" living at his parents' expense?

Vincent was devastated. Theo, alone in the family, alone in the world, had seemed to understand him. Now, like his parents and sisters, Theo saw him as the family problem. At the time, Vincent said little, and when he wrote Theo shortly afterward, he thanked him for the visit and called him his "compagnon de voyage." But Vincent insisted he wasn't willing to get a conventional job just to please his family. As for Theo's charge of "idleness," he observed that his backbreaking work as an evangelist was "a rather strange sort of 'idleness.'" In any case, he was determined to follow his own path. "It would indeed be a decisive answer (always supposing that it were possible to assume, quick as lightning, the form of a baker, a barber or a librarian); but at the same time it would be a foolish answer, more or less like the action of the man who, when reproached with cruelty for riding a donkey, immediately dismounted and continued his way with the donkey on his shoulders." Vincent closed with his customary sign-off—"a handshake in my thoughts"—but there was no mistaking his sense of betrayal.

Since Vincent didn't save his brother's letters, we don't know how Theo responded, or whether he responded at all. We do know that Vincent didn't write to his brother for nine months, the longest he ever went without writing him. But when Theo sent his brother fifty francs the following July, Vincent, like a prideful child who has been waiting for an excuse to make up with his best friend, grudgingly accepted the money—and the olive branch. "I am writing to you rather reluctantly because, for a good many reasons, I have kept silent for such a long time. To some extent you have become a stranger to me, and I to you perhaps more than you think. It is probably better for us not to go on like that." Vincent readdressed the charges Theo had made at their last visit, with an eloquence and forcefulness that suggest he had spent much of the intervening time thinking about them. It was the longest letter Vincent had ever written—a painstaking, scrupulous document, in which his need to be understood by Theo seems almost palpable, as if by explaining his life to his brother, he could explain it to himself. He acknowledged that their positions had changed. "If I have come down in the world, you have in a different way come up in it. . . . I am glad of that, I say that in all sincerity, and it will always give me pleasure." But he insisted that, in essentials, *he* hadn't changed since that day at the Rijswijk mill. "What has changed is that my life then was less difficult and my future seemingly less gloomy, but as far as my inner self, my way of looking at things and of thinking is concerned, that has not changed. But if there has indeed been a change, then it is that I think, believe and love more seriously now what I thought, believed and loved even then." As for getting a conventional job, he explained that though his journey seemed aimless to his family, there was purpose in it. "But what is your final goal, you may ask. That goal will become clearer, will emerge slowly but surely, much as the draft turns into the sketch and the sketch into the painting through the serious work done on it." Vincent compared himself to a caged bird in spring, which knows it should be out building nests and hatching young but can only bang its head against the bars. "Do you know what makes the prison disappear? Every deep, genuine affection. Being friends, being brothers, loving, that is what opens the prison, with supreme power, by some magic force." Reflecting on his ordeal in the Borinage, Vincent extended the ornithological metaphor. "What the moulting season is for birds—the time when they lose their feathers—setbacks, misfortune and hard times are for us human beings. You can cling on to the moulting season, you can also emerge from it reborn, but it must not be done in public."

In retrospect, Vincent's year in the Borinage may have been something like an alcoholic "hitting bottom," and Theo's visit may have carried the kind of galvanizing shock of a family "intervention," forcing Vincent, who had been struggling to reconcile his great obsessions—art and religion—into realizing what he really wanted to do. With this letter, he was serving notice that he had made his choice: he was determined to become an artist. And he was expressing, as plainly as his pride allowed, that Theo, his "compagnon de voyage," was a vital part of his new path.

———

The brothers entered into an unspoken partnership. Over the following several years, with the singlemindedness with which he had thrown himself into religion, Vincent worked at copy-book exercises into the night; studied anatomy texts and perspective manuals; visited museums; apprenticed himself to painters (and antagonized them until they broke with him); and filled sketchbook after sketchbook. "If I can only continue to work, somehow or other it will set me right again," he wrote Theo. Theo dedicated himself to supporting his brother. From his annual salary of 4,000 francs (excluding commissions), he sent Vincent 100 francs a month: 30 percent of his salary, about twice what a weaver earned at the time and, for a man who was also helping to support his parents and sisters, a considerable sacrifice. (When Theo got a raise, he boosted Vincent's allowance to 150 francs.) Theo also served as a one-man art warehouse, supplying Vincent with sketch pads, drawing paper, pencils, quill pens, sepia ink, art books, draftsmanship guides, prints, engravings, and anatomical illustrations of horses, cows, and sheep. Over the years, at Vincent's behest, Theo brokered introductions to other artists; forwarded letters; delivered drawings to friends; bought Vincent furniture; settled his brother's debts; put up struggling young artists in his apartment; researched painters in whom his brother expressed interest; passed along information on how to make lithographs or how to draw from engravings; aired out, varnished, or brushed with egg-white the paintings Vincent sent him; gave him feedback on his work; and sent him his old clothes—a rare instance in which an older brother got the hand-me-downs. In addition to his work at Goupil, Theo had what amounted to a second full-time job: his brother.

The brothers carried out their partnership largely by mail, as Vincent continued his peripatetic ways (during the ten post-Borinage years that remained to him he would live in eleven different places), while Theo, the still point in Vincent's turning world, spent the rest of his life in Paris. Some biographers have suggested that Vincent maintained close epistolary contact with Theo not to communicate with his beloved brother but to stay on good terms with his financial lifeline. In almost every letter Vincent dropped not-so-subtle hints ("I am still passing through a fairly difficult period right now. The cost of model, studio, drawing and painting materials keeps going up"), referred to his costs ("Of course I have to pay the people who pose. Not much, but because it happens every day it is one expense more"), or made direct requests ("Here we are at the beginning of another month, and although it's not yet a month since you sent me something, I would ask you to be kind enough to send me some more soon"). He assured Theo that the money fueled his art, not his stomach ("when I receive the money my greatest craving will not be for food, though I shall have been fasting, but even more so for painting—and I shall immediately go on a hunt for models and continue until all the money is gone"). He made frequent references to the privations he endured for his art (to pay for canvas and paint, he lived on bread and coffee for days at a time), and pointed out examples of his thrift (in Arles, he would make do with less expensive prostitutes, "the kind of 2-franc women who were originally intended for the Zouaves"). He asked for advances but complained if his monthly payment was a day late ("Am I less than your creditors? Who must wait, *they or I???*").

Yet money seemed less a motivation for writing his brother than an excuse to talk about art. In the same letter in which he pointedly mentioned being too weak to get food down, he had enough energy to go on for another six pages, rhapsodizing about his favorite hues. "Cobalt is a divine color, and there is nothing so beautiful for bringing atmosphere around things. Carmine is the red of wine, and it is warm and spirited like wine." Each letter brimmed with accounts of current projects, embellished with pen-and-ink illustrations ("I've been plodding away the last few days at a woman whom I saw pulling carrots in the snow last winter") and descriptions of scenes he wanted to sketch ("I see pictures and drawings in the most squalid little corners. I am irresistibly impelled to study them"). When, in 1882, partly at his brother's urging, Vincent began oil painting, his letters became even richer and more colorful, as if composed with the same thick brushstrokes he applied to his canvases. He told Theo what shade every inch of a painting would be. (For a model's head, he described "a flesh colour full of tonal values, with more bronze in the neck, jet-black hair—black which I had to do with carmine and Prussian blue—off-white for the little jacket, light yellow, much lighter than the white, for the background. A touch of flame red in the jet-black hair and again a flame-coloured bow in the off-white.") He discussed technical problems, evaluated artists of the past, and tested his theories about art on Theo as he had once tested his ideas about religion. "What I want to express, in both figure and landscape, isn't anything sentimental or melancholy, but deep anguish." (His postscript, asking for more drawing paper, was more prosaic: "Please remember the *thick* Ingres if you can, enclosed is another sample. I still have a supply of the thin kind. I can do watercolour washes on the *thick Ingres,* but on the sans fin, for instance, it always goes blurry, which isn't entirely my fault.") His letters to Theo seemed as necessary a part of his creative process as the paintings themselves. If he didn't describe a painting to his brother, it wasn't yet complete.

Vincent needed Theo not just as an audience for his art, but as a witness to his life. All his other relationships—with his parents, his sisters, his teachers, and his few friends—ended in misunderstanding and estrangement. Theo alone still put up with him, and it was to Theo that he detailed each twist in his melodramatic path: falling in unrequited love with Kee Vos, his widowed cousin; breaking with his mentors H. G. Tersteeg and Anton Mauve; setting up house with Sien Hoornik, a pregnant, alcoholic prostitute he planned to marry despite, or perhaps because of, the fierce opposition of his family. (In the end, he succumbed to Theo's arguments and left her.) From his brother, Vincent needed understanding, if not absolution. He felt compelled to tell Theo "all the thoughts that come into my head, without being afraid of rambling on now and then, without censoring my thoughts or holding them back." His letters to Theo constituted not only his artistic manifesto but also his confession. "If I couldn't give vent to my feelings now and then," he wrote, "I think the boiler would burst." After painting from dawn to dark, he stayed up almost every night to write. ("Dear brother, It is already late, but I want to write you once more. You are not here, but I wish you were, and sometimes it seems to me we are not far away from each other.") After he signed off ("a handshake in my thoughts, your loving brother Vincent"), he almost always wrote more—page after page—until his postscripts were longer than the letter proper. In writing, as in painting, Vincent couldn't stop. When he finally came to an end, he pleaded with Theo to write back soon.

If he didn't receive a reply promptly, Vincent confessed, he felt "absolutely cut off from the outer world."

Dealing with Vincent was such an all-consuming task that it was easy to forget—for Vincent, at least—that Theo worked six days a week at Goupil, often till late at night, frequently going on the road to inspect potential acquisitions or show paintings to prospective clients. In 1881, after little more than a year in Paris, Theo had been put in charge of the firm's annex on Boulevard Montmartre, where he developed a reputation for being a sensitive, honorable young dealer. Theo even persuaded his bosses to let him show some of the Impressionists, a controversial new group of painters scorned by the art establishment as childish amateurs. In 1884, Theo sold a landscape by Pissarro; the following year he would show Sisley, Monet, and Renoir. Although not an aggressive salesman, Theo was quietly passionate about the artists he believed in. "He was pale, blond and so melancholy that he seemed to hold canvases the way beggars hold their wooden bowls," recalled the Symbolist poet Gustave Kahn. "His profound conviction of the value of the new art was stated without vigor, and thus without great success. He did not have a barker's gift. But this salesman was an excellent critic and engaged in discussions with painters and writers as the discriminating art lover he was." The Impressionists respected Theo not just because he was one of the few dealers willing to handle their work, or because he was one of the few dealers they trusted to dry and frame their paintings properly, but because, in a notoriously cutthroat business, he was interested in them as people as much as in how much their canvases sold for. ("At times I have my doubts about which I like most, the painter himself or his work," Theo confessed.) When Albert Besnard was in sudden need of 200 francs, he came to Theo—"You are the only person I can turn to," he wrote—and Theo obliged. When the elderly Pissarro couldn't pay his rent, Theo advanced him money against future sales, sales he knew might never take place. It frustrated Theo that the work he most admired was so little appreciated. A friend observed that whenever Theo sold a canvas by an established artist for ten or twenty thousand francs "but tried in vain to obtain 400 francs for a fine painting by Pissarro, his heart was invaded by hate, an inevitable and ferocious irritation." (It was an irritation no doubt fueled by his frustration on his brother's behalf.) Like Vincent, he despaired at the foolishness of certain clients. "What can I do," he wrote his sister, "when some one demands a picture, as happened the other day, where the sun and moon must appear simultaneously?" Unlike his brother, Theo was willing to compromise: "I let it be painted."

Biographers emphasize the differences between the brothers— Vincent the ornery, unpredictable artist, Theo the practical, tenderhearted man of business. But the brothers, as Vincent liked to point out, had much in common: their tendency to melancholy, their thriftiness, their love of reading, their appetite for work, their eye for color, their fondness for long walks in "gray weather," their loneliness, their inclination to "analyze things." "How curious it is that you and I often seem to have the same thoughts," Vincent wrote. One senses that "respectable" Theo would have liked to be a little less respectable, a little more like Vincent. Although it occasioned him no end of aggravation, he admired his brother's unyielding nature and fretted that he himself was too pliable. In his letters, one can hear him trying on Vincent's persona. When he wrote his sister Lies in October 1885, it could have been Vincent speaking: "The more people one meets, the more one sees that they are hiding behind the accepted language of convention; what they really mean when they say they are sincere is so often trivial and malicious." If Theo wished he had a bit more Vincent in him, so, too, did Vincent. Though he liked to chaff Theo about playing the "lucky dog" to his *mauvais coucheur,* Vincent was delighted whenever Theo shed his buttoned-down self. It made Vincent feel less alone. In 1883, after visiting Vincent and Sien in The Hague, respectable Theo confessed that he, too, had taken in a woman from the streets, a girl from Brittany who had a tumor in her foot and couldn't work. Vincent was ecstatic. "To you and me there appeared on a cold, pitiless pavement the downcast, sorrowful figure of a woman," he wrote, with the brio of a romance novelist, "and neither you nor I passed her by, but both of us stopped and followed the dictates of our human heart." He prodded his brother for details ("I'm eager to hear how well up your woman is in artistic matters"), recommended books ("I think the works of Michelet would be something to soothe and strengthen her mind"), and urged Theo to bring her home to Holland, perhaps hoping their father would see that his Jacob could be just as embarrassing as his Esau ("Who knows whether it might not help to set right certain things concerning my own woman"). Theo did not introduce her to his parents. When he told them he was thinking of marrying the woman, Pastor van Gogh and his wife, worried that their worst fear—that Theo was taking after Vincent—was coming true, told Theo the relationship was not in keeping with "the dignity of his calling." (Perhaps not coincidentally, once he had broken with Sien Hoornik, Vincent—who, without ever having met Theo's woman, had urged Theo to marry her and have a child—began to question the woman's suitability, worried that she had a craving for "greatness," and likened her to Lady Macbeth.) The problem was solved when Theo's "patient," as he called her, having been restored to health at his expense, ran away one night and never returned.

It has been suggested that Vincent saw Theo as his alter ego. Indeed, Vincent seems to have had difficulty seeing Theo as a separate person with a life of his own. In 1883, Theo, beset by depression and anxiety, confessed he was thinking of emigrating to New York, a city said to be receptive to artistic innovation, and opening his own gallery. Blaming Theo's malaise on his profession ("it seems to me that the whole art business is rotten"), Vincent suggested a career change. "Come and paint with me on the heath, in the potato field, come and walk with me behind the plough and the shepherd, come and sit with me, looking into the fire—let the storm that blows across the heath blow through you," he wrote from Drenthe, in the northeast Netherlands, a dreary region of peat bogs and incessant rain. He urged Theo to admit to himself: "I don't want the city any longer, I want the country. I don't want an office, I want to paint." Ignoring the fact that Theo had never completed so much as a sketch, Vincent insisted that being an artist was not a matter of talent but an act of will. He pointed to fraternal precedent. "Throughout the history of art one repeatedly finds the phenomenon of two brothers being painters," he wrote, citing the Ostades, the Van Eycks, the Bretons. He even chose a specialty for his brother ("there is a famous *paysagiste* inside you"), offered to give him lessons, and calculated how much money the pair might save if they lived together as artists. "In my view it would be an *erreur de point de vue* were you to continue in business in Paris," Vincent declared. "The conclusion then: two brother painters."

It is hard to tell how serious Vincent was. He knew that if Theo gave up his job it would mean the end of his monthly stipend. (At the close of one hortatory missive he added, sheepishly, "If you could send me some money towards the end of this month. . . . I would risk buying a few shirts and drawers which I need very, very badly.") He may have been trying to shock Theo into staying at Goupil. He may just have wanted the company; he was even more lonely than usual in the moors of Drenthe, and admitted that in addition to his desire to see Theo tap his hidden talents, he could use a "comrade." There is no evidence that Theo took Vincent's career advice any more seriously than Vincent had taken Theo's advice, four years earlier, to become a baker. When his sales figures took an upturn, Theo's spirits did too, and talk of emigration ceased.

Vincent's desire for Theo to become an artist was part of his life-long battle with the father he both scorned and wanted to please. If Theo became a painter, he would be choosing Vincent and the artistic life. If Theo stayed with Goupil, he would be choosing their father and bourgeois respectability. (That Theo, with his well-cut suits and neatly trimmed mustache, bore an uncanny resemblance to Pastor van Gogh cannot have helped.) "Are you a 'Van Gogh' too?" pointedly asked Vincent, for whom the family surname had become a kind of shorthand for his father's cautious conformism, and part of the reason he signed his paintings, simply, *Vincent*.

Van Gogh or not, Vincent moved home from time to time to save money, but he and his aging father quarreled bitterly—three or four hours at a stretch, Vincent attacking all the values his father held dear. "You're poisoning my life," Pastor van Gogh would finally say. "You'll be the death of me." Though Vincent's biographers tend to paint Theo as a virtuous milquetoast who reflexively kowtowed to his intransigent brother, Theo was one of the few people who dared criticize Vincent's boorish behavior, especially when directed at their parents. On Christmas Day 1881, when Vincent refused to attend church with his family and was ordered from the house by his exasperated father, Theo was furious. "That you could not bear it there any longer is possible, and that you differ in opinion with people who have lived all their lives in the country and have not come into contact with modern life is not unnatural," he wrote. "But, confound it, what made you so childish and impudent as to embitter and spoil Father's and Mother's life in that way?" Vincent annotated the letter, answering his brother's charges point by point, and mailed it back to Theo. ("Please don't think I'm sending your letter back to offend you, I simply believe this is the quickest way of answering it clearly.") During their momentous walk in the Borinage, Theo had accused Vincent of changing. Now Vincent accused Theo of the same thing. Theo, he said, was becoming more and more like their father, determined to "maintain a certain social position—a certain affluence," while he, Vincent, was becoming less and less like him, "uglier and rougher still." But, said Vincent, "I shall be a painter, in short a creature with feeling." He invoked the memory of their walk to the Rijswijk mill. "And I see those same two brothers in earlier years—when you had just entered the art world, had just begun to read . . . *Feeling, thinking and believing the same* to such an extent—that I wonder: can those be the same two? Wonder: what will the outcome be—will they separate for ever or will they take the same path once and for all?" Vincent repeatedly, vexingly, referred to Theo as "Father II."

Their father's shadow loomed over another area of fraternal tension: the conflict between artist and dealer. Ever since Vincent left Goupil he had disparaged the art business, and now he accused Theo of bowing down before the "money devil." Referring to Eugène Delacroix's famous painting of the 1830 revolution, *Liberty on the Barricades,* he compared Theo and himself to fighters on opposite sides of the barricade—"you before it as a soldier of the government, I behind it as a revolutionary." Theo must have found it annoying that at the same time his bosses were carping at him for caring more about artistic innovation than about commerce (for being, in short, a cultural revolutionary), Vincent was accusing him of the exact opposite. But he responded mildly, whereupon Vincent, like a child whose parent won't rise to the bait, stepped up his attack. Not only was Theo a philistine dealer, he said, he wasn't even a good one. "You have *never yet* sold a *single thing* I have done—whether for a lot or a little—*in fact, you haven't even tried.*" (It was true that Theo wasn't trying hard to sell his brother's work. He had trouble enough selling the Impressionists, much less Vincent's powerful but crude drawings of gnarled old peasants uprooting carrots in the snow.) In a postscript longer than the letter itself, Vincent's fury became more generalized. "What I have had against you this past year is a kind of relapse into cold respectability which seems to me sterile and futile—the diametrical opposite of everything that is active, and of everything that is artistic in particular." He went on to blame Theo for his breakup with Sien, for his meager social life, and even for his loneliness: "A *wife* you cannot give me, a *child* you cannot give me, *work* you cannot give me. Money, yes—but what good is that to me?" Vincent said that he was speaking frankly so that Theo could see "why I can no longer think of you as a brother and a friend with the same pleasure as before."

Theo endured Vincent's baiting with Job-like forbearance. (There was more than one masochist in the Van Gogh family.) No matter how disagreeably Vincent acted, Theo kept the oath they had sworn at the Rijswijk mill. Describing Theo's love and support for his brother as part of his "every breath, every heartbeat, and every thought," their sister Lies added that "Never for one moment did he doubt the future of Vincent's art." To Lies, Theo observed, "Vincent is one of those who has gone through all the experiences of life and has retired from the world; now we must wait and see if he has genius. I think he has." At the same time, it must be said that although Vincent frequently threatened to break with Theo and end their financial relationship—a curious bargaining chip, considering it was Theo who was giving *him* money—Vincent never truly broke with his brother, either. And so Vincent's rambling, pleading, badgering, soul-searching letters continued to pour into Paris, where Theo read them, addressed his brother's needs as best he could, then placed them in the bottom drawer of his desk. After his death, his widow would find some 670 of them there.

In March 1885, Pastor van Gogh had a stroke at the front door of his presbytery and died at the age of sixty-three. In April, Vincent painted *The Potato Eaters,* his first full-scale composition and his first masterpiece. A short time later he started painting in vibrant color. Their father's death may have liberated Theo as well; in April he bought Boussod & Valadon (as Goupil's was now known) its first paintings by Monet, and the following year, he got grudging permission to devote two small, low-ceilinged rooms on the mezzanine of his Montmartre annex to the Impressionists, an arrangement tolerated as long as Theo continued to make the company huge profits from the Salon warhorses that covered the ground-floor walls.

Pastor van Gogh's death had a soothing effect on the brothers' relationship. Vincent stopped attacking Theo for being a philistine. He compared the two of them with Edmond and Jules de Goncourt, the French brothers who collaborated on their popular novels and social histories. In December 1885, Vincent urged Theo to think about "what the de Goncourts went through, and how at the end of their lives they were melancholy, yes, but felt sure of themselves, knowing that they had *accomplished* something, that their work would remain." Three months later, in March 1886, Vincent took the train to Paris and met Theo at the Louvre.

*   *   *

Acting as one's brother's keeper is especially complicated when that brother is physically or mentally disabled. In addition to helping care for the disabled sibling, the so-called normal sibling may feel unspoken pressure to make no demands of his own, lest he add to the stress of an already overburdened family. In the words of the psychotherapist Jeanne Safer, who grew up with an emotionally troubled older brother, "The sibling of the child with special needs is not supposed to have any needs." He may also feel pressure to compensate for a disturbed or disabled sibling by being "perfect." ("You shall and must be our joy and honour!" Theo van Gogh's parents pleaded. "We cannot do without it.") Sensing he is the repository of his parents' hopes and dreams, he may be driven to over-achieve. As he grows, he may have difficulty finding the middle ground: forging an identity of his own without abandoning his sibling, integrating his sibling into his life without letting him consume it.

Theo van Gogh sacrificed his money, time, health, and identity to tend to Vincent. The psychologist Stephen Bank points out that there can be a cost to the kept as well: the risk of becoming weaker, more passive, less competent. Someone who is always provided for may grow comfortable in that role—psychologists call it learned helplessness—and have difficulty becoming a separate individual able to function on his own. (Theo's all-encompassing support of Vincent was the kind of behavior that, a century later, addiction specialists would call "enabling"—behavior that, however well-intentioned, may further erode the independence of the addict.) The symbiotic relationship between keeper and kept is invariably more complicated than it may appear.

Both Homer Collyer and his younger brother, Langley, were used to being coddled. Although they had degrees from Columbia—Homer in law, Langley in engineering—they rarely worked, living with their doting, overprotective mother well into their forties. (Their father, a wealthy Manhattan gynecologist, had moved out years earlier.) After their mother's death in 1929, the brothers grew more and more reclusive, holing up in the family's four-story Harlem brownstone, accumulating possessions at a rate that would make the Collyer name synonymous with pathological hoarding. One by one, their gas, telephone, electricity, and water were turned off for nonpayment, and they lived in their dark house, moving cautiously among ever-growing piles of junk. After Homer went blind in 1934 and, several years later, was immobilized to a near-fetal position by rheumatism, Langley devoted himself to his brother: He cooked his meals; cut up his meat; poured his wine; peeled him a hundred oranges a week (a diet the brothers mistakenly believed would improve Homer's eyesight); bathed him; read him Shakespeare, Dickens, and out-of-date newspapers; and, because there was no water to flush the toilets, bottled his brother's urine and excrement in jars he stored on the second floor. At night, Langley ventured outside on foraging expeditions, dragging a cardboard box at the end of a rope, gathering discarded fruit from trash cans as well as scavenging rubbish to add to the mountains that filled their house. Returning home, he'd crawl through tunnels he'd made in twelve-foot walls of bundled newspapers, avoiding booby traps he'd set for prowlers, which, when tripped, released avalanches of detritus, to bring food to his brother. He tried to stay awake all night. "I have a way of relaxing without sleeping so I can be ready to answer my brother whenever he needs anything," he said.

Did Homer want to be kept or was he a kind of prisoner? Was Langley selfless or selfish? The truth of their entwined lives may never be known. "My brother isn't well," Langley told a neighbor. "If he dies I'm going to jump in the river. He's all I have to live for."

On March 21, 1947, alerted by neighbors to a strong odor coming from the Collyer home, police forced their way in and bored through the floor-to-ceiling mess till they found Homer's body, curled up on the floor in a tattered bathrobe. They couldn't find his brother. As police searched for Langley across the city, workers began carting away two decades' worth of accumulated debris from the house: umbrellas, bicycles, baby carriages, dressmaker's dummies, desiccated Christmas trees, toy trains, phonograph records, thousands of empty cans, reams of sheet music, hope chests, 28,000 books, six American flags, eight live cats, a two-headed baby preserved in formaldehyde, a horse's jawbone, an accordion, two pipe organs, five violins, fourteen pianos, and the canoe in which the Collyers' father had paddled each day to his job at Bellevue Hospital. In all, 187 tons were hauled away.

Eighteen days after Homer was found, a worker discovered another body, trapped between a mahogany chest and an old sewing machine. It was Langley. He had been crawling through a newspaper tunnel to bring food to his brother when he was smothered by falling debris. The trap he'd built to protect his brother had trapped him. He died ten feet from Homer, who, without Langley to feed him, starved to death a few days later. According to detectives, Langley had been turned toward Homer, his hand stretched out as if reaching for his brother.

*   *   *

Vincent arrived in Paris in poor condition. Years of neglect had taken their toll: his body was gaunt and his teeth were so rotten he could hardly chew his food. On the verge of turning thirty-three, he looked closer to fifty. Theo sent Vincent to his doctor, who replaced ten of his decayed teeth with a dental plate. He gave up his evenings at the Holland Club to take Vincent to dinner. He paid for Vincent's art classes under the renowned academic painter Fernand Cormon. He rented a larger apartment so Vincent could have a studio. "We are getting along well in the new flat," Theo wrote his mother. "You would not recognize Vincent, he has changed so much. . . . If we can keep it up, then I think he has the worst behind him; and he is going to come out on top."

Theo had always put a good face on things when reporting back to his parents. As roommates, practical, fastidious Theo and sloppy, unpredictable Vincent comprised a nineteenth-century odd couple whose misadventures might have provided raw material for a French farce had they not been so distressing to Theo. Vincent left paints on the floor for visitors to step in; he rarely replaced the caps on his oozing tubes; he propped wet paintings against the walls; he used Theo's socks to clean his canvases; he left his threadbare underwear strewn about. After a long day at the gallery, Theo would come home to find his painstakingly furnished apartment a mess and Vincent, his perennial need for engagement whetted by years of solitude, eager to deliver the oral equivalent of his letters far into the night. Whenever Theo tried to end the conversation by going to sleep, Vincent would follow him into his bedroom, pull up a chair, and keep talking. Vincent could be tender and considerate one moment, surly and unreasonable the next. Sometimes, no matter what eager-to-please Theo did, Vincent found fault. "There was a time when I loved Vincent dearly and he was my best friend but that is no longer the case," Theo wrote their youngest sister, Willemina. "He seems to think it is even worse for him because he never misses a chance of showing his contempt for me and telling me that I fill him with loathing. This makes sharing an apartment with him almost unbearable. Nobody wants to come to my house any more because there are always rows and because he is so filthy and untidy the place is an absolute shambles." Wil advised Theo to "leave Vincent for God's sake." But Theo demurred. "It is such a peculiar case. If he only had another profession, I would long ago have done what you advise me. I have often asked myself if I have not been wrong in helping him continually, and have often been on the point of leaving him to his own devices. After receiving your letter I have thought it over again, but I think in this case I must continue in the same way. He is certainly an artist, and if what he makes now is not always beautiful, it will certainly be of use to him later; then his work will perhaps be sublime."

Vincent liked to refer to Theo as a "lucky dog," but during their time in Paris, Theo's life was even more troubled than his brother's—enough to make one wonder whether Theo felt the need to prove to Vincent that he, too, occasionally needed looking after. Europe was in a depression, the art business was in a slump, and Theo was tired of fighting his bosses to show the Impressionists. Vincent was badgering him to pursue his long-held dream of opening his own gallery, but when Theo asked Uncle Cent for financial backing, he was refused. Theo had always been susceptible to psychosomatic ailments; now that he was beset by problems at work and at home, his chronic cough worsened, his face swelled up ("it has literally disappeared," wrote Andries Bonger, a close friend of Theo's who lived with the brothers for a summer), and at one point he had an attack of nerves so severe he was temporarily paralyzed. Theo told his sister Lies that he did not think he would live to see thirty.

Furthermore, Theo's romantic life made Vincent's look almost healthy. Like Vincent, Theo tended to become became infatuated with women he barely knew, while his few flesh-and-blood relationships were with prostitutes or other women of a lower social station whom he felt compelled to rescue. Theo was trying to end an affair with a disturbed young woman who had moved in with the brothers, bringing still more chaos to the household. Even an emotional Good Samaritan like Vincent felt the woman was a bad match for Theo. (In a memorable instance of the pot calling the kettle black, he described her as "seriously deranged.") Nevertheless, he advised Theo not to turn the woman out lest it drive her to suicide. The ideal solution, said Vincent, was for Theo to foist her off on someone else. He volunteered himself for the job. "I am ready to take S. off your hands," he wrote Theo, while his brother was in Holland on business, "*i.e.* preferably *without* having to marry her, but if the worst comes to the worst *even* agreeing to a *mariage de raison*." Theo did not take his brother up on his bizarre offer.

Part of the reason Theo wanted to end his relationship with the young woman was that he wanted to begin one with Andries Bonger's younger sister, an English teacher for whom he had developed a Vincent-like obsession since being introduced to her the previous year. Vincent, who summed up his romantic philosophy to Theo as "If ever you fall in love, do so without reservation," urged Theo to express his feelings. After meeting her three times, Theo abruptly proposed; the shocked girl refused him, saying that she was in love with someone else—a situation reminiscent of Vincent's ill-fated courtship of his London landlady's daughter.

Theo eventually disentangled himself from the troubled young woman. His health and his sales figures improved. So did his relationship with his roommate. As they walked the avenues of Paris, the brothers made an unusual pair: Theo striding forward in his pressed suit, polished boots, and carefully trimmed brown beard; Vincent bobbing alongside, gesticulating wildly as he pressed a point, wearing worn boots, patched trousers, a mangy rabbit's fur cap, a scraggly red beard, and a paint-spattered blue smock of the kind favored by Flemish cattle drovers. It was a heady time for the brothers, not unlike those early days when they both worked for Goupil. But their shared excitement was no longer confined to letters. Two years earlier, Vincent had never seen an Impressionist painting. *"There is a school—I believe—of impressionists,"* he had written Theo. *"But I know very little about it."* Now he and Theo were visiting the studios of Monet, Sisley, and Seurat. Now he was discussing color theory and brushstroke technique in Montmartre cafés with Signac, Anquetin, Pissarro, and Guillaumin. Vincent's own paintings burst into color ("He is trying very hard to put more sunlight into them," Theo wrote Lies); his gloomy potato fields were replaced by radiant street scenes, his peasants by boulevardiers, his birds' nests by lilies, chrysanthemums, roses, asters, sunflowers. If his paintings, which he exhibited at a few Montmartre restaurants, made the public "a little disconcerted," as one observer put it, and failed to make a single sale, they impressed his fellow artists.

Theo was expanding Vincent's world; Vincent was also expanding Theo's. He introduced his brother to Toulouse-Lautrec and Émile Bernard, whom he'd met at Cormon's. He took him to Père Tanguy's paint shop, a gathering place for young artists. Exchanging canvases with other painters, he started a small art collection for himself and Theo. He created a circle of painters and friends of which his shy, modest brother became a part. At Vincent's urging, Theo entered more fully into the Impressionist market. Almost every evening between 5:00 and 8:00, critics, artists, and collectors gathered at Theo's mezzanine outpost for spirited discussions that continued into the night at nearby cafés. Living together gave the brothers new respect for each other. Vincent, seeing firsthand all that Theo did for avant-garde artists, would never again deride his brother as a philistine ("he is no ordinary dealer who rarely spares a thought for the painters," he explained to his sister Wil). Theo saw how other painters admired Vincent's talent and were drawn to his forceful personality. He grew more convinced than ever of Vincent's genius. "It is amazing the number of things that he knows and what a clear view he has of the world," Theo wrote Lies. "This is why I am sure if he still has a few years to live, he will make a name for himself."

Like a miner too long underground who ventures into the light, Vincent eventually found the hurly-burly of Paris overwhelming. Drinking excessive amounts of red wine and absinthe, he grew increasingly cranky. "The man hasn't the slightest notion of social behavior," Andries Bonger wrote his parents. "He has no manners whatsoever. He is at loggerheads with everyone." Even Vincent's closest friend, Bernard, admitted that Vincent could be difficult: "He was vehement in speech, interminable in explaining and developing his ideas, but not very ready to argue." Painting with Vincent was a contact sport. "Close beside me he shouted and gesticulated, brandishing his large, freshly covered canvas," wrote Signac, "and with it he smeared himself and passersby with all the colors of the rainbow." Eventually, models refused to pose for him, gendarmes forbade him to paint in the streets, and, Theo wrote tersely, "because of his volatile disposition this repeatedly led to scenes, which upset him *so* much that he became completely unapproachable." Worn down, restless, disillusioned with the city (Paris, he said, had the "tainted air of a hospital"), Vincent told his brother that he was moving on again, this time to the south of France. In February 1888, two years after he had met his brother at the Louvre, Theo accompanied Vincent to the Gare de Lyon and said good-bye. Vincent had left almost as suddenly as he'd arrived. The previous evening, he had recruited Bernard to help him cover the walls of his room with his paintings—"so that my brother will think me still here," he explained. Theo was bereft nonetheless. "When he came here two years ago, I never thought we would become so attached to one another, and now I am alone again in the apartment," Theo wrote Wil. "If I can, I shall find someone to share my house with, but someone like Vincent is not easy to replace."

* * *

For all those who step in to protect a brother from a playground bully or nurse a brother on his deathbed, there are those who fade into the background, look the other way, or shrink from the task. Faced with parental loss or neglect, some siblings quarrel and compete, each trying to save his or her own skin. Under stress, some siblings abandon or betray each other. Some simply drift apart. For every Theo van Gogh there is a Herbert Silver. A seventy-two-year-old retiree in Blissford, England, Silver called the police one day in 2004 and told them that his seventy-five-year-old brother, George, with whom he shared a trailer, had died. A postmortem found that George had been dead for as long as eighteen months. Herbert hadn't noticed. He admitted that he had found it a "bit odd" when his brother failed to emerge from his bedroom day after day, month after month, but noted that "George liked to keep himself to himself, and to be honest so do I." Furthermore, he pointed out, "I'm not my brother's keeper."

How does one weigh his responsibility to his sibling against his responsibility to himself? To society? Years ago, not long after I began dating Anne, we were playing the board game Scruples, in which players are presented with hypothetical moral dilemmas. On her turn, Anne was asked whether, if she were to learn that her brother had killed someone, she would go to the police. Anne, without a moment's hesitation, said no. I was astonished. Shoplifting, perhaps even armed robbery, but murder? No, she repeated. Quoting E. M. Forster—"If I had to choose between betraying my country and betraying my friend, I hope I should have the guts to betray my country"—she said she would never turn in her brother, no matter what he had done. She knew he would have had a good reason for killing, and she knew he would never kill again.

For Anne, the question has remained hypothetical. Others have not been so fortunate. When George Atzerodt, a Booth co-conspirator, was on the run after the Lincoln assassination (assigned to kill Vice President Andrew Johnson, he lost his nerve and got drunk instead), his older brother, John, with whom he had for several years operated a carriage repair shop, considered it his duty to inform the authorities that George might be found at their cousin's home in Maryland. Four decades later, a young English soldier in South Africa faced an even more immediate choice. Driving a gun carriage in the Royal Horse Artillery during the Boer War, he saw his brother lying wounded on the ground directly in his path. Having been ordered never to swerve from his line in battle, he closed his eyes and drove the gun carriage over his brother. The London newspaper that reported the story praised him for doing his duty as a soldier. This set off a heated dinner-table argument among the teenage Leonard Woolf and his brothers. Herbert, the eldest, declared that the boy's loyalty to his brother trumped his duty to his country; Leonard declared the opposite. If Herbert had been lying on the battlefield, Leonard added, he would surely have driven over *him*, a scenario he went on to describe in such vivid detail that his mother and sister sobbed for hours at the prospect. (It should be noted that Leonard wasn't particularly close to his five brothers, none of whom were invited to his wedding when he married Virginia Stephen.)

In 1995, when David Kaczynski, a forty-six-year-old youth counselor in Schenectady, New York, read "Industrial Society and Its Future," a 35,000-word essay published in the *Washington Post*, he didn't want to believe that its author, the so-called Unabomber, who had killed three people and maimed twenty-three over the previous seventeen years, might be his fifty-three-year-old brother, Ted. Growing up in a bookish family in a middle-class Chicago suburb, David had idolized his older brother, a math prodigy with an IQ of 167 who skipped two grades and spent hours locked in his room practicing differential equations. Ted was a moody loner so withdrawn that his mother considered enrolling him in a study of autistic children run by the psychiatrist Bruno Bettelheim. The only person with whom he seemed able to sustain a connection was David, a bookish but relatively outgoing fellow who admired Ted's independence, his originality, and his uncompromising intellect. David felt honored when Ted invited him into his room to show him his coin collection, to play recorder duets he had composed, or to hear him read from Edgar

Allan Poe. "In high school, I sort of became my brother—or at least tried to," David later wrote. "I made myself into the class 'brain,' concentrating on math just like Ted. Although I had a few friends, all National Honor Society types, I grew more socially aloof and never dated. Once an all-star second baseman in our local Little League, I dropped baseball to concentrate on academics." David was proud when he finished high school at sixteen, not much older than Ted had been when he had graduated. He was disappointed when, unlike Ted, he was rejected by Harvard. "But by then I already knew that I was no match for my brilliant older brother."

Ted seemed headed for a distinguished career in theoretical mathematics. But at the age of twenty-seven, after teaching at Berkeley for two years, Ted resigned. When Ted and David were children, their father had taken them hiking, and now Ted talked of living off the land beyond reach of modern technology. In 1969, Ted and David, who was by now an English major at Columbia, spent the summer driving across western Canada, looking for land Ted could homestead. A few years later, they pooled their savings to buy a few acres in Montana, where Ted built a crude one-room cabin. He would spend the next two decades living without electricity, telephone, or running water; foraging for edible plants; tending a vegetable garden; hunting rabbits; reading history, anthropology, and political philosophy; and writing hundreds of letters to his brother and his parents, in which he railed against the encroachment of the outside world on his wilderness life. On occasion, he left the cabin to buy supplies in the nearest town, or to work a menial job for a few months to supplement the money David and his parents sent him on his birthday and at Christmas. Ted approved when David, once again emulating his brother, gave up his job teaching high school English to live alone in a lean-to without electricity or running water in the mountains of West Texas. The brothers wrote each other often from their respective retreats. But Ted's letters grew increasingly vitriolic, bristling with diatribes against the industrial world.

In 1986, David spent two weeks at Ted's cabin. It was the first time he had seen his brother in several years. Ted seemed obsessive, angry, a little unbalanced. And yet there were reassuring moments. One day, while David was sawing wood, the worktable collapsed and David fell. His first worry was that Ted would be furious because his table was broken. But Ted put a hand on his shoulder—a moment of intimacy all the more memorable because of its rarity—and asked whether he was okay. David felt a rush of love for his brother. Three years later, however, when David told Ted he intended to marry an old high school friend and move to Schenectady, thereby rejoining the world Ted had rejected, Ted said he wanted nothing more to do with him. Ted, it was clear, felt betrayed. But Ted was not too proud to ask his brother for money, and David, who found a job counseling runaways at a shelter, was concerned enough about his brother to send it.

Although David worried about Ted's mental state, he didn't connect his troubled brother to the man who for nearly two decades had been sending bombs through the mail. But in 1995, at his wife's urging, he read the Unabomber's manifesto, which argued that the bombs were a necessary extreme to call attention to the ways technology had eroded human freedoms. He found the locutions and epithets in the essay strikingly similar to those in letters Ted had written. Horrified to think that the older brother he'd idolized could be a murderer, and tormented by the knowledge that the money he'd sent him might have financed some of the attacks, David spent several months collecting evidence that might prove his brother's guilt or innocence, and agonizing over whether and how to turn his brother in, knowing that if Ted were guilty, he'd likely be executed. In February 1996, after consulting with a graphologist, David gave the FBI directions to his brother's shack. "The thought that another person would die and I was in the position to stop that—I couldn't live with that," he said later.

The brothers hadn't seen each other in almost twelve years when a manacled Ted entered the Sacramento courtroom for his arraignment. David and his mother were sitting in the front row. Ted shuffled past them without a glance. When David left his job at the shelter to assist in his brother's legal defense, hoping to help him avoid the death penalty, Ted derided his efforts, adding that he preferred death to spending his life in prison. Diagnosed by court-appointed psychiatrists as a paranoid schizophrenic (a diagnosis he vehemently rejected), Ted pled guilty and was sentenced to serve four life terms.

In the months that followed, many people praised David's decision to turn in his brother as the only ethical choice. Some condemned it as a fraternal betrayal. Ted, calling David another "Judas Iscariot," suggested that his brother's decision was less an act of conscience than an expression of sibling rivalry. "It's quite true that he is troubled by guilt over what he's done," Ted wrote, "but I think his sense of guilt is outweighed by his satisfaction at having finally gotten revenge on big brother." In 2001, David became executive director of New Yorkers Against the Death Penalty, traveling the state to speak out against capital punishment. A painfully earnest man—the teenagers he counseled had called him Mr. Rogers— David seemed to relive his decision in every speech he gave. "Brothers are supposed to protect each other," he told audiences, "and here, perhaps, I was sending my brother to his death." He says he loves his brother. He has continued to write to him, every month at first and then, as the years passed, several times a year. His brother has never written back. "I hope that Ted will someday forgive me," David says.

Who is to say which man better serves as his brother's keeper—the man who turns in his murderous brother, or the man who refuses to turn in his? Almost every Bostonian of a certain age can recite the story of Whitey and Billy Bulger, a story so melodramatic it could provide the lyrics to a contemporary Irish-American ballad. How they grew up sharing a bedroom in the Irish-Catholic enclave of South Boston in the 1940s. How hot-tempered Whitey dropped out of high school to steal cars, boost merchandise off delivery trucks, and rob banks. How Billy, his younger brother by five years, played baseball, collected matchbook covers, served as altar boy, hung out at the library, rode the trolley across town to a private Catholic school, and worked afternoons at a local meat market to pay his tuition. How, after spending nine years at an assortment of federal prisons, including Alcatraz and Leavenworth, Whitey returned to Boston and worked as an enforcer for local mobsters, killing his way up the ranks to become the city's most powerful organized-crime boss. How, after studying Greek language and English literature at Boston College, Billy considered the priesthood but went to law school and became a politician instead, finessing his way up the ranks to become president of the Massachusetts Senate.

From the late 1970s to the mid-1990s, the Bulger brothers were the two most powerful men in Boston. Billy controlled state politics from his wood-paneled chambers under the gold dome of the State House on Beacon Hill; Whitey controlled the city's organized crime from the dimly lit, low-ceilinged confines of the Triple O's Lounge in South Boston. Portrayed in the press as a classic good brother/bad brother pair, the Pericles-quoting politician and the gun-toting mobster shared certain traits. Both were intelligent, disciplined, charismatic, and ambitious. Both had a nose for power, both wielded power ruthlessly. Both were said never to forget a slight. Both were known for exacting revenge on those who dared cross them, Billy by having your legislative bill killed, Whitey by having *you* killed. When I suggested to a biographer of theirs that Whitey and Billy Bulger constituted a contemporary version of Cain and Abel, he quickly corrected me: "Cain and Cain," he said.

Despite their divergent career paths, the brothers remained fiercely loyal. Billy secured soft government jobs for family members of Whitey's underlings. Whitey, a lifelong bachelor, was godfather to one of Billy's nine children and occasionally made an appearance at a nephew's high school football game. But as Whitey's lawlessness grew increasingly well known, the brothers found it prudent to minimize public displays of fraternal affection. Serving as brother's keeper now meant staying out of each other's way. At their mother's funeral in 1980, fearing that a newspaper photographer might catch the state senate president and the state's chief mobster in the same frame, Whitey sat in the balcony behind the organist during the service, watching as his five brothers and sisters walked the casket down the aisle and out the church. On the rare occasions reporters asked about his brother, Billy was circumspect. "There is much to admire," he told the *Boston Globe* in 1988. Four years later, sounding like the enlightened modern parent who takes pains to separate his child from his child's actions (*I don't love what you do but I love you*), he told a *60 Minutes* reporter, "He's my brother. I care about him. I encourage him to come by all the time." There were occasional slips. Billy lived next door to the mother of his brother's number one hit man, and at least twice

Billy walked in on dinners at which Whitey and his hit man were discussing business. But their fraternal pas de deux was successful. There was never a hint that Billy had done anything to benefit his brother directly. (Neither, however, was there any evidence that Billy ever tried to persuade his brother to pursue a less-murderous line of work.) Nor that Whitey had done anything to benefit his brother directly, though in 1970, during Billy's first campaign for state senate, he tried—by letting it be known he planned to kill the "bum" who dared run against his brother. Billy tracked down Whitey and told him to desist in this "madness."

In 1994, shortly before being indicted on federal racketeering charges and nineteen counts of murder, Whitey skipped town. He had been tipped off to his impending arrest by the FBI, for whom, it was discovered, Whitey had been working as an informant for twenty years, during which time the agency looked the other way while he consolidated his hold on Boston's criminal underworld and committed the majority of those nineteen murders.

If Billy knew anything about his brother's whereabouts, he kept it to himself. "I do have an honest loyalty to my brother, and I care about him, and I know that's not welcome news, but . . . it's my hope that I'm never helpful to anyone against him," Billy, who by then had left the Senate to become president of the University of Massachusetts, told a federal grand jury in 2001, adding, "I don't feel an obligation to help everyone to catch him." In 2002, asked by a congressional panel investigating his brother's disappearance whether he knew where his brother was, Billy invoked his Fifth Amendment right against self-incrimination. The following year, he agreed to testify only after he was guaranteed immunity from prosecution. Billy, it seemed, had not helped his brother directly. (The same could not be said for the youngest Bulger brother, Jackie, a retired court clerk who wore a fake mustache and posed for photos to help Whitey obtain falsified identification documents.) But Billy had, indirectly, helped Whitey remain a fugitive. He admitted they'd talked on the phone shortly after his brother had fled and he hadn't reported the conversation to the authorities. He admitted that in 1997, a London bank had called him about a safe deposit box his brother had rented. Again, he hadn't told the police. But he insisted that he hadn't talked to his brother since their initial call, and didn't know where he was. Citing a faulty memory, he deftly dodged direct responses and professed ignorance of his brother's profession. "I had the feeling he was in the business of gaming, and whatever," he said. "It was vague to me." Asked whether he'd ever discussed with his brother his decision to become an informant, Billy, who had described his contempt for informants in a memoir published a year after his brother disappeared, said no. "My brother is an older brother, Congressman. He didn't come to me looking for advice." Billy made it clear that his loyalty lay with his brother, not with his brother's victims or with the state for which he worked. Some praised his stance as an honorable choice—an act of "brotherly love," a *Globe* columnist called it. Others called it an outrage. Governor Mitt Romney, siding with the latter, forced Billy's resignation from the University of Massachusetts presidency in 2003.

In 2011, after sixteen years as a fugitive, eighty-one-year-old Whitey Bulger was arrested in Santa Monica, California, where he had been living in a rent-controlled apartment three blocks from the beach with his long-time girlfriend, thirty guns, and $822,000 in cash. Escorted into a federal courtroom in South Boston for his arraignment, he spotted Billy in the second row. Nodding slightly, he flashed a grin one reporter described as "cocksure," and mouthed the word "Hi." He did not acknowledge anyone on the other side of the aisle, which was filled with relatives and friends of some of the people he was accused of killing. He was charged with nineteen murders and more than twenty counts of money laundering, extortion, loan sharking, and witness tampering. As Whitey left the courtroom, the Bulger brothers exchanged smiles.

* * *

When Vincent left Paris, he was, by his own admission, "seriously ill, sick at heart and in body, and nearly an alcoholic." After several months in Arles, the only ailment Vincent suffered from was overexertion. "I am in a constant fever of work," he wrote Theo. When he returned from the fields after a day of painting, his eyes were bloodshot, his lips sunburned, his body covered with dust, his stomach empty. He rarely ate—for much of August he lived on milk, ship's biscuits, and eggs—and went "whole days" without speaking, except to order his coffee. When the mistral, the dry, cold wind that blew down the Rhone valley to the Mediterranean, was particularly fierce, he anchored his easel to the ground with rope and iron pegs so it wouldn't blow away. When he painted at night, he fastened candles to the top of his easel and the brim of his hat. "How I wish you could see everything I see nowadays!" he wrote Theo. "There is so much beauty before me that I can do nothing but pursue it." He was painting with unaccustomed confidence. "I am beginning to feel completely different from the way I did when I came here. I no longer have doubts, I no longer hesitate to tackle things, and this feeling could well grow." Vincent had so much to report that he sometimes wrote Theo twice a day. Meanwhile, the paintings he sent to Paris were stacking up against Theo's walls, under sofas and beds. Eventually, Theo had to rent space in a back room at Père Tanguy's shop to accommodate the overflow. (During his fifteen months in Arles, Vincent would finish 185 oil paintings, 100 drawings, and 10 watercolors.) Theo's faith had been rewarded; the paintings were like nothing he had ever seen, but he knew they were great.

Theo, however, was depressed. His post-Vincent life in Paris seemed colorless. "You may do something for me if you like," he wrote Vincent plaintively, "that is, go on as in the past, and create an entourage of artists and friends for us, something which I am absolutely incapable of doing by my own self, and which *you* have been able to do, more or less, ever since you came to France." At Vincent's suggestion, Theo rented out his brother's old room to visiting artists. But it wasn't the same. Theo was having heart trouble; he suffered from sciatica; he wrote Vincent of the "emptiness" he felt. Vincent tried to buck him up. "Take as much spring air as possible, go to bed *very early,* because you must have sleep, and as for food, plenty of fresh vegetables, and no *bad* wine or *bad* alcohol," wrote the man who subsisted on bread, coffee, and plenty of bad alcohol. He reminded his brother that, as a dealer, he was a vital part of the creative process. "Now I feel that my pictures are not yet good enough to compensate for the advantages I have enjoyed through you," wrote Vincent. "But believe me, if one day they should be good enough, you will have been as much their creator as I, because the two of us are making them together." Theo, clearly, was no longer on the opposite side of the barricade. Vincent increasingly talked of "our paintings" and "our work." Now more than ever, they were *"compagnons de voyage."*

Ever since their father's death, Vincent's letters to Theo had been markedly more thoughtful and affectionate. He no longer scolded his brother if his allowance was late. He even offered to cut his expenses: "If there should happen to be a month or a fortnight when you were hard pressed, let me know and I will set to work on some drawings, which will cost us less." When Theo was asked by his bosses at Boussod & Valadon to do more traveling, even as far as America, Vincent gallantly offered to accompany his overstressed brother—at company expense, of course. "Remember that I would far rather give up painting than see you killing yourself to make money. . . ." he wrote. (It's hard to believe he really meant this, but it was courteous of him to say it.) "You understand, it would make me wretched to be forcing you to make money. Rather, let's be together whatever happens."

Vincent felt so expansive that he began to think Arles could be the setting for an artists' collective: "some sort of little retreat," as he put it, "where the poor cab horses of Paris—that is, you and several of our friends, the poor impressionists—could go out to pasture when they get too beat up." Vincent had first mentioned the idea to Theo in 1882 and had discussed it in Paris with Guillaumin, Pissarro, Seurat, and other "comrades-in-arms." Vincent's "Society of Impressionists" sounded like a cross between a medieval craft guild, the Pre-Raphaelite Brotherhood, and a monastery. Part of the goal was practical—to bring artists together to exchange ideas, pool expenses, negotiate better prices, and share profits. Part of the goal was emotional—to foster cooperation among the members of a notoriously backbiting profession, in the process relieving Vincent's isolation by providing him with a substitute family. "I want so much that we should create a life in common, a new spirit . . ." he wrote Theo, "each of us free and producing in his separate fashion, but all of us together forming one spring, a unanimous blossoming." In April, Vincent moved into a derelict two-story house near the railway station on the edge of town. He had it painted yellow, "because I want it to be the house of light for everybody." In the Yellow House, as he called it, plans for his collective took shape. There would be twelve members. Theo would be the "dealer-apostle" who handled the financial arrangements and presented their work to the public. "I think every day of this artists' association," Vincent wrote his brother.

Having shared an apartment with Vincent for two years, Theo was aware that there was hardly a man less fit for communal living than Vincent (who may have been capable of brotherhood *only* with his biological brother), but he went along with the tide of his brother's enthusiasm. Unfortunately, if there *was* anybody less fit for communal living than Vincent, it was Paul Gauguin, the charming, arrogant, self-centered womanizer on whom Vincent fixated as the second member of his association. Vincent had met Gauguin in Paris. He had been taken with his work and, perhaps even more, with his dramatic history. Five years older than Vincent, Gauguin had spent part of his childhood in Peru; had sailed around the world with the French merchant marine; and at thirty-four, in the kind of nose-thumbing defiance of bourgeois respectability sure to impress Vincent, had given up his career as a stockbroker, abandoned his wife and five children, and devoted himself to painting. It was Vincent who had persuaded Theo to show Gauguin's work, and now he pleaded with his brother to convince Gauguin to come to Arles. "The two of us will be able to live on the same money that I now spend on myself alone," he reasoned. Once again, Theo was acting as intermediary. As further bait, Vincent offered Gauguin the leading role in his proposed collective. "As there will now be several painters living together," he explained to Theo, "I think we shall need an abbot to keep order, and naturally it is going to be Gauguin."

Vincent had envisioned the Yellow House as a retreat for Theo. "From now on you can consider yourself the owner of a country house here in Arles," he had written. "Because I'm very eager to arrange it so that you'll be happy in it." But Theo's place in the Yellow House gradually became Gauguin's. ("The room you'll stay in then, or which will be Gauguin's if Gauguin comes, will have white walls hung with large yellow sunflowers.") Whether Theo felt envy or relief, he didn't say. In any case, he did his best to satisfy his brother, and when he came into a small inheritance from Uncle Cent, he decided to use part of it to subsidize Gauguin. Meanwhile Vincent was preparing the Yellow House with the nervous ardor of a bridegroom awaiting a bride whose arrival was still in doubt. He had gas lights, running water, and a stove installed. He bought beds, mattresses, a mirror, and—looking ahead to a complete "Society of Impressionists"— twelve chairs. He was, he wrote Theo in one of his near-daily updates, giving Gauguin "the prettiest room upstairs, which I shall do my best to turn into something like the boudoir of a really artistic woman." Vincent's own room, he told Theo, would be "extremely simple." Vincent was so "wild to see my pictures in frames" that he overspent his budget and was forced to live for four days on twenty-three cups of coffee and bread purchased on credit. "Well, yes, I am ashamed of it, but I am vain enough to want to make a certain impression on Gauguin with my work, so I cannot help wanting to do as much work as possible alone before he comes." At Vincent's suggestion, the two painters exchanged self-portraits. "I have been thinking of you with very great emotion as I prepared your studio . . ." Vincent wrote Gauguin. "Let us be of good heart about the success of our venture, and please keep thinking of this as your home, for I feel very sure that all this will last for a very long time." For five months the coquettish Gauguin put off the Van Gogh brothers, but, penniless and sick, he finally agreed to the deal. On October 23, 1888, Gauguin arrived in Arles.

Gauguin, who was interested in others only insofar as they could be used for his own gain, had no desire to play "abbot" in Vincent's brotherhood; he saw Vincent as a burden to be endured in return for his brother's money. Nevertheless, for a time the two painters managed a reasonable facsimile of communal life. Gauguin, the former sailor, took charge. He bought a chest of drawers and a set of kitchen utensils; he organized their finances; he took over the cooking and delegated the marketing to Vincent. They prepared their canvases and stretchers together, made their own frames together, painted side by side, shared evening strolls, and paid joint visits to brothels on what Gauguin called "nocturnal, hygienic outings." They even collaborated on a letter to Theo. "Our days pass in working, working all the time," Vincent wrote, with the enthusiasm of a child telling his parents about a summer camp roommate. "In the evening we are dead beat and go off to the café, and after that, early to bed!" It was an auspicious beginning. "I venture to hope that in six months Gauguin and you and I will all see that we have founded a little studio which will last."

Vincent's elation allowed him to close one letter with a thought touching in its simplicity and remarkable for his so rarely having expressed it before: "Goodbye again and thank you for all you do for me."

Vincent's letters soon turned less sanguine, and, in a sign that something was troubling him, less frequent. Gauguin scorned Vincent's beloved Arles (he called it, Vincent told Theo, "the dirtiest hole in the south") and found Vincent naive and uncouth (it annoyed him that Vincent never put the caps back on his tubes of paint). At times the supercilious Gauguin seemed to toy with his needy roommate—a week after his arrival, he still had not commented on many of the canvases with which Vincent had worked so hard to impress him. As winter approached, raw, rainy weather kept them cooped up in the Yellow House, where they had endless, contentious discussions about art, about color, about the painters' association. "Our arguments are terribly *electric,* sometimes we come out of them with our heads as exhausted as a used electric battery," Vincent wrote Theo. Years later, Gauguin observed, "Between two such beings as he and I, the one a perfect volcano, the other boiling inwardly, some sort of struggle was preparing." Like quarreling brothers pleading their cases to a parent, each of them complained about the other to Theo, who, once again, played peacemaker. On December 15, after only six weeks in the Yellow House, Gauguin told Theo that he had to leave. "Vincent and I simply cannot live together without trouble, due to the incompatibility of our characters," he wrote. We don't know how Theo responded, but Gauguin postponed his departure, although he grew increasingly cool and patronizing. As Vincent saw that he was losing his abbot—and his fledgling collective—he drank more, slept less, and grew progressively erratic. On December 23, Vincent explained to Theo that there were "serious problems," saying, in something of an understatement, "I think myself that Gauguin was a little out of sorts with the good town of Arles, the little yellow house where we work, and especially with me."

Theo did not reply immediately. It would have been understandable if he had been unable to give the situation his full attention. A week earlier, he had run into Jo Bonger, the English teacher to whom he had proposed the previous year. Since his rejection, Theo had written her occasionally, trying to keep his suit alive—a genteel version of Vincent's long-ago pursuit of his London landlady's daughter. Now, meeting each other again, Theo and Jo agreed to be friends. But Theo soon realized he still wanted more. Jo, who later admitted that she had engineered their "chance" meeting, shared his feelings. Theo reproposed and she accepted. "O Mother I am so inexpressibly happy," Theo wrote on December 21. "Can it really be true?"

Jo knew that in marrying one Van Gogh she was getting two. When Theo had first written her, four days after she rejected his initial proposal, he had devoted half the letter to a description of his brother, whom she had never met. "Perhaps you'll think that what I am telling you about him has nothing to do with us, at least when it comes to giving you a glimpse into my heart," he wrote, with the forthrightness of a man declaring his baggage at the border. "But having been through so much with him and having pondered his views on life, I would feel I were concealing something important were I not to tell you about my relationship with him from the start." Jo could not have guessed how large a role her future brother-in-law would play in their relationship—and how soon.

On December 24, on the eve of his departure for Holland to meet Jo's family, Theo received a telegram from Gauguin. Vincent was in the hospital. He had sliced off half his left ear with a razor. After walking to a brothel and handing the severed appendage to a prostitute of his acquaintance, he had returned to the Yellow House, where the police discovered him unconscious on his bed. Theo took the night train seven hundred miles to Arles. He found Vincent locked in a cell at the hospital. He sat with his brother all Christmas Day. "There were moments while I was with him when he was well; but very soon after he fell back into his worries about philosophy and theology," Theo wrote Jo a few days later, from Paris. "It was painfully sad to witness, for at times all his suffering overwhelmed him and he tried to weep but he could not; poor fighter and poor, poor sufferer; for the moment nobody can do anything to relieve his sorrow, and yet he feels deeply and strongly." A day later, he wrote, "There is little hope . . . If it must be that he dies, so be it, but my heart breaks when I think of it."

Shortly before New Year's, Theo received news of Vincent's recovery. On January 7, the day after Theo traveled to Holland for his engagement party, Vincent was discharged from the hospital. Vincent and his doctors believed the attack was an isolated incident, "an artist's fit," as Vincent put it. A month later, however, Vincent suffered another breakdown and was back in the hospital.

That Vincent fell apart just as his brother was flourishing was no coincidence. Among the dozens of reasons proposed for Vincent's breakdown (exhaustion, anxiety, depression, Gauguin's threatened desertion, the failure of his artist's collective, and so on), Theo's impending marriage may have played a role. In 1953, Charles Mauron, a psychoanalytically oriented critic and translator, was the first to point out that Vincent's psychotic breaks tended to coincide with developments in his brother's romantic life. Vincent's first attack immediately followed news of Theo's engagement; further episodes took place around the time of Theo's wedding and just before the birth of his child. Emphasizing the symbiotic relationship between the brothers, Mauron suggested that Vincent perceived Theo's marriage as an abandonment; that Vincent worried that he would no longer have Theo's undivided attention and that Theo's financial and emotional resources would go to his new family. This reawakened Vincent's lifelong feelings of neglect, reinforced his low self-esteem, and triggered his need to punish himself. His self-inflicted wound, in Mauron's view, was a way of trying to keep his brother close.

Others point out that the dates of Vincent's attacks don't align with signal moments in Theo's domestic life. Indeed, there is no conclusive evidence to suggest that Vincent learned of Theo's engagement until *after* he cut off part of his ear. Whenever he found out, Vincent greeted the news favorably. Vincent had pushed Theo into first proposing to Jo, and had encouraged the relationship ever since. ("I do not forget that you insisted on my getting married," Theo wrote Vincent, "and you were right, for I am much happier.") In his letters, Vincent seemed genuinely pleased for his brother, and always asked to be remembered to Jo, whom he addressed as "my dear sister." Any jealousy he felt was convincingly repressed. "Well, do you know what I hope for, once I let myself begin to hope?" Vincent wrote. "It is that a family will be for you what nature, the clods of earth, the grass, the yellow wheat, the peasant, are for me, that is to say, that you may find in your love for people something *not only to work for,* but to comfort and restore you when there is need for it." A brother's marriage, however, inevitably affects the fraternal relationship, especially when the brothers are as close as Vincent and Theo. Although Vincent was happy for Theo and Jo, he worried whether there would be room for him in Theo's new life.

Over the next few months, Theo wondered about that, too. He was making arrangements for Vincent's care, but he was also preparing for marriage—choosing fabric for furniture, interviewing prospective maids, hunting for an apartment (one Sunday he looked at fifty). His letters to Jo, who was living with her parents in Amsterdam until the wedding, were filled with practical concerns: how to word the engagement card, whether to be married at home or in church, what kind of wallpaper to put up in the salon. Just as Theo and Vincent had gotten to know each other through their letters, now Theo and Jo tentatively began exploring each other by mail. At times, Theo played the avuncular sage, recommending books and giving minitutorials on painting's "new movement"— temperate versions of the letters with which Vincent had showered him in the old days. At times he was touchingly shy. ("Will I be able to give you the happiness you have a right to expect and will it be given to us to share our thoughts and grow in each other's hearts? I hope so, but hardly dare to believe it, because that would make life seem just too beautiful.") He warned Jo not to expect too much. ("In my relationships with friends, if I may also confess, I can be rude at times and even harsh if I'm trying to make a point.") His customary reserve gradually gave way. ("I am a fortunate person and sometimes catch myself whistling or humming a tune. It's your fault. Goodbye my precious.")

But wedding plans almost always turned to worries about his brother. "You see, this afternoon I received bad news about Vincent again," Theo wrote on February 9. "Dr. Salles wrote to say he had been in hospital again since last Thursday and asked me what should be done. He was evidently under the impression that someone wanted to poison him. They put him on his own in hospital and he hasn't uttered another word since. He weeps from time to time. Poor poor fellow, how hard his life is." A week later, in a letter largely devoted to his excitement over finding some painted cloth from the Dutch East Indies that would make "the most divine curtains for the dining room," Theo closed by confessing that he still hadn't heard from his brother. "Were I not wondering about Vincent all the time, I'd be happy with the present, but he is constantly on my mind. He still hasn't written and I've heard nothing since the letter from [Dr.] Rey." February 27: "I've received another letter from Arles saying that Vincent is back in hospital, this time at the request of the neighbours, who were probably afraid of him. This time a decision has to be taken about him being committed to an asylum . . . I know you are concerned about him and about his care, so I would simply ask if I may think of you in times of sorrow and turn to you for comfort."

On April 18, 1889, Theo and Jo were married in Amsterdam's town hall. After a one-day honeymoon in Brussels, they moved into the Montmartre apartment Theo had so carefully prepared. A few weeks later, Vincent began packing and moving out of the Yellow House, whose contents were damp and mildewed after a recent flood. "I felt it deeply," he wrote Theo, "especially because you had given me all that stuff with such brotherly generosity and yet it was you alone who continued to support me for so many years till in the end I could only report this miserable outcome of it all."

*   *   *

In the century since his death, Theo van Gogh has been portrayed as a saint who sacrificed his own life to minister to his brother. Serving as one's brother's keeper, however, may not be an entirely selfless act. Evolutionary biologists point out that acting altruistically on a relative's behalf increases the chances that familial genes will be passed to future generations. The closer the degree of relatedness, the better the odds. (The biologist J. B. S. Haldane, calculating the number of relatives he would have to save to "break even," genetically speaking, quipped that he would lay down his life for no fewer than two brothers or eight cousins.)

There are other, more immediate benefits. In the case of Theo van Gogh, William Rossetti, and other "martyred siblings of literary history" (as the biographer Leon Edel called them) who take on the care and feeding of an artist with little aptitude or taste for the practical details of navigating the real world, those benefits may seem self-evident. But even when the kept brother is not a genius, the keeper may profit. Knowing that someone is dependent on him may boost the keeper's self-esteem. Making himself indispensable may allow the keeper to feel he has triumphed in an ongoing sibling rivalry, or even that he has trumped a parent; the psychologist Stephen Bank points out that someone who serves as brother's keeper may be satisfying an unconscious desire to display his competence by "outparenting" a mother or father. Caring for a disabled sibling, too, can have its rewards. Research suggests that children with disabled siblings tend to be more sensitive, tolerant, empathic, compassionate, mature, and self-sufficient. A disproportionate number grow up to become professional caretakers: doctors, nurses, social workers, therapists.

Serving as brother's keeper may provide the keeper with an identity he might otherwise lack. It has often been said that without Theo, there might have been no Vincent. It may be equally true that without Vincent, there might have been no Theo. Who would the keeper be without someone to keep?

From an early age, James Joyce's nine brothers and sisters were conditioned to meet his needs. The eldest, the favorite of both parents, and the handsome, precocious boy upon whom the impoverished family's hopes rested, James was the only Joyce to be given a college education; his siblings occasionally went hungry so their father could buy James the books he needed. Of all the Joyce children, it was Stanislaus, three years younger than James, who took the job most to heart. Young Stannie fetched his older brother books from the library, carried messages to his friends, borrowed money on his behalf, lent him his hat and raincoat, and bowled to him in the back garden for hours at a time so James could perfect his cricket swing. Stannie worshiped James; the diary he kept was more about his brother than about himself. James, in turn, treated Stannie with a contempt that made Vincent's treatment of Theo seem generous. He read Stannie's diary without permission and used incidents from it in his work. He recycled Stannie's observations, passing them off as his own in conversation with his friends. He tried out story ideas and literary theories on Stannie. "He said frankly that he used me as a butcher uses his steel," Stannie recalled. (In *Ulysses*, Stephen Dedalus refers to his brother as "my whetstone.")

Stannie was a willing partner in his own bondage. Like his brother, he wanted to be a writer, and though James offered him no encouragement—there was room for only one writer in the house—Stannie got an education by osmosis. He followed his brother to meetings of the University Literary and Historical Society, read his brother's English and French books instead of his own schoolwork, discussed his brother's essays with him, and walked miles across Dublin with his brother just to listen to him talk. "Everywhere my brother went I was sure to go like a not too amiable little lamb." He studied his brother with a mix of admiration and jealousy. "My life has been modelled on Jim's example," he wrote at eighteen. Years later, he'd admit, "Whenever I struck out for myself, I always felt a little guilty, as if I were indulging an inferior taste." Stolid, plodding Stannie, whose seriousness was a family joke, confessed to his diary that he agreed with James's assessment of him as "quite commonplace and uninteresting," and hoped some of his brother's charisma might rub off on him. Their father called him James's "jackal," and observed with contempt that Stannie shone "with borrowed light like the moon."

When James left Dublin for Paris with Nora Barnacle in 1902, one might have expected the fraternal errands to subside. But James took even greater advantage of his brother. "Tell Stannie to go to Eason's in Abbey St where I ordered and paid for a certain quantity of paper, and tell them to forward it to me," James wrote his mother. "Tell Stannie to send me the December no of S. Stephen's and to write to the Unicorn Press and to be careful of the books in my room." "Tell Stannie to send me *at once* (so that I may have it by Thursday night) my copy of Wagner's operas and if he can to enclose with it a copy of Grant Allen's 'Paris.'" Stannie was working as an unpaid clerk in an accountant's office, but spent most of his time as James's long-distance gofer. Among James's demands: send the key to his trunk; forward various addresses; pay his debts; borrow money from James's friends and send it to him; correspond with literary magazines;

comment on James's work; fact-check his stories ("Can a priest be buried in a habit?" "Would an accident at Sydney Parade be treated at Vincent's Hospital?"); deliver his manuscripts to literary magazines; send him issues in which his poems appeared; distribute copies of his work to friends; send excerpts from his diary so he could use them as an aide-memoire; write up a summary of the state of "modern English literature"; go to the hotel where Nora had worked and learn what people were saying about her; find out how Nora could obtain her birth certificate; send a copy of Nora's grandmother's will; read up on "some midwifery and embryology and send me the results of your study." (James didn't bother to explain that Nora was pregnant with their first child.) And be quick about it. "Do not delay so long executing my requests," James wrote his brother, "as I waste a lot of ink."

Stannie proved so indispensable that in 1905, James, overwhelmed by the duties of fatherhood, summoned—the word was James's—his brother to Trieste, where he served as "a kind of extra draught horse," as Stannie put it, in the chaotic Joyce household. For the next ten years, while joining James as an English teacher, Stannie kept the household afloat financially, made sure the bills were paid, fended off creditors, babysat Nora and the children when James was away, hectored James to keep at his writing, and tried to slow his brother's heavy drinking—often hunting down and extracting him from cafés (and occasionally administering a pummeling when they got home). Stannie was filling a role traditionally held by the spouses of artists, but Nora didn't care "a rambling damn about art," according to James, and even if she had, she was unwilling to perform all the tasks Stannie was. James could be a callous, condescending master ("If God Almighty came down to earth, you'd have a job for him," Nora told him). Stannie could be an overbearing, pious nag ("He was twenty but acted forty-five," observed the biographer Richard Ellmann). The brothers often quarreled—when they were on speaking terms—over James's profligate drinking and spending. James treated his younger brother like a servant, a servant who not only doesn't get paid but is forced to support his master. (Stephen Dedalus: "a brother is as easy to lose as an umbrella.") When James and his family returned, penniless, to Trieste after a sojourn in Rome, Stannie asked his brother how he planned to live with no money, no home, and no prospect of work. "Well, then," James replied, "I have you."

James was using Stannie—*abusing* may be the more accurate word— but Stannie was also using James. Without the brother around whom his adolescence had revolved, Stannie had been floundering in Dublin. In coming to Trieste, and his first paying job, "he allowed himself to rescue and be rescued," as Ellmann points out. Yet Stannie got something else from his brother. He was one of the earliest to recognize James's genius, and, lacking the confidence to strike out on his own, he had invested in that genius. He may have been basking in his brother's reflected light, but it was a bright light. Though he would never get the kind of acknowl- edgment that Vincent accorded Theo, he was part of his brother's work. Years later he would write with satisfaction that during the ten years he had kept his brother relatively sober in Trieste, James had written *Cham- ber Music* and most of *Dubliners*, rewritten the story "A Portrait of the Artist" into the novel *A Portrait of the Artist as a Young Man*, and begun *Ulysses*. Stannie served not only as his brother's errand boy but as his de facto first reader, agent, and editor. He was proud that he had given titles to *Chamber Music* and *A Portrait of the Artist*, and that he had, how- ever unwittingly, served as a partial model for characters in *Dubliners* and *Ulysses*, even if those characters were wishy-washy sorts. There were other rewards. Stannie's father adored James and loathed Stannie; Stannie may have taken pride in being able to provide for James in ways—financial and intellectual—that his alcoholic, ne'er-do-well father couldn't. James may have "cannibalized" Stannie, as one biographer puts it, but Stannie also cannibalized James.

Things might have gone on like this forever had it not been for World War I. In January 1915, Stannie was arrested and interned for four years in an Austrian castle. (From James's perspective, Stannie's stay was apparently more inconvenient than horrific; one of the few details James reported about his brother's confinement was that he had sprained his wrist playing tennis.) All that Stannie had done for James, now safely ensconced in Zurich, was taken on by a support team of admirers, with Frank Budgen, the English painter, and Harriet Weaver, the American patroness, playing major roles, and Yeats, Pound, and Eliot playing cameos. Now that Stannie, behind barbed wire, could do nothing for him, James wrote his brother only an occasional short note. By the time the war was over, James was famous and Stannie, having had plenty of time for reflection, was determined to live a life of his own. "I had not the energy to tackle him again," he wrote. When James pressed thirty-year-old Stannie for a favor, Stannie balked. "I have just emerged from four years of hunger and squalor, and am trying to get on my feet again," he wrote. "Do you think you can give me a rest?"

Over the next twenty years, the brothers would meet only three times. James, who had his own money and an ever-widening circle of sycophants, no longer needed Stannie; Stannie, who cultivated a group of friends who liked him for his own merits, no longer needed James. Without his brother to look after, Stannie married at the age of forty-three and became a revered professor of English at the University of Trieste. Without his brother looking over his shoulder, James drank more than ever, but was able to make the artistic breakthrough that led to *Finnegans Wake*. (After reading an early installment, Stannie told James it was "drivelling rigmarole.") Yet the last person James wrote to, six days before his death in 1941, was Stannie. An outspoken detractor of Mussolini, Stannie had been placed in semi-internment in Florence as an enemy alien; now James sent his brother a postcard from neutral Switzerland with the names of some people who might be able to help him. He was, at last, doing something for the brother who had done so much for him.

It was only after James's death that Stannie felt safe to resume his custodial role: assisting his brother's biographers, interpreting his life, defending his reputation. He named his only child, born two years after his brother's death, for James. He became a writer, as he'd always wanted. But, as in his teenage, diary-keeping days, he was a writer with a single subject: his brother. By the time he died on June 16, 1955 (Bloomsday), in Trieste, the city to which James had summoned him a half-century earlier, he had, in a sense, reunited with his brother so completely that, in the end, though Stannie called his memoir *My Brother's Keeper*, one might well ask which brother was the keeper and which the kept.

*   *   *

On May 8, 1889, Vincent was taken to Saint-Paul-de-Mausole, a sanitarium housed in a former twelfth-century monastery in Saint-Rémy, twelve miles northeast of Arles. "With the consent of the person in question, who is my brother," Theo had written, "I request the admission to your institution of Vincent Willem van Gogh, painter, 36 years old. . . . In view of the fact that his internment is desired mainly to prevent the recurrence of previous attacks and not because his mental condition is unsound, I hope that you will find it possible to permit him to do some painting outside of your establishment. . . . I beg you to be kind enough to allow him at least a half liter of wine with his meals." Once again, Vincent described his new home to his brother: "I have a small room with greenish-grey paper and two sea-green curtains with a design of very pale roses, brightened with touches of blood red. These curtains, probably the legacy of some deceased and ruined rich person, are very pretty in design. . . . Through the iron-barred window I can see an enclosed square of wheat, a prospect like a Van Goyen, above which, in the morning, I watch the sun rise in all its glory."

At Saint-Rémy, the attacks—psychotic episodes in which Vincent was assaulted by hallucinations and waves of paranoia—were more frequent and more severe. They were followed by periods of depression, in which he went for days and sometimes weeks without speaking or writing. Vincent was terrified "beyond measure" by the attacks themselves, during which, at various times, he tried to poison himself by eating dirt, swallowing paint, and drinking turpentine. But he was even more terrified that they would destroy his ability to paint. After each one, Vincent urged Theo to persuade the doctor to let him go back to work. He was determined to get as much done as possible before the next attack, the way "a miner who is always in danger makes haste in what he does." The newlywed Theo did what he could from Paris: he paid Vincent's fees at the asylum and provided him with a steady stream of paints, canvas, stretchers, brushes, books, art reproductions, tobacco, chocolate, newspapers, and news (Pissarro had had an eye operation; Gauguin had sent Theo some new paintings; Tanguy's mother had died). At Vincent's request, Theo sent him a one-volume edition of Shakespeare, which Vincent read and reread. But Theo agonized over what he couldn't do for Vincent. "Poor fellow, how dearly I should like to know what to do to put a stop to this nightmare . . . ," he wrote in August 1889, after another attack. "In your last letter you wrote me that we were brothers for more than one reason. This is what I feel too, and though my heart is not as sensitive as yours, I can enter at times into your feeling of being smothered by so many thoughts that cannot be resolved. Never lose courage, and remember how much I want you." Each Sunday, on his only day off from Boussod & Valadon, Theo spent the morning rearranging his brother's paintings on the walls of his apartment.

Theo had good news for Vincent about his own work. In September 1889, Vincent had two paintings at the fifth Salon des Indépendants; six months later, at the sixth Salon he had ten. "Monet said that your pictures were the best of all in the exhibition," Theo wrote. In January 1890, at an exhibition in Brussels, a Van Gogh canvas sold for the first time. "I think we can wait patiently for success to come; you will surely live to see it," wrote Theo. That same month a young art critic, Albert Aurier, published a glowing review of Vincent's work. Vincent believed it was no coincidence that not long afterward, he suffered another attack. "As soon as I heard that my work was having some success, and read the article in question," he wrote his mother after he had recovered, "I feared at once that I should be punished for it; this is how things nearly always go in a painter's life: success is about the worst thing that can happen." (Three decades after eight-year-old Vincent had destroyed his clay elephant, he was still leery of praise.) Again, Vincent's and Theo's fortunes were dramatically juxtaposed. On January 31, 1890, not long after Vincent's attack, Jo gave birth to a baby boy. Not knowing whether his brother would be well enough to read his letter, Theo wrote Vincent to announce his son's birth. "As we told you at the time, we are going to name him after you, and I devoutly hope that he will be able to be as persevering and as courageous as you." In keeping with his feelings of unworthiness—and, perhaps, of guilt—Vincent unsuccessfully petitioned them to name the boy Theo, after their father.

Vincent's spirits increasingly faltered under threat of the attacks. "I have become timid and hesitant, and live, as it were, mechanically," he wrote. He described himself as "overwhelmed with boredom and grief."

More than ever, Vincent relied on his brother. "If I were without your friendship," Vincent wrote, "they would drive me remorselessly to suicide, and coward that I am, I should end by committing it." Theo was crushed to hear his bull-headed brother sounding so meek. As winter turned to spring, Vincent grew determined to leave Saint-Rémy. "My surroundings here begin to weigh on me more than I can say," he wrote Theo. His thoughts turned to his parents, to his childhood, to Holland. "I'm haunted by a longing to see my old friends and the northern countryside again," he wrote Theo. In another letter: "What consoles me is the great, very great desire I have to see you again, you and your wife and child." Vincent's yearning for home may have seemed like a second wind. In retrospect, of course, it signified the beginning of the end.

Theo began looking for a place for his brother. The asylums in Holland were full. He invited Vincent to live with him and Jo, but Vincent didn't feel up to the hubbub of Paris. Pissarro suggested Vincent go to Auvers, a small town an hour northwest of Paris, where he could be under the care of Paul Gachet, a homeopathic doctor, psychiatrist, and amateur painter who had written a thesis on neurosis in artists. Vincent agreed to the plan; he would stop in Paris to see Theo and his new family en route. Theo's insistence that Vincent be accompanied on the train, in case he had another attack, triggered a brief fraternal contretemps. "Up till now I have done no one any harm; is it fair to have me accompanied like a dangerous beast?" Vincent complained. As always, Theo relented, knowing there was little he could do. But, like an anxious parent, Theo couldn't sleep the night before he met his brother at the Gare de Lyon. The brothers hadn't seen each other since Theo had visited Vincent at the hospital in Arles. Jo, looking out the window of the apartment, saw their carriage arrive from the station: "Two merry faces nodded to me, two hands waved—a moment later Vincent stood before me."

It was the first time Jo had met her brother-in-law. "I had expected a sick man, but here was a sturdy, broad-shouldered man, with a healthy color, a smile on his face, and a very resolute appearance . . ." she recalled. "'He seems perfectly well; he looks much stronger than Theo,' was my first thought." The brothers went right in to see Vincent's namesake. Both had tears in their eyes as they stood side by side over the baby's cradle. Vincent had brought a gift for his nephew: a painting of almond blossoms against a blue sky. Theo and Jo hung it above the piano. Vincent could see his work everywhere: *The Potato Eaters* over the dining room mantelpiece, *Orchards in Bloom* in the bedroom, *Landscape from Arles* and *Night View on the Rhône* in the sitting room. Piles of unframed canvases lay in every corner. The next morning, Vincent was up early, spreading his canvases on the floor for him and Theo to examine. Over the next few days, Pissarro, Tanguy, and Toulouse-Lautrec called on Vincent; he, in turn, called on other old Paris friends. He and Theo visited the annual Salon. He went out to buy olives, for which he had developed a taste while painting olive trees in Saint-Rémy, and insisted Theo and Jo try them. He announced plans to return in a few weeks to paint portraits of Theo, Jo, and baby Vincent. In a letter to Wil, he wrote of his visit: "It gave me great joy to see Theo again, and to make the acquaintance of Jo and the little one. Theo's cough was worse than when I last saw him more than 2 years ago, but in talking to him and seeing him close at hand, I certainly found him, all things considered, changed somewhat for the better, and Jo is full of good sense and good will." But the bustle of Paris made Vincent uneasy, and after three days he took the train to Auvers.

There he rented an attic room at the inn, and put himself under the care of Gachet, who was nearly a match for Vincent in eccentricity. (He kept a collection of death masks of guillotined murderers in his attic.) "I have found a perfect friend in Dr. Gachet, something like another brother," Vincent wrote Wil, "so alike are we physically, and mentally, too." By all accounts, he lived quietly, simply, and productively (seventy paintings in seventy days). "When I heard much later he had been interned in a lunatic asylum in the Midi, I was much surprised," wrote the innkeeper's daughter, "as he had always appeared calm and sweet to me." Gachet, meeting Theo at his gallery on June 4, said that he believed Vincent was completely cured. Theo may have believed it, too, when he and his family visited the following Sunday. Vincent met them at the station, presenting his four-month-old nephew with a bird's nest. They lunched outdoors at Gachet's, where Vincent, carrying his namesake in his arms, introduced him to the doctor's barnyard menagerie of cats, dogs, chickens, rabbits, ducks, and pigeons. Later, they took a long walk. Vincent told Theo he hoped that this would be the first of many visits; indeed, he tried to persuade him to move his family to the country, for the sake of their health. They discussed renting a small house nearby where Vincent could spend weekends with Theo and his family. Afterward, Vincent wrote to Theo and Jo: "Sunday has left me a very pleasant memory; in this way we feel that we are not so far from one another, and I hope that we shall often see each other again." In a letter to his mother describing the visit, he added, "it is a very reassuring feeling for me to live so much closer to them."

Indeed, Vincent seemed far healthier than Theo. It had been a difficult spring. Theo's sales had been disappointing, his bosses were pressuring him, and with a new baby at home, he got little sleep. His chronic cough grew explosive, his limbs trembled, he had difficulty eating. Ever since giving birth, Jo had been in and out of bed because of postpartum blood loss. Most upsetting of all, the baby fell seriously ill—Theo blamed contaminated cow's milk—and Theo and Jo were terrified they might lose him. By late June, Theo was so exhausted and anxious that he did something highly unusual: he poured out his worries to his brother in a letter that began, points out biographer Jan Hulsker, not with Theo's usual salutation "Mon cher Vincent" but the more emotional "Mon très cher frère Vincent." After describing the child's condition, the normally circumspect Theo confessed his other worries, with a force that suggests he had been bottling them up for some time: Jo's health (each night he could hear her moaning in her sleep); their living situation (should they move to a larger apartment on the first floor? to Auvers, to be near Vincent? to Holland, to be near the family home?); his work (should he leave "those rats" Boussod and Valadon and open his own gallery at last?); his finances (he was now the sole support of his wife, child, mother, two of his sisters, and Vincent; whatever happened, they would all have to tighten their belts). In this catalogue of woes, Theo identified one comfort: Vincent was in good health. "You have found your way, dear brother, your carriage is already nearing its destination and can stand up to a good many knocks." It was an unusually long, rambling, emotional letter for Theo. Indeed, it resembled one of Vincent's, by turns worried, self-pitying, and sentimental. After unleashing a torrent of self-doubt, Theo turned to his brother. "What do you think, old fellow?"

The old fellow was taken aback. Theo's sudden fragility shook him. After so many years of leaning on Theo, Vincent wasn't prepared to resume the role of elder brother. His response was uncharacteristically cautious. He expressed concern about the child ("I feel how exhausting it must be and I wish I could help you a little bit"). Though he had pressed Theo for years to leave his job, he now vacillated ("What do you want me to say about the future, which perhaps, perhaps, will be without the Boussods? That will be as it will be"). Of one thing he was certain: he wasn't in such rosy shape as Theo suggested. "I dare not count on my health never letting me down again. And don't hold it against me if my illness should return." It was as if Vincent, witnessing Theo's breakdown, felt he had a rival for the role of needy brother; he required Theo to remain the pillar of the family, the "lucky dog." After all, if Theo couldn't take care of himself, how could he take care of Vincent?

Nevertheless, concerned for his brother, Vincent traveled to Paris, where he and Theo visited Tanguy's paint shop and had lunch with Toulouse-Lautrec. But the visit did not go well. Vincent wasn't pleased with the way his paintings were stored at Tanguy's, and he complained that there wasn't enough space to display his work at Theo's apartment. Jo was recovering from her illness, Theo was coughing worse than ever, and, though out of danger, little Vincent was still sick, wailing through the night. The brothers discussed the idea of Theo quitting the business. Jo, worried about expenses, argued against it. But their discussions were interrupted by old friends wanting to see Vincent, and Vincent, tense and exhausted, cut short his visit and returned to Auvers. There, he wrote his brother and sister-in-law a brief, agitated letter, acknowledging that "we are all rather distressed and a little overwrought." He suggested that any decision about leaving Boussod be postponed. "You rather surprise me by seeming to wish to force the situation," he wrote. (Coming from a man who *always* forced the situation, the observation must have struck Theo as peculiar.) In a subsequent letter, Vincent wanted to make it clear that they couldn't count on him. "I generally try to be fairly cheerful, but my life too is menaced at its very root, and my steps also are wavering. I feared—not so much, but a little just the same—that being a burden to you, you felt me rather a thing to be dreaded."

In Paris, Theo had told Vincent that he planned to give his employers an ultimatum, allowing them eight days to respond to his demand for higher pay. It was an uncharacteristically reckless step for Theo, just the kind of thing Vincent would have done. The deadline passed without a response. On July 21, more than two weeks after issuing the ultimatum, Theo, convinced he had made a horrible mistake, terrified he'd be jobless just when he'd started a family, told his employers he wanted to stay. The news would have relieved Vincent, but though Theo wrote his mother about his decision on July 22, he neglected to tell his brother. Might he have been embarrassed to explain to Vincent that he had caved in? That he had tried to be like his uncompromising brother but had lacked the nerve? That he was, in the end, his father's son? In any case, Vincent was preoccupied by the possibility that Theo's crisis of confidence might mean an end to his financial and, perhaps, emotional support. Vincent had always seen a vital connection between Theo and his own very existence. Over the years he had written that were Theo to withdraw his support it would be as if he were to "cut off my head"; that "I'll pay you back or die in the attempt"; that "my life or death depends on your help"; that "whatever you can spare is as absolutely necessary to me as the air I breathe." A kind of syllogism may have taken root in Vincent's unconscious: without Theo, there could be no painting; without painting, there could be no life; therefore, without Theo, there could be no life.

On the morning of July 28, Theo received a message from Dr. Gachet: "With the greatest regret I must disturb your repose. Yet I think it my duty to write to you immediately. At nine o'clock of today, Sunday, I was sent for by your brother Vincent, who wanted to see me at once. I went there and found him very ill. He has wounded himself." Theo rushed to Auvers, where he was told that on the previous evening Vincent had borrowed a revolver from his innkeeper, saying he wanted to scare away the crows that often bothered him as he worked. Instead, he had walked to a nearby farmyard and shot himself in the abdomen. Clutching his stomach, he staggered back to his room. "I shot myself," he told the innkeeper. "I only hope I haven't botched it." When Theo arrived, he lay down next to his brother on the bed, unable to stop weeping. "Do not cry," said Vincent, "I did it for the good of us all."

Although Dr. Gachet hadn't been able to remove the bullet, Vincent was well enough to talk to Theo for most of the day. "He was glad that I came and we are together all the time . . ." Theo wrote Jo that evening. "Poor fellow, very little happiness fell to his share, and no illusions are left him. The burden grows too heavy at times, he feels so alone. He often asks after you and the baby, and said that you could not have imagined there was so much sorrow in life." Late that night, Theo, sitting at Vincent's bedside, told him that he would do everything he could to help him get better and that he hoped he would be spared further attacks. "The sadness will last forever," Vincent replied. Not long afterward, Vincent had trouble breathing. He closed his eyes. Theo got on the bed beside him and cradled his brother's head in his arm. "I wish I could pass away like this," murmured Vincent. Half an hour later, at one in morning on July 29, at the age of thirty-seven, he did.

The following afternoon, Theo was part of a small group of friends and admirers that climbed the hill to the cemetery, overlooking the wheat fields, where the coffin, covered with sunflowers and yellow dahlias, was lowered into the grave. "In the assembly some people cry," wrote Émile Bernard, recalling the scene in a letter to Albert Aurier. "Theodore Van Gogh, who adored his brother, who had always supported him in his struggle for art and independence, did not stop sobbing painfully." Dr. Gachet made some remarks. Theo spoke a few words of thanks through his tears. At one point during the service, Theo fainted. "It was as if the brother called his brother from the grave," wrote Bernard. Shortly after returning to Paris, Theo wrote to his mother. "One cannot write how grieved one is nor find any comfort. It is a grief that will last and which I certainly shall never forget as long as I live; the only thing one might say is that he himself has the rest he was longing for. . . . Oh Mother! he was so my own, own brother."

For years, Theo had tried to keep his brother alive; now he tried to keep his brother's memory alive. He asked Aurier to write Vincent's biography, but

Aurier was finishing a novel. (Two years later, when he was ready to begin, Aurier died suddenly of typhoid fever.) He asked Durand-Ruel to lend one of his gallery rooms for an exhibition of Vincent's paintings, but the art dealer declined, deciding the public might find them disturbing. So Theo asked Émile Bernard to help him put up Vincent's paintings—"as many as possible"—in Theo's apartment as a kind of informal memorial exhibition. Two years earlier, on the eve of Vincent's departure for Arles, Bernard had helped Vincent decorate his bedroom with Vincent's work to make Theo feel that his brother was still there in spirit. Now Bernard helped Theo hang Vincent's canvases all over Theo and Jo's apartment. It was a way of letting people get to know Vincent's work; it may also have been a way of helping Theo feel that his brother was still there. "I wish you could see it," Theo wrote to his sister Wil. Referring to a critic who had recently disparaged Vincent's paintings, he added, "You would get something out of it, and you would see that, unlike what Monsieur Beauborg said in his article, these canvases are not the work of a sick mind, but of the ardor and humanity of a great man."

In the months following his brother's death it became clear that Theo had needed Vincent as much as Vincent had needed Theo. Without his brother, Theo fell apart. His health went downhill with astonishing speed. His chronic cough degenerated into bronchitis; his doctor prescribed medicine to help him sleep, but the side effects made his life a misery. "They gave me hallucinations and nightmares night and day to the extent that I would have jumped out of the window or would have killed myself in one way or another if I should not have stopped taking them," he wrote Wil on September 27. "I was literally crazy." Without the medicine, the cough came back worse than ever, accompanied by hoarseness, a bad cold, episodes of paralysis, and inflammation of the kidneys so severe he went eight days without urinating. Theo's behavior became increasingly erratic, increasingly like Vincent's. Discussing a minor matter with his bosses (a painting by a French Orientalist Vincent had admired), Theo grew agitated and belligerent, then abruptly resigned, determined at last to establish himself as an independent dealer, as Vincent had pressed him to do. (Realizing that Theo wasn't himself, his bosses agreed to save Theo's job until he was well again.) He seemed capable of talking only about

Vincent, of seeing only people who had known Vincent. He pored over the drawerful of his brother's letters. He grew obsessed with carrying out his brother's projects. He attempted to rent the Café du Tambourin, where he and Vincent had often wined and dined, in order to establish a society of painters. Out of the blue he sent a telegram to Gauguin: "Departure to tropics assured, money follows—Theo, Director." He consulted his brother's doctor. "I have a feeling that my head is spinning and whatever I write gives me a feeling of dizziness," he wrote Gachet. "It's again the nerves that have got the upper hand." Like his brother, he went mad. Five days after Jo's birthday on October 4, he suffered a complete mental and physical collapse. "He then became violent," wrote Camille Pissarro to his son Lucien. "He who loved his wife and his son so dearly, he wanted to kill them." On October 12, Theo was hospitalized. According to Andries Bonger, writing to his parents, "Rivet [Theo's doctor] said that his case is far worse than Vincent's, and that there is not a spark of hope."

A month later, when he was well enough to travel—albeit in a straitjacket—Theo was transferred to the Institution for the Mentally Ill in Utrecht, where he retreated into the kind of wordless stupor Vincent had experienced after his attacks, punctuated by psychotic episodes in which he tore at his clothing and had to be placed in isolation. When his wife visited, Theo did not recognize her; perturbed and incoherent, he knocked over a table and chairs and the visit was ended. One day, his doctor, trying to rouse Theo from his torpor, read aloud a newspaper article about his brother. "The only interest he had was for the name Vincent," the doctor recalled. Theo died on January 25, 1891, six months after his older brother, at the age of thirty-three. Doctors in Paris had diagnosed Theo as suffering from dementia paralytica, the terminal stage of syphilis (probably contracted during his premarital visits to prostitutes). But in his final medical records, the "cause of disease" was listed, perhaps no less accurately, as "chronic illness, excessive exertion and sorrow."

Chapter Seven
Under the Influence

Harry began to find his way back to us by heading in the opposite direction. Through our grandmother, a Unitarian who dabbled in Quakerism, our mother learned of the American Friends Service Committee, a group that sponsored work projects around the globe (reforming American prisons, building African schools), the kinds of things Mum would have loved to do herself if she hadn't had four children and a full-time job. For Harry, AFSC started out less a way to save the world than a way to get away from home. The summer after his junior year in high school, he hitchhiked up to a small town in western Vermont where, on the grounds of an old tuberculosis sanitarium, he worked at a state institution that housed more than six hundred developmentally disabled children. Harry and twelve other high school volunteers helped them with their "daily living skills," which, in most cases, meant making sure they didn't hurt themselves or anyone else as they brushed their teeth, ate their meals, and used the bathroom. Many of the children had been abused or abandoned by their parents. Many had severe emotional difficulties. Harry remembers one seven-year-old boy, the son of a married white woman who'd had an affair with a black man. Not wanting anyone in their small town to know about the boy, the white mother and her white husband had kept him locked in the basement, tossing food down to him and ignoring his cries. Now the boy stomped around all day muttering "Fuck fucking fuck"—presumably the extent of the vocabulary he'd absorbed in his childhood home. For a seventeen-year-old from a picture-perfect suburb, Harry's Vermont summer was a mind-expanding experience.

Harry's fellow volunteers were a motley collection of brainy loners, aspiring hippies, proto-socialists, and melancholy folkies from across the country. There was lots of late-night rapping about the establishment, lots of guitar playing. Sometimes they sang for their supper at nearby churches—"Puff, the Magic Dragon," "Where Have All the Flowers Gone?," and all the other songs Harry had hated singing with Mum on our nursing home missions. Best of all, there was the possibility of sex. After coming of age in an all-boy family and an all-boy school, Harry realized for the first time that his interest in the opposite gender might be reciprocated. Among people he would recall fondly as "outsiders and misfits," Harry felt at home in a way he never had before. When he returned to Dedham at the end of the summer, the prospect of resuming his old life seemed crushing. He felt he had changed so much, only to come back to a place where nothing had changed. It was at this point, alone in an empty house, that he stood at his bedroom window, wondering whether he should jump.

Ned, Mark, and I had no idea of the exhilaration Harry had felt in Vermont or the despondency he had felt on coming home. When he hitchhiked down to the Cape, where the rest of us were on an end-of-summer vacation, Harry seemed the same slightly prickly older brother who emerged from his room only to dominate us on the croquet pitch or the tennis court. But after his taste of freedom, he was determined to get still farther away. The following summer, he mopped floors at a welding-supply store until he'd saved enough money to travel across the country with a friend. One August dawn I drove him to the turnpike entrance ramp, from which he would hitch to his friend's house in Delaware. I don't remember what we talked about on the drive, or whether we talked at all, but I remember the envy and admiration I felt as I headed back toward my less-than-hip job as a day camp counselor and watched my brother, thumb out, recede in the rearview mirror. After his freshman year in college, Harry spent a second summer with AFSC, painting houses for the elderly in rural Michigan, where he fell in love with another volunteer, an olive-skinned, raven-haired girl of such beauty and sweetness that Ned, Mark, and I were stunned into silence when Harry brought her home for a visit. After his sophomore year, Harry worked as a busboy at an Italian restaurant until he'd saved enough to fly to Australia, where he got a job on a ranch in the outback north of Adelaide. He was about as far away as he could get from home and still be on this planet.

Harry had told the ranch owner he knew how to ride; in fact, his equestrian experience consisted of a few half-hour lessons he'd taken as a child. On the first morning, he was too proud to admit he'd never saddled a horse. He watched the other ranch hands, thinking it couldn't be *that* difficult. But as he cinched his saddle, he noticed them nudging one another and chuckling. The moment Harry hoisted himself onto the horse, trying desperately to look casual, the horse bolted. (Later, the jackaroos, as Australian cowboys are called, told him that the horse they had given him, the aptly named Tuffy, was so dangerous that no one ever rode him—except greenhorns like Harry.) Unfortunately, Harry hadn't cinched Tuffy's saddle tightly enough. It slid under the horse, Harry along with it. Soon, he was being dragged by the foot across the hard ground. Eventually, galloping through a stream, Tuffy shrugged off Harry, who banged his head on a rock and woke up that afternoon in the manager's home. Years later, when he told us the story, he would laugh. At the time, Harry, who prided himself on never showing weakness, was so mortified that he considered walking away from the ranch and never coming back. Realizing, however, that he was dozens of miles from the nearest town, he stayed. He was given a gentler horse, Old Chester, and he spent the next four months herding sheep and cattle, mending fences, castrating bulls, and hanging out with the foul-mouthed jackaroos. At night, he lay in his bunk, plowing through the fattest novels—*Middlemarch, Great Expectations, Moby-Dick*—that he'd been able to cram into his backpack.

Leaving the ranch that winter, Harry spent a few weeks picking tobacco in New Zealand before setting off across Southeast Asia. Determined to travel as far as he could on a few dollars a day, he made his way through Malaysia, Thailand, and India. Soon after arriving in Delhi, however, he found himself doubled over with stomach cramps. (He suspects the culprit was a half-eaten popsicle he found on the street, which, in keeping with Colt sibling dinnertime strategy, he gobbled up before someone else could gobble it up first.) After five days of misery he was able to get a flight home. From the airport, my father rushed him to the hospital. Over the following weeks, to the horror of our parents and the alarm of his doctors, Harry would lose thirty pounds from his already spare frame, withering away to a skeletal 115. I remember visiting him in the hospital and being appalled—and, I am ashamed to admit, slightly gratified—at the sight of my invincible brother seated, as he was throughout my hour-long stay, on a portable steel toilet, hospital johnny hiked up, unshaven, and vulnerable, speaking in a barely audible croak.

With the help of the Centers for Disease Control in Atlanta, the infection was eventually identified as a new strain of shigella, a bacterium resistant to most antibiotics used at the time. After two weeks in the hospital, Harry was well enough to come home. By then, he had made a decision. Before leaving for Australia, he had been a social studies major with vague plans of becoming a teacher or maybe doing something in public health. Now, whether it was the memory of the children he'd cared for in Vermont, the legions of sick people he'd seen in Southeast Asia, or the experience of his own illness, the boy who hated the sight of blood decided to go into medicine. He would be the first doctor in our family for as far back as anyone could remember.

Even when Harry was at home, however, he still seemed 10,000 miles away. That summer, he took organic chemistry, a course he needed in order to switch to the premed track. Friends house-sitting in Cambridge invited him to crash on their couch. But when the owner found out there was an extra person living there, Harry had to leave. Rather than move home, Harry—determined to preserve his newfound independence—spent the last two weeks of summer school sleeping under a fir tree outside the physics lab.

Harry didn't talk much about his adventures, and I didn't ask. Even had he confided in me, I was so preoccupied with my own world I might not have heard. By the time he came back from Australia, I was a sophomore at the same college he had worked so hard to get away from. I hadn't intended to go to Harvard. Well aware that generations of family members had preceded me, I was determined to rebel—by attending Yale. But Yale refused to cooperate, and I ended up at Harvard, where my father, who worked in the development office, had convinced me to apply. Looking back, I wonder whether I had wanted Yale because I didn't want to share a college with my older brother. It seems equally possible that I ended up at Harvard because I wanted to keep up with him.

I arrived at college determined to experience everything I hadn't experienced in high school, and then write poems about it. I vowed to read every book in Widener Library; to drink through all 187 foreign beers on the menu at the Wursthaus; to memorize Yeats's *Collected Poems* as I worked the breakfast shift in the freshman dining hall dishroom; to lose my virginity. My first day, in a paroxysm of ambition, I tried out for a play, auditioned for a singing group, signed up to work on a literary magazine, looked into tutoring inner-city kids, took a yoga class, and chatted into the night with a chestnut-haired government major from California I wouldn't see again till graduation. But having swanned through my provincial prep school, with its graduating class of forty-two boys, I felt lost at Harvard, which seemed populated by intensely blasé Manhattanites who smoked clove cigarettes, subscribed to *The New Republic,* and knew that George Eliot was a woman. Four days after I'd unpacked my father's old army duffle—luggage I had hoped would make me seem simultaneously rugged and ironic—I was aghast to find myself in my father's office, weeping in front of him for the first time since I was a child. Dad listened quietly, assured me things would get better, told me that he and Mum thought the world of me.

I have always remembered Dad's kindness to me that day. What I hadn't remembered, until the evidence stared up at me from my journal thirty-eight years later, was that before I found my father, I had gone looking for my older brother. I wonder how many years it might have saved us if I had found Harry. I wonder what I would have said to him, what he would have said to me, whether I would have cried in front of him. But he wasn't in his dorm room, so I tracked down my father instead.

I wouldn't see Harry till we were home for Thanksgiving. Back on familiar turf, in our familiar roles, I wouldn't have dreamed of telling him that I had needed him. It would be a long time before I looked for Harry again.

My feelings of inadequacy ran deep. I wanted to be a great poet, but I had the sneaking suspicion that my prosaic background left me nothing to write about. I longed to be a coal miner's son like Lawrence, a consumptive like O'Neill, an Irishman like Yeats—or just to have been born in Brooklyn. Lacking such bona fides, I did what I could. I devoured literary biographies and back issues of *The Paris Review* for clues to the writing life. When I read that Hart Crane composed his poems while listening to Ravel's *Bolero,* I bought the record and played it over and over as I wrote, until my roommates threatened to strangle me. When I read that Baudelaire smoked a pipe, I bought a pouch of Balkan Sobranie and took to puffing pensively. When I read that Ernest Hemingway wrote "as soon after first light as possible," I set my alarm and was at my desk by dawn. When I read that James Baldwin wrote after everyone else in his house had gone to bed, I waited till my roommates were asleep, then tiptoed out to the living room to write until I dozed off. Having no idea who I was, I became an amalgam of affectations, like one of those composite characters Mum taught us to draw when we were kids.

From my research, one thing was clear: the most important prerequisite for becoming a writer was an aptitude for unhappiness. Rimbaud, Crane, Kerouac, Thomas, Jarrell, Kees, Fitzgerald, Hemingway—how exquisitely miserable my role models were! The early 1970s were a particularly propitious time for tormented writers. Confessional poetry was at its most loquacious, and the Boston area was especially high-decibel ground. Lowell was teaching at Harvard, in between trips to McLean Hospital; Sexton lived a few suburbs over from my hometown; and Wellesley-bred Sylvia Plath and her suicide had recently been immortalized in *The Savage God,* a dog-eared copy of which every English major seemed to be equipped.

I longed to be a confessional poet, but I had nothing to confess. I was determined to develop some problems of my own—or at least to exude a pheromone of distress. I cultivated a look of Pre-Raphaelite melancholy and talked blithely about how depressed I was. (When a friend told me I resembled the title character in Henry Wallis's painting *The Death of Chatterton*, I swelled with pride.) I abandoned Monet, Renoir, and Pissarro in favor of Munch, Ensor, and Schiele. Like Lana Turner awaiting her destiny at Schwab's, I sat for hours in the sub-sub-basement of Widener Library, writing poems about cemeteries and gargoyles, waiting to be discovered by the *New Yorker*. I composed the first seventy-nine pages of a novel about a sensitive young writer overwhelmed by the insensitivity of the world around him. I wrote down everything I did or said or thought in a succession of numbered journals, the current volume of which I carried everywhere and produced whenever I felt even more self-conscious than usual, scribbling in its pale-green pages with an air of sheepish apology, as if I had received an unexpected call from the muse that I just had to take. At one point, believing my genius couldn't be contained in a single volume, I kept *two* journals, one a repository of poignant similes, witty aperçus, and other poetic raw material, the other a blow-by-blow account of what I read for class, what I ate for lunch, what I dreamed at night, and other momentous details of my daily life—all of which I assumed would be of vital interest to future literary scholars who, long after my death, would comb through my "juvenilia" for clues to my oeuvre. And I drank.

Alcohol was not new to me. When I had gulped down my first beer at sixteen and been infused by a sudden, golden warmth, I had an epiphany: *This* is what my father found on the way home from work at night. Liquor seemed to have an effect on my self-confidence as immediate and prodigious as that of spinach on Popeye's biceps. In high school, my friends and I had drunk whenever possible, but the opportunities had been few: a jelly jar of gin pilfered from a parental liquor cabinet, a beer or two drained at the once-in-a-blue-moon party we happened to get wind of. At college, there was an unlimited supply: half-gallons of Almaden at poetry workshops; cases of Schlitz at proctors' parties; kegs of beer at dances; tureens of sticky sangria at cast parties; buckets of Hawaiian Punch and grain alcohol at fraternity blowouts; tumblers of Black Russians at the alumni receptions for which my a capella group performed; goblets of cognac at final club dinners; bottle after bottle of bourbon, scotch, and vodka in the bars that lined Mass Ave; shelf after shelf of anything I wanted at the package store, which I now knew as "the packy." As if alcohol wasn't enough, other culturally sanctioned substances were readily available. By the time I got to college, the sixties revolution I had longed to be part of had ended, but the drugs were still around. With the Vietnam War all but over, and flower power having wilted to a desultory residue of Watergate hearings and aging, burnt-out rock groups, I could no longer justify their use on sociocultural grounds, but I did them anyway, consuming whatever was put in front of me the way an anthropologist in the field doggedly eats every bite of the native fare provided by his indigenous hosts. And, after years of trying to shame my parents into quitting, at the very moment when cigarette packs were first required to carry a label warning that their contents "may be hazardous to your health," I took up smoking myself. How could I be a bona fide poet without a drink in one hand and a cigarette in the other?

I started slowly, but, bringing to bear the competitive instincts honed at the Colt kitchen table, I drank with a certain ambition, as if the alcohol itself had been spiked with the divine afflatus, as if I believed that by drinking like Hart Crane, I might be able to write like Hart Crane. In time, however, the quantity and quality of the poems I wrote decreased in proportion to the amount I drank. Late-night literary conversations became increasingly sodden. The mellifluous vocabulary of poetry (pantoum, villanelle, sonnet, strophe, sestina, anapest, caesura, dactyl, spondee, trochee) gave way to the bruised vocabulary of drinking (wrecked, toasted, wasted, basted, plastered, blitzed, soused, fried, smashed, stewed, pissed, polluted, totaled, bombed, hammered, loaded, lubricated, trashed, fucked up). I had read that the Eskimos had their sixty words for snow; my friends and I had nearly that many for inebriation. Our favorite—a word so redolent of unconscious self-loathing it's amazing we could bring ourselves to utter it—was *shitfaced*, whose pronunciation varied according to the amount of alcohol ingested. The more we drank, the more we'd emphasize the second syllable: "Shi'FACED," we'd suddenly roar in one another's faces, apropos of nothing. (In its etymological defense, I might point out that *shitfaced* was a versatile word, capable of being dismantled into its component parts and redeployed with subtly different shades of meaning: *getting shitty* implied a slightly higher blood alcohol level than *getting faced*.) I abandoned my plan of drinking my way around the world at the Wursthaus—too expensive, too bourgeois—in favor of downing pints of Guinness at the Plough & Stars, a cozy pub whose Irish overtones seemed far more literarily useful, or draining twenty-five-cent drafts at Whitney's, a blue-collar hole-in-the-wall patronized by solitary middle-aged men whose silence I assumed bespoke an oracular wisdom and not a pie-eyed stupor as we marinated in the evening light, a tableau vivant I convinced myself was not pathetic but Hopperesque.

I viewed my drinking as a necessary adjunct to my poetry, but it served another, less overt purpose. I had spent my first eighteen years trying to be the good son, the one my parents didn't have to worry about. I was tired of being Gallant, who, I now realized, was an insufferable suck-up. I wanted a turn at being Goofus—or, as I preferred to interpret him at the time, Rimbaud. But my transgressions were less flights of the imagination than boorish frat-boy behavior: stealing beer mugs from bars; urinating in public; breaking bottles; lobbing trash cans into the street. (Even then, I hedged my bets; before I threw the trash cans, I looked around to make sure no police were in the vicinity.) On a visit home, listening to my mother fret about my brothers, I was suddenly annoyed. "*I* have problems too," I blurted out. (I felt a sibling rivalry, it seems, even when it came to dysfunction.) Mum was taken aback. I'm not sure she really wanted to know that her happiest son was unhappy. She asked the right questions anyway. She was ready to listen. But I wasn't ready to tell her. I aspired to being an enfant terrible, yet I still wanted to be a good boy.

Through it all, I convinced myself I was having a good time. Indeed, in my journals, moments of exuberance surface through the fog: walking home from Boston jazz joints in the rain after the subway shut down for the night; singing with my friends in the echoey bowels of deserted parking lots; dancing to Motown in the off-campus apartment we called Xanadu, the top floor of a four-story rattletrap that visibly swayed during our parties like the joint-is-literally-jumping sharecropper shacks in 1930s cartoons; rappelling down the side of a friend's dormitory at dawn as a milk truck clattered by. At some point, however, I went from *wanting* to have problems to *having* problems. I can't pinpoint the moment when this metamorphosis occurred. Perhaps it was the night when, at the end of a long, bibulous evening, a friend drove a carful of us the wrong way through a one-way underpass, and, while the other passengers screamed at him to turn around, I cheered him on. I called myself a poet but I couldn't even see that this nihilistic escapade was a metaphor for my own unraveling life. Drinking had started out as an adjunct to the poetry; over four years of college, poetry had become an excuse for the drinking. If, as I began to suspect, I couldn't write like Hart Crane, at least I could drink like Hart Crane. Senior year, I was invited to be part of a reading sponsored by a local literary magazine that had accepted one of my poems. It was a big opportunity for me. At a Kentucky Derby party that afternoon, I drank so many mint juleps that by the time I took the stage that evening, I could barely make out the words on the page.

Deep down I knew that my drinking had nothing to do with poetry. I had arrived at Harvard determined to feel everything, and I convinced myself that alcohol would assist me in that task. "Only connect!" I had written in my journal after reading E. M. Forster freshman year, and as I wandered from place to place, person to person, party to party, I thought I was doing nothing *but* connecting. I see now, of course, that I was doing everything in my power to *keep* from connecting. Harry had gone ten thousand miles to get away; I stayed close to home but found another way to remove myself. At some level, I must have understood this. My poetry—more confessional than I realized at the time—was, I see now, all about missed connections: estranged brothers, distant fathers. (Curiously, I never connected my downing drafts at Whitney's with my father downing cocktails at the end of the day; if I had, I would have had to admit that I was drinking far more than he ever did.) I only knew that as long as I was holding a bottle, the night seemed to hold possibility. Eventually, however, the bartender shouted last call, the music ended, the dancing stopped, the lights came up, and the night always ended the same way, as I observed in my journal, in a rare moment of honesty: "And once again I find myself cold and alone, wandering the three o'clock streets."

The connection I most wanted to make, of course, was with the opposite sex. I was mortified beyond measure that, despite embarrassed make-out sessions with girls who were almost as nervous as I, I was, technically, still a virgin. In my desperation, I made reconnaissance missions across the river to those establishments whose pinups I'd found so alluring in high school and watched bored strippers and baggy-pants comics on the stage of the erotically-if-oxymoronically-named Pilgrim Theatre, telling myself that I was bearing witness to the last remnants of traditional burlesque and my visits, therefore, had something of an educational component. On a college glee club tour of Europe, after evenings spent singing Renaissance motets in ancient cathedrals, I'd search out the city's red-light district as if I were a sociologist conducting cross-cultural research, eyeing the prostitutes hungrily but never getting closer than the far side of the street. After a summer digging ditches in Southern California, I took a bus to Tijuana, determined, at last, to lose my virginity. But after patrolling the streets for several hours, trying to decide which dingy bar might yield the most accessible options, I couldn't find a bank that would cash my traveler's checks on a Sunday, and had to take the bus back to San Diego in my still-uncorrupted state. I told myself that if things went on this way much longer, I'd go to New York and audition for *Oh! Calcutta!*, and somehow, with all that onstage nudity, I couldn't help getting laid. Or I'd join a cult—one of those loosey-goosey ones in which even the ugliest people were permitted to take part in the orgies. In the end, I was spared such lengths. One night at a party at Xanadu, an older woman (maybe even as ancient as twenty-four or twenty-five), a friend of a friend, who was at least as drunk as I, was waiting for me when I went to bed. Though grateful to have lost my virginity, a week later, after a visit to the college health services, I learned that I had gained a case of the crabs—a fact I noted casually in my journal as if it were just another occupational hazard of the writing life. But the whole business left an enduring residue of shame.

All the time I was wandering around Cambridge in confusion, Harry was buckling down to his premed program. He and I were not only at the same college, we were, after his year in Australia, in the same graduating class. Though we lived only three blocks from each other, we might as well have been on opposite sides of the world. What little time Harry didn't spend in libraries and laboratories he spent playing chess with his roommates and working as a bartender to save money for medical school. (He rarely drank himself.) I spent my time editing literary magazines and singing with my all-male a capella group, whose members constituted a posse of substitute brothers. I was still a little intimidated by my real brother. Harry had worked with disabled children, hitchhiked across the United States, herded cattle in Australia, traveled across Southeast Asia, nearly died in India, and been awarded conscientious-objector status during the war—just the kinds of experiences I dreamed of being able to cite in the author's biography I envisioned on the back of my first book of poems, under a photograph of the brooding author. By contrast, I had taught suburban summer-campers to make lanyards, crossed the United States by Greyhound bus, toured Europe with my college glee club, and been enormously relieved when, nine months after I registered, the draft was abolished. But there was something more. Harry and I had gone to college to try on new selves, and now we avoided each other, as if our shared childhood was a secret we didn't want anyone else to stumble upon. Friends who found out I had a brother couldn't understand why I never invited him over, why I never mentioned him. How could I? Harry knew who I really was beneath my literary camouflage—after all, he had heard me chant the word *looties,* heard me sing the *Beverly Hillbillies* theme song twenty times in a row, seen me writhe under the pressure of a surgically applied noogie. In any case, after searching for him the first week of freshman year, I never walked the three blocks to see him again. Instead, I wrote poems about the distance between us.

One night during sophomore year, on my way to meet some friends at a bar, I saw a man with a familiar-looking mop of curly black hair studying the notices on a bulletin board. It was Harry. Telling myself I shouldn't keep my friends waiting, I kept walking. Was I worried I'd be embarrassed by him—or that he'd be embarrassed by me? Senior year, I ran into Harry on the street near his dorm. We talked. According to my journal, "I tried to explain some things to him." What things? That I was drinking too much? That I felt lost? That I didn't understand how we had grown so far apart? That despite the distance between us, I still felt inexplicably bound to him? One afternoon, I saw the movie *On the Waterfront,* and when I heard Brando say, "You was my brother, Charlie. You should have looked out for me a little bit," I found myself tearing up.

A few months later, we graduated, and Harry was off to Alabama to work in a mental hospital, and I was off to write poetry in Paris.

Little did I know that Ned was no less lost than I. When I started college, Ned had three more years of high school, years he wouldn't have to share the campus with me. But our mother began teaching there, and her shadow was far larger than mine. She was not only a wildly popular art instructor, but a Pied Piper to the idiosyncratic, the quirky, and the confused—words that might have described Ned at the time. Seeking guidance from his teacher-mother, however, was the last thing Ned was likely to do. Ned joined the outing club, rowed varsity crew, starred in plays, and sang in the glee club and the a capella group. Girls melted over his McCartneyesque solo on the Beatles' "If I Fell." But he still felt something of a failure. "Looking back, I think I unconsciously decided that since I couldn't succeed as much as my older brothers, I was going to go the other way—and *not* be successful," he says now. He gravitated toward a group of similarly disaffected classmates whose motto was "Fuck it." Friday nights, wearing the old green canvas jackets they'd bought at the Army Navy store, they'd wait outside the packy for someone over the age of eighteen willing to buy a bottle of Jack Daniel's for them. Taking it to a friend's house, they'd drink, smoke pot, and listen to music until someone passed out.

Ned was happier in the summer, away from home, when he cleared out a room for himself in the barn of our grandparents' place on Cape Cod and worked at the local fish market, unloading trucks, prying open quahogs, filleting striped bass. It seemed an extraordinarily cool job to me, the kind Kerouac would have had if he'd *had* a job. At night, Ned and his friends found as much excitement as they could in a quiet resort community: stealing bottles of parental booze; tossing cherry bombs; executing tire-squealing, sand-spraying 360s on the beach at night in Dad's ancient Comet, which was known to Ned's friends as the White Bomb, not for its velocity but for its decrepit appearance. (Years after Mark had nearly fallen through the rotting floorboards of our old Ford Fairlane, Ned discovered that the holes in the floorboards of the Comet made a handy emergency disposal chute for joints whenever a police car hove into view.) One summer morning we looked out the window of our grandparents' house and instead of the familiar Stars and Stripes flying from the flagpole we spied a red-and-yellow McDonald's banner—plunder from one of Ned's nocturnal exploits. Another morning we came down to the beach to find BONZO DOG BAND scrawled in red paint on a boulder, words that to our grandmother, as she came down for her morning swim, must have seemed as inscrutable as the words *mene mene tekel upharsin* had seemed to Belshazzar. The handiwork of a drunken friend of Ned's who had felt compelled to immortalize the name of his favorite rock group, the words would resist Ned's scrubbing and more than a decade of salt spray before they faded.

I had always suspected that beneath our old reflexive strife Ned and I were more alike than we cared to admit. But on visits home, we moved warily and politely around each other. At his high school graduation, I read what friends had written about him in his yearbook, below a photograph in which he sat cross-legged on the bow of a boat, brandishing a beer. Their commentary was a farrago of allusions and in-jokes, none of which I understood. I didn't know my brother. I didn't have a clue.

Ned applied to Harvard because he felt he was supposed to, because his older brothers had, but his grades weren't good enough and he wound up at a small Connecticut college with an acclaimed theater program. During his freshman year, I drove down to New London with my parents to see him in *The Madwoman of Chaillot*. At the height of my suffering-poet period, I envied Ned the dark, dreary, down-at-heels city where Eugene O'Neill, one of my heroes, had been so miserable. (Unbeknown to me, Ned loved O'Neill, too, and later told me that while I had been drinking twenty-five-cent drafts at Whitney's, he had been drinking twenty-five-cent drafts at the Dutch Tavern, an old O'Neill hangout.) Ned had traded in his army jacket for a sheepskin coat that, with his new mustache—much thicker than my own painstakingly cultivated weedy strip—made him look like a younger version of the Marlboro Man. Though Ned vowed to work harder in college, he spent a good deal of his time at parties. One night, after an evening of drinking, he and his friends broke into the kitchen of the downtown hotel in which, coincidentally, O'Neill's older brother had spent his last years at the bar, and stole several tubs of ice cream. They were gulping it down when Ned noticed a potted palm he thought might look good in his dorm room. He began dragging the heavy container across the lobby, but when he tried to maneuver it through the revolving door, it got stuck. The night watchman came running. Ned was too drunk and too stubborn to retreat without his prize, and the guard punched him over and over before he was able to crawl out to the car in which his friends were waiting. When he came home for Christmas, Ned still had a black eye that, he explained to our parents, he had acquired in a fall. When he told me the real story, I was impressed. Ned was a far more authentic enfant terrible than I.

A few nights later, Ned came home with the other eye black, too. He and a few friends from high school had been drinking in a dicey part of Boston when they'd been hassled by a group of young men. Ned's friends had fled; Ned had taken refuge in a phone booth, which his attackers rocked until it tipped over. I felt chastened. One black eye seemed a badge of honor; two seemed a little sad. Ned spent much of the vacation in his room, the shades drawn.

Not long before going back to college, Ned had a fierce argument with our mother. Ned retreated upstairs, and I followed. I urged him to talk to Mum, to repair their relationship. He shook his head, trembling, trying to hold back tears. "It's too late," he said. "It can never be fixed." He added, bitterly, that ours was the most screwed-up family he knew. I protested that ours was no worse than some, and a lot better than many. I said that at least we brothers got along. Ned eyed me as if I were crazy. "Brothers are supposed to look out for each other, they're supposed to be close to each other," he said. "We're nothing like that."

While the rest of us were pulling away from the family, Mark was longing to pull the family together. But with Harry and me at college and Ned spending as much time out of the house as possible and then going off to college himself, Mark was, in essence, the only brother still at home. After years of not being able to get a word in edgewise at the dinner table, he was alone with our parents in a suddenly quiet house. In some ways, Dad, whom he adored, was the closest thing Mark had to a brother at the time. Dad and Mark tossed a ball in the backyard, entered parent-child tennis tournaments, went to Harvard football games together, and watched the Red Sox and the Bruins on TV—all the stuff Dad had once done with Harry and me. When Dad came home from work with a few drinks under his belt, Mark tried to ignore it. With his brothers gone, Mark relied even more on his pack of friends. Every Saturday morning after breakfast, they'd gather in someone's backyard for all-day nerf football games, breaking for interludes of street hockey or walks down to the Plaza to hang out over milk shakes at Friendly's. When I was home, Mark and I would kick a soccer ball or play knee hockey, and Mark's delight at being included was palpable. Preoccupied with my "problems," however, I'd cut short our game to return to Cambridge, in case there was a party I might be missing.

If only we had spent more time together beyond the gravitational forces of home, my brothers and I might have acknowledged one another's fitful evolution. But on the rare occasions we were all in one place—Thanksgiving, Christmas, a few days at the end of summer—we quickly, unwittingly, resumed our familiar roles: Harry the loner, Ned the rebel, Mark the baby of the family, me the peacemaker. Even as I worked so hard to become someone new myself, I wouldn't allow my brothers to change. There were good times: playing table hockey, laughing at old jokes, sharing popcorn at a movie. But for the most part, we remained in our own spheres. We no longer fought, or even argued much. It might have been better to have had that contact than none at all. But while I lamented the distance between us—"I think there should be no relationship closer than that of two brothers," I wrote in my journal—I did nothing to bring us together. "When it came time for me to leave," I wrote after one visit, "I had the sensation of blowing it—not getting down to the mind-bending conversations I know we could and should be having." The summer after Harry and I graduated from college, our grandfather died. We met for the funeral on a drizzly July day in the small Rhode Island town where he had grown up. After the service, as my brothers and I shouldered Gramps's coffin through the church, it struck me how united we must have seemed to the people we passed. Outside, we slid the coffin into the hearse, and scattered to our separate lives.

Christmas was the one time we tacitly agreed to be a family, to let the comforting rituals lull us into recapturing some of our early happiness: trimming the tree with Mum's hand-painted ornaments, crowning the top branch with Harry's angel; listening to Dad read "The Night Before Christmas" in his gravelly voice; standing shoulder to shoulder as we sang "O Come All Ye Faithful" at midnight mass; walking home together through the sleeping town. At seven on Christmas morning, Mark, the only one of us still young enough to want to get up early, would knock gently on our doors: "It's time for stockings," he'd say. Harry, Ned, and I would groan, but we'd trudge into our parents' bedroom to open the stockings Mum had filled by the fireplace. Afterward, the smell of bacon lured us down to the kitchen, where Dad was fixing a scrambled-egg-and-English-muffin breakfast. We grumbled good-naturedly about the family tradition that said every last dish had to be washed before we were permitted to file into the living room for presents. Led by Harry, we joined in fraternal choruses of exaggerated oohs and aahs as each box was opened. Clearing away the wrapping paper and ribbons, we agreed that even though Mum had declared it was going to be a "lean Christmas" (triggering fraternal singalongs of "I'm Dreaming of a Lean Christmas" à la Bing Crosby), it hadn't been lean at all.

One Christmas morning, when I was twenty-one, we gathered in the kitchen, where Dad was cooking our traditional eggs-and-bacon break-fast. The previous evening, Dad had been at a party at a neighbor's house. He had come home late, slurring his good nights, clearly incapable of accompanying us to midnight mass. Now he stood at the stove, thick-voiced, heavy-lidded. No one said anything. Mum quietly folded napkins and slipped them under the forks on the table. Harry, Ned, and I leaned against the counter. For years, we had ignored our father's drinking, as one might ignore a low-grade fever, and now we pretended, as we always did, that nothing was wrong. I think we might have gone on pretending forever if Mark—at thirteen the youngest, the smallest, the sweetest, the one who found it hardest to make himself heard, the one to whom our father was closest—hadn't spoken through his gathering tears. "Dad," he said quietly, shaking his head. "You drank too much last night and it makes me so sad when you do that." Our father continued arranging lines of bacon on the paper towel as his eyes filled.

It would be several years before he quit drinking for good. But that moment in the kitchen was, I think, what persuaded him to stop.

Chapter Eight

Brothers, Inc.: Chico, Harpo, Groucho, Gummo, and Zeppo Marx

Watching the first few scenes of *The Cocoanuts*, a 1929 film set in a well-appointed but down-on-its-luck Florida hotel, moviegoers settled in for what seemed to be a routine tale of star-crossed lovers and double-crossing crooks. Twenty minutes in, a curly-wigged fellow in a battered top hat and a tattered trenchcoat five sizes too large saunters into the hotel lobby, followed closely by a man wearing the kind of bowl-shaped hat that might suit an organ grinder's monkey, a corduroy jacket five sizes too small, and the grin of a child who's knows he's about to get away with something. The grinning man speaks in an exaggerated Italian accent; the top-hatted fellow doesn't speak at all, though he carries a walking stick topped with a rubber bulb that he honks as he scurries after every young woman who enters the lobby. Unusual guests, to be sure, but no stranger than the cigar-waggling hotel manager, who wears a swallowtail coat, wire-rimmed spectacles, and unnaturally rectangular eyebrows that, like his shiny black mustache, appear on closer inspection to be made of shoe polish. The only normal-looking man on the premises is the desk clerk, a stiff, well-groomed chap in a double-breasted suit who might have stepped from the pages of a men's catalogue.

Spotting potential guests, the manager and the clerk, hands extended, stride across the lobby toward the new arrivals, who, hands extended, stride toward their hosts. The four men stride right past each other like proverbial ships in the night, setting off a cockeyed quadrille in which they chase each other around and over the sofa. When the chase subsides, the following things occur: the silent fellow eats the buttons off a bellboy's jacket; the grinning man wrestles the bellboy for possession of the empty suitcase; the silent fellow begins hurling fountain pens into the wall as if they were darts; the manager and the grinning man swap nonsensical quips ("Would you like a suite on the third floor?" "No, I'll take a Polack in the basement") as matter-of-factly as if they were chatting about the weather; the silent fellow climbs over the front desk and rips up the letters in the pigeonholes; the manager helpfully hands the letters up to him for shredding; the silent fellow brushes some glue onto a wad of sealing wax, gobbles it up, and washes down his meal with a swig from the inkwell.

The four characters play off one another so instinctively—except, perhaps, for the handsome clerk, who, as if realizing he can't keep up, disappears midway through the proceedings—that their nonsense appears to make perfect sense. Many moviegoers refused to believe that four such mismatched characters, who seemed almost to belong to four different species, could have been played by brothers.

One suspects they could have been played *only* by brothers. And even then, perhaps only by Groucho, Harpo, Chico, and Zeppo Marx.

*   *   *

When I was seven or eight years old, I was browsing the bookshelves in the playroom of my grandparents' house when I came across a children's book called *The Five Chinese Brothers*. Based on an ancient folktale, it tells the story of five lookalike brothers, each of whom possesses a unique power. One can swallow the sea, one has an iron neck, one can stretch his legs endlessly, one can survive fire, and one can hold his breath forever. The sea-swallowing brother is unjustly accused of a crime and sentenced to be beheaded. On the night before his execution, the brother with the iron neck secretly takes his place. The executioner swings his axe in vain. The judge sentences the brother to drown, but the brother with the stretchable legs steps in. One by one, each brother uses his singular gift to help the condemned man avoid execution. Finally, the judge gives up and pardons the prisoner.

I was fascinated by the book. The protagonists were as fantastic as comic book superheroes, and yet they happened to be brothers. What if my brothers and I had such powers? What would they be? Would we work well together? At that age it was hard to imagine us working together at all. Harry preferred doing things on his own, whereas Ned and I couldn't operate a Kool-Aid stand for more than half an hour without squabbling and tearing it down.

Brothers who have been rivals since childhood, brothers who have painstakingly carved out their own fraternal niches, and even brothers who have always been close might find pursuing their careers in the company of a sibling or two a little claustrophobic. Yet ever since Aaron served as Moses's spokesman, brothers have worked together. They have ruled kingdoms (Charlemagne and Carloman); owned department stores (the Strauses); manufactured soap (the Levers); made wine (the Gallos); operated circuses (the Ringlings); performed standup comedy (the Smotherses); made furniture (the Stickleys); founded advertising agencies (the Saatchis); started banks (the Lazards); robbed banks (the Barkers); run Mafia families (too many to count); overseen drug cartels (the Félixes); sold cars (the Renaults); performed on the flying trapeze (the Wallendas); made music (the Beach Boys); produced movies (the Warners); written musicals (the Shermans); organized labor unions (the Reuthers); led posses (the Earps); and starred in sideshows (Chang and Eng, the original Siamese Twins). Although the intimacy and complexity of the sibling bond can make such collaborations fraught and highly combustible, it can also make them rich and successful.

When I was a child, I often spent my allowance on Smith Brothers Cough Drops, whether I had a cough or not. I liked the grown-up taste, the tongue-stimulating sensation of the initials "SB" molded onto each lozenge, and the old-fashioned package, on which the heads of the bearded Smiths, looking like retired Civil War generals, faced each other over what I assumed to be their names, "Trade" and "Mark." But I especially liked the sound of the word "Brothers" in the company title, which conjured intimacy, solidity, durability, trustworthiness—all the things I longed for in my own sibling relationships. I'm not sure I would have forked over my dime for Smith *Cousins* Cough Drops.

*   *   *

Left to their own devices, the Marx brothers might have turned out very differently. Chico wanted to be a professional gambler, Harpo a piano player, Groucho a doctor, Gummo an inventor, Zeppo a boxer. Their mother had other plans. Harpo, with an inordinate amount of help from a ghostwriter, famously described Minnie Marx as possessing "the stamina of a brewery horse, the drive of a salmon fighting his way up a water-fall, the cunning of a fox, and a devotion to her brood as fierce as any she-lion's." Born Minna Schoenberg in Dornum, Germany, she spent her childhood crisscrossing the country by wagon with her father, a traveling magician-cum-ventriloquist, and her mother, a yodeler-cum-harpist. In 1879, when she was fourteen, the family emigrated to New York, where Minna—now Minnie—worked five years in garment-industry sweat-shops before marrying Samuel Marx, a tailor from Alsace chiefly remem-bered for the ineptitude of his sewing, the excellence of his cooking, and the endlessness of his pinochle games. The young couple settled in Yorkville, an immigrant neighborhood on Manhattan's Upper East Side, where Minnie gave birth to five boys, and immediately began plotting to hoist them above their working-class origins.

Long after Minnie Marx was dead, Groucho liked to say, "Our mother treated us all equally—with contempt." In fact, Minnie neither treated her sons with contempt—the intensity of her affection would leave lasting scars—nor did she treat them equally. From the beginning, she favored her eldest son, Leonard, who would one day be known as Chico. Perhaps it was because an earlier child had died of influenza at the age of seven months, and her grief intensified her attachment to the next. Perhaps it was because Leonard was a robust baby: fair-skinned, blue-eyed, and slightly chubby, like his mother. Or because he had a flirtatious, manipu-lative personality not unlike hers. Or because he was bright. When he chose to attend, Leo did well in school. His ability to solve complicated math problems in his head led teachers to assume he'd become a bookkeeper. But he preferred to apply his mathematical gifts elsewhere. By the time he was a teenager, Leo was running away from home, fighting in the streets, betting on boxing matches, hustling pool, and playing all-night crap games in the back room of a cigar store on Lexington Avenue. There would be a lifelong tendency among his brothers (and some biographers) to dismiss his excesses as the endearing, boys-will-be-boys antics of a congenital scamp, but there was ample evidence early on that the eldest Marx brother was a compulsive gambler. After he quit school at twelve to work in a lace factory in Brooklyn, he'd bet away his paycheck long before he got home. To cover his losses, he stole from his own family. His parents knew that if something went missing—his grandfather's silver-headed cane, his father's tailoring shears, the one-dollar gold Ingersoll watch his younger brother Adolph had been given for his bar mitzvah—it would likely turn up in the window of the pawn shop on East Ninety-Eighth Street. Yet Leo's attitude was so confident, his lies so inventive, and his mother so doting that he got away with almost everything. Hoping to divert her beloved eldest son from juvenile delinquency, Minnie bought him an old upright piano and paid for weekly lessons. Leo demonstrated a distinct aversion to practicing, but he was a quick study and was soon performing in saloons and nickelodeons. For his finale, he played audience requests, blindfolded, with a bedsheet covering the keyboard.

Like his mother, Leo had chutzpah to spare, and occasionally double-booked jobs, in which case he recruited his brother Adolph—"Ahdie"—who looked so much like him that few people could tell the difference, to play one of the engagements. (When they were older, Chico would take advantage of their resemblance to cover up his affairs, insisting to outraged husbands that the culprit had been his brother, known by then as Harpo.) Younger by fifteen months, Ahdie was his brother's temperamental opposite. Leo was his mother's child, brash and determined, all restless forward motion; Ahdie was his father's, mild and tolerant, content to let life take him where it may. Leo was facile and sharp; Ahdie was a slow learner, barely able to read and write before dropping out of school in second grade and turning to his older brother for instruction. "In a short time he taught me how to handle a pool cue, how to play cards and how to bet on the dice," the younger brother recalled. Leo used his gift for accents to talk his way out of trouble in the German, Irish, and Italian neighborhoods that surrounded their Jewish enclave; Ahdie carried an apple or an old tennis ball to bribe his way past streetcorner bullies. Leo imitated the way people spoke; Ahdie, embarrassed by his high, squeaky voice, imitated the way people looked. Trailing after his older brother, Ahdie, too, seemed headed for a life of gambling and petty thievery, but he gradually drifted off to explore the world on his own. Between the ages of fourteen and nineteen, he worked as a pie sorter in a bakery, delivery boy for a grocer, apprentice to a butcher, bellhop at a theatrical hotel, janitor in a Bowery saloon, packer for a greeting card distributor, dogwalker for an actress, stockboy in a department store, pin setter at a bowling alley, cigarette boy at a German social club, ragpicker at a textile house, and piano player at a Long Island brothel, where he pounded out his two-song repertoire, "Waltz Me Around Again, Willie" and "Love Me and the World Is Mine," over and over, varying the tempo and the octave. His mother worried that Ahdie lacked ambition, especially compared with his older brother, who walked the streets at a trot. Years later, he would recall, "It went without saying that I was the untalented member of the family."

If Minnie found Leo the most irresistible of her children, she found Julius, who would be better known as Groucho, the least appealing. Julius had darker skin, coarser hair, a bigger nose, a frailer body, and a slight walleye. From an early age, Julius sensed his mother's disappointment—which, to a sensitive, quick-to-take-offense boy, felt like contempt. Furthermore, by the time Julius came along, his lookalike older brothers had already paired off, developing their own in-jokes and secrets, leaving him to fend for himself. Nearsighted Julius wasn't as good as Leo and Ahdie at stoop ball, and he disdained as childish the card games they spent every spare moment playing. He found something else to interest him, something his brothers cared nothing about: books. He devoured the Frank Merriwell stories and Horatio Alger's rags-to-riches tales. He developed a rich vocabulary and a stinging wit to hide his loneliness and clear space for himself in a crowded household. But it seemed unfair to him that Leo, who stole from his own family, could do no wrong in his mother's eyes, while he, the dutiful son who did well in school and turned over to his parents the dollar a week he earned singing in the boys' choir at the Episcopal Church on Madison Avenue, received only indifference; that Leo, who rarely practiced, should get the only piano lessons the family could afford, while he, who had the best ear of the brothers, had to teach himself to play. Julius's resentment of Leo, and his distrust of the world in general, was so evident that his mother called him *Der Eifersüchtige*—"The Jealous One." That his mother spoiled his younger brothers—Milton (the future Gummo), a sickly child with a rheumatic heart, and Herbert (the future Zeppo), the baby of the family, born nine years after Milton—only reinforced Julius's sense of neglect. As did the fact that, like Leo and Ahdie, the two youngest Marx brothers eventually paired off, too, leaving Julius, the middle child, odd man out. His peripheral status made him all the more determined to be noticed. "Groucho was the most serious, and he was the most ambitious," a neighbor recalled. "He wanted to be somebody."

In later years, the Marx Brothers would reminisce about their early days through the forgiving scrim of nostalgia: playing prisoner's base and one o' cat; stealing peaches from the orchard behind Jacob Ruppert's Park Avenue mansion; wrestling in their cramped, three-bedroom apartment on East Ninety-Third Street, where the door was always unlocked and a parade of relatives and neighbors dropped by to drink coffee or play cards. But their childhood was shadowed by a sense of deprivation that fueled their desire to escape. The four older brothers shared a double bed, two at each end. "We never went hungry, at least not *too* hungry," said Groucho. "But there was generally some kind of brawl at the dinner-table over who would get what." (Years later, when the brothers started making good money in vaudeville, Harpo once ordered one of everything on a restaurant menu just because he could.) The brothers weren't together much—Leo off gambling, Ahdie wandering the city, Julius in school, Milton sick at home, and Herbert too young to be part of things—but when they were, they were a five-person wrecking crew. "The boys were wild and [their father] couldn't control them . . ." recalled a neighbor. "The place would be a shambles, especially if Mrs. Marx left them alone. They would tear down the draperies." At a cousin's wedding reception, Ahdie and Julius encountered a urinal for the first time. They jumped on it glee-fully until the pipe ruptured, flooding the hall and bringing the festivities to a halt.

Minnie was determined that her children do better than their feckless father. She had an alternative role model in mind: her younger brother, Adolph Schoenberg, who had quit his job as a pants presser, changed his name to Al Shean, and become one of the highest-paid entertainers in vaudeville. Once a month, Uncle Al came to visit, decked out in matching fedora and spats, twirling a gold-headed cane, and exuding a cologne-scented nimbus of prosperity as he regaled his nephews with tales of life on the stage. Minnie took them to the theater to see their uncle perform; at home, they imitated his routines, capably enough that she decided one of them should try show business. The logical candidate was her piano-playing eldest, but Leo was an irresponsible hell-raiser. Ahdie had no apparent talent, Milton stammered, and Herbert was too young. That left Julius, who, though homely and awkward, had a decent soprano. Though Julius was the best student among the brothers, Minnie pulled him from school in the sixth grade. Julius had dreamed of being a doctor but was eager to please the mother who never seemed pleased with him, and he went on the road as a female impersonator in a small-time vaudeville group that billed itself as the Leroy Trio. Though his first tour ended badly (the other two "Leroys" ran off with his earnings, stranding him in Cripple Creek, Colorado), and though he would forever resent having his education halted because his eldest brother wouldn't pull his weight, Julius found, in the attention of strangers, something he'd never gotten at home. "For the first time in my life," he recalled, "I felt like I wasn't a nonentity."

One by one, his brothers were conscripted into the act by maternal fiat. Milton didn't stammer when he sang, so in 1907, Minnie dressed him and Julius in straw boaters and white duck suits, paired them with a sixteen-year-old girl, and dubbed them the Three Nightingales. The girl sang off-key, fell in unrequited love with Julius, and wasn't cost-effective (she couldn't share a hotel room with the male Nightingales), so Minnie replaced her with a boy. The trio met with a measure of success until its opening night at Henderson's Coney Island, when Minnie learned that the theater had promised its customers a quartet. Hurrying to Manhattan, she strode down the aisle of the Thirty-Fourth Street nickelodeon in which nineteen-year-old Ahdie was plying his two-song repertoire, and ordered him to follow her. On the el train back to Coney Island, Ahdie changed into the white duck suit she'd brought, while Minnie screened him from fellow passengers with newspapers and taught him the words to "Darling Nelly Gray," telling Ahdie to fake the bass part, where he could do the least damage. She marched him into the wings, and, as the band struck up the Nightingales' cue, shoved him onstage. Looking across the footlights at what he later remembered as "a sea of hostile, mocking faces," Ahdie was terrified. "With my first look at my first audience I reverted to being a boy again," he recalled. "My reaction was instantaneous and overwhelming. I wet my pants."

Minnie might have chosen Leo for the act had she been able to find him. While his brothers were touring, Leo worked a succession of jobs that took him far from Yorkville: pool hustler, lifeguard, circus wrestler, flyweight boxer, whorehouse pianist. In 1911, he was working in Pittsburgh as a song plugger when he formed a duet with a singer, adopted his barber's Italian accent, and joined the vaudeville circuit as "Marx and Gordoni." In 1912, while playing in Chicago, Leo attended a performance of the Three Marx Brothers, as they were now called, in nearby Waukegan. Leo hadn't seen his brothers in several years, during which time they had evolved from a singing act peppered with a few jokes to a comedy act with a few songs thrown in. (Gummo would later say that the Marx Brothers, unable to sing or dance, ended up comedians by default.) For the past year they had been performing "Fun in Hi Skule," a Julius-written version of a vaudeville comic staple, the school act. As the curtain went up, red-wigged Ahdie, playing a dim-witted student, entered the classroom with an orange for his crotchety old teacher, played by Julius. Glancing into the orchestra pit, Ahdie was shocked to see Leo at the piano. Ahdie reacted in typical Marx Brothers fashion: he let out a yell and threw the orange at his older brother. (It was not the first time a Marx Brother had ad-libbed, nor would it be the last.) Leo caught the orange and threw it back, triggering a free-for-all. "When Groucho and Gummo saw what was going on they started whooping too," Harpo recalled. "We heaved everything we could get our hands on into the orchestra pit—hats, books, chalk, erasers, stilettos. The piano player surrendered. He climbed up onto the stage, sat at one of the school desks, and joined the act." The Three Marx Brothers had become Four.

*　*　*

More than a century before Minnie Marx sent her sons out on the vaudeville circuit, Mayer Amschel Rothschild, a junk-dealer-turned-coin-trader-turned-banker in the Jewish ghetto of Frankfurt, sent his four younger sons to different European commercial capitals—London, Paris, Vienna, and Naples—to establish branches of the family business. (He kept his eldest son by his side.) The fraternal diaspora mimicked those traditional fairy tales in which brothers are dispatched into the world to seek their fortunes. In the Rothschild version, the brothers ended up controlling much of European finance and amassing the largest private fortune in the world. Their sibling bond would be enshrined in the family coat of arms. In addition to a menagerie's worth of heraldic beasts, it contained a clenched fist holding five arrows, each symbolizing a brother.

Parental ambition is one spur to fraternal collaboration. Brotherly example is another. In 1844, twenty-two-year-old Heyum Lehmann, the second son of a Bavarian cattle dealer, emigrated to the United States. He worked for three years as a peddler in Alabama until he had enough money to send for his younger brother, Mendel. Henry and Emanuel, as they now called themselves, ran a dry goods and cotton trading business ("H. Lehman and Bro.") for three more years before sending for their younger brother, Maier (soon to be known as Mayer) and repainting the sign over their store to read "Lehman Brothers"—a name it would keep long after its three founders died and the company had evolved into one of the world's most respected banks, a name it would keep right up until the company itself died in 2008. Similarly, in Roaring Twenties Philadelphia, Fayard Nicholas taught his toddler brother, Harold, the dance steps he saw each night on the stage of the Standard Theater, where his parents played in the house band. By the time Fayard was eighteen and Harold was eleven, the tap-dancing Nicholas Brothers were the featured act at New York's Cotton Club and the toast of the Harlem Renaissance.

It was hardly surprising that "the Mayo Boys," as their neighbors in southeastern Minnesota knew them, went into medicine. Will and his younger brother, Charlie, were sons of a country doctor. As children in the 1870s, they swept and dusted their father's office, drove him on his rounds, accompanied him on autopsies, and learned anatomy by playing with the bones of a Sioux warrior he kept in an iron kettle. As they grew older, the brothers served their father as ersatz nurses: rolling bandages, applying poultices, fitting plaster casts, heating surgical instruments, handling sponges during operations, and, occasionally, dressing wounds. Dr. Mayo discussed case histories with them, took them to medical society meetings and assigned them Gray's *Anatomy* and Paget's *Lectures on Surgical Pathology.* "We were reared in medicine as a farmer boy is reared in farming," recalled Will, admitting on another occasion that "It never occurred to us that we could be anything but doctors."

It also never occurred to the Mayo boys that they could be anything but partners. Both became surgeons, dividing their work according to their talents: Will operated below the neck (the abdomen and pelvis), while Charlie operated above the neck (eyes, ears, nose, throat, brain). For more than a decade, until their caseloads made it impossible, each assisted at the other's surgeries. People from around the world came to the Mayo Clinic, either to be operated on by the brothers or to watch them operate. Visiting surgeons might observe Will as he resectioned a stomach, then go to a neighboring theater to see Charlie perform a thyroidectomy, then hurry back to watch Will remove a gallbladder. "Dr. Will" and "Dr. Charlie," as they were known, remained as close as they had been in childhood. They shared a bank account and lived next door to each other. (Their plan to build a passageway leading to a communal study between their homes was vetoed by their wives, who pointed out that they already spent more than enough time together.) Will, the more polished public speaker, reaped the greater share of the glory, but Charlie seemed never to resent it, and Will always accepted honors and awards "on behalf of my brother and myself." One of Will's friends remarked, "I believe if Dr. Will were elected President of the United States he would accept the office in the name of his brother and himself." After Charlie died in 1939 at the age of seventy-three, Will lived only two months without his brother.

None of their Dayton, Ohio, neighbors could have predicted what the two youngest Wright brothers would end up doing. But they could have guessed that whatever it was, they'd do it together. "From the time we were little children my brother Orville and myself lived together, worked together and, in fact, thought together," wrote Wilbur, a month before his death. Their father, a bishop of the United Brethren Church, hoped that Wilbur, the older brother by four years, would follow him into the ministry, but he encouraged his children to pursue whatever sparked their interest. Their interest was sparked by anything that involved building. As children, the brothers made sleds, wagons, kites, chairs, a foot-powered lathe, and a paper-folding machine. After Orville dropped out of high school to construct his own printing press from scrap, they launched a weekly newspaper, with Wilbur as editor and Orville as publisher. A few years later, they opened a shop where they made, sold, and repaired bicycles. In 1896, twenty-nine-year-old Wilbur read in the newspaper that Otto Lilienthal, a German engineer known as "the Flying Man" for his predilection for strapping on willow-and-muslin wings and jumping from high places, had died in a gliding accident. Ever since their father had given them a toy helicopter made of cork, bamboo, and tissue paper when Wilbur was eleven, the brothers had been intrigued by flight. Now they read everything available on the subject. They spent each day constructing model kites and gliders in their workroom behind the bicycle shop, rigging up a bell system to warn them when a customer arrived and they were needed to change a tire or true a wheel. They spent each evening discussing wing warp, lift and drift, lateral control, and equilibrium. For a few years, they treated flight as just another engineering puzzle to be solved. But by the end of October 1900, after spending five weeks testing their first manned glider in the fickle winds above the dunes of Kitty Hawk, North Carolina, the brothers had found their life's work.

*   *   *

From 1912 to 1918, the Four Marx Brothers worked the vaudeville circuit, performing four shows a day, six days a week, forty weeks a year. Like animal species that evolve to fill separate niches within an ecosystem, they carved out increasingly distinct characters on stage, exaggerations of the off-stage roles they had carved out within their family. Leo, the manipulative charmer who had used his flair for dialect to survive the streets of Yorkville, became the crazy-like-a-fox "Eye-talian" sharpie always on the lookout for a score. Ahdie, the wide-eyed dreamer with the flexible features, became the puckish, rubber-faced, loose-limbed innocent. (When Minnie sent Ahdie his yodeling grandmother's old harp, he taught himself how to play—resting it on the wrong shoulder for a year before realizing his mistake—and worked it into the act.) Julius, the bookworm, became the know-it-all purveyor of sardonic barbs and scattershot non sequiturs. Milton, tallest and blondest, played the ingenue, whose main job, as one reviewer put it, was "to look handsome."

Those characters were refined in 1914, when, with bookings scarce, Minnie asked Al Shean for help. One night, after seeing his nephews' show, Shean sat down at the kitchen table with a sheet of butcher paper and wrote a new act, accentuating the strengths of each brother and exaggerating their differences. He gave Julius all the monologues; made Leo's immigrant con artist more of an amiable, wisecracking kibitzer; transformed Milton into a white-gloved, cane-carrying dandy; and gave Ahdie, who had been relatively garrulous in the school act, more physical bits and fewer words. When Ahdie protested, his uncle told him that his voice undercut his whimsical appearance and the act would be better if he didn't talk at all. Not long afterward, a reviewer praised Ahdie's pantomime but added: "Unfortunately the effect is spoiled when he speaks." Ahdie swallowed his pride, relinquished his three lines, and never uttered another word onstage. (His performance would be so convincing that to the end of his career many people pitied him for being "a poor, deaf mute.") Later that year, after a show in Galesburg, Illinois, the brothers were playing poker with Art Fisher, a monologuist on the bill, when Fisher, dealing the cards, also dealt the names that would forever define them. "This one's for you, Harpo," he said, tossing a card toward Ahdie. "This one's for you, Chicko," he said, tossing one to Leo, and so on, thus immortalizing Ahdie's musical trademark, Leo's prodigious appetite for the opposite sex (the *k* was later dropped by a careless typesetter), Julius/Groucho's perpetual air of dissatisfaction, and Milton/Gummo's hypochondriacal habit of wearing gumshoes, even when it wasn't raining. Spur-of-the-moment inventions, the nicknames became their stage names and, eventually, the names by which almost everyone, including some of their children, would call them, names that would make it even more difficult for their audience—and for the brothers—to separate their onstage and offstage selves.

Over time, the brothers also acquired their visual trademarks. Harpo was always on the lookout for new props with which to communicate wordlessly. He purloined a rubber-bulbed klaxon from a taxi, stuck it under his belt, and learned to honk it as expressively as most actors use their voice. During a rainstorm in San Francisco, he ducked into a pawnshop and bought a baggy old trenchcoat; he wore it on stage the next day and, over time, added pockets and panels out of which maps could be extracted and silverware could pour. Groucho, who had started smoking cigars in his teens to look "manly," found they were useful onstage, giving him time to think of snappy comebacks as he puffed. During one performance, Groucho began scooting across the stage in a stooped, bent-kneed, hurry-up lope not unlike that of a father running alongside his child's bicycle as he teaches him to ride. The audience loved it. In 1921, the brothers were appearing at Keith's Flushing in Queens when Groucho's wife gave birth to their first child at Lenox Hill Hospital on the Upper East Side. Groucho spent every spare moment at the hospital with his new family. One night he stayed so long that by the time he got to the theater it was too late to glue on his horsehair mustache, which needed several minutes to dry, so he smeared some greasepaint across his upper lip.

Combined, the brothers sparked a kind of spontaneous comic combustion, transforming their drapery-pulling, urinal-stomping youth from dross into art. Although their act had a script, the brothers deviated from it at the slightest whim, trying to top one another, trying to throw each other off stride, trying to keep from getting bored. (The brothers were forerunners of the improv groups that would flourish a half-century later.) They'd play leapfrog, sit on ladies' laps, climb the backdrop, guzzle water out of a goldfish bowl, and swallow the goldfish. "We always played to ourselves, never the audience," recalled Groucho. "Sometimes we got to laughing so hard at ourselves we couldn't finish." During a performance in Ann Arbor, Michigan, Groucho was singing a mock aria ("La Donna è Mobile") in "double-talk Italian," accompanied by Chico on the piano, when Harpo ran onstage, bumped Chico off the piano stool, and began to play a quickstep-march version of "The Holy City." Whereupon Groucho knocked Harpo off, Chico knocked Groucho off, and Harpo knocked Chico off. The round robin of brotherly one-upmanship continued until Chico was on the piano stool, Harpo was on Chico's shoulders, and Groucho was crouching behind them, his arms reaching around Chico, all three singing and playing a six-hand, three-key, three-voice version of "Waltz Me Around Again, Willie."

Although the brothers had gone their separate ways in Yorkville, their decade on the vaudeville circuit—a survival-of-the-fittest procession of interminable train trips, one-dollar hotel rooms, and indigestible boardinghouse food—brought them closer, as they teamed up to defend themselves against unscrupulous producers, crooked theater managers, and spitball-throwing audiences. To save money on trains, the brothers often bunked in a single berth, as they had in childhood. In each new town, their first stop was the pool hall, where Chico offered to play anyone in the house for five dollars, while his brothers made side bets with the onlookers. On southern swings, they carried blackjacks in their back pockets as they left the theater each night, in case any local bullies insisted on mixing it up with the city slickers. Years later, Harpo would tell his son, "If I didn't have four brothers to help me fight my way through what we all had to go through, I'd never have made it."

The brothers applied their all-for-one, one-for-all philosophy to the opposite sex. In later years, many of the stories they told of their vaudeville days centered on their carnal exploits: making group expeditions to "hookshops"; posing next to their billboards after the show in hopes of attracting local girls; being chased by the husbands or fathers of the girls they'd attracted. Minnie encouraged her sons to pursue loose women. She didn't want them trapped into marriage, which not only might break up the act she'd worked so hard to assemble but would require her to share her boys. Her favorite son, with his crooked smile and key-shooting piano turn, was the most promiscuous. Chico's pick-up technique was straightforward. "He'd walk up to a girl and say, 'Do you fuck?'" recalled Groucho. "And many times they said yes. By the time any show opened he'd fucked half the chorus." (All his life, Groucho would envy Chico's prowess with women.) Chico often recruited dates for his brothers. Other times, they inherited his hand-me-downs. In one of numerous incidents whose casual misogyny makes the skin crawl, Chico, after having sex with a girl at their boardinghouse, turned the gaslight low, told his brothers to wear their matching silk shirts, and invited them to take a turn. (The lookalike ruse would be recalled in the film *Duck Soup*, when Chico and Harpo dress up like Groucho in an attempt to bed the gullible Margaret Dumont.) Small wonder that when thirty-one-year-old Chico, to Minnie's dismay, married a nineteen-year-old secretarial student and installed her in the chorus, Harpo, Groucho, and Gummo saw nothing wrong in pinching their sister-in-law's fanny as she passed in the hallway, or trying to steal a kiss whenever Chico wasn't around. Betty complained to her husband, who laughed it off and explained that the brothers had always shared their girls. But he agreed to talk to them. "You don't do that to wives," Chico explained.

The Marx Brothers' all-for-one ethos went only so far: some brothers were more valuable than others. In 1918, as World War I dragged on, Minnie took Gummo aside and pointed out that while Chico was married and Zeppo was too young for the service, if Groucho or Harpo were drafted, the act couldn't survive. If Gummo was willing to serve, however, she believed the others might be spared. Gummo was relieved. To him, the prospect of battle seemed less terrifying than being onstage. Gummo hated performing, because whenever he got nervous he stammered. (To compensate, he searched the dictionary for synonyms to each word that gave him trouble.) After eleven years in the act, the sacrificial lamb went eagerly to his fate, which turned out to be rather pleasant. Made an "acting corporal" by someone who recognized him as a Marx Brother, Gummo was stationed in Chicago, where his chief contribution to the war effort seems to have been procuring chorus girls for his senior officers. Meanwhile, Minnie, wanting to keep the name "The Four Marx Brothers," ordered seventeen-year-old Zeppo to join the act. When Minnie called, Zeppo (as he had been dubbed for doing chin-ups as avidly as Mr. Zippo, a trained chimpanzee of some renown) was working as a garage mechanic, lifting weights, chasing girls, getting in fights, carrying a gun, and stealing the occasional automobile. Tall, blond, muscular, and stammer-free, Zeppo slid easily into Gummo's straight-man role. He slid less easily into the fraternal quartet offstage. When Zeppo developed a crush on an eighteen-year-old named Ruth and hired her to be his dancing partner, Groucho stole her away and married her. Zeppo's resentment would outlast the marriage.

In 1924, the Marx Brothers made the improbable leap from vaudeville—"the slums of entertainment," in Ben Hecht's words—to Broadway. They remained untamed. Asked by a nervous producer what kind of show the brothers planned, Groucho once replied, "I don't know. We'll stick four Jews up against the wall and see what happens." Groucho was only partly kidding. On the first out-of-town tryout of *The Cocoanuts*, there was so much ad-libbing that the show ran long by forty minutes. Director George S. Kaufman, who also co-wrote the book, worked through the night, cutting choruses and dance numbers. The next night, the show ran even longer. *The Cocoanuts* would have 377 performances on Broadway, each unique. One night Groucho, following Margaret Dumont offstage, began leaping from one side of her long-trained evening dress to the other as if he were playing hopscotch; another night he landed on the train itself, stranding Dumont in her whalebone corset. (Dumont chose to go trainless thereafter.) Another night, during a quiet scene between Groucho and Dumont, Harpo persuaded a blond chorus girl to scamper across the stage, shrieking, with a horn-tooting Harpo in hot pursuit. Groucho wasn't fazed. "First time I ever saw a taxi hail a passenger," he observed. When Harpo chased the girl back across the stage in the opposite direction, Groucho was undaunted. "The nine-twenty's right on time," he said, checking his watch. "You can always set your clocks by the Lehigh Valley." The brothers had such difficulty recalling all their ad libs

("Do you remember what I said when I tripped you?" Groucho would ask Dumont) that a stenographer was hired to take notes at each performance. Theatergoers, never knowing what might happen, returned again and again. The golfer Bobby Jones saw *The Cocoanuts* twelve times, the columnist Heywood Broun twenty-one.

Offstage, the Marx brothers ran no less amok, engaging in an incessant stream of what child psychologists would, decades later, refer to as "testing behavior." At a party thrown by the *Animal Crackers* songwriters Bert Kalmar and Harry Ruby, the brothers began tossing food, silverware, dinner plates, and coffee cups out the hotel window onto the roof of the garage. Harpo and Chico had the piano teetering on the sill before their hosts managed to stop them. When Irving Thalberg, the brilliant young MGM producer known as "The Boy Wonder," kept the brothers waiting for their first appointment, they blew cigar smoke through the cracks in his closed door until Thalberg emerged to see whether there was a fire. Kept waiting a second time, they dragged his steel file cabinets over to the door and trapped Thalberg in his own office. During yet another meeting, Thalberg abandoned them for a story conference elsewhere and returned to find them sitting naked in front of a roaring fire, roasting potatoes they'd ordered up from the studio commissary. "He never walked out on us again," boasted Groucho.

A disproportionate number of the Marx Brothers' pranks involved humiliating women. At the theater, the brothers hid beneath the makeup table in the ladies' dressing room, mercilessly commenting on the physical attributes of female cast members as they made quick changes during the show. Although they considered every woman fair game for pinches, kisses, and lascivious remarks, the brothers' favorite target was Dumont, the majestic, grand dame of an actress who, as J. B. Priestley noted, could be shot out of a cannon without disturbing her dignity. Onstage, the brothers subjected her to constant physical assault, clutching, grabbing, and pawing at her with the determination of piglets rooting for position at their mother's flank. Offstage, the brothers were no less determined to upset her equilibrium. On the train for the road tour of *Animal Crackers,* after Dumont had retired to her berth, the brothers ganged up on the conductor, pulled off his pants, and threw him on the sleeping Dumont, who woke up screaming. In Indianapolis, Groucho convinced the hotel detective that Dumont was a notorious prostitute. When the unsuspecting actress took the detective to her rooms to demonstrate that nothing could be further from the truth, Groucho emerged carrying a douche bag ("You sneak," he hissed at Dumont, eyeing her companion, "I don't know why I put up with this"); whereupon Dumont and the detective walked into her room to find Chico lying on the bed in his underwear reading the *Daily Racing Form* ("Oh, you got another guy—well, I'll be back in half an hour"); whereupon bare-chested Zeppo emerged from the closet, a hotel towel around his waist ("Just because I'm the youngest, you take my money, but you never get around to me"); whereupon Dumont, in tears, entered the bathroom to find a naked, grinning Harpo in the tub, a four-in-hand Windsor knot around his penis.

Part of their behavior—behavior that today would be recognized as sexual harassment or even assault—was an act, an extension of their ribald onstage characters. Part was a continuation of the casual objectification of women, not unusual for the times, that had been encouraged by their mother during their vaudeville days. Part of it was having been raised in an all-male environment—Minnie being considered "one of the boys"—and never outgrowing it. (Which might also explain why so many Marx brothers' pranks involved nudity—their own or someone else's. Indeed, their habit of summarily stripping male visitors of their clothes came to seem an unofficial Marx Brothers greeting ceremony.)

Many people—men and women alike—found the brothers difficult to work with. The beleaguered Dumont threatened to quit on an almost daily basis. When Paramount executives wanted to punish the temperamental young actress Lillian Roth, they made her appear in *Animal Crackers*. "It was one step removed from the circus," recalled Roth of the atmosphere on the set. The brothers were habitually late, and even after they finally assembled, it was hard to keep them corralled. Harpo would drift off to play his harp, Chico would disappear to call his bookie, Groucho would find a corner in which to read the *Wall Street Journal,* Zeppo would be off somewhere doing deep knee-bends. After working on the scripts for *Monkey Business* and *Horse Feathers,* S. J. Perelman, who described the brothers as "capricious, tricky beyond endurance, altogether unreliable, and treacherous to a degree that would make Machiavelli absolutely kneel at their feet," decided he'd had enough. "I'd rather be chained to a galley oar and lashed at ten-minute intervals than work for those sons-of-bitches again."

Although the Marx Brothers combined seamlessly onstage, they did most of their offstage preparation alone. "How can you write for Harpo?" Kaufman observed. "What do you put down on paper? All you can say is, 'Harpo enters,' and then he's on his own." Harpo worked backstage and at home, testing potential props, practicing his pickpocketing, adding pouches to his capacious raincoat, playing his harp, and dreaming up sofa-jumping, chandelier-swinging, curtain-riding gags. Chico, who considered rehearsal an intrusion on his card-playing, prepared very little. "I don't think Chico ever knew what the plot was about," observed the screenwriter Nat Perrin. "I don't think Chico ever looked at any of the lines but his, and hardly those." He'd show up at the theater at the last minute, stroll onstage without makeup, and—though his memory for numbers was so prodigious that after a brief look at a dollar bill he could recite its eight-digit serial number backwards and forwards—forget his lines.

Of all the brothers, Groucho was the most involved in the show. He worked with the writers, helping shape the story lines and polishing the gags. Although Groucho was an inspired ad libber (the only actor, it was said, that Kaufman ever allowed to improvise onstage—as if he had a choice), what sounded like stream-of-consciousness was often the product of meticulous experimentation. For the two Thalberg pictures, *A Night at the Opera* and *A Day at the Races,* the brothers, harking back to their vaudeville days, tested key scenes on the road in front of live audiences—four shows a day, six days a week, for four weeks—before shooting the movie. After each show, Groucho and the writers huddled backstage, chewing over what had gone well and what hadn't. Working by what he acknowledged was "trial and error," Groucho would try a line every possible way: changing the order of the words, mispronouncing them, experimenting with tone and inflection, accenting different syllables. On the *Races* tour, when the line "Is he dead or has my watch stopped?" wasn't getting much of a laugh, Groucho rephrased the question as a statement—"Either he's dead or my watch has stopped"—and the house erupted. In the famous tutsi-frutsi scene, Chico, peddling a racing guide to Groucho, says, "One dollar and you remember me all your life," whereupon Groucho replies, "That's the most nauseating proposition I ever had." Groucho wasn't sure whether *nauseating* was the optimal word. Over 140 stage performances, he tried a variety of substitutes: *obnoxious, revolting, disgusting, offensive, repulsive, disagreeable,* and *distasteful.* "The last two of these words never got more than titters," Teet Carle, a Marx Brothers publicist, recalls. "The others elicited various degrees of ha-has. But *nauseating* drew roars." Carle asked Groucho why he thought *nauseating* was so much funnier, expecting his boss to propound an elaborate theory of comedy. "I don't know," Groucho replied. "I really don't care. I only know the audiences told us it was funny."

Groucho's perfectionism was rooted in anxiety. By now, the outsider in the family was the acknowledged leader of the act (in part, no doubt, because it mattered the most to him). When Alexander Woollcott reviewed the Marx Brothers' Broadway debut, he assumed, like most people, that Groucho was the eldest. By *Duck Soup,* Groucho was getting top billing. As in childhood, however, Groucho was sensitive to any slight. It peeved him that Woollcott's review had been headlined "Harpo Marx and Some Brothers." His insecurity was especially evident when it came to his brothers' musical solos. In the middle of Harpo's moment in the sun, he'd wander onstage and urge: "Play softer. We can still hear you." The writer George Seaton recalled standing in the wings with Groucho during a tryout performance of *A Day at the Races.* "The audience was applauding Chico, who was doing an encore. Groucho walked right out on the stage and said jokingly, 'If you come near a tune, play it.' He thought he would get a big laugh, but the audience hissed him instead." Groucho, who always believed that *he* had deserved the piano lessons, stomped offstage. Sometimes, when Chico was in the midst of his solo, Groucho would retreat to his dressing room and read.

Groucho may have felt excluded by his older brothers, who roomed together on the road, shared an apartment in London during the brothers' English tour, had dressing rooms in the same complex at MGM, and usually went out together after the show while Groucho met with the writers.

Groucho never blamed Harpo, the brother to whom he felt closest, and for whom he would name his son. But he never forgave Chico for being Minnie's favorite.

Groucho had another reason for resenting Chico. When Chico joined the act, he had taken over from Minnie as manager, bringing the same head for numbers and devil-may-care approach to negotiations that he brought to the craps table. His congenital optimism served as a counterweight to Groucho's expect-the-worst philosophy. When the brothers despaired of breaking out of vaudeville into the legitimate theater, it had been Chico who bucked them up, sweeping them along in his enthusiasm, telling them that their luck was about to change. "Harpo and I were always very timid," admitted Groucho. "We didn't think we would ever be successful. But Chico was a gambler and he felt differently . . . He gave us courage and confidence." In 1919, when vaudeville was dying, it had been Chico who, over a game of pinochle, convinced a producer to sign them to a three-year theater contract. In 1928, when the talkies were taking the country by storm, it had been Chico who buttered up Paramount's head, Adolph Zukor, into giving them $25,000 more than he'd planned to film *The Cocoanuts*. In 1934, when Paramount concluded that the brothers were no longer box office draws, it had been Chico who persuaded his bridge-playing buddy Thalberg to sign them for the pictures that turned out to be their biggest hits.

Chico could make deals for the brothers, but he couldn't be trusted with the money. "We quickly learned never to let Chico hold the salary," said Groucho. "He'd blow it on a card game or at the track." To pay off gambling debts, Chico would hurry to the box office before his brothers so he could pocket their salaries in addition to his own. Other times, he'd forge their names on checks. Eventually, the brothers set up secret banking codes to safeguard their transactions. Groucho and Harpo fretted about the unsavory company Chico kept. According to Harpo, the brothers' tour of England in 1922 had been hastily arranged by Chico because he worried that a hustler he'd hustled in Cleveland was out for revenge. In 1925, in Detroit on a post-Broadway tour, Chico walked off the stage in the middle of a scene, saying he needed some air. He never came back. Groucho, Harpo, and Zeppo had to finish the show alone,

Groucho playing Chico's part in addition to his own. The police theorized that a record-setting heat wave had disoriented Chico, but the truth was more prosaic. Before the show had left New York, Chico had lost $30,000 shooting craps and was worried that the mob was after him. The brothers feared that this time he might turn up at the bottom of the river. Three days later, Chico called. He was in Cleveland and planned to return to Detroit that night.

On the vaudeville circuit, Groucho always sent part of his paycheck home; Chico gambled his away. After the move to Broadway, Groucho visited their mother nearly every day; Chico, who lived much closer to her Queens apartment, had to be pushed to drop by. Groucho resented that no matter how irresponsible Chico was, onstage and off, he was still getting away with murder. So Groucho punished Chico with his caustic wit, berating him for his sloppy performances and profligate ways. When Chico gave Groucho a dog for his birthday, Groucho named it for his eldest brother and took particular delight in calling out, "Here, Chico!" when its namesake was around. Chico would chuckle, refusing to get upset. Beneath Groucho's resentment lay envy and self-doubt. In a letter to a friend, Groucho described his eldest brother: "He is a diminutive, dynamic combination of Ponzi and Casanova, who disregards all the laws of life and constantly snaps his fingers in fate's kisser—he gambled with everything—but who knows, maybe he has the right idea?"

No matter how much the brothers argued, they always swallowed their differences for the sake of the act, joining forces against anyone outside the fraternity. Long after Groucho had stolen Ruth away from Zeppo, Zeppo lost his grip on Ruth during a dance number, and she fell into the orchestra pit. Convinced that Zeppo had dropped her on purpose to get back at her for jilting him, Ruth insisted that Groucho fire his brother: "Either he goes or I go." Groucho told Ruth she could go. (She didn't.) Before shooting started on *A Day at the Races,* Betty convinced Chico that he deserved more camera time. Chico promised to bring it up with his brothers. He came home from the studio boiling mad. "Betty, don't ever interfere with me and my brothers again! Just remember one thing: There's only room for two prima donnas in the act. Not three. Groucho and Harpo need the limelight. I just need the act to be good." A few years later, when Chico's adolescent daughter, Maxine, made disparaging remarks to her friends about her father's womanizing, Harpo asked to see her. She went to his dressing room. Harpo began to pace. Though he never raised his voice, he told her to keep her thoughts to herself. "I can't stomach disloyalty," he said. The eternally dyspeptic Groucho might grouse about Chico's gambling, but when Chico ran up debts, he helped pay them off.

*   *   *

Like the Marx Brothers (or the Five Chinese Brothers), fraternal partners often divide the work according to talent or taste. Thus Aaron, the kinder, gentler, more articulate older brother, served as spokesman for his stern, uncompromising, tongue-tied younger brother, Moses, enabling the two of them to play an Old Testament version of good cop, bad cop. Thus General William Howe, commander of the British Army in North America during the Revolutionary War, coordinated the attack with his older brother Richard, an admiral in the Royal Navy. Thus, the seventeenth-century Dutch painters Jan and Andries Both combined their talents on a single canvas, Andries painting the figures into his brother's landscapes. Like Jack Spratt and his wife, each brother contributed something the other lacked; together, they combined to make a whole.

If Joseph Montgolfier, a restless, easily distracted eighteenth-century Frenchman who dreamed of floating above the clouds, hadn't had a more pragmatic brother, the hot-air balloon might never have gotten off the ground. After watching laundry dry over an open fire one day and noticing that the heated air rose and made the sheets billow, Joseph experimented with several rudimentary box-kite-like prototypes before recruiting his younger brother Étienne, a practical fellow who had taken over the family papermaking business. With Joseph as the idea man and Étienne as technical advisor, the Montgolfiers built ever-larger hot-air balloons. (Étienne also served as publicist for the team; having lived in Paris, he was more presentable than shy, unkempt Joseph.) On September 19, 1783, with Louis XVI and Marie Antoinette looking on at Versailles, the brothers launched the first aircraft to carry passengers—a sheep, a duck, and a rooster, all of whom seemed oblivious to the magnitude of the occasion as they floated over the French countryside for eight minutes and two miles at an altitude of 1,500 feet before descending safely to the earth. Two months later, another "Montgolfière," as their invention was called, became the first aircraft to carry humans—but not the brothers, whose father had given them permission to forsake the papermaking business only if they promised never to go aloft themselves.

The fraternal division of labor at Walt Disney Productions was even more sharply defined. Walt, the younger brother, was the puckish, charismatic, creative genius who chose the subjects, outlined the stories, and worked with the animators. Roy, eight years older, was the cautious, sensible businessman responsible for financing his brother's visions. When Walt caught Roy talking to people on the creative side, he'd order his brother back to his own office. The animator Dave Hand described a meeting in which Roy complained that Walt's movies were costing too much. "There was complete silence," Hand recalled. "Then Walt's loose eyebrow shot up at an unusually sharp angle, and turning to Roy in an uncompromising matter-of-fact straight-from-the-shoulder answer, said quite simply, 'Roy, *we'll* make the pictures, *you* get the money.' That was that."

Like the Montgolfiers and the Disneys, collaborating brothers often have complementary personalities. Mayer and Emanuel Lehman, who ran the family cotton brokerage after their older brother Henry succumbed to yellow fever in 1855, made an effective team because Mayer, a sociable fellow who relished taking risks, was all "buy, buy," while Emanuel, cautious and quiet, was all "sell, sell." (As family tradition had it, Mayer made the money and Emanuel made sure they didn't lose it.) The Mayos, too, fit together like yin and yang. Will was a dignified, austere, ambitious man to whom it seemed natural to take responsibility for the clinic's administration. Charlie, mischievous, folksy, and droll, was better one-on-one with the patients. If a business plan needed fine-tuning, colleagues turned to Will; if a tense patient needed reassuring, they turned to Charlie. ("Everybody likes Charlie, don't they?" Will once remarked to his sister-in-law. "They aren't afraid of him. No one ever claps me on the back the way they all do him." He thought a moment. "But I guess

I wouldn't like it if they did.") When Mayer Rothschild sent his sons abroad, he matched each of them to the European country most suited to his personality. Amschel, the eldest, who stayed in Frankfurt, lived on a princely scale but was a cautious, deliberate, joyless prude. Salomon, the second son, used his talents for flattery and ingratiation to navigate the treacherous diplomatic shoals of anti-Semitic Vienna. Nathan, the London Rothschild, was a thrifty, truculent bull of a man who scorned frippery and acted swiftly and decisively. The geographical synchronicity faltered with Carl, a nervous, taciturn fellow who clung to his faith—his family nickname was "mezzuzah boy"—amid the hurly-burly of Naples. But it resumed with the youngest brother, James, a sophisticated dandy who collected art, bought the Lafite vineyards, and entertained lavishly at his palatial Paris home and his three châteaux.

It would be hard to find two brothers less alike than George and Ira Gershwin. As a child, George misbehaved in school, stole from neighborhood stores, and fought so frequently that his nose assumed a permanent crook. His older brother, Ira, excelled in school and spent his spare time reading Henry James, Gilbert and Sullivan, and the Elizabethan poets. After their parents bought a secondhand piano, twelve-year-old George traded the streets for the keyboard, and by fifteen, had become the youngest song plugger on Tin Pan Alley. Ira, for whom the piano had been intended, was a self-described "floating soul" who haunted libraries and movie houses, composed occasional light verse, and bounced from one dead-end job to another until, at the age of twenty-one, he tried putting some words to one of his younger brother's songs. "I always felt that if George hadn't been my brother and pushed me into lyric writing," he recalled, "I'd have been contented to be a bookkeeper." George was a slim, leonine man who looked like a Spanish noble. He lifted weights, did sit-ups and push-ups religiously, danced divinely, and was adept in every sport he attempted. Ira, a squat, portly fellow with glasses, looked like Hollywood's idea of an accountant; he played an occasional round of golf but was "a hard man to get out of an easy chair," as a friend observed, and preferred sedentary pursuits like poker and Scrabble. George was a restless night owl who loved parties and travel, brimmed with boyish exuberance, and exerted a magnetic pull in every room he entered. Ira was a contemplative homebody who retreated to the outskirts of parties. George was a sexually voracious man who never married. Ira married at twenty-nine and was a devoted husband until his death fifty-seven years later. George was a compulsive worker who could dash off four hummable tunes in an afternoon. Ira was a craftsman who would fuss over a single line for days. And yet these fraternal opposites produced hundreds of the most memorable songs in American history, in which words and music inhabit each other so thoroughly it is hard to believe they didn't come from a single source.

Some collaborating brothers are remarkably similar. A century before George and Ira Gershwin worked side by side, Jacob and Wilhelm Grimm wrote at facing desks almost every day for fifty years. Unlike the Gershwins, the Grimms had been inseparable from childhood. Born a year apart in Hanau, Germany, the eldest of six children, Jacob and Wilhelm played hide-and-seek together, walked hand-in-hand together, read together, were tutored together, collected books together, and slept in the same bed together throughout their youth. Although Jacob, the elder brother, was somewhat more introverted and ambitious, both were brilliant students who studied twelve hours a day, graduated at the head of their high school classes, and went into the law, determined to live up to the expectations of their father, a prosperous magistrate who died when Jacob was eleven. In 1805, when Jacob took a job in Paris and they were briefly apart for the first time, nineteen-year-old Wilhelm wrote, "When you left, I thought my heart would tear in two."

A few years later, realizing that their hearts lay less in law than in philology, the brothers began studying German folklore. Over the following half-century, working opposite each other in their shared study, they co-authored volumes on German legends, German grammar, and ancient German law, as well as assembling the collections of fairy tales for which they would be remembered. Even after Wilhelm married and fathered three children, the brothers continued to live under the same roof and adhere to the same strict schedule. Wilhelm's wife kept the house as quiet as possible, accepting that the brothers' primary allegiance was to their work and to each other. "All you could hear was the scratching of their pens, and sometimes Jacob's frequent little coughs...." recalled Wilhelm's son. "I cannot imagine that anyone would dare interrupt this sacred silence."

The nineteenth-century French writers Edmond and Jules de Goncourt were separated by eight years, and their personalities were polar opposites. Edmond, the elder, was reserved, sincere, sentimental, deliberate, and responsible. Jules was witty, volatile, exuberant, mischievous, and spoiled. Yet their sensibilities were so similar that they were able to write in a single voice, co-authoring more than two dozen novels, plays, histories, and works of criticism. "The strange thing is that although we are absolutely different in temperament, taste, and character, we are absolutely identical in our ideas, our judgements, our likes and dislikes as regards other people, and our intellectual perspective," they wrote. "Our minds see alike and see with the same eyes." Following their mother's death in 1848, they lived together for a quarter-century without spending more than a few hours apart, locked together by their distrust of the outside world as well as by their devotion to each other. "When we are parted, we each feel the lack of the other half of ourselves," they wrote. "We are left with nothing but half-sensations, a half-life; we are incomplete like a book in two volumes of which the first has been lost."

Fraternal co-authors were something of a fad in nineteenth-century France, but the Goncourts were the only literary brothers close enough (and, perhaps, neurotic enough) to keep a journal together. Each night for almost nineteen years—with Jules sitting at the table holding the pen, and Edmond standing behind him and looking over his shoulder, sometimes speaking, sometimes listening, in a process Edmond called "dual dictation"—they recorded their impressions of the day, employing, for the most part, the first person plural. Literary critics have never been able to attribute any particular passage to one brother or the other. Their novels and plays were deemed stuffy and old-fashioned, but their journals—a gossipy bouillabaisse of dinner parties, brothel visits, opening nights, mistresses, revolutions, literary backbiting, court intrigue, high-society scandal, and flagrant name-dropping (Flaubert, Zola, Verlaine, Baudelaire, Maupassant, Wilde, Turgenev)—provided a delicious portrait of Second Empire Paris. In 1870, when the thirty-nine-year-old Jules died of syphilis, a despondent Edmond abandoned the journal for several months before resuming. In 1886, he began publishing the *Journal des Goncourt* (underscoring their fraternal unity by using the singular surname). "This journal is our nightly confession," he wrote in the preface, "the confession of two lives never separated in pleasure, in work or in pain, the confession of two twin spirits, two minds receiving from the contact of men and things impressions so alike, so identical, so homogeneous, that this single confession may be considered as the effusion of a single ego, of a single *I.*" The journal would come to an end in 1896 when Edmond died, thirteen days after making a final entry in which he described an amusing after-dinner anecdote told him by Montesquieu.

*   *   *

In 1931, the Marx Brothers moved to Hollywood, where they made the string of movies that cemented their fame. Off-screen, however, the brothers had gone their separate ways. Most had wives and children. When Chico was home, he could be an irresistibly charming husband and father. Reading the funny papers to his daughter, he performed each comic strip in a different accent. Visiting his wife in the hospital after an operation, he soft-shoed into her room in top hat, white tie, and tails. "He could display a quality which only the Yiddish word *schmeikel* can describe: a charm based on the need to be adored," his daughter, Maxine, observed. Having been his mother's favorite, Chico sought the adoration of women for the rest of his life. He was unfaithful on his honeymoon and as often as possible thereafter. "His trailer on the film set was used mainly for seducing purposes," wrote the Marx biographer Joe Adamson, "and he would arrange for his girls to be hired as extras, just so they'd be handy." The brothers joked publicly about Chico's excesses ("There are three things that my brother Chico is always on—a phone, a horse, or a broad," Groucho said) but worried that his philandering would jeopardize their success. When Chico began to juggle his one-night stands with a not-so-secret long-term affair with a teenage actress, they laid down the law: he could cheat on his wife, but he had to be discreet. Divorce, they told him, was out of the question.

They were even more concerned with his gambling. When Chico

wasn't playing high-stakes poker with studio executives, he was crossing the border to the Agua Caliente Jockey Club, a racetrack near Tijuana favored by the Hollywood crowd, where he might lose ten thousand dollars in an afternoon. Or he was betting on boxing matches and throwing lavish postfight parties in a double suite at the Ambassador Hotel for a slew of big-time gamblers and small-time starlets. People liked betting with Chico because he always gave them generous odds, and if his opponent was losing, he'd up the odds to make the bet more interesting. Whether he won or lost didn't seem to matter. "If I lose today, I can look forward to winning tomorrow," he explained. "And if I win today, I can expect to lose tomorrow. A sure thing is no fun. Groucho and Harpo like sure things, but there's no fun in security." One can only hope the story is apocryphal that during the filming of the climactic scene in *A Day at the Races*, Chico, betting with an extra, put his money on the horse that, according to the script, was destined to lose. Asked why, Chico said, "The odds were fifteen to one."

In *Growing Up with Chico*, Maxine Marx painted a less-cavalier portrait of her father's addiction. At family dinners, Chico was often on the phone to his bookie. On their cook's nights off, he took his wife and daughter to the Clover Club, where he'd gulp down his food and head for the illegal gambling tables in the back. Just as the young Chico had pawned his father's shears to pay a gambling debt, the middle-aged Chico sold off the family furniture. "Nothing was unhockable," wrote Maxine. "For years, mother refused to let him buy a house because she was afraid he would sell it without telling her, and we would be out on the street." They rented, moving, over the years, from opulent to less fancy to modest. Worried that mobsters were after him, Chico would disappear for a few days, telling his family he was taking a vacation.

Harpo, who also gambled, told Chico all he had to do was quit after he'd lost a preset amount. Groucho, who wouldn't even roll dice for the lunch tab at the MGM commissary, told Chico gambling was a waste of time and money. Chico would promise to slow down but then go on a spree. In 1937, he was sued by the widow of a gambler who'd been shot dead with Chico's check for $2,000 in his pocket. When she'd tried to cash it, the check had bounced. Groucho and Harpo issued Chico an ultimatum: either he let them take over his finances or they wouldn't sign their new three-picture contract with MGM. Chico, who couldn't afford to stop working, acquiesced. The brothers would save almost $300,000 for Chico over the next few years. But in 1940, when he ran up huge debts to some mobsters, Chico begged his brothers for the money. They refused. He hired an attorney and threatened to sue. Disgusted, they told him to take his money and go ahead and die broke. He went through it in a matter of weeks.

Harpo's path had diverged sharply from Chico's. After the brothers' Broadway debut, Alexander Woollcott, the *New Yorker* writer whose review had made them stars, had adopted Harpo no less completely than if he were an orphan or a stray dog. ("He was in love with Harpo," Groucho observed, "but in a nice way.") Overnight, Harpo was transplanted from the raffish demimonde of cardsharps, bookies, and horseplayers to the hallowed literary precincts of the Algonquin Round Table, where he bore witness to the verbal jousting of Dorothy Parker, Robert Benchley, and Heywood Broun. He spent his summers at Woollcott's private seven-acre island in Vermont, playing badminton, anagrams, and croquet, as blithe as a boy at summer camp. "I had begun to pay myself back with interest for everything I'd missed out on when I was a kid," he wrote in *Harpo Speaks!* "I wasn't having a second childhood. It was my first real childhood." Under Woollcott's auspices, Harpo become a Zelig of the twentieth-century literary world, meeting and beguiling Noel Coward, Somerset Maugham, and George Bernard Shaw. His trust in the essential benevolence of the world allowed him to adapt to almost any situation. In 1933, at Woollcott's instigation, Harpo became the first American artist to perform in the Soviet Union. Although there was a ticklish moment at the Polish-Russian border when customs inspectors opened his trunk and found two revolvers, three stilettos, four hundred knives, half a dozen bottles marked POISON, and a trove of red wigs, false beards, and rubber hands, Harpo's solo act met with ovations wherever he appeared.

One of the great ironies was that Harpo, the second-grade dropout whose handwritten prop list included "sizzers," "telliscoap," and "karit," was taken up by the Algonquinites, rather than Groucho, the hair-trigger wit who had actually read the books they had written. The few times he joined the Round Table for lunch, Groucho felt unwelcome. Where Harpo was content to listen, Groucho, an autodidact who felt lifelong embarrassment over his sixth-grade education, tried hard to impress. (One member found Groucho "arrogant and superior" and referred to him as "Harpo's Bad Brother.") Groucho may have been especially defensive because he had literary aspirations of his own. Backstage, while Chico and Harpo played cards and chased women, Groucho read *The Atlantic* or *War and Peace*. In 1925, he published a few squibs in *The New Yorker*. When a piece he wrote was reprinted in H. L. Mencken's *The American Language,* he was over the moon: "Nothing I ever did as an actor thrilled me more." In Hollywood, he helped start his own Round Table, a weekly lunch with Perelman, Benchley, Ben Hecht, and Charles MacArthur. They called themselves the West Side Writing and Asthma Club. At the MGM commissary, Groucho sat at the writers' table rather than with his fellow stars. "I'm essentially a writer who unfortunately went into show business," he liked to say.

Groucho's literary aspirations became a sore point in his marriage. His wife wanted the proverbial Hollywood life of parties, premieres, and nightclubs. Groucho, whose idea of a good time was having his writer friends over for Gilbert and Sullivan sing-alongs, preferred to stay at home, monitoring his investments, strumming his guitar, and playing with his son and daughter. If Chico went through life seeking the attention he had gotten from Minnie, Groucho sought to give his children all the attention Minnie hadn't given him. When they were babies, he'd rush home between shows to change their diapers, bathe them, and feed them. As they grew, he read aloud to them, told them Grouchified versions of Little Red Riding Hood and Jack and the Beanstalk, introduced them to classical music, took them to movies and baseball games, played pool and Ping-Pong with them, helped them with homework, and shot home movies of them on family vacations. Having been on the road since the age of fourteen, Groucho threw himself into domestic life: choosing the menus, doing the shopping, managing the household finances, being both breadwinner and homemaker. Groucho had forbidden his wife to work as an actress; now he usurped her role as a mother. The more useless Ruth felt, the more useless Groucho made her feel, belittling her opinions, chipping away at her self-confidence with withering remarks. Increasingly unhappy, Ruth spent more time out—at the parties Groucho refused to attend, at the nightclubs he detested. Groucho masked his insecurity with his aggressive wit; Ruth masked hers with alcohol.

Zeppo liked the perks of being a Marx Brother. He bought a yacht and a Rolls-Royce for himself, furs and jewelry and a pair of Afghan hounds for his wife, and a mansion to house their possessions. But he didn't like being a Marx Brother. Like Gummo, Zeppo suffered from stage fright. "My career on the stage is practically ruined, because I am afraid of my brothers," he confessed to an interviewer in 1929. "I'm the youngest, and from the moment I first went on I would look over at them, who had already been established as comedians, and if I caught them smiling, even good-naturedly, over what I was saying or doing, I would become self-conscious to the point of unhappiness.... It's developed an inferiority complex in me." Zeppo, who sought relief in psychoanalysis, had always felt on the edge of the fraternal group. Like Gummo, he had been relegated to playing the straight man, the secretary, the amanuensis, the one the others bossed around. Indeed, the name Zeppo would become a kind of joke, a synonym for bland superfluousness. That he was paid less than his brothers only underscored his lowly status. Offstage, his ideas were disparaged or ignored. Groucho used to say that the only sure way to test out a gag was to try it out on Zeppo—if he liked it, they threw it out. Yet even Groucho admitted that offstage, Zeppo was the funniest brother. By definition, however, the straight man wasn't supposed to be a comedian. "I knew I could get laughs," said Zeppo, "but I wasn't allowed to with the Marx Brothers." In 1930 he got his chance. When Groucho had an emergency appendectomy in Chicago, Zeppo, who understudied all three brothers, donned a swallowtail coat and a greasepaint mustache and performed Groucho's part so faithfully that friends of Groucho's were unaware of the switch till they came backstage. Zeppo's triumph, however, was tempered by the fact that the audience didn't seem to notice that nobody was playing Zeppo's part.

In 1934, after sixteen years with the Marx Brothers, Zeppo quit the act to join a talent agency. "I'm sick and tired of being a stooge," he wrote in his resignation letter to Groucho. "You know that anybody else would have done as well as I in the act. When the chance came for me to get into the business world I jumped at it. I have only stayed in the act until now because I knew that you, Chico and Harpo wanted me to." If Zeppo hoped that his brothers would make at least a pro forma attempt to argue him out of it, he was disappointed. When Irving Thalberg wondered aloud whether three Brothers should get paid as much as four, Groucho replied, "Don't be silly—without Zeppo we're worth twice as much."

Groucho wasn't far off. Their next two pictures, *A Night at the Opera* and *A Day at the Races,* in which Zeppo was replaced by a similarly insipid, good-looking young actor, grossed twice as much as their previous two. (The movies, however, lacked a certain frisson that came from knowing all four leads were real-life brothers.) But the Marx Brothers themselves were running out of steam. When they cavorted in *Races,* Chico was forty-nine, Harpo forty-eight, Groucho forty-six. They were, as one of their screenwriters uncharitably put it, "old men trying to be pixies." After performing together for nearly thirty years, they were sick of the act, sick of their characters, and a little sick of one another. A line from *Go West,* a 1940 clunker, seemed inadvertently pertinent: "You love your brother, don't you?" Groucho, eyeing a dilapidated Harpo, asks Chico. "No," Chico responds, "but I'm used to him."

In 1941, between takes for *The Big Store,* Groucho told a reporter that it would be their last picture. "Our stuff is simply growing stale," he said, as his older brothers listened. "So are we. What happened to us is that we were defeated by our own specialty. The fake mustache, the dumb harp player, and the little guy who chased the ladies, all were funny at first. But it became successively harder with each picture to top the one before. We couldn't get out of the groove, without getting out of the movies. So we decided to get all the way out." Breaking up, Groucho acknowledged, "means a certain amount of sadness. But everything passes, sadness included. Anyhow, I prefer never to work again than to make another Marx Brothers picture."

*   *   *

The Brothers Grimm are often characterized as a model of fraternal collaboration to which each brother contributed in equal measure. Yet in a 1822 letter, Wilhelm admitted to a friend that he had spent most of his life "submitting" to his brother's will. Even in the most balanced partnerships, one brother usually takes the lead. As with the Grimms—and the Mayos, and the Wrights—it is often the elder brother, but occasionally, as with the Marxes and the Disneys, a younger brother, thanks to talent or personality, becomes the driving force. On his deathbed, Mayer Rothschild made his sons promise that they would remain united, cooperating in all their business decisions. Yet "the five Frankfurters," as they were known, were co-equals only in theory. Third-born Nathan, the most ambitious, soon became "the commanding general," as Salomon half-joked, who made his brother "marshals" do his bidding. Although they likened him to Napoleon and chafed at his bullying tactics (after one sneering communiqué from London, even the obsequious Salomon was emboldened to complain, "One just doesn't write that way to one's family, one's brothers, one's partners"), they acquiesced for the sake of the family business. Indeed, though all of the brothers quarreled, in the end there was no one else they trusted so much as one another.

There was no question that the name Gershwin meant, as the journalist Isaac Goldberg put it, "Principally George, Incidentally Ira." Ira agreed. Saying that the word *genius* applied only to his younger brother, he did whatever he could to allow that genius to express itself. He took care of George's business affairs by paying his bills and making his travel arrangements. "He was under the spell of his brother's overwhelming personality, as the rest of us were," observed the playwright S. N. Behrman. The director Rouben Mamoulian recalled being summoned to George's apartment to hear the *Porgy and Bess* score for the first time. "George was the orchestra and sang half of the parts, Ira sang the other half," he recalled. "Ira was also frequently the audience. It was touching to see how he, while singing, would become so overwhelmed with admiration for his brother that he would look from him to me with half-open eyes and pantomime with a soft gesture of his hand, as if saying, '*He* did it. Isn't it wonderful? Isn't *he* wonderful?'"

There were numerous reasons why it was Jesse and not Frank who emerged as the de facto leader of the James gang, the one the others called "Captain"—although Frank was four years older, a Confederate veteran, and had ridden with an embryonic version of the gang for a year before sixteen-year-old Jesse was allowed to join. Part of it was personality. Frank was a studious fellow who, before the Civil War, had wanted to be a teacher. (Partial to Shakespeare, he was said to have quoted the Bard during one robbery.) Jesse, who quit school at thirteen, was impetuous, cocky, mischievous, and unusually talkative—even as he held up trains and shot bank tellers. "Jesse laughs at everything—Frank at nothing at all," wrote John Newman Edwards, a purple-prose journalist who burnished the James legend in a series of worshipful articles. "Jesse is light-hearted, reckless, devil-may-care—Frank sober, sedate, a dangerous man always in ambush in the midst of society." Part of it was ambition. Frank shrank from the limelight. Jesse wrote letters to newspapers about the gang's deeds, likening himself to Caesar, Napoleon, and Alexander the Great. Part of it was looks. Frank was slim, long-faced, and dark-haired. Jesse was stronger and handsomer, with sandy hair, blue eyes, broad shoulders, smooth skin, and a turned-up nose—a more memorable countenance for the wanted posters. Jesse's name, too, was catchy, alliterative, easy on the tongue. Part of it was the division of labor. Frank was the detail man who studied the maps, planned the escape routes, counted the money, and handed out shares. Jesse was the big-picture man who exhorted the gang to ever-riskier exploits. In a profession in which the more violent a man was, the more his peers respected him—and the more his enemies feared him—Jesse took greater relish in his work. Small wonder that Jesse was the James people wrote ballads about.

Indeed, Frank's heart may not have been fully in his work. In 1882, Bob and Charley Ford, the last remaining members of the gang, shot Jesse in the back for the $10,000 reward. (Old West gangs were a growth industry for brothers; at various times, the James gang had four fraternal subsets: the Jameses, the Youngers, the Millers, and the Fords.) Seeming almost relieved that his fate was no longer tied to his infamous brother's, Frank turned himself in. Jesse's death, however, had satisfied the state's thirst for revenge, and after a sixteen-day trial, Frank was acquitted. Yet he seemed unable to settle down. Over the succeeding twenty-eight years he lived in St. Louis, New Orleans, and Dallas, among other places, and worked quietly but honestly as a horse-race starter, livestock trader, burlesque house doorman, racetrack commissioner, telegraph operator, shoe salesman, and, with his old gang-mate Cole Younger, reformed desperado in a traveling stage show celebrating the fading Wild West. After his mother's death in 1911, Frank and his family moved into the house in which he and Jesse had grown up. In the four years that remained to him, he gave tours of the farm to curious tourists for twenty-five cents.

*   *   *

After twenty-two years as a quartet, and seven more as a trio, the Marx Brothers weren't quite sure what to do on their own. Chico acted in a play and did a radio show, but found that whenever he tried moving beyond his Marxian character, audiences complained. So he donned his green Pinocchio hat, polished up his "Eye-talian" accent, formed his own orchestra ("Chico Marx and His Ravellis"), and toured the country, telling jokes, singing the old songs, waving a baton in front of the band for a few bars, performing his key-shooting piano solo, and gambling away his paychecks as quickly as he earned them.

Chico's life was unraveling. His wife had put up with his philandering for decades, but in 1941, the year the brothers broke up, she learned that Chico had had a fling with a young friend of their daughter's. She agreed not to divorce him, but from then on, they ate and slept separately. Although Chico treated his gambling losses with customary bravado—"The first crap game I played I lost $47,000 in one night," he told a reporter. "But I learned as I went along. In time I was able to lose more than that"—he was, increasingly, whistling in the dark. In 1947, he had a heart attack at the Las Vegas nightspot where he was performing. Doctors told him he could no longer tour, and Chico announced his retirement. Two years later, after running up some gambling debts, he was back on the road. But there was less demand for his solo act, and he was forced to play a grueling schedule of one-night stands reminiscent of the old vaudeville days. Once or twice a year, he persuaded Harpo to join him, and they'd reprise their Marx Brothers antics. Chico could still wow people backstage with his serial-numbers-on-a-dollar-bill trick, but the impetuous, dashing gallant who had always taken the stairs two at time was a lonely, plodding, diminished old man who claimed to be fifty-five but was sixty and looked seventy. Chico, said Groucho, was the family's "lost soul."

If Chico was fading, his former partner in crime had been reborn. Well into middle age, Harpo had been a womanizer and gambler to rival his older brother, albeit less publicly. But in 1936, at the age of forty-nine, the man Walter Winchell called "Hollywood's most reluctant bride-groom" married a former Ziegfeld Follies showgirl. Harpo and Susan would adopt four children in the next eight years. Having grown up in a big family, Harpo longed for a big family himself. "I wanted to have a child at every window," Harpo explained, "waving to me when I came home." He converted the dining room into a poolroom; installed a Ping-Pong table on the patio; hung the jacaranda with year-round Christmas lights; and filled the house with dogs, cats, hamsters, goldfish, a turtle, a monkey, and more than a hundred birds. He gave up smoking, gambling, and staying out late; he got home each evening in time to play with his children, who called him Harpo, not Dad. At bedtime he lulled them to sleep by playing "Annie Laurie," the first solo he'd played in vaudeville, on the harp.

With Groucho's help, Harpo had invested wisely in the stock market. He could afford to pick and choose his projects. He tried a few non-Marxian roles, including a summer stock production with his old friend Alexander Woollcott, who was godfather to Harpo's eldest son. But when he tried to make a Harpo movie on his own, the studio refused to finance the film unless Groucho and Chico appeared in it, too. As the years went by, Harpo occasionally got out his wig and trenchcoat to perform at char-ity fund-raisers, or to perform with Chico, who was by then a charity in himself. But show business took second place to family. In the fifties, Harpo moved to Palm Springs, where he built a house on the edge of a golf course, not far from Zeppo and Gummo, and spent his days practic-ing the harp, playing golf and bridge, painting landscapes he donated to charities, and spending time with his wife and children. As a teenager,

Harpo had been considered the least likely to succeed of the brothers; as a grown-up, he was the happiest.

Of all the brothers, Groucho was the most determined to leave the Marx Brothers behind. He performed in several plays, developed a few radio shows, and appeared in a movie with the Brazilian singer Carmen Miranda. (His best line came offscreen when he remarked, "I played second banana to the fruit on Carmen Miranda's head.") But the only role people wanted him to play was Groucho. In 1942, he joined a dozen other movie stars in a "Hollywood Victory Caravan" that crossed the country by train, selling war bonds along the way. At their final stop, in Washington, D.C., they were met by a huge crowd. As the stars disembarked, the crowd applauded each iconic face. Then a slender middle-aged man in a suit, looking more like a tax lawyer than a movie star, climbed down. He was met with silence. The man climbed back aboard the train, dabbed some greasepaint on his upper lip, stuck a cigar in his mouth, and reappeared, waggling his eyebrows and assuming a bent-knee walk. "Doesn't anybody want little old Groucho's autograph?" he called, as the crowd cheered the most recognizable mug in show business.

In 1947, Groucho agreed to host a new quiz show called *You Bet Your Life*. *Newsweek* observed that using Groucho as a quizmaster was like selling Citation to a glue factory. But the show was a hit on radio, and, three years later, an even bigger one on TV. There were Marxian elements: the show's theme song was "Hooray for Captain Spaulding"; a young announcer named George Fenneman served, as Groucho put it, as "the male Margaret Dumont"; and Groucho was his famously acid self. But when the producers advised him to wear his swallowtail coat and greasepaint mustache, Groucho balked. "The hell I will," he snapped. "That character's dead." (He did consent to grow a real mustache, a symbolic nod to his immortal character, and to wear a hairpiece, noting that "If the sponsor and the network want to see me with a full head of hair, there will be the devil toupée.") While Chico and Harpo would be stuck playing their Marx Brothers characters into old age, *You Bet Your Life* allowed Groucho to evolve into at least a cousin of his stage self. In 1951, nineteen years after appearing on the cover with Chico, Harpo, and Zeppo, Groucho appeared solo on the cover of *Time*, in an article titled "Trademark Effrontery." After forty years as a member of the Marx Brothers, Groucho, the middle child, stood alone in the spotlight.

The most successful brother was, however, the least happy. Groucho would marry three times—all sweet, naive, would-be actresses many years younger, who, in the face of a hypercritical husband, ended up drinking heavily. In public, Groucho played the lecher: pinching fannies, making risqué remarks, and stealing kisses. Like an adolescent determined to prove his he-man bona fides, he larded his conversation with words like *fuck* and *broad*. But he harbored lifelong feelings of sexual inadequacy and was terrified of intimacy. His son theorized that Groucho felt threatened by strong, smart women who reminded him of his domineering mother, and so he married vulnerable, tractable gentile girls barely out of adolescence. Having spent most of his life in the company of his brothers, Groucho was truly comfortable only with men—the crowd of writers with whom he discussed books and politics, the flock of aging comedians with whom he traded quips over lunch at the Hillcrest Country Club, the brothers who constituted an impermeable five-member club of their own. Chico's daughter believed that all the Marx brothers had "a basic contempt for women"; if so, Groucho's contempt was rooted in self-loathing. "I don't care to belong to any social organization that would accept me as a member," Groucho famously remarked on resigning from the Friars Club. He could have been speaking about women.

As Groucho's children grew older, he pushed them away, too. Surpassingly proud when his son became one of the top young tennis players in the country, Groucho rushed from the soundstage to attend his matches. But when Arthur, hoping to please his father, became a writer, Groucho, whose fondest dream was to be accepted as a literary man, treated him no less disdainfully than he had treated S. J. Perelman. When his nervous son showed him a few chapters of his first novel, Groucho read for an hour, then threw the pages aside, exclaiming, "Amateur Night!"—and recommended that he burn them. Groucho adored his older daughter, Miriam, a precocious tomboy with a wit almost as caustic as his, but he couldn't help criticizing her. When Miriam was a homesick college freshman on the far side of the country, Groucho, in an otherwise affectionate letter, wrote, "Perhaps it's the excess weight that you've put on that's responsible for your pessimism. I've always been under the impression that fat people are happy—maybe you're just an exception." It was as if he were talking to Margaret Dumont onstage, not writing a letter to his insecure eighteen-year-old daughter. Like his wives, Miriam would turn to drink, spending decades in and out of hospitals for treatment of alcoholism. She would stop drinking at the age of fifty, as the father she had worshiped was dying.

The only brother able to move beyond his Marx Brothers role onstage, Groucho was the only one unable to move beyond it offstage. He had developed his character to keep the world at bay, and the character became indistinguishable from the man. "Groucho never knew how to talk normally," said the actress Maureen O'Sullivan. "His life was his jokes." At movies, he kept up an audible running commentary ("My God, she's crying already!" Groucho exclaimed when *Now, Voyager,* starring the histrionic Bette Davis, opened with a scene of raindrops pelting a windowpane), which fellow moviegoers would shush angrily until they'd identified the source, at which point they'd ask for his autograph. Groucho grumbled about having to be "on," but ever since his mother had pulled him out of sixth grade to put him on stage he'd been conditioned to give audiences what they wanted. So he pinched bottoms, pestered pretty girls for kisses, insulted strangers. He'd answer the phone or sign letters using the names of his old characters. When Groucho visited the hospital after his grandson was born, recalled his daughter-in-law, "He did the Hack-enbush routine up and down the halls." His life became a kind of nonstop performance. In 1961, an elderly T. S. Eliot wrote Groucho, saying he was a fan and asking for an autographed photo. Groucho sent him a studio portrait. The author of *The Waste Land* (which, it must be noted, has a certain Grouchoesque eclecticism) thanked him but said he would prefer one in full Groucho regalia. Groucho complied. The two men became pen pals. A few years later, when Groucho was in London, Eliot invited him to his home for dinner. In the week prior, Groucho, the would-be intel-lectual, boned up, reading *Murder in the Cathedral* twice, *The Waste Land* three times. At dinner, all Eliot wanted to talk about was the courtroom scene in *Duck Soup.*

The older Groucho got, the more venomous his jokes became.

"Groucho feels he has to live up to the legend," said the screenwriter Julius Epstein. "He *has* to be insulting to everybody; he feels they expect him to treat them like he treated Margaret Dumont." Indeed, most of his victims went home thrilled that they had been insulted by the great Groucho; it was like being punched on the street by Jack Dempsey. But not everyone. Groucho was walking with a friend when a man approached them and told Groucho, "Everyone tells me I look like you when you were young." Groucho looked at the man. "If I'd looked like you," he said, "I would have killed myself." The man, retreated, speechless. Shy and vulnerable as a child, Groucho scorned weakness in others and had learned to attack before others could attack him. He could be brutally judgmental, but he judged no one more harshly than himself. When a fan remarked how pleased he was to meet the famous Groucho, Groucho demurred. "I've known him for years," he said, "and I can tell you it's no pleasure."

*   *   *

It seems something of a miracle that the Marx Brothers managed to perform together for more than three decades. Indeed, brothers don't have to be "one soul placed in two bodies," like the Goncourts, to collaborate successfully. For some, friction can be a motivating force. The identical twins Mike and Bob Bryan have been the best doubles tennis team in the world for much of the new millennium, their fraternal synchronicity enabling them to beat numerous opponents with more raw ability. Yet they fight each other almost as fiercely as they did when they were children. In one early-round match in 2009, Mike yelled at Bob, who jabbed the butt of his racket into Mike's crotch. Mike doubled over and fell to the court. When he was capable of speech, he smiled up at his brother: "Got me, asshole." Then Mike rose to his feet and the twins closed out the match as if nothing had happened. After they played poorly in an early-round victory at Wimbledon in 2006, the brothers had a fistfight in the backseat of the car en route to their rented house. Inside, the battle continued: Mike kicked Bob in the stomach, Bob smashed Mike's guitar. Then they made up and went on to win the championship. "Neither of us will ever play with another partner," says Mike. "So we never worry about offending the [other] guy . . . We'll always get over it."

Sometimes, however, the very familiarity that can make a fraternal collaboration so effective can end up destroying it. Much of the Everly Brothers' appeal derived from their siblinghood. Their father, a coal miner turned musician who taught them how to sing and play guitar, encouraged their similarity. The brothers looked alike, dressed alike, wore their hair alike, and, though the younger brother, Phil, had a naturally higher voice, they sounded alike. On stage, they stood close to each other, heads together, sharing a microphone, their two voices blending into one seamless sound. In 1957, "Bye Bye Love" made them overnight stars.

From the beginning, though, Don, two years older, was the better guitar player, the more sophisticated musician, and the natural leader. He sang the solos, performed the introductions, wrote most of the original songs, and made most of the decisions. Phil, a more easygoing fellow, didn't mind deferring. "I was always a younger brother and basically followed pretty much what went down," he recalled. (When the brothers served in the same unit during a six-month hitch in the Marine Reserves, Don was named platoon leader.) As their fame grew, however, Phil began to chafe at his secondary role. The brothers had never been particularly close, but their early success had yoked their lives together. They had masked their differences for the sake of the act. Now they began asserting their individuality. They styled their hair differently. They bickered over their musical direction. In the mid-sixties, the Beatles and the Rolling Stones were ascendent; the Everlys, though still in their twenties, seemed part of an earlier era. Phil was content to perform their old hits; Don, intent on being taken as a serious artist, wanted to experiment. Phil liked playing the lucrative, tuxedo-and-bright-lights casino dates of Las Vegas; Don preferred jeans-and-T-shirt rock clubs. On tour, they stayed in separate hotels, arrived independently to concerts, and prepared in separate dressing rooms. Their wives didn't get along. Their friends had to choose sides, and to be in one brother's camp meant you were excluded from the other. And yet moments after an offstage shouting match, they'd step onstage and deliver a flawless performance. Eventually, they kept their distance even onstage: from cozying up to one microphone, heads together, they moved to a double mike and, eventually, to separate microphones. But they were reluctant to split up; only as the Everly Brothers could they make that kind of money.

During a 1973 performance, Don, who had drunk several margaritas before the show, began going flat, missing words, singing the wrong verses, and making incomprehensible comments between numbers. At the end of one song, as Don took a bow, Phil smashed his guitar, walked into the wings, and announced, "I'll never get on a stage with that man again."

Over the next decade, the brothers met only once, to bury their father after he died of lung cancer. Each pursued a mildly successful solo career. For several years, Don refused to play their old Everly Brothers hits, Phil occasionally played one or two. Then in 1983, ten years after their split, they agreed to settle "the big southern feud" as they called it, by playing several concerts. "I don't want to end my life on negative terms with my brother," said Phil. When they met for their first rehearsal, not having seen each other in eight years, they bear-hugged. Then, recalled Don, "We just walked up to the microphone and said, 'Right, it's "Bye Bye Love" in the key of A.' Everybody knew it and away we went."

If conflict can rupture a fraternal partnership, it can also propel it to greatness. Although Wilbur and Orville Wright were the closest of brothers, their working relationship thrived on an almost childlike contrariness. "One of them would make a statement about something very important, and then there would be a long pause," remembered their niece, Ivonette. "Then the other would say, 'That's not so.' 'Tis too.' 'Tisn't either.'" Their assistant, Charlie Taylor recalled, "They'd shout at each other something terrible. I don't think they really got mad, but they sure got awfully hot." One morning after a particularly vehement argument the night before, Orville arrived at the shop and admitted to Charlie that he'd been wrong and they should do it Will's way. Soon afterward, Will came in and said he'd been thinking it over and maybe Orville was right. Whereupon the argument began again, each brother defending the position the other had taken the night before. The brothers not only enjoyed their debates—

"I love to scrap with Orv," Will said—but found them essential to their work, a kind of Socratic dialogue that enabled them to home in on a solution. "Honest argument is merely a process of mutually picking the beams and motes out of each others' eyes so both can see clearly," Will explained to a friend.

Scholars argue over which Wright made the greater contribution to the invention of manned flight, but the brothers themselves gave no thought to the issue. They were sparring partners but never rivals. It didn't matter which brother made a breakthrough as long as they moved closer to their common goal. "No matter what either one did, the other seemed sure to take the next needed step," wrote their biographer Fred Kelly. "It was almost as if they were deliberately taking turns."

In September 1902, the brothers made their third annual trip to Kitty Hawk to test their latest glider. That year's model was more stable than its predecessors, but every so often it would slide sideways and crash to the ground no matter what the pilot did. The Wrights couldn't figure out why. One night, Orville drank more coffee than usual and was unable to fall asleep. He lay awake in their tent, mulling over the problem. He realized that as the glider went into its sideways slide, the fixed vertical tail not only failed to keep the glider on its path, it also collided with stationary air, pushing the craft into what would one day be called a tailspin. Orville concluded that if the tail were able to move, the operator, by altering the tail's angle, could exert pressure on the higher wing and might thus be able to control the turn. In the morning, Orville explained his idea to his brother. After a moment's reflection, Wilbur agreed with Orville's assessment. Then he suggested that the movement of the tail be coordinated with the movement of the wing, so that the operator, by shifting his hips, could tilt the wings and alter the tail's angle at the same time. It was Orville's turn to agree. Orville's solution and Wilbur's addendum constituted a Eureka moment in the invention of the airplane—a simple but elegant solution in which, like the wing and the tail, they acted in concert.

They would spend a year back in Dayton perfecting a motor before returning to Kitty Hawk. On the cold, blustery morning of December 17, 1903, a little more than three years after they had made their first glider, Orville climbed into the operator's cradle. (The brothers took turns making their test flights, and it was Orville's turn.) With Will jogging alongside, his hand on the right wingtip, the machine, with Orville at the controls, rose, dipped, and rose again.

* * *

By the 1950s, when people thought of the Marx Brothers, they thought of Groucho, Harpo, and Chico. The more famous the older brothers had become, the further Gummo and Zeppo had sunk into obscurity. People often got them confused. Discharged from the army, Gummo had returned to his first love: inventing. He tried to market a new kind of cardboard laundry box, but nobody bought it; he invented a skidless tire, but on a test drive, the car drove right out of its wheels. He opened a successful dress business, "Gummo Marx Inc.," but the Depression intervened and the company went bankrupt. (It is unclear whether sales were helped or hurt when Gummo's brothers dropped by the showroom, trying on the merchandise and chasing customers away.) The three older brothers persuaded Zeppo to take Gummo into his talent agency; once again, the two younger brothers paired off. Gummo, a soft-spoken, good-natured fellow, proved to be a highly successful agent, known for his honesty, often working on a handshake basis. (Zeppo took a more aggressive approach. At a nightclub, trying to persuade the writer Norman Krasna to become a client, he punched out a drunk who had been pestering Krasna. "Does the other agency give you that kind of service?" he asked the startled writer.) In the early 1950s, Gummo sold the agency and limited himself to representing his brothers. He moved to Palm Springs, where he bought a house on the golf course and lived quietly with his wife. Although he was still a hypochondriac, quick to give family and friends the details about his latest doctor's appointment, he had the well-fed look and contented air of a country squire.

Gummo never regretted leaving the act. He admired his brothers, but he was happier in the background. He joked gracefully about their fame. ("I attribute their success entirely to me," he told A. J. Liebling. "I quit the act.") Yet Gummo may have been more valuable to the Marx Brothers out of the act. He was their agent; he was also, in Harpo's words, their "den mother." (Many years earlier, when Gummo married, Minnie had given her new daughter-in-law the lowdown on her sons: "Groucho is the fairest man you will ever meet, but he is a little hard. Chico is the black sheep of the family. Harpo is my sweetheart and Gummo is my mother.") Whenever a brother had a problem, he turned to Gummo, the family fixer. When Minnie stormed out of Arthur's seventh birthday party, offended by something Ruth had done, Groucho asked Gummo to smooth things over. When Harpo got cold feet about marrying Susan, Gummo assured him she was the best thing that had ever happened to him. When Groucho worried that he might not be able to deliver a speech he'd written, he asked Gummo to pinch hit. ("And don't forget," Groucho warned, "Big Brother is always watching.") When Harpo's heart began to fail, he turned to Gummo, who seemed to know every doctor in Southern California, for advice. When Chico died, Gummo made the funeral arrangements. "I was the one who took care of these things," he said. "Not because I wanted to, but because I was expected to."

Zeppo, too, was happier out of the Marx Brothers. His talent agency, Zeppo Marx Inc., became the third largest in Hollywood, with a client list that included Clark Gable, Jean Harlow, and Lana Turner. For some time, however, there was one glaring omission: the Marx Brothers. "They probably didn't think I was good enough," Zeppo said later, adding, "But a lot of good writers and directors and actors and actresses thought I was good enough. I had 250 clients." When the brothers finally signed on, only after dependable Gummo joined the agency, Zeppo found them as difficult to handle as their directors had. "Whatever kind of deal I would get them, they would want to change," he said. In 1938, Zeppo negotiated a remarkably good contract for *Room Service*, but Groucho sniffed that he should have gotten them more. Feeling as unappreciated as he had on stage, Zeppo refused to work with them after that, turning them over to Gummo.

In 1949, Zeppo left the agency and started a series of business ventures: he bred racehorses with Barbara Stanwyck; he bought a grapefruit farm (and sold shares to his brothers); he ran a fishing business from a boat named *The Marx Brothers*. He retired to Palm Springs with his wife and two adopted children, where he bought a house near Gummo's and spent his time lifting weights, puttering in his machine shop, playing high-stakes poker and golf, and getting into fights that occasionally landed his name in the police blotter. In 1959, Zeppo, now divorced, married a twenty-nine-year-old showgirl who, in turn, divorced him fourteen years later to marry his next-door-neighbor, Frank Sinatra. Not long after the divorce, seventy-two-year-old Zeppo was accused of beating his latest girlfriend "about the face and head and pulling her hair and attempting to break her nose," in the words of the police report. Zeppo dismissed the incident, which took place in the driveway of the country club, as "just a little pushing and shoving" over a credit card, but was ordered by the court to pay $20,690 in damages to the woman, who went on to marry the Mafia boss Jimmy "The Weasel" Fratianno.

Zeppo never liked reminiscing about the glory years. In one of his rare interviews he said that he had "hated" being in the Marx Brothers. "The only fun I got out of it was the chorus girls," he recalled. "And laying all of them, or as many as I could."

Though Zeppo and Gummo saw each other every day for lunch, and Chico, Harpo, and Groucho rarely let more than a few days go by without phoning one another, Harpo's son Bill could recall seeing all five Marx brothers together only once beyond the confines of the Hillcrest Country Club. And yet, as if they needed to be physically proximate, they never lived far from one another. In his late sixties, Groucho bought a weekend cottage in Palm Springs, where Harpo, Gummo, and Zeppo now lived. (Chico, who couldn't afford a second home, was the only Marx Brother who didn't have a place there.) At infrequent family gatherings, "the boys," as they referred to one another, formed their own insular group, sharing a language that even their wives and children couldn't speak. If there was no dish-throwing or drape-pulling, there was tall-tale-telling from their vaudeville days. They had shared women, they had shared roles, and now they shared stories—at different times, they'd tell the same tale about a different brother, as if when something happened to one Marx brother, it happened to all of them. At evening's end, they'd sing verse after verse of "Peasie Weasie," the patter song with which they'd always concluded their vaudeville act. "That the brothers loved each other more than they did any collection of wives, daughters, or sons is hard for me to admit," recalled Chico's daughter, Maxine, "but I think it was the case."

More and more, what brought the brothers together was their worry over Chico. In 1956 Chico was forced to stop touring because of his heart condition. The following year, the IRS sued him for $77,564 in back taxes. His brothers put up the $25,000 the government accepted as an installment. To get by, Chico filed for Social Security. Gummo squirreled away $10,000 in his safe as an emergency fund for his eldest brother. "Most mornings I'd get a call from him. 'Gummy,' he'd say, and I knew what was coming. 'I had some bad luck last night and I need three hundred dollars.' So I'd give him that, and another three hundred, and then five hundred, and before I knew it the ten thousand was gone." Every so often, Chico sold his membership in the Hillcrest Country Club to pay off a gambling debt, but his brothers always bought it back.

The brothers' greatest sacrifice for Chico wasn't financial but artistic. For decades, producers had been trying to get Groucho, Harpo, and Chico to reunite onscreen. For Chico, who was near bankruptcy, they did. In 1957, they appeared in what was, even for the Marx Brothers, a stretch: an adaptation of *The Story of Mankind*, Hendrik van Loon's history of civilization. Harpo played a speechless Isaac Newton, Chico a fifteenth-century monk, Groucho the seventeenth-century Dutch settler who bought Manhattan from the Indians. It was advertised as the last Marx Brothers movie, but the brothers weren't in a single frame together, which made sense historically if not dramatically. According to most reviews, their last film was also their worst. Two years later, the brothers, coming together again for Chico's sake, began work on a situation comedy. Gaunt, exhausted, and hobbled by arteriosclerosis, Chico struggled to remember his lines, and his scenes had to be reshot again and again. No company was willing to insure the ailing actor, and the pilot was never completed. On October 10, 1960, Chico made his last television appearance, playing four-handed bridge. He lost.

For years Groucho had joked, with a mix of envy and spite, that Chico would die in bed, but the bed would belong to another man's wife and the cause of death would be a bullet fired by an angry husband. In October 1961, five months after suffering another heart attack, Chico, aged seventy-four, died in his own bed in a modest bungalow in one of the less-expensive neighborhoods in Beverly Hills, where he was living with his second wife, an actress twenty-nine years younger. He was broke. "I wish I were Groucho so I could help you out," he said to his daughter not long before he died. She told him she wouldn't exchange him for anyone.

Chico's alter ego wouldn't last much longer. In his later years, Harpo was treated as a cherished national treasure. Even Groucho, who found fault with everyone, couldn't help saying nice things about him. "He inherited all my mother's good qualities—kindness, understanding, and friendliness," Groucho said. "I got what was left." In the years after his brother's death, Harpo suffered a series of heart attacks himself, and though he still played his harp every morning, his stage appearances grew rare. In 1963, seventy-four-year-old Harpo appeared at the Pasadena Playhouse for a fund-raising concert. Wearing his customary raincoat, sneakers, and battered top hat, he performed some of his iconic routines without a word, as he had for fifty years. After he shuffled offstage, the emcee, Allan Sherman, told the crowd that they had witnessed Harpo's final performance. Harpo wandered out from the wings. The audience cheered. Raising his hands to quiet them, Harpo said, in his soft voice, "Now, as I was about to say in 1907 . . ." The audience roared—and then listened raptly as Harpo poured forth a fifteen-minute string of stories. In September 1964, Harpo checked into the hospital for a coronary bypass. Two days later, he died. Groucho wept when he got the news. It was the only time his son ever saw him cry.

Groucho was alone. The two brothers to whom he had been closest were gone. Many of his writer friends were dead. Margaret Dumont died a year after Harpo. His third wife left him two years after that. He was largely estranged from his children. The fourteen-year run of *You Bet Your Life* had ended one month before Chico's death, and, though Groucho made occasional TV appearances, prostate trouble, hearing problems, arthritis, depression, and a series of minor strokes kept him at home. His doctors forbade him to smoke cigars. He occasionally invited people to dinner, but shooed guests out the door before eleven, when he'd put on his polka-dot pajamas, get in bed, and watch the nightly rerun of *You Bet*

Your Life, playing the game along with the contestants, preening when he got the right answer. Whenever an old Marx Brothers movie came on TV, he'd watch.

Groucho made the three-hour drive to Palm Springs less and less often. At infrequent dinners with Zep and Gum, as he called them, they'd talk about Minnie, about the old vaudeville days, about Chico's escapades. Of his two surviving brothers, Gummo was the one to whom Groucho was closer. (In an unguarded interview, Groucho would call Zeppo "cold-blooded.") But he couldn't help needling his milder, more vulnerable brother, treating him, as he had onstage, as his stooge. With Chico gone, it seemed as if Groucho needed a brother to pick on, and Gummo was a safer target than short-tempered Zeppo. Indeed, the worst that Gummo, ever the diplomat, would say of Groucho was, "He should have been a Quaker. He was stern. I don't quite understand what made him tick the way he did."

Groucho would have a bizarre final act. In 1971, an ambitious young actress was hired to answer his mail. Depending on to whom one talked, Erin Fleming was either a caring, attentive companion who revitalized Groucho's career and gave him a reason to live, or a controlling, abusive gold digger who exploited a dying man. Either way, she took charge of his life. She prodded him into giving a series of one-man concerts, in which Groucho, his lope slowed to a halting shuffle, his rat-a-tat delivery faded to a mumble, told jokes from Marx Brothers movies, showed a film clip or two, and sang a few old vaudeville songs—performances that audience members, some of them gotten up in greasepaint mustaches, false noses, and wire-rimmed glasses, tended to find either poignant or pitiful. (After seeing his brother's show in Los Angeles, Zeppo pronounced the spectacle "sad.") At times, Erin was solicitous and attentive; at times she'd scream at Groucho in front of guests, humiliating him as he had humiliated his three wives. Groucho's children intervened, kindling a long, costly court battle for custody. In early 1977, Groucho was hospitalized with a broken hip, and his condition deteriorated rapidly. When Gummo, depressed since the death of his wife a year earlier, and distraught over Groucho's situation, died on April 21, at the age of eighty-four, Groucho, not far from the end himself, wasn't told.

In his final months, Groucho, surrounded by nurses he no longer had the strength to pinch, roused himself enough to crack an occasional joke. When George Fenneman visited, he helped a nurse transfer Groucho from his wheelchair to his bed, putting his arms around him and swiveling him onto the mattress. "You always were a lousy dancer," growled Groucho, clinging to his old *You Bet Your Life* announcer. But age, illness, and painkillers had softened him. When his daughter-in-law, a woman he had always disliked, came to visit, Groucho kissed her—not the joking, lascivious smooch of yore but a flurry of affectionate, needy, apologetic pecks. "He kissed her about fifty times," recalled Nat Perrin. "He would never have stopped if she hadn't gotten tired of bending over." When the screenwriters Norman Panama and Julius Epstein visited with their wives, Groucho mustered a ghost of his familiar leer for the women. "They both love me," Groucho murmured. "Everyone loves you, Groucho," Panama said. "Yes," Groucho said faintly. "Everyone except me."

Slipping in and out of consciousness, Groucho died on August 19, 1977. Zeppo, who had sided with Erin Fleming in the custody dispute, learned of his brother's death from the evening news. The last Marx brother would die of lung cancer two years later at the age of seventy-eight.

A quarter-century earlier, on a summer evening in 1954, Harpo and Susan Marx hosted a party in their Beverly Hills home following Groucho's wedding to his third wife, a former model forty years his junior. It was the first time the five brothers had been together in several years.

Groucho was standing by the piano, singing a mock love ballad to his new wife, when he suddenly nudged the accompanist off the piano bench and started playing a rollicking tune, *"Ist das nicht ein Schnitzelbank?"* It was their mother's favorite song from the old "Fun in Hi Skule" act, a song they had sung hundreds of times in towns and cities across the country in their vaudeville days. Few of the guests knew it. But for his four brothers, it was a siren call. Sitting in different corners of the room, they took up their parts. For a few minutes the wedding was forgotten, the guests were forgotten, and the Marx Brothers were together again.

Chapter Nine

Aerogrammes

Sifting through a chest of old letters not long ago, I came across a sheaf of aerogrammes postmarked Buenos Aires and addressed to me in Paris. I had moved there after graduating from college, intending to write poetry in a garret on the Left Bank. I had no clue how I would support myself. Fortunately, a well-connected uncle got me a job with a company that sold cigarette lighters and electric shavers, a job to which Rimbaud surely would never have stooped. By day, I crunched numbers for marketing reports. By night, I holed up in my apartment—not quite the Left Bank garret I'd envisioned, but a decent-size studio in a disappointingly fashionable arrondissement on the Right Bank—and, like Harry in Australia, plowed my way through the longest novels in the English language. I must have written about my loneliness—although I'm sure I wasn't brave enough to use the word—to Ned, who had taken a year off from college and, through that same benevolent uncle, gotten a job in Argentina.

A month into my stay, the landlord's wife slipped an aerogramme under my door.

Just got your letter. It sounds like you're not too impressed with the situation over there. The first thing I want to say, George, as everyone has told you, I'm sure—it's a bitch the first month or so, language worst of all. It makes the loneliness all the worse (it did for me!). But shit, man, if you let it dwell on you that things are in a bad news way, things'll go like shit. Just try to find something positive to think about whenever you're down. Christ, I've had it bad here off and on but when I realize how much I could be gleaning from this experience, I get disgusted for feeling sorry for myself.

Ned, who had been in Argentina for six weeks before I arrived in Paris, went on to write of weekdays checking and rechecking budget data, weekends riding horses and eating grass-fed beef at his boss's ranch in the pampas. I envied how settled he sounded. But it comforted me to know that Ned had gone through some of the same things in *his* foreign country that I was going through in mine. It felt strange to have my younger brother counseling me, but because he was seven thousand miles away, I was able to listen. I took his cursing to be a measure of his concern, and when, in the midst of those "shits," he used my name, I was touched.

With the Atlantic between us, Ned and I entered into a sporadic epistolary relationship. I looked forward to finding, when I got home from work, a flimsy sky-blue aerogramme with his familiar, hastily penned, left-handed printing on the front. Ned wrote about his love of Argentina, I wrote about my growing affection for Paris. Occasionally, we talked of family. At Thanksgiving Ned admitted that it was strange not to be home, eating turkey and playing touch football. "I wouldn't have minded being there," he admitted. If our correspondence wasn't exactly Jamesian in its profundity, it was a start. We could, it seemed, stop playing Got You Last and talk to each other—at least if we were on separate continents. Ned had left behind his Marlboro Man sheepskin coat when he went to Argentina. I had brought it with me to France. On cold winter days I wore it as I walked the streets of Paris, and thought of my brother in Buenos Aires. When Ned wrote to suggest we meet in Europe that spring and bum around North Africa together, I urged him eastward. In the end, Ned couldn't save enough money to cross the Atlantic, although he spent several days casing the docks of Buenos Aires, trying to find a freighter that would take him. So he hitchhiked up through Latin America to Massachusetts. I wandered around Spain and Morocco before flying home. That summer, we met in a bar on Cape Cod and traded travelers' tales. We talked about O'Neill and Kerouac. We got drunk. As we staggered out into the windy August night, it felt as if we were finally becoming brothers.

Ned wasn't the only brother to write to me in Paris. Near the bottom of the chest, I was surprised to find a letter from Harry. After telling me about his first year at medical school, he skipped a few lines and wrote, seemingly out of the blue:

> I'm sorry I grew apart from you over the years, George. When I was younger, I'm not sure why, I really had to shut myself off from people— maybe I felt too vulnerable. Anyways, I can't change what I've done or been. But I feel like over the last few years I've been getting myself together and I feel real . . .

The next line, obscured by a strip of blue paper where, years ago, the unfolded aerogramme had stuck on its own glue, was indecipherable no matter how I held it up to the light or carefully tried to peel the paper away. What did he feel, I wondered. Lucky? Hopeful? Glad?

The last few lines, however, were clear:

> Anyways, I hope we can be closer in the future. I always cared for you tho I never liked to show it.
>
> Much love,
your bro'
Harry

* * *

I wish I could say that these first brave bids for fellowship immediately flowered into unbreakable fraternal bonds. Back home, however, we resumed our separate orbits: Ned in college in Connecticut, Harry in medical school in Ohio, Mark in boarding school in New Hampshire, me in graduate school in Maryland, where, after what turned out to be a glorious year in Paris, I had moved to get a master's degree in writing poetry.

In graduate school, the chicken-or-egg relationship between poetry and alcohol blurred still further. One night, driving with friends through East Baltimore on our way home from a surpassingly drunken evening, I found myself reciting "When You Are Old," Yeats's confession of unrequited love for Maud Gonne—one of the poems I'd memorized freshman year in the Harvard dishroom—to the rusted metal speaker at a Jack in the Box drive-through. "What can I get you?" a tired, disembodied voice crackled, as my fellow poets howled. "What can I get you?" If only I had known.

On graduation day, one of the poets threw a final bacchanal. My head still hurt from a party the night before, so I sipped a Coke and watched things disintegrate around me. One poet crawled off on her hands and knees, moaning, to vomit in the bathroom; a fiction writer staggered from person to person, shouting insults before passing out on the floor; a long-haired poet threw a glass of bourbon at his prostrate friend, prodded him with a boot, and yelled at him to get up; a Coleridge-loving senior on whom I had a Yeats-like crush walked out the door in disgust, saying "Fuck all of you." The drunken excess that, when I was in its eye, had seemed an exuberant expression of Rimbaudian *dérèglement de sens* now seemed merely pathetic. The party ended when a Jagger-lipped poet ran outside into the blinding afternoon light, dancing with what seemed to be ecstasy but turned out to be fury as he darted into traffic, screaming incoherently at the cars rushing by on their homeward commute. Another sober poet and I wrestled him, thrashing and ranting, back to his apartment, where his wife sighed and herded him inside.

In the fall, I moved to New York, where I wrote poems, auditioned for shows, and waited tables. I drank less, but I was drifting and aimless, like a sailboat in irons.

Not long afterward, a few years since that Christmas in the kitchen with Mark, Dad stopped drinking. For good measure, he stopped smoking, too.

He and Mum went into couples therapy and began the long, slow process of getting to know each other again. As my brothers and I watched their cautious reconnection, I think we realized that whatever happened between our parents, *we'd* have to begin sticking together. I recalled what Mum used to say to us in the old days when we couldn't stop fighting: "Someday your father and I will be gone and you'll only have each other."

It occurred to me that if my parents could change, I might be able to change, too. I moved back to Baltimore and started work at a magazine. My first assignment was to spend a night at a hospital emergency room and describe what I saw. In my poetry days, I had dismissed doctors (and lawyers and bankers and businessmen) as pillars of the bourgeoisie—they weren't *artists*—but as I watched them stitch up knife wounds and comfort feverish children, I was embarrassed by my arrogance. It occurred to me that this was what my older brother spent his life doing. What else about my brothers had I blinded myself to?

Though I went into journalism in order to have what I had always disdained as a "real job," I found that I loved it. I stopped writing poetry. I wasn't, it seemed, going to be the next Rimbaud. But I no longer wanted to be. Other changes followed with an ease that made them seem inevitable. I quit smoking, my drinking slowed to an occasional beer or two, and I fell in love with a girl whose vitality and optimism seemed as enviable to me as drinking myself insensate had seemed a few years earlier. On our first date, I found myself sipping a single beer for three hours because I didn't want to miss a word she said.

I don't think it was a coincidence that my awakening came not long after my older brother had begun to find contentment himself. Harry loved medicine, and he loved his medical school, an unconventional institution in Ohio where Benjamin Spock, the antiwar pediatrician whose baby-care book had served as our mother's gospel, had taught for several years. After his experience with AFSC, Harry wanted to work in rural, underserved areas; now he spent his summers with a team of medical students driving from town to town in the foothills of eastern Kentucky, offering blood screenings and rudimentary physicals. Far from Harvard, far from Boston, paying his own way through school, Harry finally felt free of his family. At the same time, he began to find his way back toward us. When he came east on vacation, he was less reserved, more at ease. One Christmas he brought home a nursing student he'd been seeing. Harry seemed a different person around Sandy. He smiled more. He seemed happy—a word I wouldn't have thought to apply to him since the days we'd played catch with Dad in the old Dedham backyard. As I watched them, I couldn't help wondering whether this woman knew the real Harry. Had she played Monopoly with him? Had he put her in a half nelson? But the more I saw them together, the more I realized that perhaps it was *I* who didn't know the real Harry. My older brother was growing up. I didn't want to be left behind.

Backpacking home from South America had given Ned a dose of confidence and a taste for travel. Determined to finish college while spending as little time in the classroom as possible, he embarked on what seemed, from my vantage point, like a series of stirringly picaresque adventures. He acted in summer stock. He delivered boats to the Caribbean. He sailed on a two-masted schooner from Cape Cod to Puerto Rico, studying marine biology and maritime history while learning how to sew sails and steer by the stars. When a hurricane hit just before his ship entered the Sargasso Sea, Ned was one of the few on board not to get seasick. When the students took turns at the helm while checking the long lines, Ned was the only one able to maneuver the 120-foot boat close enough to snare a buoy on his first attempt. Arriving in San Juan Harbor at the end of the voyage, Ned found a job crewing on the *Romance,* a square-rigger that took honeymooners island-hopping in the Caribbean. Varnishing the gunwales, scrambling up the rigging to release the topsails, drinking rum in palm-shaded ports, Ned felt, for the first time, that he truly fit in. At winter's end, the captain invited him to stay with the ship and spend a year cruising to the South Pacific. Ned had dreamed of sailing around the world but felt it was his duty to finish college. He reluctantly returned to school, where he made the Dean's List for the first time. But he sometimes wondered whether he'd made the right choice. Thirty years later, when Ned and his wife went on an eco-tour of the Galápagos Islands, they sailed by a volcanic cliff on which, for more than a century, sailors had painted the names of the vessels on which they passed through these waters. Ned felt a twinge when he saw the name *Romance*.

Mark, too, would leave home. When he was thirteen, my parents sent him to boarding school, thinking a change might do him good. Mark wasn't bullied at his new school, but he was still the smallest in his class, and though he made friends, he felt homesick and a little lost. I returned from my year in Paris in time to attend his ninth-grade graduation. In a snapshot Mum took, Mark looks eager and adoring, while I, sporting a weaselly Fu Manchu and recovering from a bout of dysentery acquired in Marrakesh, look emaciated and out of it. We seem as mismatched as Harry and I in the photo taken just before Harry left for boarding school.

In high school, Mark came into his own. He played on the varsity soccer, ski, and tennis teams. At home, he was finally big enough and good enough to compete in any sport we played. Indeed, he became the best tennis player of us all and spent summers teaching at a tennis camp, where he was a favorite with both campers and counselors. Mark loved working with kids. Around the same time, to my grateful relief, he also found that he loved physical labor—mowing lawns, shoveling snow, and all the other chores I had spent years trying to worm out of. He liked the discipline, as well as the gratification of immediate, tangible results: a closely cropped yard, a freshly cleared driveway. When he was sixteen, Mark spent his spring break pitching hay and mucking manure at our aunt's dairy farm in Virginia. He counted it as one of his best vacations ever. Mark still fretted that he wasn't as accomplished as his older brothers, but he worked hard, did well in school, and was prized by the admissions office for being such a persuasive tour guide. At his graduation, we watched Mark receive the prize for sportsmanship and school spirit. As he showed us around the campus, everyone seemed to know him. After the ceremony, Dad took a picture of the brothers—the first picture in many years with all four of us in the same frame. I'm grinning sheepishly; Ned is laughing, look-ing past us at someone out of camera range; Harry has an arm around

Mark; Mark, in his commencement robes, seems exhilarated at being surrounded by his brothers. We look happy.

The more we began to establish our own lives, the closer we grew as brothers. In the fall of 1980, newly graduated from college with a degree in theater studies, Ned moved to New York to become an actor. He got headshots taken, made hundreds of copies of his resume, and bought an answering machine. He found an apartment share in Hell's Kitchen. He got a job as a waiter at Steak & Brew, one of those all-the-watery-beer-you-can-drink places of which I had once been so fond. I had been back in New York only a few months myself, sleeping on a friend's couch on the Upper West Side and trying to be a freelance writer. Neither Ned nor I had any money, so we'd walk the city, talking of Paris, Buenos Aires, and our fledgling careers. Spending time with Ned away from home, I began to appreciate his deadpan sense of humor, his curiosity, his willingness to try new things. He introduced me to sweet Italian sausage from Greenwich Village butcher shops whose floors were furred with sawdust, and empanadas from hole-in-the-wall Argentinian joints along Eighth Avenue, where he bantered in Spanish with the countermen. One afternoon in Times Square we watched a tourist get fleeced at three-card monte, and Ned quietly pointed out how the shill hustled up business and the lookouts corralled the marks while keeping an eye out for police. When he came to dinner with some of my friends, Ned was drawn into talking a little about his time at sea. Afterward, my friends all said how great my brother was.

But having spent much of the previous two years on the ocean, Ned found New York claustrophobic and the theater business dispiriting. After playing leads in college, where he'd rehearse a single scene for hours, he found it hard to get accustomed to cattle calls, in which he'd file onstage with nine other actors, get eyeballed for a few seconds by three people behind a desk, and then be dismissed as not the right "type" as another ten actors filed in. When Ned got cast in the chorus of a nonpaying show, he had to drop out after a few weeks to keep his waiting job so he could pay the rent. The restaurant was so filthy that several times he had to position himself as he took an order so that his customers couldn't see the cockroach traversing the wall behind him. To get to his apartment, he had to walk a gauntlet of massage parlors, porn shops, junkies, and hustlers. (I remember a haggard-faced prostitute hailing us on Eighth Avenue. "Going someplace?" she purred. "Yes, I am, thank you," Ned replied. She looked at him for a moment and then screamed, "Fuck you, you smartass kid.") To get to his room, Ned had to negotiate hallways that smelled of urine, a superintendent who was perpetually drunk, and three locks on his apartment door. His bedroom window, which had been painted shut, looked onto an airshaft so narrow he could read the numbers on the digital clock in the apartment across the way. Ned said he felt as if he were living at the bottom of a well. At night, he was kept awake by the crash of bottles tossed down the shaft by his upstairs neighbors.

As the months went by, Ned spent less time walking the city and more time in his apartment, reading pulp novels. His college girlfriend broke up with him. One day Ned and I met for lunch in Central Park, and Ned, talking about his life, began to cry. I put a hand on his shoulder and tried to console him. He shook his head. "I'm sorry," he kept saying through his tears. "I'm sorry."

Not long after that, Ned decided to leave New York. Mum and Dad drove down from Massachusetts to retrieve him. Mum told me later that on his final day in Manhattan, on a last walk through Times Square, Ned played three-card monte and lost twenty dollars.

While Ned and I were in New York, Mark and Harry were in Ohio. It was surely no coincidence that Mark chose to go to college not far from where his eldest brother was in medical school. Several years earlier, before Mark left for boarding school, Mum had asked Harry to talk to him about the facts of life. Mark, of course, had insisted that he already knew everything he needed to know, but when Harry began quizzing him, he realized that Mark was as clueless as the rest of us had been at that age. (Mark later confessed that what scant knowledge he possessed had been gleaned from sneaking peeks at Mum's copy of *Our Bodies, Our-selves*.) Thereafter, knowing how lonely boarding school could be, Harry had stayed in touch. When Mark got to college, he and Harry visited each other, went to concerts together, talked on the phone. When Mark acquired his first girlfriend, Harry listened to him rhapsodize about the ups and counseled him through the downs. When Mark felt lonely and anxious, Harry told him how lonely and anxious *he* had felt at Mark's age. Far from home, Mark found something of a second father in Harry. Harry, who may have felt it easier to confide in Mark than in brothers closer to his age, found in Mark another path back to his family. Mark eventually transferred to college back east, but whenever he felt low, he'd dial Harry's number.

After his summers teaching tennis, Mark knew he wanted to work with children, but he worried that being a gym teacher and coach might not be considered sufficiently ambitious, so he majored in elementary education. He spent part of his senior year on the Zuni Indian Reservation in New Mexico, helping fifth-graders with their reading and writing, and showing them how to hit a forehand on the dilapidated neighborhood court. After graduation, he got a teaching job in the mountains of northern New Hampshire. Mark had always been good with kids, but keeping twenty-six fifth- and sixth-graders in order was a challenge for a guileless twenty-two-year-old. Mark knew no one in his new town, and though he'd never had trouble making friends, he was too busy trying to keep up with his work to socialize. There were happy moments—he coached the high school JV soccer team to the league championship, and each Friday night he treated himself to a beer and a Salisbury steak at the local diner, chatting with the owner and watching the Bruins on the overhead TV. But as winter came on, and his students went stir crazy, and his apartment on the top floor of a rooming house seemed especially cold and bleak, Mark got depressed. He did a good job of hiding it. When Ned and I came for a ski weekend, we were impressed by how grown-up our younger brother's life seemed. We had no idea that after we left on Sunday afternoon, Mark would return to his room in the gathering darkness, stare at the stacks of papers he had to grade, and worry about how he'd get through the next five days. Often, in those dark times, he'd call Harry, who'd talk him through his anxiety.

By the end of his year in New Hampshire, Mark wasn't sure he was cut out to be a teacher. He didn't know what he wanted to do, but he knew he wanted to get away. He had heard there was good money to be made canning salmon in Alaska, so he decided to spend the summer there. Our parents worried that he might not be able to handle it, and though I was impressed with Mark's resolve—driving across the country to find a job in Alaska was more adventurous than anything I'd ever done—I, too, wondered whether my sensitive youngest brother was ready for it. I remember spreading out a map of the United States on the dining room table and planning a route for him: suggesting campgrounds, giving him the names of friends to stay with, recommending sights not to miss, and surely conveying the message that if only he followed his older brother's advice, he'd be okay. Feeling guilty that I hadn't paid more attention to him when he was a child, I tended to be overprotective just as he was trying to assert his independence. One June morning, trying to disguise their nervousness, our parents waved as they watched Mark pull out of the driveway in his beat-up Chevy Nova, equipped with a cheap two-man pup tent, the map I'd annotated for him, an AAA TripTik Dad had gotten him, and a bag of peanut-butter-and-jelly sandwiches Mum had prepared.

Driving all day, sleeping in his car at night, following none of my recommendations, Mark got to Alaska in five days. He found a job in a cannery on the Kenai Peninsula, where he worked eighteen-hour shifts hauling chunks of frozen salmon from the freezers to the cutting tables, using a sledgehammer to break up the fish, hoisting them onto conveyer belts, and boxing them for shipping. At the end of the day, he and his new friends from around the world ate cheeseburgers, drank cheap beer, and listened to bands in local bars before collapsing in their sleeping bags in the tent city of seasonal workers that bloomed on the edge of town. Mark's routine left him exhausted but invigorated. He was on his own five thousand miles from home and yet for the first time in his life he didn't feel homesick. He was doing something none of his brothers had ever done and he was doing it without any help from his family. In August, when the fish moved south, Mark and his friends moved too, getting cannery jobs in Ketchikan, where they bunked in a boardinghouse, five to a room. At the end of the summer, salmon season over, Mark drove back across the country with a friend, singing along to the radio, trolling for new stations as they passed out of the previous station's range, flashing their high beams at passing truckers so the drivers would know when it was safe to cut back into the right lane, and getting a kick out of it when the truckers flashed their brights back to say thanks. I happened to be at home when Mark rolled into the driveway. Stepping from the car, tanned and fit, a thousand dollars in his pocket, my little brother looked like a man.

Mark would remain in Boston. He took a job on the grounds crew at the school for the blind where our father worked as a fund-raiser and quickly made himself an indispensable employee. He worked six days a week, volunteered for extra assignments, rarely used his vacation time, and never took a sick day unless he was practically at death's door. Outside work, Mark had a circle of devoted friends, and he was the one who made sure they got together—organizing Saturday morning basketball games, golf weekends, dinners out, trips to Fenway Park.

Mark lived only twenty minutes from Ned, who had gotten a job as a carpenter's helper. As a child, Ned had always loved building things, and now he found even the "grunt work" satisfying. After a long day of driving nails, caulking holes, and installing drywall, he'd spend the evening building himself a tool box or making a bookshelf for Mum and Dad. Nevertheless, he fretted that he should be doing something more conventionally "important." It stung when a great-uncle told him, "Don't worry, you'll find a real job soon." He'd always been interested in the news, so he took night classes in broadcasting and, eventually, wangled an internship at a Boston television station. He started out fetching coffee and delivering stories off the wire-service ticker, but in time he was allowed to write short news items and assist in the editing room. By his own admission, Ned had always been easily bored—among the reasons he loved traveling was that he saw something different every day—and journalism offered a never-ending procession of different stories. For six months he worked as a carpenter's assistant by day and a news intern by night. When he was offered a full-time job at a station in Duluth, Minnesota, he bought an old orange VW Bug for six hundred dollars and drove west, engine light flickering the entire way. He was twenty-six. The station was tiny, the market minuscule, the salary a hair's breadth above minimum wage, and the climate subarctic. Ned had one decent pair of shoes and an old blue blazer of Dad's to wear on the air. But he had found what he wanted to do. When I was home for a visit, Mum and Dad showed me tapes of his stories—Ned interviewing old fur trappers and talking with Native Americans about how they harvested wild rice. With his good looks, resonant voice, and insatiable curiosity, he was a natural.

Ned rose rapidly up the television food chain: from Duluth (the 116th-largest market in the country), to Jacksonville (60th), to Raleigh (32nd). In each new place, he followed his customary when-in-Rome policy. In Duluth, he canoed the Boundary Waters; in Jacksonville, he lived near the beach and ate oysters and fried cooter; in Raleigh, he became a connoisseur of barbecue and earned the nickname "Ocean Boy" because, whenever he got the chance, he'd drive three hours to the Outer Banks to windsurf. In 1988, he returned to Boston (the 5th-largest market) to be a reporter at the station where he had interned. When Ned started in television news, he had set a goal: to be in a top-ten market within five years. He had done it in four. Looking back, he admits that part of his motivation was proving to his older brothers that he could succeed. "I always held myself up to you guys at high school," he says. "You always did so well in academics and in sports." He and his girlfriend, a producer he had met in Duluth, bought a reproduction saltbox on a quiet cul-de-sac in a Boston suburb. On his days off Ned used his carpentry skills to fix up the house. They got a dog, a mutt named Teddy, who was not much larger than Penny. Whenever they could get away, they headed down to Cape Cod.

Where once my brothers and I had been just as happy to spend time apart, we now went out of our way to spend time together. When they were on their home turf, I could see them not just as their childhood selves—people to react against or compare myself with—but for who they were. After medical school, Harry had gone into family practice, one of the least-well-paid specialties but one that offered maximum patient contact and unlimited opportunity for working with needy rural populations. When I visited Harry in Virginia, where he and Sandy had moved for his residency, he had been up all night delivering a baby. It had been a difficult birth, and as he described it I was bowled over by the drama of his work and the matter-of-factness with which he talked about it. Over the years, whether from the suffering he had seen as a doctor, from the influence of the effervescent Sandy, or just from the weathering effects of time, Harry's sharp corners had been rubbed smooth. I had always prided myself on being the "sensitive" brother, but when I finally gave him a chance, Harry turned out to be a good listener. And when we played a round of golf for the first time in ten years, I found that Harry's killer instinct had toned down to a mildly competitive proclivity. He still won.

Staying with Ned at his house outside Boston, I admired the shelves he'd made, the dogwoods he'd planted, the sun porch he'd built by himself. Over dinner, we talked about family but also about books, politics, and history, subjects that, in years past, Ned might not have raised with his supposedly more intellectual brother—or that his supposedly more intellectual brother might not have deigned to raise with him.

One fall, my girlfriend, Anne, and I invited Mark on a five-day canoe trip in the Everglades. At the last minute, Anne's brother dropped out of our planned foursome, so Mark had the difficult task of paddling solo. It was a grueling vacation: nine or ten hours a day of canoeing, sometimes fighting our way across wind-whipped bays scalloped with two-foot waves, sometimes picking our way through mangrove labyrinths while clouds of mosquitos dined on us. Muscular from his outdoor work, Mark was not only a powerhouse paddler but an uncomplaining expedition member, keeping his cool and his sense of humor long after I had lost both. We spent Thanksgiving swaddled in mosquito netting on a tent platform deep in the mangrove wilderness, scarfing down a noodle-and-ham mush. It was one of the best Thanksgivings I'd ever had.

Each June, our parents rented a house on Cape Cod and we gathered for a week or two, just as we had when we were children. At an age when my friends' parents, facing each other alone across the dinner table now that their children were gone, were drifting apart or divorcing, Mum and Dad seemed to be converging. They still had different interests: Dad had his tennis, his yard work, his men's club, his Red Sox; Mum, in addition to teaching art and English, now taught Holocaust studies and death education, volunteered with AIDS patients, wrote poetry, organized peace vigils, and meditated. But whether they were showing us photos of a recent trip to Costa Rica or working together in the garden, we could see that there was no one with whom either of them would rather decipher a Spanish menu or dig up a dandelion.

We brothers, too, seemed to be getting a second chance. On the Cape, we played all the games that in childhood had ended in tears or double chicken wings. If there was tension over a close play at home plate or a disputed word in Scrabble, we let it go. If, in the presence of our parents, we began reverting to our old roles, we'd catch ourselves. We admired one another's areas of expertise. Harry was still the master of any game he played. Ned was the handyman around the house and the captain of the waterfront. Mark was our pool sharp and lobsterman, and, as Dad got older, the substitute breakfast chef. I fancied myself the fisherman-in-residence, if only by virtue of the fact that I spent more time with a line in the water. But whenever one of my brothers pulled in a lunker, I was as happy as if I had caught it. (Almost.) One evening Harry reeled in a striper and brought it to a family cookout. As people oohed over his catch, Harry smiled and shook his head, "George showed me what lure to use," he said. "He's the real fisherman in the family." I felt as if I had been knighted.

On the tennis court, we still tried hard to win, but we realized it wouldn't kill us if we lost. When a brother fired off an ace or executed a passing shot, we applauded it. On crucial points, I no longer prayed for my opponent to double-fault. Harry and I had mellowed with age, and with Mark in the mix, things could never get too tense. In what seemed a curious refutation of the transitive principle, Harry usually beat me and I usually beat Mark, yet Mark, in a kind of Möbius-strip twist, usually beat Harry. It was as if none of us dared beat our older brother—unless he was so much older that a victory wouldn't threaten the pecking order. We invited Ned to join us, but he always begged off, saying he wasn't good enough and didn't want to ruin our game.

Yet it didn't feel right when one of us was missing; only when the four of us were together did things seem balanced. Sometimes we'd all cook dinner, chatting, listening to music, moving from refrigerator to stove to table, putting a hand on a brother's shoulder as we maneuvered around him with a hot saucepan, tossing a spice bottle or a can of tomato paste to a brother across the kitchen, joining in on the chorus as Ned launched into a hilariously over-the-top rendition of "Shake Your Booty." We always made more food than we needed, as if we were still afraid we'd have to fight over the last drumstick on the platter. We still ate as if we were in a race. Colt girlfriends invariably observed that they'd never seen anyone eat as fast as their boyfriend—until they met his brothers. But we no longer rushed from the table. We lingered, prolonging the conversation. Later, we'd play Trivial Pursuit or shoot pool, as the Red Sox game crackled on the radio. Occasionally, we played guitar with Mum and sang the old songs from our stint as nursing home troubadours.

On our last day, Dad always insisted on getting a picture of "the four boys." We'd make a show of grumbling, but we were secretly pleased, I think, to gather on the back steps, Harry looking squarely into the camera, me trying to come up with witty alternatives to "say cheese," Ned surreptitiously pinching Mark, Mark trying not to crack up. It was an excuse for us to have our arms around one another.

But the undertow had not entirely receded. One summer afternoon, we were playing that classic New England blood sport, croquet. Harry, as always, was several wickets ahead, so far ahead, in fact, that Ned, Mark, and I joked about teaming up against him to make the game interesting. And then we began to do just that, each of us ignoring the next wicket to go after Harry's ball. We didn't care which of us won; we just didn't want Harry to—which, of course, made Harry all the more determined. I remember him sending Ned's ball down the hill, where it rolled and rolled until it came to rest in a distant patch of poison ivy. The shot was within the rules, but it was executed with the kind of mercilessness we hadn't seen from Harry in years. We redoubled our efforts, this time without the smiles. The old Harry would have responded by putting his head down and annihilating us. Now, in a voice husky with suppressed emotion, he said that if we were going to team up against him, he wasn't going to play. Ned shook his head. "Don't take it so seriously," he said. "It's just a game."

Suddenly, Harry and Ned were shouting at each other—Harry arguing that ganging up on him wasn't fair, Ned that Harry was too competitive. Mark and I, standing among the wickets, mallets in hand, were dumbfounded. There hadn't been a cross word among the four of us in years. That it was between Harry and Ned was astonishing. Ned's teenage battles with me were the stuff of family legend, but Harry and Ned had hardly seemed to be on each other's radar when we were growing up. And yet thirty-two-year-old Harry and twenty-nine-year-old Ned had turned on each other with the abruptness of dogs who, frisking happily, suddenly go for each other's throats.

I could see that our teaming up against Harry carried behind it the accrued frustration from all those childhood losses at football and Pounce. I could also see how watching his brothers unite against him might have provoked Harry's old feelings of being an outsider in his own family. And how Harry's seemingly effortless dominance in croquet that day might have tweaked Ned's old feelings of frustration at not being as athletic as his older brothers. I had never seen Harry that angry. Indeed, all through adolescence, Harry had kept things so tight inside that I had never really seen him lose his temper. It was what I had always been most afraid of. "Come on, let's deal with this right now," Harry kept shouting at Ned. For a time, Ned shouted right back. But then he shook his head and began to walk away. "It's not worth it," he kept saying tersely. Harry followed right behind him: "Come on, let's do it, don't be a chicken, let's get it out right now." Harry later told Mark and me that he meant he wanted to talk things out with Ned, to get at the source of the tension between them. At the time, Mark and I assumed he wanted to fight—and we knew Ned had never been one to back down from a challenge. Indeed, as Ned strode across the field toward the water, I thought he was leading Harry farther from the house so they could punch each other where our parents couldn't hear them. Mum, who was making a cup of tea in the kitchen, remembers hearing the shouts and worrying it was the end of us as a family.

Although the yelling seemed to go on forever, it may have lasted a minute or two. In the end, Harry and Ned went off in opposite directions to cool down. The tension dissipated, like a hurricane that suddenly veers out to sea and spends itself.

The croquet incident was so unexpected because by then some of us had started families of our own and the dramas of our childhood seemed progressively distant. Harry recently told me he had always reckoned that Mark or I would be first to marry because we were "the least screwed up." But Harry ended up leading the way, as usual. One evening in 1982, he called to tell me he and Sandy were getting married. I was pleased but not surprised. I was surprised, however, and very pleased, when he asked me to be his best man. That summer, in the backyard of Sandy's parents' house in the foothills of Santa Fe, I stood at my brother's side. Like the bride and groom, the celebration was low-key (Harry went jacketless), homey (Sandy's mother served turkey casserole), and nontraditional (a mariachi band). It was a measure of Sandy's gameness and Harry's affection for his family that the newlyweds spent the first night of their honeymoon camping in the mountains with the groom's parents and brothers, an expedition aborted when a lightning storm of biblical intensity forced us to flee to a motel whose name—the De Anza Motor Lodge—still triggers laughter at family gatherings thirty years later. Graciously insisting that the bride and groom take one of the two available rooms, the rest of us squeezed into the other, talking happily through the evening in a scene that struck me as a kind of fulfillment of my Darien-era vision of fallout-shelter bonding.

Marriage changes the geometry of a family, altering the angles of each relationship within it. Merely by requiring time and attention, it can cause siblings to drift apart or even drive a wedge between them. (A friend told me that he and his brother hadn't spoken in five years, ever since he'd criticized his sister-in-law's parenting skills. During our entire conversation, he never used his brother's name, referring to him, when syntax demanded, only as "my former brother.") Sandy, a quintessential caregiver, brought us closer. One of five sisters herself, Sandy liked large families, liked her husband's brothers—although she'd been a bit nonplussed when, the day she met us, Ned accidentally steamrollered her in a game of touch football—and we liked her. Her lack of competitive fire had a mellowing effect on our own contentious tendencies, and her mere presence helped lower the testosterone level at any fraternal gathering. Indeed, having a sister-in-law gave us a hint of what it might have been like to have had a sister when we were growing up.

Two years after the wedding, Harry called to tell us that Sandy was pregnant. After his residency, they had moved to New Mexico, where Harry had taken a job with the Indian Health Service on the Zuni Reservation. Sandy was in her twenty-sixth week when her water broke. The regional hospital said not to bother bringing Sandy in. There was nothing they could do for a baby born that early. If Sandy could stay pregnant one more week, they would see her. The alternative, they said, was to have the baby at the local hospital and bring him or her home to die. Harry made some calls. He found a hospital in Phoenix that had had some success with very small preemies, though the odds were still bleak: a 50 percent chance that the baby would survive and be normal, a 25 percent chance he'd survive but be severely impaired, a 25 percent chance he'd die. Harry helped Sandy into their car and sped three hundred miles to Phoenix, where Ian was born, his umbilical cord wrapped around his neck. He was twelve inches long and weighed one pound, fifteen ounces.

Sandy took a room in a nearby boardinghouse so she could be with Ian every day. Each weekend, Harry drove five hours to Phoenix, where he and Sandy stood vigil in the Neonatal Intensive Care Unit, gazing down at their son in his heated plastic isolette, a tube in his throat connecting him to the ventilator that enabled him to breathe, a ganglion of lines tethering his shoe-sized body to a bank of monitors, a cacophony of alarms ready to sound if his heartbeat, his temperature, or his blood pressure dipped or spiked. Harry and Sandy's medical skills were of no use; they weren't even allowed to hold their son until he was ten days old. Harry called Mum and Dad frequently. All his life he had prided himself on his independence, but as he started his new family, he needed his old one.

When Ian was two months old, Dad and I flew out to Phoenix. Although he had gained more than a pound, Ian was still so small that he could wear only the Cabbage Patch doll clothes Sandy bought at a nearby toy store. His arms and legs looked as brittle as twigs. His skin had the translucence of wax paper. I tried to keep my eyes on my nephew and not on the blinking lights or squiggly lines of his heart monitor, which, every few minutes, beeped loudly and made my own heart jump. Ian was eerily still, except for the nearly imperceptible swell of his chest with each breath and the occasional flicker of his raisin-sized gray eyes. As we stood by his isolette, I couldn't help thinking of the incubator Harry, Ned, and I had watched so hopefully when we were children. On the last day of our visit, I put on a mask and gown. Sandy placed Ian, swaddled so that only his face was visible, in my arms. He felt like a small wounded bird.

Ian was in the ICU for four months. Even after Harry and Sandy brought him home, he would be tethered to an oxygen canister and an apnea monitor for three more months, and there would be years of worry over whether he had been brain damaged (no) or was developmentally delayed (no). Ian's homecoming happened to coincide with Mark's senior-year teaching stint in Zuni. Mark lived in a trailer down the street but spent most evenings at Harry and Sandy's, playing backgammon, watching baseball on TV, cradling his nephew in his arms, and giving Harry the kind of reassurance Harry had always given him. By the following June, when we gathered on Cape Cod, Ian was out of the woods—a smiling eight-month-old baby whose uncles competed to fuss over him. Two years later, after Sandy nearly lost her life during an ectopic pregnancy, she and Harry adopted a baby girl, naming her Maya.

That same summer I brought Anne to our family reunion. I had met Anne when she interviewed me over lunch for a job at a magazine. I ate a lot of tekkamaki and I took the job. Though I had been immediately attracted to her omnivorous intelligence (not to mention the mesmerizing kissability of her lips), I was still getting over a long relationship with my Baltimore girlfriend. Anne and I became friends. I brought her to Cape Cod because I knew that while I might not be ready for a relationship, it might be in my best interests to keep her close until I was. I wanted Anne to approve of my family and, perhaps even more, I wanted my family to approve of her. (I don't think I could have gotten serious about someone who didn't get along with my brothers; at the same time, I couldn't imagine someone *not* getting along with my brothers.) The two-way vetting was a success on both counts. Anne, who has one brother, to whom she is uncommonly close, knew how important siblings can be. Coming from a small family, she found the rambunctious clamor of our large one invigorating, though she didn't believe me when I told her we'd fought tooth and nail when we were young. She teamed up with Harry in Trivial Pursuit and crushed the rest of us (he had sports and science sewn up, she had literature and film); she helped Ned chop onions for his famous bouillabaisse; she took long hikes with Mark, picking ticks off the backs of each other's legs as they talked about the idiosyncracies of their respective families. Later, Anne would joke that going out with me was like getting four brothers for the price of one.

A year later, Anne and I spent a few days with Harry, Sandy, and Ian in Zuni. It was October 1986, and we arrived just in time to see the Red Sox play the Mets in game six of the World Series. Boston led three games to two—one more victory and they'd be champions for the first time since 1918. When the Red Sox took a one-run lead in the seventh inning, Harry and I, too nervous to watch, retreated to the kitchen, where we listened, fingers crossed, from what we thought was a safe distance, while Anne and Sandy stayed in the living room and shook their heads at the foolishness of men. When the Red Sox manager pulled Roger Clemens after the seventh inning, we begged him not to; when the Mets tied it up in the eighth inning, we groaned and pounded the table; when Mookie Wilson's routine grounder found its way through Bill Buckner's legs in the tenth inning to win the game for the Mets, we nodded understandingly through our tears. It had been too good to be true. Later, as I was brushing my teeth, I heard Harry in Ian's bedroom, talking quietly to his two-year-old son, telling him about the Red Sox: summarizing their benighted history, touching on the near misses of 1967 and 1975, invoking the names Yastrzemski, Conigliaro, and Fisk, and explaining that although the team had lost, there would be a seventh game and they would try again. It was important, Harry told Ian, to keep trying.

Perhaps because I am a middle child, I have always had a hard time making choices. Despite the Colt family's seal of approval, I dithered unconscionably before asking Anne to marry me. But our visit to Zuni helped me see what marriage and fatherhood could look like. Indeed, I might never have gotten around to either had it not been for Harry's example. Eventually, I proposed. On the other hand, like all my brothers, once I make a choice, I commit to it wholeheartedly. I persuaded Anne that, approaching our mid-thirties, we should try to start a family right away—like a few seconds after we got engaged.

When it came time to choose a best man, I didn't hesitate. I chose Harry and Ned and Mark. (I even added a fourth, my cousin Henry, who is also one of my closest friends.) At the rehearsal dinner, Harry, Ned, and Mark joined Mum and Dad in singing a toast to Anne. Mark played guitar, Harry banged on a tambourine, and Ned threw in some solo do-si-dos that brought down the house. The following day, I stood in a corner of our Manhattan loft and watched each of my brothers walk down the makeshift aisle escorting a bridesmaid—Harry jacketless, bolo-tied, frizzy-haired, Ned looking like a Brooks Brothers ad in his crisp pinstriped suit, and Mark, eyes already welling up, in a blue blazer. They were followed by the ringbearer, four-year-old Ian, and the flower girl, two-year-old Maya. And then Anne walked down the aisle, three months pregnant. As I saw her tummy bulging ever so slightly beneath a specially fitted flapper-era gown, my happiness was complete.

Six months later, Anne and I brought Susannah home from the hospital. As we experienced the blinding fear and humbling ignorance of new parents, convinced that each sniffle was the harbinger of pneumonia, I felt new respect for Harry and Sandy, who had gone through a genuine life-and-death struggle with their first child and never complained. (I also instantly forgave Mum and Dad for any and all errors they might have made when I was a child, thunderstruck by the realization that they had gone through this *four* times, all when they were far younger than Anne and me.) When Anne and I discussed whom to ask to be Susannah's godfather, the choice, again, was simple: there was no one we trusted more than Harry. Over the following months and years, during each new crisis—real or imagined—I turned to Harry, who, as a doctor, father, and brother, gave me advice medical, parental, and fraternal. Harry could reassure me that when Susannah spat up her dinner or skinned her knee, it wasn't the end of the world. And when Susannah developed a truly serious illness, when it really did seem as if it might be the end of the world, it was Harry I called time after time.

One April morning in 1990, seven months after Susannah was born, I was at my office in midtown Manhattan when my father called. Mark had been in an accident. Shortly before dawn, while he was on his way to work, his car had gone off the road and hit a tree. A passing motorist had called 911. An ambulance had rushed him to the nearest hospital— the same hospital in which he had been born twenty-eight years earlier. Mark had suffered what the doctor called "severe internal injuries" and was about to go into surgery. Accustomed to taking notes for my job, I transcribed, on a bright yellow *While You Were Out* message pad, some of the words I heard over the telephone: "lacerated kidney," "crushed pancreas," "may lose spleen." Looking at the pad, I couldn't bear to think these words had anything to with my brother.

The surgery, which, as the doctor delicately phrased it, put Mark's internal organs "back in their proper places," was successful. It was performed by a man who had been a few years ahead of me in high school, a bluff, good-natured fellow who had rowed crew on a boat I had coxed. He had gone on to become one of those "uncreative" doctors I'd once scorned. Now I thanked God for the fact that he hadn't chosen to be a poet instead. Although he predicted that Mark would be hospitalized for up to three weeks, Mark was out in five days. The staff was amazed at how fast he recovered, attributing it to his great physical condition.

A few days before Mark was released, I got a call from my mother. There was more news. In a tearful conversation in his hospital room, Mark had told her that he had a gambling problem.

Mark would tell us later that he had started gambling when he was a sophomore in college. He had worked the breakfast shift in his dormitory kitchen, and one morning the cook had shown him and several other students how to place bets on sports events with a bookie in a neighboring town. Mark had enjoyed the adrenaline rush of risking a few bucks. Over the following eight years, however, what had started as a lark turned into a habit. After a hard day at work, he'd go home to his apartment, place small bets on a few games, then stay up and watch them on TV. With money on the line, even the most insignificant contest between also-rans took on the intensity of a World Series game seven. Gambling, Mark told us, gave him confidence and helped keep his anxiety at bay. "Gambling was something I thought I was good at," he says. "And that could mask that I felt a failure in other parts of my life."

It seemed impossible to us that Mark, who wore his emotions on his sleeve, had been able to keep his gambling a secret. I recalled a few occasions on which he had spoken with surprising intensity about some obscure game between West Coast basketball teams he'd stayed up late to watch. But he had always loved watching sports, ever since those childhood evenings in the den with Dad. Mark's gambling, like Mark himself, had been careful, well-organized, and informed by the characteristic Colt frugality. (Part of the reason we were so shocked was that we couldn't imagine ourselves risking even a dollar or two, even on a sure thing.) Mark never bet large amounts, always paid his bills on time, and never got into debt. Later, his therapist told him she had never seen such a thrifty gambler. But gambling had gradually consumed his thoughts until he was rushing home every night to scour the sports pages and call his bookie to bet on a game in which he otherwise had no interest. Just as I used to think drinking made me feel more alive when in fact it had only helped me avoid life, Mark believed that gambling gave him control when, in fact, it had made him so anxious and distracted that he had lost control of his car.

When Mark entered therapy, it became clear that the forces that had led to his gambling involved all of us. I was reminded of our childhood games of Crack the Whip. The boy at one end could be running slowly, even walking, but when he changed direction, the centrifugal force grew as it passed through each person; by the time it reached the whip's end, it was so strong that the last one in line, running too fast for his legs to keep up, spun off and tumbled to the ground.

At the suggestion of Mark's counselor, the six of us entered family therapy. Three or four times that spring, Harry flew in from Wisconsin,

I took the shuttle up from New York, Ned drove in from Boston, Mark came from work in Watertown, and our parents drove over from Dedham to meet with a psychologist in a suburb not unlike the ones in which we had grown up. In the morning, lying in bed in SoHo, Anne and I read Babar aloud to Susannah, who was on the verge of saying her first words. In the afternoon, sitting in a semicircle in an office with wall-to-wall carpeting and Winslow Homer reproductions, my brothers, parents, and I sorted through layers of misperception, unspoken hurts, unvoiced accusations, and old wounds so deeply buried it seemed impossible they could ever heal. It was as if we, too, were learning to speak a new language.

I had assumed that I was there to help Mark, to help fix things, to be a sensitive listener, to be, perhaps, something of a therapist myself. Then, one afternoon, as we were discussing our peaceful early years in Dedham, I began to talk about how close I had felt to Harry and how confused I had been at the gulf that had opened between us. I was surprised to find myself unable to stop crying. Harry explained that his pulling away had nothing to do with me. He talked about how, as a teenager, he had just been trying to survive, and to do that, he'd felt he had to distance himself from his family. I'd had no idea how much Harry had hurt because he worked so hard to conceal it. He told us that when he had been moved up to the third floor at the age of nine, he had felt exiled, not promoted.

It was at this point that my father reached into his pocket, pulled out his wallet, and unfolded the ancient, crumbling photograph of Harry and me, taken when we were children. And it was at this point—in a moment so fraught with symbolism that I wondered later whether it had really happened—that the snapshot split in two and fluttered to the ground. At the time, I thought it could only mean that our family had been irreparably fractured. It did not.

Chapter Ten

The Lost Brother:
John and Henry David Thoreau

On New Year's Day of 1842, a twenty-six-year-old schoolteacher named John Thoreau was stropping his razor in the family home in Concord, Massachusetts, when the blade slipped and nicked the ring finger on his left hand. It was a slight cut, barely deep enough to draw blood, and John bandaged the wound. A few days later, his finger began to throb, and when he removed the bandage on Saturday, January 8, he found that a portion of the skin was necrotic. That evening he went to the town doctor, who found no cause for concern and redressed the finger. Walking home, however, John began to feel pain in other parts of his body—pain that quickly grew so severe he was barely able to stagger into the house. When he woke the following morning, he found it difficult to open his mouth. That night, his body began to shudder with excruciating spasms. Lockjaw had set in.

In 1842, lockjaw was a disease with which many Americans were familiar. A bacterial infection named for the muscle spasms that make it difficult to speak or swallow, lockjaw (now known as tetanus) triggers spasms not only in the jaw but throughout the rest of the body. As the throat eventually, irrevocably, constricts, breathing becomes impossible; most lockjaw victims die by suffocation. An 1809 painting by Sir Charles

Bell, a Scottish surgeon and medical illustrator, depicts a soldier dying of the disease: jaw tensed, neck flexed, fists clenched, toes curled, eyes bulging, back arched so acutely that a medium-size dog could walk underneath. It is a painting that hurts to look at. A vaccine for the disease would not be developed for more than a century. In John Thoreau's day lockjaw was invariably fatal.

On Sunday, John's younger brother, Henry, came home from Ralph Waldo Emerson's house, where he had been living and working for the past eight months, to look after John. Henry was a devoted and tireless nurse to his brother, but there was little he could do other than hold him through his spasms and keep him company when they subsided. On Monday, a doctor summoned from Boston told John there was no hope. Death would be painful, he said, but it would come quickly. Though John's parents, his two sisters, and his brother were agonized, John, whose spiritual beliefs were more traditional than those of his pantheistic brother, was calm: "The cup that my Father gives me, shall I not drink it?" At times John was delirious, at times almost pacific. "His words and behavior throughout were what Mr. Emerson calls manly, even *great*," Emerson's wife, Lidian, reported. Her letters, written to her sister after John's death and based on Henry's testimony, are the best account we have of John Thoreau's last hours: "After J. had taken leave of all the family he said to Henry now sit down and talk to me of Nature and Poetry, I shall be a good listener for it is difficult for me to interrupt you. During the hour in which he died, he looked at Henry with a 'transcendent smile full of Heaven' (I think this was H's expression) and Henry 'found himself returning it' and this was the last communication that passed between them." On Tuesday, January 11, at two in the afternoon, John Thoreau died in his brother's arms.

When Henry returned to the Emersons' that evening to tell them of his brother's death, they were impressed with the young man's self-possession. Often prickly and headstrong, Thoreau was surprisingly calm. On Wednesday morning, he came back to pack up his clothes and move home. "I love him for the feeling he showed and the effort he made to be cheerful," wrote Lidian Emerson. "He did not give way in the least but his whole demeanour was that of one struggling with sickness of heart." Thoreau's composure may have reflected his extensive reading of the Stoic philosophers. It may also have resulted from what twentieth-century psychologists would identify as the first stage of grief: denial. For nearly two weeks after his brother's death, Henry sat in the Thoreau home, listless, passive, silent. His sisters led him outdoors, hoping that his love of nature would revive him, but he remained unreachable. Then, on January 22, eleven days after his brother's death, Henry's jaw began to stiffen, his muscles to spasm. The doctor was perplexed; lockjaw was not a contagious disease, and there was no sign of any cut. Yet the symptoms were unmistakable. There was nothing to do but wait for the end. Even the unflappable Emerson, writing a letter to his brother William after returning from a lecture he'd given in Boston, was driven to uncharacteristic typographical excess: "My pleasure at getting home on Saturday night at the end of my task was somewhat checked by finding that Henry Thoreau who has been at his fathers since the death of his brother was ill & threatened with *lockjaw!* his brother's disease. It is strange—unaccountable—yet the symptoms seemed precise & on the increase. You may judge we were all alarmed & I not the least who have the highest hopes of this youth."

The symptoms were indeed precise, but they were psychosomatic. Henry did not have lockjaw; what he had was a grief so profound that he had assumed the earmarks of his brother's fatal illness.

*   *   *

History does not record the reaction of the Thoreau parents to the death of their eldest son, but Henry David Thoreau's extraordinary response illustrates how devastating the death of a sibling can be. And yet, just as the sibling relationship in psychology has been minimized in comparison with the Oedipal drama, the loss of a sibling has, in the hierarchy of grief, been subordinate to the loss of a child. Those mourning the death of a brother or sister often say that they have been made to feel the loss is not theirs to grieve, that it "belongs" to their parents—an example of what some psychologists call "disenfranchised grief," the frequently unacknowledged loss experienced by supposedly peripheral survivors:

ex-spouses, lovers, gay partners, grandparents, friends. Surviving siblings report that would-be comforters are far more likely to comment, "How awful for your parents" than "How awful for you." (Hallmark didn't begin to sell sibling-specific bereavement cards until the 1980s, long after they had produced cards addressing the loss of parents, grandparents, and children.) The handful of researchers studying sibling loss tend to have lost siblings themselves and, finding no help in the medical literature, sought their own answers.

Losing a brother or sister may be especially traumatic at an early age, when the loss, painful enough in itself, is often compounded by the fact that siblings are unlikely to get much support from parents consumed by their own grief. In 1867, when her favorite son died in a skating accident two days before his fourteenth birthday, Margaret Barrie retreated to her darkened bedroom, leaving her six other children to fend for themselves. After several days had passed, an older sister told six-year-old James, the bewildered youngest son (and future author of *Peter Pan*), to go to their mother and remind her that she still had another boy. Even after Mary Todd Lincoln spent five weeks in bed mourning the death of her eleven-year-old son, Willie, to typhoid fever in 1862, she found it difficult to be with eight-year-old Tad, because he reminded her of his absent older brother. She stopped inviting Tad and Willie's best friends to the White House because, she wrote their mother, "It makes me worse to see them"—and thus further isolated her youngest son.

"It has been aptly said that the surviving sibling becomes a double orphan," write Stephen Bank and Michael Kahn in *The Sibling Bond*, "losing not only a sister or a brother but also an emotionally available parent." Those who have lost a sibling when young speak of the unspoken pressure to avoid making demands on grieving parents, to have no needs of their own, to "be good." In a study of 159 adolescents and adults who had lost a sibling in childhood, more than half had never discussed the death with anyone in their family. Such unacknowledged grief can surface years later as depression, often when the survivors' own children reach the age their sibling was when he died.

The loss of a sibling can be calamitous at any age. "My beloved brother's death has cut into me, deep down, even as an absolute mutilation," wrote the sixty-seven-year-old Henry James to Edith Wharton, after William's fatal heart attack. One often reads of a widow or widower who, in apparently good health, dies not long after the death of a beloved spouse. The same can be true of brothers. After my wife's father died at the age of ninety-five, Anne and I were shocked when his younger brother started to deteriorate with astonishing speed. Bill had looked up to—and had tried to live up to—his older brother since they were children. Though for the past ten years they had lived on opposite coasts, they had spoken to each other every Sunday afternoon. Those phone calls, Bill's last tangible connection to his siblings, his parents, and his childhood, were a fraternal umbilicus. When they stopped, Bill began to stop, too. His wife and sons could not reverse his slide. Severely weakened, he fell, hit his head, and was taken to the ICU, where he died less than six weeks after his brother.

*   *   *

When most people think of Henry David Thoreau, they think of the Hermit of Concord, the epitome of independence—as if he'd lived his entire life in his one-room cabin on Walden Pond. In fact, Thoreau spent only two years in his cabin (which was, at times, as bustling as a Left Bank café), and for much of his life he was dependent on others for emotional and financial sustenance. During his first twenty-four years, Henry relied heavily on his older brother.

Born two years apart, the Thoreau brothers were unusually close. As children, they shared a trundle bed. John usually fell asleep right away; Henry lay awake watching the stars. It isn't surprising that on his deathbed, John Thoreau asked his brother to talk to him of nature. Had it not been for John, "the family naturalist," as one Thoreau biographer calls him, Henry's lifelong absorption in the natural world might never have taken root. (John's detailed list of Concord birds was Henry's first field guide, the template for the hundreds of natural history charts Henry would one day assemble.) Whenever they weren't in school, they were exploring Concord: digging for arrowheads along its riverbanks, spearing eels in its ponds, watching for hawks over its meadows, sledding its hills, building boats and paddling them on its streams until darkness fell. They invented

Indian names for each other, pretending to be braves of the Wampanoag tribe that only a few decades earlier had prowled these same woods. They carved their initials side by side on the railing of the old red bridge over the Concord River. On summer mornings they'd wake before dawn to hike to the cliffs at Fair Haven in order to watch the sunrise. On summer nights they'd build a fire on the shore of Walden Pond, hoping to attract the fish. "We caught pouts with a bunch of worms strung on a thread," Henry later recalled, "and when we had done, far in the night, threw the burning brands high into the air like skyrockets, which, coming down into the pond, were quenched with a loud hissing." After John's death, Henry would remember those early days in a poem: *For then, as now, I trust, / I always lagg'd behind, / While thou wert ever first, / Cutting the wind.*

Although far less is known about John than about his famous brother, the available evidence agrees that while they shared many interests, they had very different personalities. (Edward Emerson's observation that "These brothers were just enough unlike to increase the interest and happiness of their relation" has the whiff of the politic.) The terms used by their fellow Concordians to describe John ("genial," "pleasant," "serene," "loving," "saintly minded," "a bright spot," "a flowing generous spirit," "the life of every gathering") were near-antonyms of those they used to describe Henry ("shy," "silent," "rigid," "brusque," "unsympathetic," "in the green apple stage," "an odd stick"). John was said to be an extroverted version of the father for whom he had been named, an easygoing pencil manufacturer too tenderhearted to be much of a businessman. Henry was said to have inherited his contrary ways from his mother, an ambitious, garrulous woman (her hard-of-hearing husband occasionally feigned deafness to tune out her voice) who ran a boardinghouse in the Thoreau home. John was comfortable in his skin; Henry's didn't yet seem to fit. Even as a child, Henry was a distant, defensive, irascible fellow who looked at the ground when he talked to you—an embryonic version of the man Nathaniel Hawthorne would describe as "the most unmalleable fellow alive." At school, none of their classmates could remember Henry ever playing with them in the yard. He preferred, they said, to stand on the sidelines and watch. (A leading local lawyer found Henry so solemn he called him "the Judge," and Thoreau's schoolmates took up the nickname.) John, by contrast, would sit by the hour on the fence outside the schoolhouse and regale his classmates with stories and jokes, making them laugh until it hurt. John was the more popular brother. He was also considered the more promising. And if his sister Sophia's portrait of him can be trusted (one biographer, deeming it "atrocious" and calling the painter "feebly artistic," suggests that it cannot), John was better-looking than Henry, his nose less prominent, his chin stronger, his features more aquiline, his mouth curled into a winsome half-smile rather than a quizzical frown, his hair shorter and more kempt.

If Henry was chagrined at being unfavorably compared with his older brother, he didn't show it. No one in Concord thought more highly of John than did Henry himself. He called John his "good genius." John was not only a beloved older brother but a father figure as well; Henry looked up to him as he couldn't look up to their amiable but feckless father. John's gregariousness also had an unintended fringe benefit for his brother. Henry drew all the companionship he needed from his older brother, allowing him to indulge his reclusive side, to withdraw even more than he might have otherwise, to become even more himself. Emerson, who was among Thoreau's closest companions in adulthood, famously remarked that Thoreau had no friends. That may have been true after John's death. But for the first twenty-four years of Henry's life, he had a friend, a best friend.

The brothers were parted in the fall of 1833 when Henry went off to Harvard. (Although John was considered the more promising, Henry was the more bookish, and by the time Henry was of college age the family finances were in better shape than they had been two years earlier, when John finished his education at the age of sixteen and went to work as a teacher.) Henry frequently came home to see his family or to recuperate from an illness. When they weren't together, the brothers wrote each other playful, affectionate letters. After graduation, Henry, at loose ends, biding time in his father's pencil-making operation, turned again to his brother, suggesting that after John finished the school year they head west to search for teaching jobs. "It is high season to start," wrote Henry, with youthful brio. "The canals are now open, and travelling comparatively cheap. I think I can borrow the cash in this town. There's nothing like trying." Although John agreed to the proposal, nothing came of it, and Henry, of course, would ultimately choose to do his traveling in Concord. But in the fall of 1838, Henry convinced his older brother to leave his teaching post in Roxbury and join him in running Concord Academy, a small private school Henry had opened a few months earlier. Under Henry, it had done well enough, but with the universally admired John taking over as preceptor (what might today be called headmaster), the first families of Concord seemed even more willing to entrust their sons and daughters to the school. Soon there were twenty-five children enrolled, and a growing waiting list.

Unsurprisingly, the Thoreaus had somewhat unusual ideas of what constituted good teaching. "We should seek to be fellow students with the pupil," wrote Henry, "and we should learn of, as well as with him, if we would be most helpful to him"—a credo that could serve as mission statement for many a progressive school over the following century. The Thoreau brothers didn't neglect the traditional subjects. John taught grammar, geography, and mathematics in the downstairs classroom. Henry, by virtue of his Harvard education, handled the more advanced courses upstairs, including Latin, Greek, French, physics, algebra, geometry, and natural history. The brothers could be just as strict as their public-school counterparts. Henry kept one pupil after school nearly an hour because he had omitted an "et" while reading a Latin sentence. Yet some of the curriculum raised eyebrows among more pedagogically conservative Concord parents. Each morning, following prayers, one of the brothers offered a brief talk (on the beauties of the seasons, for instance, or on the existence of an all-powerful being), a sort of philosophical palate cleanser to set the stage for the day's work. There were field trips—to the office of the *Yeoman's Gazette* to watch the compositors set the day's news in type; to Pratt's gunsmith shop to observe the regulating of gunsights; to Fair Haven Bay to learn surveying; to the banks of the Concord River to watch John and Henry apply a fresh coat of tar to the bottom of their latest handmade boat. Students who boarded with the Thoreaus were taken to local lectures; one evening, for instance, they heard Emerson speak on literature at the Lyceum. Saturday mornings were devoted to composition. ("N.B. Writing will be particularly attended to," noted a newspaper announcement for the school.) "The boys sometimes write their lives or those of some venerable Aunt Hannah or Uncle Ichabod," one student wrote to his parents, adding that he himself had composed two themes on less personal topics: birds and berries, subjects on which one of his instructors would write a great deal in the years to come. "Mr. Thoreau reads [a]loud those compositions which he thinks will please the scholars, which sometimes occasions a great deal of laughter."

Concord Academy students spent an unusual amount of time out of doors. Recess was extended to half an hour (three times the norm), during which period the classroom windows were opened to provide fresh air for the children when they returned—apparently something of a revolutionary concept. At least once a week, the Thoreau brothers led the entire school into the surrounding countryside to pick blackberries, gather chestnuts, search for arrowheads, study flowers under a magnifying glass, take a swim, or row on one of the town ponds, while their teachers told them about the life cycle of the frog or about the Indians in whose footsteps they followed. (John, ever-thoughtful, occasionally brought melons from his garden for the students, or cut strips of birch bark and bent them into drinking cups for thirsty girls.) Each spring John and Henry provided the students with small hoes so they could plant their own vegetables in an old potato patch Henry had plowed next to the school. A good deal of the Concord Academy curriculum consisted of precisely what the Thoreau brothers would have been doing even if they hadn't been teaching—a continuation of the fraternal explorations they'd undertaken since childhood.

John, who joked and played games with the students at recess, was the favorite. He talked to them "like an affectionate big brother," according to one student; wrote them playful letters; and put them at their ease. Many years later, a former student would compare him with Arnold of Rugby, the legendary headmaster immortalized in *Tom Brown's School Days*, adding, "To me that man seemed to make all things possible." John thought more of others, it was said, Henry thought more of himself. Henry was "respected," recalled one student, while John was "loved." Although

Henry got along well with the students, they thought him a little stiff and standoffish. The boys called him "Trainer Thoreau"—*trainer* being their nickname for *soldier*—because his erect posture and long, measured stride had a bit of military starch. They occasionally teased him. Once they cut out a picture of a booby from the almanac and passed it around, laughing and saying it reminded them of Henry. At the same time, Henry seems to have been one of those gifted, idiosyncratic teachers whom students always remember. Long after his death, elderly Concordians would recall in detail Henry's morning talks, his original way of explaining things. After an outbreak of profanity among the male students, for instance, he brought them together and said: "Boys, if you went to talk business with a man, and he persisted in thrusting words having no connection with the subject into all parts of every sentence—Boot-jack, for instance— wouldn't you think he was taking a liberty with you, and trifling with your time, and wasting his own?" Henry then shoehorned the word *boot-jack* into a sentence at frequent intervals to illustrate the absurdity of swearing. There was something marvelous about a teacher who could tell the month of the year by what flowers were in bloom, who could find arrowheads seemingly on demand, who told them that a cobweb was a handkerchief dropped by a fairy, and who once shot a sparrow for his students so they could examine it more closely. (Those who can't imagine the animal-loving Henry toting a flintlock shotgun to school may be interested to know that both Thoreau brothers were enthusiastic young marksmen; indeed, after shooting the sparrow, Henry, when no other game came in view, took potshots at a snowball balanced on a fencepost.) At the end of each day, as Henry was heading home, a child or two, hoping to hear more of his stories, would reach for his hand. Louisa May Alcott, a student at Concord Academy and herself something of a rebellious loner, had a schoolgirl crush on Henry she never entirely outgrew. Years later she drew a fictional portrait of him in her novel *Moods,* writing "power, intellect, and courage were stamped on his face and figure, making him the manliest man that Sylvia had ever seen."

These were halcyon days for the brothers. Henry, who had started writing poetry, expressed his joy at being reunited with John—and revealed the extent of his identification with him—in a poem titled "Love":

We two that planets erst had been
Are now a double star,
And in the heavens may be seen,
Where that we fixed are. . . .

That double star would be threatened when they fell in love with the same woman, setting off an interlude in the life of the Thoreau brothers that, if it hadn't ended so sadly, could have furnished the ingredients for a Preston Sturges screwball comedy, complete with love-besotted poetry, two marriage proposals, a priggish clergyman, a maiden aunt named Prudence, and a giraffe. In 1839, Ellen Sewall, the lively, intelligent seventeen-year-old daughter of a prominent Unitarian minister from Scituate, had come to Concord, where her aunt boarded at the Thoreaus', for a two-week stay. She spent much of that time with the Thoreau brothers, who escorted her to their favorite spots for hiking, rowing, berrying, and arrowhead-hunting. Henry also took her to gape at the "camelopard" exhibited in Concord by a traveling show. Evenings, there were suppers at which the Thoreau brothers played music, Henry on the flute. At one such gathering, the young people tried their hand at phrenology, which was in vogue at the time, and took turns interpreting the bumps on one another's heads. When Henry, "reading" Ellen's cranium, announced that she had no bumps at all, the rest of the group howled with laughter; according to phrenology, a bumpless head indicated that its owner was either a genius or an idiot.

Henry was smitten by the end of the first day, John not long thereafter. They each responded according to character. Henry confided in his journal, writing poems in Ellen's honor. *One green leaf shall be our screen, / Till the sun doth go to bed, / I the king and you the queen* began one; another echoed the double-star poem he'd written about his brother. *As 't were two summer days in one, / Two Sundays come together, / Our rays united make one sun, / With fairest summer weather.* Five days after Ellen's arrival, Henry sounded like an old hand at courtship, at least in the safety of his journal: "There is no remedy for love but to love more." However, he wasn't such a fool for love that he sacrificed *all* his principles. When Ellen asked him to accompany her to church one Sunday morning, he refused. All outdoors, he informed her, was his place of worship. John was more socially sophisticated than his brother. (One can't imagine Henry writing to a friend, as John did shortly before Ellen's arrival, "there is naught here save a few antiquated spinsters, or December virgins, if you will; and well may I sing, 'What's this dull town to me? no girls are here.'") He was also more forward; after Ellen departed, finding that she had left behind some arrowheads, he sent them to her, along with a flirtatious letter and a mounted insect as an in-joke. (A third young Concordian, a vacationing Harvard student, was also enamored of Ellen, but, seeing her monopolized by the Thoreau brothers, retired from the fray.) For her part, the young girl seems to have felt strongly, too; according to her own account, she cried all the way to Lexington in the stage coach and, on arriving home in Scituate, wrote to her aunt that her fortnight's visit had been one of the happiest times of her life. By then, her name had been carved into the railing of the old red bridge over the Concord River—between the initials of the Thoreau brothers. Four weeks later, on the last day of August, at the start of a long-planned boat trip, John and Henry would paddle beneath those initials.

Who knows what really happened between the brothers on that voyage? We have only Henry's account, written six years after the journey and four years after John's death and intended, in part, as a memorial to his brother. But thoughts of Ellen must have hung between them as they plied the river in the boat in which they had courted her so recently. When they returned, John left immediately for Scituate, where he had a successful visit, although Ellen's five-year-old brother kept calling him "Henry." Over Christmas vacation, the Thoreau brothers made a joint pilgrimage to see Ellen. Afterward, they expressed their sibling rivalry in gifts. Henry, perhaps sensing that Ellen's father needed wooing as much as Ellen, sent Reverend Sewall a book of poems by Jones Very, under whom Thoreau had studied Greek at Harvard. John, covering several bases at once, sent some South American opals for Ellen's natural history cabinet, some books for her eleven-year-old brother Edmund, and a long letter to five-year-old George, which closed, "I send you Sir nothing but a letter, and now if sister has read it through to you very carefully you may give her a kiss for me and wish her a Happy New Year!!" Whereupon Henry trumped his brother by sending Ellen some of his own poems, including one in which he recalled their afternoons on the river. The Thoreaus competed not only for Ellen but for her brothers. John made a special friend of George, while Henry was so taken with Edmund that he wrote him a famously enigmatic love poem, "Sympathy" (*Lately alas I knew a gentle boy, / Whose features all were cast in Virtue's mould . . .*). Whether Thoreau's feelings for Edmund were a projection of his feelings for Ellen or his feelings for Ellen were a projection of his feelings for Edmund is a subject of controversy among Thoreau scholars.

It is not known whether the Thoreau brothers discussed their common interest in Ellen, but it is likely that at some point Henry dutifully stepped aside so that his elder brother might pursue his suit. The following summer, after Ellen revisited Concord, John made two trips to Scituate. On the second, while he and Ellen were walking on the beach—and Aunt Prudence had tactfully paused to rest on some rocks—John proposed. Ellen accepted. By the time they reached home, however, she realized she had made a mistake; Henry was her preferred Thoreau. In any case, her mother made her break off the engagement, certain the news would dismay Ellen's father, a hard-line Unitarian who disapproved of Emerson and his circle. John returned, despondent, to Concord. Henry may have felt sorry for his brother, but he also saw new hope for himself: "Night is spangled with fresh stars," he wrote in his journal. In November, Henry proposed to Ellen in a letter. Her father was furious—Henry, being the "transcendental brother," as he sardonically referred to himself, was an even more objectionable son-in-law than John—and insisted she write in a "*short, explicit* and *cold* manner to Mr. T." and refuse him. She did. (Four years after rejecting the Thoreaus, Ellen married a Unitarian minister and went on to have ten children. But her feelings for the brothers endured. At some point she scissored out all references to them in her diary, and, late in life, told her daughter she had felt almost in love with both of them.)

Whether Henry was really in love with Ellen, with Edmund, with the idea of love, or with whatever his brother loved, is not clear. Neither is the interlude's effect on the brothers' relationship. Some biographers believe that the brothers grew less close. There is, for instance, no evidence of their taking another trip together after their voyage on the Concord. But that may have been for other reasons. In January 1841, two months after Henry's proposal had been refused, John came down with a cough he couldn't shake. Although Henry would describe his brother as a "sturdy oak," John had always been less robust than he. John occasionally suffered from nosebleeds so violent that he fainted, and there were days when what he called "colic" (but was more likely early-stage tuberculosis) kept him housebound. Even when healthy, he weighed only 117 pounds. John soon grew too weak to teach. Henry didn't wish to continue without his brother, and on April 1, 1841, they closed their school.

If there was a growing distance in their relationship, Ellen Sewall may not have been the only cause. During the years he taught school with his brother, Henry was also undergoing a period of ferocious intellectual growth, fueled in large part by his new friendship with Emerson. Henry began to keep a journal; started to write poetry; was introduced to Margaret Fuller and other leading thinkers of the day; became a Transcendentalist; published in *The Dial*; lectured at the Concord Lyceum; and, given the run of Emerson's vast library, expanded the ambitious program of reading he had started at Harvard, plowing through Aeschylus, Virgil, Goethe, and Fenelon in the original. It was as if he had a second, separate life, a life of the mind he couldn't share with his brother. Though John was intelligent and well-read (on January 27, 1841, he and Henry had taken the affirmative in debating Bronson Alcott at the Lyceum on the topic "Is it ever proper to offer forcible resistance?"), he didn't share his brother's intellectual seriousness. While Henry enjoyed teaching and was, in his way, good at it, there is little doubt that, even had John remained healthy and the school doors open, Henry eventually would have defected. With Emerson's support, Henry was beginning to identify himself as a writer.

Henry found in Emerson, who was fourteen years his senior, not only a mentor but the wise, paternal figure his own father had never been and for whom his brother had stood in. For Emerson, too, the relationship filled familial needs. During the previous three years, he had lost two brothers, for whom he had the deepest affection and the highest hopes, to tuberculosis. When Emerson met Thoreau, he may have found in this brilliant, peculiar young man a rough-hewn surrogate for his late brothers. Furthermore, Emerson had lost his father on the eve of his eighth birthday, and though he was the third of six sons, he had, in many ways, become the head of the family; as his own brothers died, he became an elder brother to many young writers, of whom Thoreau was the most promising.

In the early years of their relationship, Thoreau worshiped Emerson as devoutly as a young boy ever worshiped his older brother. In one of his early poems, "Friendship" (a subject to which he would return all his life), Thoreau writes of *Two sturdy oaks I mean, which side by side, / Withstand the winter's storm, / And spite of wind and tide, / Grow up the meadow's pride, / For both are strong.* Whether the poem referred to his new friendship with his illustrious neighbor or to his deep-rooted bond with his beloved brother can't be determined; likely both were on his mind. Both were vital to Henry. The intellectual stimulation he couldn't get from John, he got from Emerson; the easy affection he couldn't get from the emotionally removed Emerson, he got from John. (Like all Concordians, Emerson was fond of John, who had built him a bluebird house and had thoughtfully taken his son Waldo to a traveling daguerreotypist for his portrait, a portrait that became even more precious to Emerson after Waldo died a few months later.) But Emerson inadvertently, unknowingly, challenged John for Henry's attention. Henry appeared to make a choice when, three weeks after the Thoreau brothers closed their school, he accepted Emerson's invitation to move into his home for a year. In return for room and board, Thoreau would serve as handyman, carpenter, chimney sweep, gardener, intellectual foil to Emerson, playfellow for his four children, companion to Lidian, and, during Emerson's frequent absences on lecture tours, man of the house. Thoreau ostensibly made the move for financial reasons, but any post-Ellen awkwardness in his relationship with his brother must have made it easier to leave. The Emerson house was only a short walk from the Thoreaus', and Henry, no doubt, returned home for frequent dinners. It was from Emerson's house that, eight months after he had moved in, he hurried home to be at his dying brother's side.

*   *   *

If lockjaw was a common phenomenon in 1842, "sympathetic illness" was all but unknown. One of the first references in the medical litera- ture would appear more than a century after Thoreau was stricken, when psychiatrist Erich Lindemann, in a 1944 study of 101 patients grieving the death of a loved one, found numerous instances in which their grief had been complicated by "the acquisition of symptoms belonging to the last illness of the deceased." Two decades later, in a study of 58 children whose psychiatric conditions were linked to the death of a sibling, the psychologist Albert Cain found that nearly half had suffered "hysterical identifications" with the sibling's prominent symptoms, including pains, convulsions, asthmatic attacks, and, in one case, paralysis. Cain noted that these symptoms may be delayed (as in Thoreau's case) "when there is necessity for maintaining the morale of others."

Cain also found that these hysterical identifications were usually associated with a sense of guilt. In half of the children he saw, guilt "was rawly, directly present," even five years or more after the sibling's death. "Such children felt responsible for the death, sporadically insisted it was all their fault, felt they should have died too, or should have died *instead* of the dead sibling. . . . They mulled over and over the nasty things they had thought, felt, said or done to the dead sibling, and became all the guiltier." Their guilt led to depression, accident-proneness, punishment seeking, constant testing behavior, and other forms of acting out. Cain observed that surviving siblings often sensed that their parents wished that *they*, not their sibling, had died.

Cain was studying psychiatric cases. Feelings of guilt, however, are common after most sibling deaths. When his fourteen-year-old brother, Jack, was killed in a horrific table saw accident, twelve-year-old Johnny Cash felt as if he, too, had died. The boys had been inseparable. When not working side by side in their father's Arkansas cotton fields, they swam, climbed trees, and fished. "Jack was my big brother and my hero: my best friend, my big buddy, my mentor, and my protector," Johnny recalled. Jack had been the golden boy in the impoverished Cash family, a strong, considerate, reliable fellow who planned to become a preacher. Johnny was a scrawny, cigarette-smoking rebel. At night, while Jack studied the Bible, Johnny listened to blues and gospel on the radio. On the day of Jack's death, Johnny had begged his brother to come fishing with him; Jack said he couldn't, that the family needed the money he earned making fence posts in the high school agriculture shop. Afterward, Johnny kept thinking that if only he'd been able to persuade Jack to go fishing, his brother would still be alive. The guilt he felt was reinforced by his father, who, when drunk, told Johnny *he* should have been the one to die. During Johnny Cash's subsequent decades of drinking, drug use, and other self-destructive behavior, it seemed almost as if he was taking his father's words literally.

Guilt may encourage a surviving sibling to feel he must stand in for his dead brother. The concept of a "replacement child" goes back to the Bible. After Cain killed Abel, Eve gave birth to a third son, whom she called Seth, from the Hebrew word for "set" or "appointed," believing God had sent him to her as a substitute for her dead son. (The Bible does not tell us whether Seth followed in Abel's footsteps, careerwise, but in *Antiquities of the Jews,* the first-century historian Josephus refers to Seth as "a virtuous man" and "of excellent character.") As in Eve's case, the notion of a replacement child can be taken literally, when parents conceive a child to replace a child who has died, often giving the newborn his deceased brother's name. (In Albert Cain's study, there were a few instances in which grieving parents renamed a *living* sibling for the dead child.) Nine months and ten days after the death of their first child, Salvador, to a gastrointestinal infection at the age of twenty-one months, Salvador and Felipa Dali had a second child, whom they also named Salvador. The second Salvador grew up in the shadow of the first. His brother's photograph hung over his parents' bed, his toys still lay scattered in the house, and his memory was invoked constantly by his parents, who referred to him as a "genius." When the second Salvador was five, they took him to his brother's grave and told him he was the reincarnation of his dead brother. Desperate to prove to his parents that he was unique, he became a tantrum thrower, an intentional bedwetter, and a lifelong exhibitionist. In his histrionic life and Surrealist art, he sought the attention he never got from his parents. "All the eccentricities which I commit, all the incoherent displays are the tragic fixity of my life," he wrote. "I wish to prove to myself that I am not the dead brother, but the living one."

Surviving siblings may feel unspoken pressure to replace the lost sibling by living up to his example or by living *for* him—keeping him, in a sense, alive through themselves. One way to do that is to assume part of his identity. That identification can be physical: Henry David Thoreau trying on John's illness; Robert Kennedy wearing Jack's old navy jacket; six-year-old Joshua Fleck asking, after the death of his identical twin to brain cancer, that a piece from Shayne's blue blanket be sewn into his own matching blue blanket; the professional football player Arnaz Battle tattooing the face of his younger brother, who drowned at the age of three, on his arm so that, as Battle put it, "he would always be with me."

That identification can be figurative, as when a surviving sibling takes on some of the personality traits or ambitions of the lost sibling, a phenomenon psychologists refer to as "living for two." (The expression is made literal by the southern folk superstition that when one twin dies, the surviving twin inherits his strengths. Thus Elvis Presley grew up believing, as his mother assured him, that he had inherited the talents of his stillborn twin, Jesse.) Seventeen-year-old Vladimir Ulyanov (Lenin) read widely in radical politics, but when his older brother, Alexander, who had introduced him to the work of Karl Marx, was hanged for his part in the attempted assassination of the tzar, Lenin grew determined to translate theory into action. The young Bill Tilden was a naturally gifted tennis player but didn't take the sport seriously until his beloved older brother, a talented amateur who had taught him the game, died of pneumonia when Bill was twenty-two. After that, said a friend, "Nobody ever worked so hard at anything as he did at tennis." Ranked seventieth in the country at the time of his brother's death, he was world champion four years later. When twenty-three-year-old army scout David Weir was killed in Baghdad in 2006, his eldest brother, Chris, a twenty-seven-year-old financial officer from Tennessee, volunteered to complete his brother's service, one of numerous instances in which someone has enlisted after his brother has been killed in battle. Following his younger brother John's death, the landscape architect Frederick Law Olmsted, co-creator of New York's

Central Park, looked after his sister-in-law and her three young children. Eventually, Olmsted and his sister-in-law would marry and have four more children of their own, in a kind of organically evolving levirate marriage: the tradition, widely practiced in the ancient world and still found in some parts of India and Africa, in which the brother of a deceased man is obligated by law or custom to marry his brother's widow.

"Living for two" can be an inspiration and a burden. When his devout, sweet-tempered older brother was killed in the Korean War, thirteen-year-old Jerry West, suspecting his parents would rather *he* had died, took out his bitterness on the basketball court. "The pressure I felt was to compensate, to account for my brother David's death," he later said. Competing with an inner fury that was almost frightening, he would become one of the greatest players in history. He would also suffer periodic bouts of crippling depression. When seven-year-old Arthur Nixon, the fourth of five brothers in Whittier, California, died of meningitis in 1925, his twelve-year-old brother Richard felt guilty, believing that a rock thrown by a neighbor had contributed to his brother's death, a rock from which he felt he should have been able to protect his younger brother. "I think it was Arthur's passing that first stirred within Richard a determination to help make up for our loss by making us very proud of him," his mother recalled. "Now his need to succeed became even stronger." Eight years later, Richard's older brother, twenty-three-year-old Harold, the handsome, dashing, devil-may-care golden boy of the Nixon family—all the things Richard felt he wasn't—died of tuberculosis. Richard "sank into a deep, impenetrable silence," according to his mother. When he emerged from his depression, twenty-year-old Nixon, already a stridently ambitious young man, became even more driven. "From that time on, it seemed that he was trying to be *three* sons in one," said his mother. (His failed 1960 presidential campaign was made more excruciating by the fact that his opponent, John F. Kennedy, exemplified many of the qualities that Harold Nixon had possessed.) Though Richard Nixon would eventually win the presidency and become the most powerful man in the world, he felt a lifelong sense of inadequacy—he'd never be as handsome, charming, or graceful as his older brother. And, in the end, he would lose that power by self-destructing, as if he felt at some level that he didn't deserve his success.

In *Maus*, a graphic memoir detailing his parents' experience as Jews in wartime Poland, the cartoonist Art Spiegelman describes the difficulty of being raised in the shadow of a "ghost-brother"—an older brother he never knew who had died during the war at age five or six. "I didn't think about him much when I was growing up," writes Spiegelman, who was born after his parents survived Auschwitz and came to the United States. "He was mainly a large, blurry photograph hanging in my parents' bedroom. . . . The photo never threw tantrums or got in any kind of trouble . . . It was an ideal kid, and *I* was a pain in the ass. I couldn't compete." In 1944, after his older brother, Joe, died while carrying out a secret bombing mission over the French coast, Jack Kennedy told a friend that for as long as he could remember, he had defined himself through his competition with his brother. Now that brother was gone. Yet the competition would never end. He would forever be compared with a brother whose greatness had been made permanent by death. "I'm shadowboxing in a match the shadow is always going to win."

The stress of being a replacement child can be corrosive. Although there is no way to identify the precise strands that combined to turn the young Adolf Hitler into a mass murderer, the psychologists Stephen Bank and Michael Kahn believe that his status as a replacement brother was a crucial factor. Before Adolf's birth, three Hitler children had died in infancy, and his parents were desperate to cauterize their grief by raising a healthy son. When Adolf was eleven, his elder half-brother, Alois, who resented Adolf's favored status, quarreled bitterly with their father and ran away to England, where he was arrested and jailed for theft. Later that year, Adolf's six-year-old brother Edmund died of the measles. Hitler's bedroom overlooked the cemetery wall behind which Edmund had been buried; according to neighbors, he spent countless hours sitting on that wall, staring into the graveyard. After Edmund's death, the outgoing, well-mannered boy who had excelled in school became a problem child, brooding and defiant. "Torn between fulfilling the father's angry demands to be a perfect replacement sibling and the exiled Alois's call to be impulsive, Adolf Hitler turned inward and became openly hostile to everyone's expectations," wrote Bank and Kahn in *The Sibling Bond*. "His status as a replacement child (five times over), in the context of an already overclose maternal relationship and a strict father, can be seen as a major organizing factor in the development of Hitler's sadism and his arrogant claim to superiority and invulnerability."

*   *   *

On the surface, Thoreau's psychosomatic lockjaw was a dramatic measure of his identification with his beloved older brother, no doubt exacerbated by the trauma of nursing him during the last two days of his agonizing death. Henry and John had shared much of their lives. They had attended school together, taught together, explored Concord together, taken vacations together, even fallen in love with the same woman. Now they were sharing the same illness. Thoreau himself saw it this way. On March 14, writing of John's death to a friend, he explained, "I have been confined to my chamber for a month with a prolonged shock of the same disorder—from close attention to, and sympathy with him, which I learn is not without precedent." Indeed, Thoreau identified so strongly with his brother that he may unconsciously have felt he couldn't go on without him. Conversely, he may have felt guilty that even before his brother's death, he *had* begun to "go on without him" by pursuing a career as a writer and by moving away from home—and away from his ailing brother. Thoreau's illness may also have been an expression of "survivor guilt," that phenomenon by which someone may feel intense guilt after surviving an accident fatal to others.

But Thoreau had other reasons to feel culpable. In his psychobiography of Thoreau, Richard Lebeaux points out that despite the reverence he felt for his older brother, Henry surely also felt rivalry—for their parents' love, for their students' affection, for their neighbors' approval, and, most recently and keenly, for the heart of Ellen Sewall. "Because he loved his brother so much, Thoreau experienced unbearable guilt," writes Lebeaux, who believes that John's death was the central event in Thoreau's life and in his growth as an artist. "His psychosomatic illness could be interpreted as a way of punishing himself and trying to share the fate of John, thereby relieving his guilt." Had such a theory been expressed in 1842 pre-Freudian Concord, it would doubtless have been considered as ludicrous as a teacher who believed he could learn from his students. And yet it is possible that Thoreau sensed among the townspeople, on some level, disappointment that saintly John and not irascible Henry had been the Thoreau brother to die.

On January 27, two weeks after John's death and three days after Henry's symptoms began to fade, Henry's grief was compounded when five-year-old Waldo, his favorite among the Emerson children, died of scarlet fever. "I feel as if years had been crowded into the last month," he wrote on February 21, two days after opening his journal for the first time since John's death. Friends said of Thoreau that it seemed as if a part of him had been torn away. To the outside world, he struggled to put John's death into perspective. "Soon the ice will melt, and the blackbirds sing along the river which he frequented, as pleasantly as ever," he wrote Lucy Brown, Lidian's sister, on March 2. "The same everlasting serenity will appear in this face of God, and we will not be sorrowful, if he is not." One senses Thoreau trying to talk himself back into health. But his despair surfaced in his journal. "My life, my life! why will you linger? Are the years short and the months of no account? . . ." he wrote on March 11. "Why, God, did you include me in your great scheme? Will you not make me a partner at last?" Two days later, in his journal, he was again philosophical: "The sad memory of departed friends is soon incrusted over with sublime and pleasing thoughts, as their monuments are overgrown with moss. Nature doth thus kindly heal every wound. By the mediation of a thousand little mosses and fungi, the most unsightly objects become radiant of beauty." But his entry of March 26, two and a half months after John's death, was more raw. "Where is my heart gone?" he asked. "They say men cannot part with it and live." By mid-April, he had moved back to the Emersons', but he was still too weak and despondent to work in the garden.

If Thoreau's psychosomatic illness and severe depression can be considered a form of symbolic death, it would lead to a corresponding rebirth. As spring moved into summer, Henry's brave words about nature's healing powers took root, and he began to find in its matter-of-fact cycle of death and regeneration a measure of consolation. A key Transcendentalist tenet was a belief in the spiritual significance of natural events. John had kindled his interest in nature; John's death made nature seem even more vital. Wandering the woods and fields he had explored with his brother, he felt closer to John, a feeling he would express in a poem, "Brother Where Dost Thou Dwell?" written sixteen months after John's death:

> *Where chiefly shall I look*
> *To feel thy presence near?*
> *Along the neighboring brook*
> *May I thy voice still hear?*
>
> *Dost thou still haunt the brink*
> *Of yonder river's tide?*
> *And may I ever think*
> *That thou art at my side?*

Henry not only immersed himself in nature, he began to write about it. In April, Emerson had suggested he review five recent books of natural history for *The Dial*. (Devastated by the death of his son, Emerson was trying to prod his surrogate son back to life.) "Natural History of Massachusetts" was Thoreau's first nature essay and, in retrospect, it is clear that he had found his calling. Written with a naturalist's powers of observation and a poet's gift for description, Thoreau's "review" was a freewheeling discussion of the themes he had been wrestling with in the aftermath of John's death: the inevitability of change, the fragility of life, death and rebirth. He wrote of spring's annual renaissance with an exuberance approaching ecstasy, concluding, "Surely joy is the condition of life." In finding recovery and renewal in nature, he began to find recovery and renewal in himself. "It was the beginning of a very creative six months of work, it was a big step toward staking out his own special subject matter, and it was a significant move away from 'Dialese' and the Emersonian manner to a style of his own," writes Robert Richardson in his intellectual biography of Thoreau. "His characteristic form and his characteristic style both emerged over the remaining months of 1842." Thoreau's creative surge (by the end of the year he had completed a second nature essay, started a third, and composed a lecture on Raleigh—whose heroic life and noble death may have brought John to mind) was matched by his physical industriousness (he worked in his father's pencil-making operation, helped build a new family house, and planted gardens for both the Hawthornes, who would be moving to Concord that summer, and the Emersons). Even before John's death, Thoreau had been feeling adrift: he had lost a possible spouse, been deprived of a job, and was beginning to doubt his future as a writer. The death of the brother with whom he so identified would nearly kill him. But it would also force him to find his own identity. "His discovery of himself came directly and rapidly out of the tragic losses of January," concludes Richardson. "It is almost as though John's death freed him."

*　　*　　*

In *The Wound and the Bow*, Edmund Wilson argues that suffering often furnishes the raw material for art. The psychiatrist George Pollock, noting how many writers, artists, and musicians lost siblings in their youth, suggests that grief may spur creativity as a kind of compensation. Pollock cites James Barrie, the six-year-old boy whose older brother died in a skating accident. Their mother had done little to hide her preference for that older brother, a handsome, charming scholar and athlete. After David's death, his small, grave, apparently unexceptional younger brother attempted to comfort his near-catatonic mother by impersonating him: dressing in David's old clothes, assuming his mannerisms, even learning his characteristic whistle. When replacing his brother failed to work, James, in the years to come, more successfully diverted his mother by writing stories and plays and reading them aloud. Writing, observes Pollock, became James's way of getting his mother's attention. One of the stories he told her would evolve, decades later, into *Peter Pan*, which Barrie, surely thinking of his lost brother, subtitled "The Boy Who Wouldn't Grow Up."

Although psychologists have only recently turned their attention to sibling loss, writers have for centuries tried to come to grips with it in literature. The Roman poet Catullus memorialized his dead brother in several poems, including a formal tribute that ends with the famous salute *ave atque vale* ("hail and farewell"), and a starkly haunting lamentation ("You, brother, have destroyed my happiness by your death: all my soul is buried with you . . ."). After his younger brother John died in a shipwreck in 1805, William Wordsworth was so stricken he could write no poetry for several months. But then he began work on *Elegiac Verses,* in which he sought to immortalize his brother. "I shall . . . never be at peace till, as far as in me lies, I have done justice to my departed Brother's memory," he wrote a friend. Samuel Clemens felt crushing guilt after his younger brother, Henry, died in a riverboat explosion at the age of nineteen. Clemens had gotten his brother a job on the boat, and would have been on board, too, had he not debarked a few days before the accident. Throughout their boyhood in Hannibal, Missouri, the restless, mischievous older brother had tormented the exasperatingly well-behaved younger brother—pelting him with clods of dirt, dropping a hollowed-out watermelon on his head from a third-story window. But he had also looked out for him, and by the end of adolescence, Samuel felt that the pensive Henry was one of the few people who knew him well. Eighteen years after the accident, Clemens would resurrect an exaggerated version of Henry in his first novel. "He is Sid in *Tom Sawyer,*" wrote Mark Twain in his autobiography. "But Sid was not Henry. Henry was a very much finer and better boy than Sid ever was."

Writing about a lost brother is, of course, a way of keeping him alive. Tolstoy and Thomas Wolfe are among the novelists who have dealt with the death of a brother in their fiction; Uwe Timm, Mikal Gilmore, and Brent Staples have struggled with it in memoir; Eugene O'Neill rendered it in drama. For Jack Kerouac, writing about his older brother, Gerard, was a way of trying to keep *himself* alive. Much of Kerouac's short life, in fact, could be seen as a search for the nine-year-old boy who died of rheumatic fever when Kerouac was four. After Kerouac met Neal Cassady, the charismatic car thief who would become his muse, he told Allen Ginsberg that Cassady might well be Gerard reborn. In *Visions of Cody,* his worshipful novel about Cassady, Kerouac declared, "Cody is the brother I lost." The real brother would be enshrined in *Visions of Gerard,* an impressionistic novel about the "saintly" boy "who warned me to be kind to little animals and took me by the hand on forgotten little walks." Kerouac came to believe that Gerard was, in a sense, the author of his books—that his elder brother was alive and speaking through him.

But if his brother's death fueled Kerouac the writer, it devastated Kerouac the man. Gerard had served as a buffer between his meek, impressionable younger brother and their domineering mother. The mother's grief for her older son, along with her subsequent overprotectiveness of her younger son, placed even more strain on an already confused Oedipal relationship. For years after his brother's death, Jack, beset by nightmares, slept in his mother's bed, an arrangement his mother did nothing to discourage. His self-esteem suffered as his mother simultaneously babied him—long after he had grown—and compared him with the angelic brother with whom he could never compare. "It should've been you that died, not Gerard," she'd say. Kerouac did his best to oblige her, pursuing a lifelong course of self-destructive behavior that left him broke, broken, and alcoholic. He was living with his mother when he died of a hemorrhage caused by acute liver damage at the age of forty-seven.

*   *   *

It is interesting to speculate what would have become of Thoreau had his brother not cut his finger that New Year's Day. John, of course, had drawn Henry into the social life of Concord to the extent that he was able, and, under his continuing influence, Henry might have been drawn in still further. Without John, Henry became, if anything, even more reclusive. But had John Thoreau lived, wrote Edward Emerson, and had Ellen Sewall accepted Henry's proposal, "who shall say but that the presence of these blessings would have prevented his accomplishing his strange destiny? For his genius was solitary, and though his need for friendly and social relation with his kind was great, it was occasional, and to his lonely happiness the world will owe the best gifts he has left."

Further, John's death seemed to kindle in Henry a new sense of purpose, as if he needed to make something of himself not only to live up *to* John but to live *for* him. Twenty-three months before his brother's death, he had mused in his journal: "On the death of a friend, we should consider that the fates through confidence have devolved on us the task of a double living, that we have henceforth to fulfill the promise of our friend's life also, in our own, to the world." Without John's death, Henry might never have become Thoreau.

On July 4, 1845, three years after John's death, Henry moved into the cabin he had built near Walden Pond. "I went to the woods because I wished to live deliberately," he would observe, in one of the most famous sentences in American literature. He also went there to write about John, about the fourteen-day voyage they had taken six years earlier, a voyage that had become an emblem of Henry's deep feeling for his brother. He began to think of the trip as fodder for a book—his first, a sort of memorial tribute to John. Each morning, sitting at his old Concord Academy desk, overlooking the place where he and his brother had spent so much time, he wrote about that memorable journey, reliving their days on the river, bringing John back to life.

The work went well. By the following summer, he had finished a first draft of *A Week on the Concord and Merrimack Rivers*. He read aloud from the manuscript to friends who made the walk along the northern edge of the pond to his cabin. After hearing an excerpt on a cold March evening in 1847, Bronson Alcott wrote in his diary:

> The book is purely American, fragrant with the life of New England woods and streams, and could have been written nowhere else. Especially am I touched by his sufficiency and soundness, his aboriginal vigor,—as if a man had once more come into Nature who knew what Nature meant him to do with her,—Virgil, and White of Selborne, and Izaak Walton, and Yankee settler all in one. I came home at midnight, through the woody snow-paths, and slept with the pleasing dream that presently the press would give me two books to be proud of—Emerson's "Poems," and Thoreau's "Week."

"Presently," in *A Week*'s case, would stretch to two years. Even after he had submitted it to publishers, Thoreau, a notorious perfectionist, continued to revise the manuscript; given its subject, he may have found it especially hard to let go. In any case, even with Emerson and Hawthorne lobbying on his behalf (Emerson, touting it to an editor, called it "pastoral as Isaak Walton, spicy as flagroot, broad and deep as Menu"), *A Week* was turned down by four publishers. A fifth finally agreed to take it on, as long as Thoreau would repay the printing costs if the book didn't sell. *A Week on the Concord and Merrimack Rivers* was finally issued on May 30, 1849, ten years after the trip that had inspired it, seven years after John's death.

Thoreau had retreated to Walden in order to "simplify" his life, but the book he wrote there was anything but simple. *A Week* (for dramatic purposes, the two-week trip was compressed into one) is, on the surface, a travel narrative, recreating the brothers' voyage in the *Musketaquid,* the fifteen-foot skiff they'd built in the spring and named after the Indian word for the Concord ("Grass-ground River"). As a travel narrative, *A Week* is rather tame. Although Thoreau compares the Concord with the Nile and invokes "the Scythian vastness of the Billerica night," the Concord was a gently flowing river, the end-of-summer weather was balmy, and the brothers' experience seems as sweetly innocent as a Boy Scout camping trip. (Their most thrilling adventure may have been the hot pursuit of a runaway melon that had floated downstream.) Spliced at frequent intervals into the narrative are loosely related Thoreauvian riffs: on the fish of the Concord River; on the arrival of the white man in North America; on the Roman satirist Aulus Persius Flaccus; on traveling on the Sabbath; on epitaphs; on waterfalls, and so on. As Emerson observed to a potential publisher, "The narrative of the little voyage, though faithful, is a very slender thread for such big beads & ingots as are strung on it." (Many of these beads and ingots were first published in *The Dial* and subsequently squeezed into the manuscript over the years, making *A Week* something of an anthology: *Thoreau's Greatest Hits, 1841–1849.*) Strewn here and there are snippets of popular song, excerpts from the *Gazetteer,* scraps of poetry, and a commonplace book's worth of quotations from Homer, Confucius, Jamblichus, Chaucer, Tennyson, Ossian, Aubrey, Sadi, Chateaubriand, Simonides, Mencius, Bokhara, John Smith,

Sieur de Monts, Gower, Goethe, and Mother Goose, to name a very few. The book's overstuffed, kitchen-sink quality makes it seem, at times, the work of a graduate student who can't finish his dissertation.

A Week is a curious memorial. Thoreau never mentions John by name, never describes him. Indeed, after the epigraph (*Where'er thou sail'st who sailed with me, / Though now thou climbest loftier mounts, / And fairer rivers dost ascend, / Be thou my Muse, my Brother*—) the word *brother* appears only twice. Thereafter, John becomes part of "we" and "us," making the two brothers seem almost as if they are one, as in Henry's "double star" poem. Several years earlier, Thoreau had taken on John's illness; now it was as if he were absorbing his brother's persona. The brothers seem extraordinarily close as they head north, singing as they row: naming the islands they pass; identifying the birds overhead; pausing under a willow to slice open another melon from Henry's garden; camping on the shore, using their mast for a tentpole and their sail for a tent; drinking cocoa boiled in river water; eating fish they'd caught, berries they'd picked, and the occasional loaf of bread purchased from a local farmer; reading the 1839 *American Gazetteer* by the light of a lantern; talking of old friends by the campfire; sharing a buffalo skin and a blanket (as they had once shared a trundle bed); lying awake together listening to the wind on the water. It may have been the nearest the brothers ever came to their childhood dream of being Indians.

Thoreau nowhere mentions his brother's death, but images of death abound: a fisherman swinging a scythe in the meadow, "himself as yet not cut down by the Great Mower." Frequently comparing life to a river that runs inexorably to the sea, Thoreau ruminates on transience and permanence, on decay and renewal, on time's passage, on the thin line between sickness and health—themes he had wrestled with and written about since John's death, and which he would wrestle with and write about for the rest of his life. ("Some are reputed sick and some are not. It often happens that the sicker man is the nurse to the sounder," wrote Thoreau, surely thinking, perhaps guiltily, of John's final days.) But Thoreau accepts life's cycles, acknowledging that while his brother is dead from the smallest accident, *he* is still alive: "we walk on in our particular paths so far, before we fall on death and fate, merely because we must walk in some path." In short, life, like the river on which he and his brother paddled, goes on.

On the eve of their final day, the wind changed and came out of the north. "That night was the turning point in the season," Thoreau wrote. "We had gone to bed in summer, and we awoke in autumn." It was cold and breezy. The brothers were on the river before dawn. Hoisting their sail, with wind and current at their backs, they flew downstream, covering the fifty-mile return journey in a single exhilarating day Thoreau would always remember. That evening, their boat arrived at its familiar spot on the Concord riverbank, the faint depression it had left on the bulrushes still apparent. The brothers, wrote Thoreau, "leaped gladly on shore, drawing it up, and fastening it to the wild apple-tree, whose stem still bore the mark which its chain had worn in the chafing of the spring freshets." Nothing had changed, and yet when he wrote these lines, six years later, Thoreau knew that everything had changed.

Writing *A Week* was a way of what a psychologist would now call "working through" John's death. On that account, it may have been a success. The book itself was a critical and financial failure. (Another book written at Walden would make Thoreau's reputation, if not his fortune.) Although some reviewers found it thoughtful and original, many more were annoyed by the digressions. "We come upon them like snags," wrote James Russell Lowell, "jolting us headforemost out of our places as we are rowing placidly up stream or drifting down." The publisher did little to promote *A Week,* and of 1,000 copies printed, only 219 were sold. In 1853, a wagonload of 706 unsold copies appeared at the Thoreau home; their author lugged them armful by armful upstairs to his attic bedroom. "I have now a library of nearly nine hundred volumes," he wrote drily in his journal, "over seven hundred of which I wrote myself." Thoreau was dismayed that his first book, his memorial to John, had been so poorly received. To pay off the $290 debt—a fortune to someone who had lived on 58 cents a week at Walden—he would have to make pencils, thousands of them, over the next few years. For the rest of his life, when, occasionally, people wrote to him requesting that he sell them a copy of *A Week,* which could no longer be found in bookstores, he was uncharacteristically, almost pathetically, grateful.

Years after his brother's death, according to Sophia, Henry was rarely able to mention his brother by name. If it happened to be mentioned by others, tears came to his eyes. In 1854, when he told his new friend Daniel Ricketson about John, Thoreau turned pale and had to go to the door for air. Ricketson said it was the only time he ever saw Thoreau show deep emotion. For a long time after John's death, Thoreau refused to sing. But singing eventually became a link to John. A friend recalls that the only time he heard Thoreau "speak" of his brother was when he sang "Tom Bowling," a sentimental ballad about a drowned sailor he had often sung with John. (*His form was of the manliest beauty, / His heart was kind and soft, / Faithful, below he did his duty, / But now he's gone aloft.*") It became Thoreau's favorite song, and when friends heard him sing it—or "Row, Brothers, Row," which reminded Thoreau of his weeks on the river with John—in a voice as gruff as his personality, they knew of whom he was thinking.

For several years, Thoreau had nightmares on the anniversary of his brother's death. Even as he regained his equilibrium, he suffered periods of depression. "What am I at present? A diseased bundle of nerves standing between time and eternity like a withered leaf that still hangs shivering on its stem," Thoreau wrote in his journal in January 1843, a year after John's death. "A more miserable object one could not well imagine." He found it painful to walk past Emerson's barn, on which hung the bluebird house his brother had made. Then, too, there was the *Musketaquid,* the boat Henry and John had built. During the summer after John's death, Thoreau had often visited the Hawthornes. One evening, after dining with his friends, Thoreau and his host went for a row in the *Musketaquid.* Afterward, Thoreau offered to sell the boat to Hawthorne for seven dollars. The offer was accepted, the buyer noting that he wished he could "acquire the aquatic skill of its original owner at as reasonable a rate." It is said that Thoreau sold the boat because he needed the money. No doubt he did, but he may also have parted with it because the boat was a too-painful reminder of John; indeed, the date was August 31, three years to the day since he and John had set off in that same boat on their memorable trip. The following April, on the eve of moving to Staten Island, where he would tutor Emerson's nephew, Thoreau asked Hawthorne for one last ride in his old boat, which its new owner had rechristened *Pond Lily*. In early spring, there was still ice on the river. They rowed up the North Branch of the Concord, put ashore, and climbed a snowy hill. On their return, the boat was leaking, so they clambered aboard a large cake of ice and floated back down the river, towing the *Pond Lily* behind them.

"A man can attend but one funeral in the course of his life, can behold but one corpse," Thoreau wrote, after walking the Cohasset shore in 1849 and coming upon scores of corpses from the recently shipwrecked Irish brig *St. John*. For Thoreau, John's death would reverberate when his sister Helen died of tuberculosis two weeks after the publication of *A Week*; when he was dispatched by Emerson to Long Island in 1850 to search for the body and manuscripts of the shipwrecked Margaret Fuller; when he served as pallbearer for twenty-three-year-old Lizzie Alcott, who died of scarlet fever in 1858; when he handled the funeral arrangements for Emerson's mentally disabled brother, Bulkeley, who died in 1859; and when he nursed his father, John Thoreau Sr., in the months before he died that same year. Wrote Thoreau: "I perceive that we partially die ourselves through sympathy at the death of each of our friends or near relatives. Each such experience is an assault on our vital force."

As Thoreau struggled to put John to rest, his relationship with Emerson became increasingly vexed. Despite trying to help him get *A Week* into print, Emerson had been frustrated by Thoreau's endless revisions and disappointed in the final product. But the tension had deeper roots. Emerson, fourteen years older, had been a father figure for Thoreau. After John's death, he became something of a surrogate brother as well. (Emerson, of course, knew what it meant to lose a brother, having lost three to tuberculosis.) Thoreau began to feel less comfortable about following the beat of Emerson's drum. Accusations that he was an imitation of Emerson had long rankled him. After meeting Thoreau in 1838, Lowell had written that the young poet echoed Emerson's tone and manner so completely that "With my eyes shut, I shouldn't know them apart"; ten years later, in *A Fable for Critics*, he publicly lampooned Thoreau as a literary thief who "follows as close as a stick to a rocket, / His fingers exploring the prophet's each pocket." Although Thoreau was grateful to Emerson for all he had done for him, he chafed under the weight of his debt. For someone who prided himself on his autonomy, he found it galling to be so dependent. Even at Walden, where he wrote what would become the bible of independent living, he was living rent-free on Emerson's land. He sensed Emerson's exasperation with his lack of tangible literary accomplishment, with the seeming lack of ambition in the young man he had hoped might epitomize the "American Scholar" he'd called for in his 1837 Harvard Phi Beta Kappa address. (Twenty-five years later, in his eulogy for his friend, Emerson could not help sounding a note of disappointment that "instead of engineering for all America, he was the captain of a huckleberry-party.") Thoreau, of course, had ambitions. Increasingly, however, they were ambitions that weren't Emerson-approved. Indeed, Thoreau was in the process of outstripping his mentor, though it would not be fully apparent till long after both had died. Throughout the forties, Thoreau began slowly, painfully, to assert his literary and emotional (if not financial) independence. As in many mentor-disciple relationships, an affiliation that had been paternal had become fraternal, and the sibling rivalry began to emerge.

There were other strains. Thoreau and Emerson were moving in different directions, in different circles. Thoreau's world was growing— geographically—ever smaller, Emerson's ever larger as he became a writer of international stature. Thoreau was becoming increasingly solitary, Emerson increasingly social. (Emerson wrote an exasperated mock-letter in his journal: "My dear Henry, A frog was made to live in a swamp, but a man was not made to live in a swamp. Yours ever, R.") There was tension on the domestic front, too. Thoreau had lived at Emerson's for a total of two years and ten months—eight months longer than he had lived at Walden Pond. (Recalled Emerson's son, "He was to us children the best kind of an older brother.") Even the preternaturally serene Emerson must have felt a twinge when, far from home on a lecture tour, he received a letter in which Thoreau cheerily informed him that Emerson's three-year-old son, Edward, had asked him, "Mr. Thoreau, will you be my father?"

(Thoreau had added, not entirely helpfully, "So you must come back soon, or you will be superseded.") And he cannot have been oblivious to the bond between Thoreau and Lidian, for whom Emerson himself found it difficult to show affection. It is likely that Thoreau was, for a time, and in his own awkward way, in unrequited love with Emerson's wife; it is possible that he felt an unconscious rivalry with his benefactor for her affections, echoing his rivalry with his brother for the hand of Ellen Sewall.

Both men had exacting ideals of friendship; each found it impossible to live up to the other's. It is ironic that, as they wrote essays about the importance of friendship, both men were, at some level, profoundly lonely—Emerson since the deaths of his first wife, his brothers, and his son Waldo, Thoreau since John's death. Even more ironic, they discussed their loneliness with each other. Their friendship became increasingly knotty; there were periods of polite estrangement. They complained about each other in their journals, like schoolgirls quarreling via their diaries. In 1857, Thoreau wrote about their friendship as if it had ended, in lines, according to the biographer Henry Seidel Canby, "which for the expression of personal grief are not equalled elsewhere in Thoreau's Journal or the letters, except at the death of his brother John." Although their frayed relationship never irrevocably tore, neither did it ever entirely mend.

*　*　*

The loss of a sibling changes the fraternal hierarchy. After Joe Jr.'s death, Jack became the eldest Kennedy brother, inheriting all the hopes and ambitions their father had invested in Joe. "It was like being drafted," Jack told a reporter. "My father wanted his eldest son in politics. 'Wanted' isn't the right word. He demanded it." Jack was now living for two, as his old Choate headmaster pointed out in a letter to Jack's parents: "I'm sure he never forgets he must live Joe's life as well as his own." During the 1952 race for the Senate seat that was to have been Joe's, the notion of Jack as a "replacement brother" became a campaign selling point. "John Fulfills Dream of Brother Joe Who Met Death Over the English Channel" was the headline on an eight-page brochure. As Jack took Joe's place, Bobby took Jack's place, serving as his campaign manager—the role Jack would have filled for Joe. The order of succession in the Kennedy family was as clear as that of the English throne. "Just as I went into politics because Joe died, if anything happened to me tomorrow, Bobby would run for my seat in the Senate," Jack said in 1959. "And if Bobby died, our young brother, Ted, would take over for him."

In 1968, it was Ted's turn. "Like my brothers before me I pick up a fallen standard," he said in a speech eleven weeks after Bobby's death. In the space of twenty-four years, through a series of almost unimaginable tragedies, Ted Kennedy had gone from being the youngest of four brothers to being the eldest. (On inauguration weekend in 1961, Jack had presented him with a cigarette box, engraved with the words, "And the last shall be first.") For the erstwhile baby of the family—the least promising Kennedy, the butt of his brothers' jokes, the chubby one his sisters wanted to cover in football, the one who would describe himself as having been in "a constant state of catching up"—the burden proved overwhelming. Kennedy's subsequent stumbling—the alcohol, the partying, the women—could be interpreted not just as the grief and confusion of a man struggling to live up to his martyred brothers but as acts of self-preservation by a man fighting off the fate decreed for him by his father. His was a nearly unwinnable task: there were those who couldn't forgive him for not being his brothers, and there were those who couldn't forgive him for being so much like them.

Kennedy began to catch up to his brothers only when he stopped trying. After losing the Democratic nomination in 1980, he abandoned his quest for the presidency and settled into life as a senator—not, perhaps, the prize his father had wanted, but the political niche for which he may have been best suited. He was a natural legislator. Now he threw his full energy into the job. Remarried to a woman who made him happy, he seemed, finally, to be his own man.

In 1994 I wrote a magazine profile of the then sixty-two-year-old senator. As I followed him through the halls of Congress for a week, I could see ample evidence of his vestigial status as youngest brother. He was deferential, conciliatory, willing to compromise, eager to please—the very qualities that helped make him, some say, the best politician of all the Kennedy brothers. But this quintessential youngest brother had become the only Kennedy brother who lived long enough to have gray hair. He had assumed responsibility as the family patriarch, watching over not only his own children and grandchildren but his brothers' children and grandchildren; walking fatherless nieces down the aisle; showing up at graduations; remembering birthdays, baptisms, and confirmations. At the same time, he had assumed responsibility to his country for representing what was left of the Kennedys. And if he seemed to have made his way out from under the shadows of his brothers, it was clear those shadows would always be there.

At week's end, I interviewed the senator in his two-bedroom pied-à-terre on a quiet street in Boston's Back Bay. The walls and tables, like those of his Senate office, were covered with family photographs and memorabilia. I had been advised by a Kennedy aide not to ask him anything about his brothers until late in the interview, not because he would refuse to speak about them but because he would get so tied up emotionally that "although the words would come out, he wouldn't be there" for the topics that followed. It was good advice. When I finally asked Kennedy how he felt about being surrounded in his homes and offices by pictures of his brothers, inarticulateness descended as suddenly and inexorably as static on a radio. As long as we'd stuck to the safe ground of legislation or the pleasant ground of children and grandchildren, his voice had been rich, lively, and relaxed. Now it was slower, thicker, softer. He bumped awkwardly along, stumbling over words, having trouble completing even a single sentence. "Well it's interesting because . . ." he said. "I mean the things that sort of catch you may . . . in terms of my brothers and family members, you're not quite sure when these things are going to come. You can pass different pictures and, you know, walls, for a very considerable period of time and then something will sort of catch it, you know, something will reawaken . . . waken you."

He could have stopped after a sentence or two but he blundered ahead—the youngest sibling, still trying to please. A man who was usually in perpetual motion was now motionless. His hands rested on the table, like those of a child saying grace. His face got even redder than usual, swelling with effort. It was clear to me that the meaning lay not in the words themselves but in the silence that separated them.

The week before I met him, he had given the eulogy at Jacqueline Kennedy Onassis's funeral. Now I asked whether her death had marked an end of an era for him, as it seemed to for many Americans who had never met her. His voice dropped even lower, his always watery eyes got more so, and he talked in jerks and pauses, like someone trying to get traction in mud. "It has . . . I mean for me it was an individual . . . human being . . . as . . . mention in terms of the members of my family . . . I think it was a rollback to another time, bringing back all kinds of recollections and memories." He and I both knew he was talking about the death of his brother John; the message was in the body language, and the words were a meaningless overlay. He meandered a bit more, then said, almost in a whisper, "It just created a very powerful . . . moment and . . . you know, I mean you can't anticipate those kind of factors, but it was for real . . . certainly was for me." He was silent a long moment. He had wound down to the end.

*   *   *

As he entered middle age, Thoreau spent less time with writers and philosophers, more with farmers and fishermen; less time at his desk, more in the forest. "I think that I cannot preserve my health and spirits," he wrote, "unless I spend four hours a day at least—and it is commonly more than that—sauntering through the woods and over the hills and fields, absolutely free from all worldly engagements." "Sauntering" makes it sound as if his daily hikes were casual neighborhood strolls intended to burn off a few calories; in fact, they were systematic research expeditions. As he put it, "I go out to see what I have caught in my traps which I set for facts." To harvest those facts, Thoreau dressed himself up as a sort of one-man natural history lab. Clad in browns and greens for camouflage (making him look, he said, "the color of a pasture with patches of withered sweetfern and lechea"), he wore an oversized straw hat with the lining gathered in midway to form a "scaffold" on which to transport botanical specimens (kept moist, he said, by "the darkness and the vapors that arise from the head"); carried a walking stick (its edge marked in inches and feet for measuring the length of a pickerel or the depth of the snow) and his father's old flute instruction book (in which to press flowers and plants); and sported pockets custom-tailored to accommodate his notebook, Thoreau Pencil, spyglass, microscope, jack-knife, twine, ruler, and surveyor's tape (as well as any sticks, stones, seeds, nuts, or apples he came across that required further scrutiny or digestion). Despite being weighed down like a Yankee peddler, Thoreau, employing what a friend referred to as "his grave Indian stride," was able to cover as many as thirty miles in a single day, often leaving Ellery Channing—the sometime poet who, since John's death, had become the closest thing Thoreau had to a hiking partner— huffing and puffing in his wake. Just as the young Thoreau had struggled to keep up with his older brother, Channing was always a few steps behind the indefatigable Thoreau; just as John had been the personable member of the fraternal pair, Thoreau seemed positively affable next to the moody, grandiose Channing. Though Thoreau was only four months older than Channing, there was no doubt who was the older brother in this relationship, no doubt who was "cutting the wind."

Thoreau found himself approaching nature less transcendentally and more scientifically. He kept careful notes on the level of the rivers, the depth of the snow, the temperature of the ponds, the size of the seedling roots, the number of rings on the tree trunks, the blossoming of the flowers, the leafing of the plants, the colors of the morning and the evening skies, the arrival and departure of the birds. He collected and identified more than 800 of the 1,200 known plant species in the county. His attic bedroom doubled as a natural history museum in which, on shelves he'd made of river driftwood, he arrayed his pressed plants, lichens, birds' eggs, hornet's nests, arrowheads, spear points, Indian hatchets, and minerals, as well as a supply of nuts, of which, says Channing, "he was as fond as squirrels." He brought home birds' nests to dissect, crow scat to examine, snapping turtles to measure, peepers to study (they escaped and took up temporary residence in the family piano). He spent hours in close encounters with the local fauna; watching a tortoise lay its eggs, monitoring a hawk's nest until the fledglings flew away. "He knew the country like a fox or a bird," said Emerson, recalling a walk on which Thoreau "drew out of his breast-pocket his diary, and read the names of all the plants that should bloom on this day, whereof he kept account as a banker when his notes fall due." Thoreau's goal was nothing less than to classify and catalogue each stage in the development of every plant and animal in Concord. (In the early 1860s Thoreau would begin to enter his accumulated data on vast charts that tracked the natural history of each day of each month over the course of his eight years of observation.) At the same time, to make his modest living, he was working as a surveyor, mapping the boundaries of the land he had first explored with his brother.

Some biographers dismiss Thoreau's late-life obsession with natural science as a comedown from the moral and philosophical musing for which he is best known. (Emerson considered it a tragic waste of talent, and Thoreau himself worried that in focusing on the facts of the natural world he might lose sight of its poetry.) Others maintain that it was a leap forward, pointing the way toward what we now call conservation ecology. True, Thoreau was interested in science, but there was something more going on. Not only was he trying to document every last detail of the natural world around him, he was trying to become part of that world himself. On hot summer days, like an early prototype of John Cheever's Swimmer, he made a point of stripping and swimming in every pond or creek he came to; sometimes he waded down entire rivers end-to-end in nothing but his hat; once, he stood so long in a pond, observing bullfrogs, that a passing farmer assumed his own father had gone drinking and lost his way home. He'd follow a fox's trail by its scent; catch bees, release them and try to track their flights; flap his elbows at his sides and utter "something like the syllables *mow-ack* with a nasal twang and twist in my head" to attract the flocks of geese that flew overhead; feed mice and birds from his palm; scratch frogs' noses with his finger; catch and release fish with his bare hand; let snakes coil around his leg; tame a flying squirrel and watch it glide across his room. (He returned it to its hemlock tree the next day.) "I wanted to know my neighbors, if possible,—to get a little nearer to them," he said. More, he wanted to *be* them. He said he sometimes felt like a hound or a panther, and confessed to an occasional urge to devour a woodchuck raw. Reading his journals one senses in him a growing ambition to be as wild as the wilderness itself—either to devour the wilderness, or to let it devour him. Seventeen years after he wrote love poetry to Ellen Sewall, he found a new paramour. "There was a match found for me at last," he wrote in December 1856. "I fell in love with a shrub oak." After John's death he had looked for his brother in nature. Now he wanted to become part of nature. He wanted, perhaps, to rejoin John. It may not be too much to say that Thoreau's famous observation on staying close to home—"I have travelled a great deal in Concord"—reflected an unconscious desire to stay close to John and the places they loved.

For Thoreau's obsession with nature's cycles was entwined with increasing thoughts of his own natural cycle. "I think that no experience which I have to-day comes up to, or is comparable with, the experiences of my boyhood . . ." he wrote in 1851, four days after his thirty-fourth birthday. "In youth, before I lost any of my senses, I can remember that I was all alive, and inhabited my body with inexpressible satisfaction." Thoughts of his childhood were juxtaposed with thoughts of his own end. "The woods I walked in my youth are cut off," he wrote, after hiking to Walden Pond, where part of the forest had recently been razed. "Is it not time that I ceased to sing?" Where once he had risen with John before dawn to watch the sunrise, now he hiked at midnight under the full moon, delighting in the way his familiar world was transformed under a softer light. As we grow older, he observed ruefully, "we have more to say about evening, less about morning." He wrote increasingly of loss: the slaughtering of the wild pigeons, the dwindling of fish, the disappearance of the Indians. In autumn, he liked to row his boat filled with willow leaves that had fallen from the tree under which the boat was moored. He was fascinated by leaves; he compiled a list of the order in which local trees budded and leafed; he catalogued the sequence and gradations of their tints as they aged and decayed. "How beautifully they go to their graves!" he wrote, adding, "They teach us how to die."

It had been John, of course, who taught Henry how to die. And when Thoreau's own death came, there was a sense that he had long been ready. On December 3, 1860, Thoreau was out in the snow counting rings on a cut hickory tree. He came down with a cold, which spiraled into bronchitis, which lured tuberculosis—the family disease—from dormancy to full-blown virulence. By January 1862, it became apparent that the forty-four-year-old Thoreau would not recover. Every account of his death stresses his acceptance. "During his long illness I never heard a murmur escape him, or the slightest wish expressed to remain with us," his sister Sophia wrote. "His perfect contentment was truly wonderful. None of his friends seemed to realize how very ill he was, so full of life and good cheer did he seem." Indeed, during his last months, "the most unmalleable fellow alive" became patient, pleasant, almost charming—a lot, in fact, like John. He held court for a parade of friends, neighbors, and even strangers who knocked at the door, some of whom he had long treated with indifference or scorn, telling them stories, describing his previous night's dreams, consoling those who sought to console him. He refused opiates, telling Channing that he "preferred to endure with a clear mind the worst penalties of suffering, rather than be plunged in a turbid dream of narcotics." Kept awake by pain, he'd ask his sister to rearrange the furniture so that it might cast interesting shadows on the wall. When he could no longer manage the stairs, his rattan day-bed, which he had built himself and used at Walden, was brought down from his attic bedroom to the front parlor. There he lay, no longer surrounded by his birds' nests and arrowheads but by the flowers, fruit, jars of jelly, and game given him by neighbors, a generosity that moved him to comment, "I should be ashamed to stay in this world after so much has been done for me. I could never repay my friends." (His sister records the story as evidence of his heartfelt gratitude, but it is hard not to suspect an underlay of the mordant Thoreauvian wit.) Even then, Thoreau insisted on being helped to the table so he could eat with his family, saying, "It would not be social to take my meals alone." By temperament and choice, Thoreau was a Stoic— woe to those who, hiking with him, had complained about the pace—but as he lay in his bed, he may also have been thinking about the grace with which his brother had faced death. Death, of course, had been another way, the final way, in which John had gone before him, "cutting the wind."

His brother was much on his mind. Though emaciated and coughing uncontrollably, Thoreau worked whenever he had the strength, trying to keep up his correspondence, to organize his manuscripts, to edit several nature essays for *The Atlantic,* to complete his catalogue of Concord's biota. When he could no longer hold the pencil in his trembling fingers, he dictated his letters and editorial changes to his sister, even as his voice faded to a whisper. When he could no longer see to read, Sophia read to him. He spent some of the last months of his life going over *A Week*. His *Walden* publisher had offered to reissue it; to Thoreau, it must have seemed a measure of vindication for the book that was so close to his heart. Once again, he was back on the river with his brother. On the morning of May 6, he gave a longtime friend, a former Concord Academy student, an inscribed copy. Below the epigraph (*"Be thou my Muse, my Brother"*) he had taped several strands of John's hair. A little later, he asked Sophia to read aloud from the last chapter, which describes that giddy final day of the trip, when the brothers flew at astonishing speed toward home. After she read the sentence, "We glided past the mouth of the Nashua, and not long after, of Salmon Brook, without more pause than the wind," Thoreau reportedly said, "Now comes good sailing." A few moments later, he died.

Chapter Eleven
The Colt Men

On a warm spring evening in 2011, we have gathered for dinner at my house in western Massachusetts. Harry and Sandy have come down from Maine to stay with us. Ned and his wife, Cathy, are staying with Mum and Dad at their retirement community twenty minutes south. Mark has driven out from Boston. The meal is a farewell dinner of sorts. Ned and Cathy leave this week for Islamabad, where Ned will start a new job with an international relief organization. Harry leaves next week for India, the country in which, after getting so sick thirty-eight years ago, he started on the path to becoming a doctor. He'll spend five weeks of his sabbatical leading a group of medical students through the Himalayan foothills, offering health care to local villagers. It is rare that all four brothers are together. This afternoon, as I mowed the lawn, I felt the anticipatory flutter in my stomach I always feel when I know I'll be seeing them. With Ned traveling the world and our parents in their eighties, we never know when—or whether—the whole family will be together again.

Mum and Dad sit at either end of the table, canes hanging on the backs of their chairs. Dad turned eighty-seven a month ago. After operations on his back, knee, and Achilles tendon, his balance is iffy, and when he negotiates the kitchen steps, we four brothers hover around him like Secret Service agents around the president. An injured shoulder and a bad hip have left eighty-year-old Mum with a hitch in her step. But neither parent has lost anything mentally. (Dad insists he didn't have much to lose to begin with.) Mum belongs to two meditation groups, participates in poetry workshops, shows her paintings, and practices tai chi. Dad serves on the retirement community's fund-raising board, tutors local children, organizes a weekly men's lunch, and monitors his beloved Red Sox. At home, they are almost always together: weeding in Mum's Buddha garden; working at their desks side by side in their shared study (Dad paying bills, Mum Googling poems); preparing dinner in the kitchen; holding hands under the covers as they talk in bed at night. Not long ago, Dad, out of the blue, said to me, "Well, your mother and I have been having an awful lot of fun for the last twenty or twenty-five years"—an admission that, for him, was tantamount to Stanley Kowalski bellowing "STELLA!"

As I look around the table, I am, as always, startled to be reminded that my brothers and I are well into middle age. At fifty-eight, Harry is the only one who still has all his hair; he's also the only one who has gone gray. But his physique is so trim, his face so smooth, and his curly silver mop so thick that strangers often assume he's the youngest of the brothers. Ned's hairline has retreated and his face and stomach are a little fleshier these days, but he still turns heads. (My daughter thinks he resembles Gregory Peck.) I have a yarmulke-size bald spot, and no matter how much I exercise I can't rid myself of an incipient second chin. Even the youngest of us is no spring chicken, his face weatherbeaten from decades of working in the sun. Mark is shorter, sturdier, and stronger than his brothers, but over the years his red hair has turned brown, his freckles have faded, and he no longer looks like the exception that proves the rule. Indeed, the older we get, the more we resemble one another, as if we are converging on some sort of happy Colt medium.

We join hands around the table. Dad talks about how wonderful it is to be together, his voice a little husky, the way it gets when he's on the home stretch of *The Night Before Christmas.* Then he launches into his old high school grace: *Bless this food to thy use* . . . Over spaghetti and salad, we catch up on one another's lives: Ned's and Harry's travels, Mark's golf game, my new crab apple trees. Ned is about to undergo his first colonoscopy. Harry and I offer him sage counsel on laxative preps. (Where once we reported back to our younger brothers on the teachers they'd inherit, we now report back on cholesterol screenings, PSA tests, stretching exercises, and remedies for cracked heels.)

Then Harry recalls singing in the St. Paul's choir, triggering a flurry of brotherly memories: the little manila envelopes we got on payday, the black-and-white vestments that made us look like fluffy penguins, the excitement of staying up to sing at midnight mass on Christmas Eve. Ned remembers that on Palm Sunday we'd whip one another with palm leaves all the way home. Mark recalls how, before the early service on Easter, the elderly women of the church served us breakfast in the parish hall, complete with foil-wrapped chocolate eggs and yellow marshmallow bunnies. "What was that song we always sang at Easter?" Harry asks. It comes to us at the same moment and we launch into "RELEASE BARABBAS UNTO US!" in mock-operatic voices, surprised at how much of it we remember. From there, it isn't much of a leap to the Colt Family Singers and their nursing-home gigs. I recall the time when, in mid-"Kumbaya," an elderly man cried out, "Would you please SHUT UP!" Mum reminds us of how the women used to weep at the sight of handsome Ned in his lederhosen. "That's because I wasn't wearing any underwear," Ned says.

And the past rushes back. A single name or phrase culled from our fraternal lexicon is enough to set us off: Candy Cobb (the unattainable beauty across the street in Darien, at whose house we first listened to *Meet the Beatles*); Freddie Miller (Ned's pop-eyed friend, whose father, it was said, had a bullet or a BB—no one was quite sure which—lodged in his skull after being shot as a peeping Tom); Lumpkins (the bed-and-breakfast near our grandmother's house in Virginia where Ned kept us in stitches with his fake snoring); *Woo Dip Har* (the dish Mum always ordered at the forlorn faux-Polynesian restaurant we patronized on special occasions); Mr. Lammons (the father who liked to chase kids through the graveyard and goose them); Miss Zimmer (the dental hygienist on whose pillowy, white-uniformed breasts we'd rest our heads as Dr. Sweetnam drilled into our candy-lacquered teeth). Ned and I talk the most: me filling in details and making corrections, Ned cracking jokes, often at his own expense. But Harry contributes frequently, and though Mark doesn't remember the earlier stuff, he chimes in as we move forward through the years. We laugh so hard and talk so fast, overlapping, that Mum and Dad can't catch everything. But they look on, smiling, pleased to have "the four boys" under one roof. Although our wives don't understand all the references, they laugh along, too. My teenage son gazes from uncle to uncle as he listens, astonished at the evidence that his father had a childhood. At a certain point, however, I'm aware only of my brothers. It's as if it's just the four of us again, a world unto ourselves.

*   *   *

My brothers and I could never have imagined, during our splintered adolescence, how close we would become. Having spread out across the country and around the world, we have all, except for Ned, returned to New England, slowly moving back toward home, toward one another.

After four years in New Mexico, Harry and Sandy took jobs in Wisconsin, where they stayed seven years before heading to rural Maine. Although they left, in part, because their tidy suburb reminded Harry a little too much of Darien, it did not escape Harry's notice, or ours, that, having moved across the country from his family, he had, over the years, reversed the journey. Their house in Maine sits on thirty-eight acres of meadow and forest that roll down to a lake. Sandy keeps three horses, two dogs, a cat, a rabbit, and a dozen chickens, whose eggs Harry sells at work. Harry spends his spare time tending an ever-expanding vegetable garden. At the height of summer, the hillside, brimming with pumpkins, peppers, corn, tomatoes, and potatoes, is as voluptuous as a Grant Wood landscape. In winter, Harry can ski twenty miles through the woods without seeing a car. He is a long way from suburbia.

Sandy works as a geriatric nurse practitioner at a nursing home. Harry works as a family physician: delivering babies, freezing warts, setting broken arms, counseling addicted young adults, helping elderly patients with end-of-life decisions. He also serves as director of the practice's residency program, helping coordinate the training of thirty young physicians, a task that requires organizational skill and tactful but occasionally firm leadership—attributes not unlike those needed by the eldest sibling in a large family. As a clinician, Harry is known for his sensitivity, bred in part, perhaps, by the medical emergencies in which he nearly lost his wife, his son, and his youngest brother. The young man who spent summers working with disabled children now spends part of his off-time working with underserved populations overseas.

That Harry's specialty is family practice seems fitting. His house in Maine has become a family gathering place. For many years, until our parents grew too old to make the trip, it is where we celebrated Christmas, observing the familiar rituals of our youth with a new generation of Colts: the singing of carols on Christmas Eve; the frying of eggs and bacon on Christmas morning; the chorus of mock "oohs" and "aahs" as a jar of homemade piccalilli from a distant cousin is unwrapped under the tree (a spruce cut from the woods behind the house), atop which perches Harry's old construction-paper angel, her cherry-red robe faded to pale pink. There are new traditions, too: Sandy, clothes dusted with flour from baking pies, decorates the windows with candles and pine swags; Harry, wearing the bell-festooned jester hat someone gave him as a joke, leads us on sledding runs behind the barn and skiing expeditions across the snow-covered lake. Harry shudders to imagine what his life might have been like had he not met Sandy at a medical school party more than three decades ago, or had they not had Ian, now a twenty-seven-year-old businessman in Singapore, and Maya, a twenty-four-year old college student in Maine.

Harry still relishes competition, but these days, it's mostly with himself, whether swimming laps or producing the plumpest of raspberries. Each time he studies for the medical boards, he frets that he won't do well. Each time he scores in the 99th percentile. (He has always been a good test taker.) When Harry took up growing vegetables, he became a certified master organic gardener, though he pooh-poohs the achievement, observing that if you can say "mulch" with a straight face, you're well on your way to horticultural competence. He remains disciplined and driven, surely the only Colt brother capable of adhering to a no-dessert policy for more than a single evening. At the same time, the boy who bristled with suppressed feeling has become, if not fully laid back, at least fairly well tilted. Harry's informality expresses itself most noticeably in his take on fashion. He wears pants till the cuffs are frayed, T-shirts till they are in shreds. The bolo tie he wore to my wedding is, if not the only cravat in his closet, the only one I've ever seen on him, and when Dad's retirement party was held at a jackets-required Boston club, he arrived in an ill-fitting corduroy number he'd bought for five dollars at the Salvation Army on the drive down from Maine. Harry lives simply and wastes nothing, a philosophy that dovetails nicely with his approach to finance. For decades, he and I vied for the title of stingiest brother. Harry has cut his own hair for forty years; I shave with razors till they are as dull as butter knives. But after Harry had a swimming pool installed four years ago—for reasons of health, he hastened to assure us—I believe I took sole possession of the crown. (Our house came with a decrepit pool, but I haven't opened it in four years, unwilling to spend a cent to fix its torn liner.) We kid Harry about his dangerous drift toward profligacy, but note that he still wears tattered seventeen-year-old swim trunks as he does his laps.

These days, Harry is the older brother I always wanted during the dark years of his adolescence, and of mine. He is the one my younger brothers and I turn to: for medical information, for help in understanding the challenges faced by our aging parents, for advice on career decisions. He's the one whose guidance I seek along the way stations of fatherhood: from croup and head lice to mononucleosis and tonsillitis; from allowances and the facts of life to teenage drinking and driver's ed. The brother to whom I was once afraid to talk is now a patient listener. The brother who was once so competitive that he'd quit a game rather than admit defeat now bursts into laughter after a muffed shot on the tennis court. The brother who kept his distance from the family is now the family mediator. At our parents' fiftieth-anniversary party, it was Harry who not only served as emcee but gave his own heartfelt toast. Once again, I have followed my older brother's lead: into marriage, into parenthood, into country life, into middle age. Approaching my sixties, I feel safer knowing that Harry is still ahead of me, breaking trail.

Twelve years ago, Anne and I moved to western Massachusetts after twenty years in Manhattan and five years of envying Harry's life in rural Maine. We bought an old brick farmhouse that overlooks a valley and backs up against a forest. That spring, Harry drove 250 miles with his favorite shovel and an assortment of seeds from his private stock to help me start a vegetable garden of my own. He showed me how to turn the soil, leavening the sandy brown earth with moist black compost; how to plant pumpkin seeds in small hills, four seeds to a hill; how to trace a shallow trough for the tiny lettuce seeds by dragging a finger lightly across the soil; how to pay out the seeds between thumb and forefinger as if dealing from a deck of miniature cards. Sitting in the earth, as we sat in our backyard sandbox so many years ago, we worked hard, pausing occasionally to catch up on each other's lives while over the course of the weekend the garden transformed from a bumpy, weed-filled tangle to a quilt of rich chocolate rectangles.

Several years after we married, Anne and I were having dinner with friends when the conversation turned to a movie star who had made the tabloids for inviting a young reporter to have sex with him in the backseat of his car. One of our friends observed that there were two types of men: front-seat guys (the kind women want to settle down with) and backseat guys (the kind they want to fool around with). Julie said I was definitely a front-seat guy. Anne, bless her heart, protested, saying *she* considered me a backseat guy. But I was, deep down, I knew, a front-seat guy who had tried hard for a time to pass. At the doctor's office recently, I was asked to fill out a form assessing my current health. One section was devoted to alcohol, cigarette, and drug use. As I reported my intake at one beer every month or two, my years of excess felt so distant that the questions seemed absurd. Where once I aspired to a life of Goofus-worthy dissipation, I have, in the end, embraced my inner Gallant. I look back fondly but quizzically at the eighteen-year-old who, arriving at Harvard, wrote in his journal: "I want to make each minute count." At fifty-seven, I have the same goal, but a different idea of how to achieve it.

After Susannah was born, Anne and I tried to have another child. Following three years of miscarriages, infertility, and adoption discussions (during which time we turned often to Harry and Sandy, who had gone through so much to have their own two children), Henry's birth, nearly six years after Susannah's, seemed something of a miracle. I had been secretly hoping for another girl. I loved being father to a daughter, and, having grown up in an all-boy family, I knew too well what could go wrong with sons. Now, of course, I'm overjoyed to have a daughter *and* a son, though when Henry tracks mud into the kitchen or leaves his pajamas on the bathroom floor, I cannot fathom how Mum survived four of us. I sometimes wish, however, that Henry had a brother (or three), or Susannah a sister, so they could know what it's like to have a same-sex sibling. I would have preferred to have more children—despite the Sturm und Drang, I'm glad I grew up in a large family. But thanks to my waffling, Anne and I got started late, and by the time the second arrived there was no time left to try for a third.

Because of the age and gender differences, Susannah and Henry's sibling rivalry is minimal. They coexist peaceably. (I recall a spring evening seven or eight years ago when I couldn't find them at dinnertime. A knot of worry tightening in my chest, I searched for them outside, and discovered them behind the barn, lying in the grass, watching bats zigzag across the sky. The Colt household rarely saw a scene that pacific.) But sometimes I miss the ambient bedlam in which I grew up. At the same time, remembering how my brothers and I squandered our brotherhood when we were young, I want my children to realize how lucky they are to have a sibling, and when I catch them in a rare moment of discord, I have to bite my tongue to keep from saying, "Someday your mother and I will be gone and you'll only have each other."

My own competitive instincts have faded with age. I no longer reflexively measure myself against every man I meet, although I experience a twinge of satisfaction when I beat a younger cousin in tennis; when I lap the fellow in the next lane at the college swimming pool (until he gets out of the water and I see he is the white-haired emeritus professor of philosophy); or even when, donating blood, I squeeze the rubber ball so hard that my pint bag fills before that of someone who was hooked up before me. When our dog barks and I tell him to be quiet and he barks again and I tell him to be quiet again, I am reminded of Ned and me in childhood, each unable to let the other have the last word. I still strive mightily to beat my brothers in tennis or golf or Cranium, but when Harry lands a seven-letter gem on a triple word score in Scrabble, when Ned finds five times as many quahogs as me in half the time, or when Mark outswims me to the orange buoy, I feel that in some way I partake in their achievements. When Ned was named Distinguished Graduate by our high school a few years ago—and rated a glossy spread in the alumni magazine, headlined "Journalist, Mentor, Global Citizen"—I considered it a feather in our fraternal cap, although, unlike William James, who refused election to the American Academy of Arts and Letters because his brother Henry had been elected several months earlier, I would readily accept the honor if it were to come my way, too. A few months ago, when Harry, signing a communal sixtieth anniversary card for Mum and Dad, pretended to write, "I love you more than my brothers do," we all laughed.

When I was young, I wondered why my biological brothers couldn't be more like my friends. Now, when I hear someone describe his buddy as "the brother I never had," I feel lucky. I *have* a brother. Three of them. Five years ago, when Anne was diagnosed with breast cancer, their response was immediate: Mark offered to take care of the children while we were in New York for the surgery; Harry volunteered to come down on his week off to stay with us while Anne recuperated; Ned phoned from the Middle East to offer his support. Over the following months, Harry called regularly and listened to me vent about oncotype scores, radiation dosages, and hormonal therapy options. He made an occasional judicious comment, his honesty far more comforting than the nervous reassurance I'd hear from well-meaning friends. After we talked about Anne's treatment, he always wanted to know how *I* was doing. Mark visited often, and his emotional and physical warmth was no less helpful, though I worried that, in his joy at seeing Anne postsurgery (a new procedure that was more than a lumpectomy but less than a mastectomy), he'd hug her so hard that he'd dislodge her hundred-plus stitches. Ned kept in touch by e-mail from around the world, and merely thinking about the cataclysmic events he witnessed in his work helped me keep my problems in perspective. My three brothers were, I realized, not unlike the tag-team wrestlers of my old fantasy, each with his own strengths, each ready to step in and help out.

Eighteen years after Harry and I hid in his kitchen during the sixth game of the 1986 World Series, the Boston Red Sox played the New York Yankees for the American League pennant. The Sox lost the first three games, then stormed back to force a game seven. That night, there was near-constant phone contact between my house in western Massachusetts, Mark's house in eastern Massachusetts, and Harry's house in Maine, where Harry was watching with Dad. Even as the Sox took a big lead, we reminded each other not to get our hopes up, that there was still a lot of baseball to be played. (Nine-year-old Henry, wearing his Red Sox cap, crossing his fingers and making sure I crossed mine, didn't understand why, at crucial moments, I kept disappearing into the kitchen, unable to watch. "You've got to *believe*, Daddy," he'd say. "We can do it.") Even after it was 10–3 in the bottom of the ninth, I didn't dare relax. When Pokey Reese threw to first for the final out, Anne couldn't fathom why I wasn't jumping for joy; I was, of course, waiting for the umpire to announce that the game would have to be replayed because the Red Sox had won.

I called Mark. His phone was busy. I called Harry. His phone was busy, too. I learned later that they had been on the line with each other from the eighth inning on—and that, still later, Ned had called Harry and Dad from Malaysia to celebrate. The telephonic round robin would repeat itself a week later when the Red Sox won their first world championship since 1918.

A few years ago, when Ned was home for a visit, I asked him whether he ever thought about settling down. He shook his head. "I don't want to be someone whose main goal in life is mowing the lawn and waiting for the mail to arrive," he said. In 1992, two months after marrying the TV producer he'd met in Duluth, Ned and his wife headed to Eastern Europe, where Ned spent five years as a freelance radio and television reporter covering the breakup of the former Yugoslavia. The brother with whom I used to play Civil War was now risking sniper fire to cover a real civil war. One night, when my six-month-old son had croup and I was dozing on his bedroom floor in a haze of humidifier mist, with the NPR station on low, I was awakened by a familiar voice describing some new atrocity in the Balkans, against a background of crackling gunfire. ". . . This is Ned Colt reporting from Sarajevo," the voice concluded. The contrast between our lives seemed unreal. Yet Ned was still Ned. One day I got a letter in which he had enclosed a snapshot of a dingy-looking store over whose door a sign read "LOOTIES." The word was, Ned informed me, Slovenian for "crazy."

As the war came to an end, NBC offered Ned the job he'd always wanted: network foreign correspondent. Over the next dozen years, he lived in Hong Kong, Beijing, and London, covering wars, revolutions, and natural disasters in more than eighty countries. (In my address book, Ned's crossed-out entries take up six or seven times the space of those of his more sedentary brothers.) For much of that time we saw Ned only on our television screen, walking toward the camera in a tan shirt, khaki pants, and, often, a flak jacket, microphone in hand, face focused in an expression of concern as he detailed the latest international disaster against an ever-changing background: a bombed-out street in Afghanistan, a coastal settlement washed away by a tsunami in Sri Lanka, an earthquake-scarred village in Kashmir, a bullet-pocked city in Iraq. Over the years, the boy who worried he couldn't live up to his high-achieving older brothers has, in many ways, outstripped them. He is certainly the best-known of us. He has made (and spent) the most money. In childhood, Ned was often identified as Harry's or George's brother. Today Harry and I are proud to be known as Ned's brothers—though I was a little hurt when, at my twenty-fifth high school reunion, a faculty wife on whom I once had a crush draped herself over me until she realized I wasn't Ned.

The adolescent who worked hard to separate from his family now works hard to be part of it, faithfully calling our parents every Saturday, calling his brothers on every birthday (and after every crucial Red Sox game) whether he's in Baghdad or Borneo, sending postcards from so many different places that at one point my daughter had a not-too-shabby international stamp collection. Ned gets back for the holidays when he can; when he can't, we'll get a call on December 25 and hear him, ten thousand miles away, launch into his inimitable rendition of "I'm Dreaming of a Lean Christmas." Each summer, Ned organizes our family reunion on Cape Cod, arranging his vacation so he can drive Mum and Dad to the house and get them settled, often after having taken three flights for sixteen hours across eight time zones. Whenever Ned comes to the States, his luggage contains an international bazaar of gifts: shirts from Bali for his brothers, knockoff Cartier watches from Singapore for his nieces, rugby shirts from Hong Kong for his nephews. Ned is the least parsimonious of the brothers, whether saving business-class travel kits for his nieces or helping fund the college tuition of a young Afghan he met on assignment in Kabul. Ned sends mail-order delicacies on Dad's birthday, flowers on Mum's birthday and Valentine's Day. The mother and son who once fought so furiously have had an online Scrabble game going for years, Mum from her study in Massachusetts, Ned from his hotel room in Amman or Moscow or Jerusalem. Mum told me it used to seem as if their relationship always went back to the day she thrust Ned into a cold shower, but no longer. The last time she said good-bye to him, she told him that if something were to happen to her before they saw each other again, it was okay because she felt fully loved by him. Ned told her he felt the same.

Several years after his first marriage ended, in part because their jobs kept them away from each other so much, Ned met the woman who would become his second wife, a beautiful, well-read, tennis-and-Scrabble-playing TV producer who relishes adventure almost as much as he does. (They celebrated Ned's fiftieth birthday by swimming with great white sharks in South Africa, Cathy's fiftieth by swimming with whale sharks in the Philippines.) Although Ned doesn't have children, partly because he's been on the road most of his adult life, partly because he felt his own childhood was sufficiently difficult, he has been a virtuoso uncle, in some measure because he has remained a bit of a kid himself—dropping to his hands and knees to play with my daughter when she was a toddler, patiently answering my son's questions about the relative firepower of rocket launchers and bazookas when Henry was in his military hardware phase. When Henry's fourth-grade class was asked to write about their hero, Henry chose his uncle Ned, and was delighted when Ned declared his favorite subjects in school to have been Recess and Lunch. As one of Henry's godfathers, Ned is responsible for the provision of cool presents—Henry is surely the only one in his class with a T-shirt that reads "Fallujah Fire Rescue"—and spiritual guidance. "I lead by example," Ned tells Henry. "Whatever I do, you do the opposite." But Ned takes his charge seriously. When ten-year-old Henry was in tears over grounding out in a baseball game, Ned told him about the time in fourth grade he'd gotten so frustrated after striking out yet again that he had stood at home plate and sobbed, "I can't play . . . I can't play." When Henry was eight, Ned gave him a remote-controlled motorboat named, according to the box in which it came, the *Fast Lady*. We rowed out to the middle of a lake for her maiden voyage. Henry carefully placed her in the water, but no matter how he manipulated the joystick, the boat went in circles. The *Fast Lady*, it seemed, had a fatal design flaw even Ned couldn't fix. Henry's face fell. But Ned saved the day, launching into a verbal riff that made the *Fast Lady's* failure seem heroic: a maritime calamity on the scale of the *Titanic*, a historic disaster we'd been exceptionally privileged to witness.

The boy who never turned down a dare remains the most adventurous of us, the only one who has bungee-jumped, scuba-dived, played elephant polo, fired an AK-47, walked barefoot over hot coals, or owned a motor-cycle. When we go fishing, he's the one who gooses the throttle on the boat and takes the waves head-on; when we go hiking, he's the one who wants to bushwhack through the woods, catbrier be damned; when we go mountain biking, he's the one who invariably takes a jump too fast and ends up sailing over the handlebars. Age has begun to temper Ned's penchant for derring-do but not his stubbornness. Passing an electric cattle fence the last time we were in Cape Cod, Ned put a finger on the wire, just to see how strong the current was. (Very.)

It's not so much that Ned loves taking risks but that he's so inquisitive. The less-than-avid high school student is something of an autodidact—the most likely of us to look up a word in the dictionary, a butterfly in a field guide. (And yet when he went back to school at fifty-four, earning a master's degree in public administration from Harvard's Kennedy School of Government, the boy who hadn't gotten into Harvard thirty-five years earlier came within an A– of getting straight As.) Where once he shied away from family word games, he has become an expert crossword puzzler and a voracious reader, thanks in part to all those eighteen-hour plane flights. A few summers ago, we went hiking along a stream near my home. Ned was curious about everything: stepping into the woods to sniff a fern; wondering why one mountain laurel bush had bloomed while another remained entirely green; stopping to help a pudgy black caterpillar off the path and asking whether it would become a moth or a butterfly. While our wives sat on the bank, Ned and I waded out through the cold water and clambered onto a rock. As we talked about what kind of fish might be swimming past us, Ned picked up a stick that had gotten caught in the current and tossed it back in. "Let's see how far it gets downstream," he said.

Ned is the most sophisticated of the brothers. He knows where to find the best cannoli in Boston's North End, how to order unlisted house specialties in Chinese restaurants, what obscure microbrewed IPA we might like to try on our next get-together. On a recent family trip to Poland for our cousin Henry's wedding, Ned drove us all over the countryside, guided Dad's wheelchair over the dirt paths of Auschwitz and Birkenau, and tracked down obscure provincial restaurants where, using the pidgin Croat he'd picked up covering the war in the Balkans and more hand signals than a third-base coach, he managed to make a parade of local delicacies appear on our table. Ned is also the most practical—able to fix a leaky faucet, repair a window sash, build a shed. The boy who loved pushing Matchbox cars around the sandbox has taught himself to drive a tractor, operate a forklift, and run a woodchipper. At family reunions, he's the brother covered with poison ivy rashes and tick bites, tramping through the woods with a chain saw and a fully loaded workbelt, pulling down the tree-devouring bittersweet and nailing up bat houses.

Ned retains some of his youthful self-doubt. He says he gets especially anxious when he's working on deadline or ad-libbing on camera. To me, he seems remarkably cool under pressure. Several years ago, he and I were trolling in the bay when my line snagged on a lobster pot. A few tugs on the rod didn't free it, so I grabbed the line and yanked. The line slipped through my hand, whereupon I made the breathtakingly stupid mistake of wrapping it once around my hand and tugging harder. We were in a rip and, though the engine was off, we were drifting rapidly away from the lobster pot, the line tightening around my hand. Embarrassed—I was the alleged fisherman—I said nothing to my brother at the helm. The line gnawed into my skin, the flesh whitening around it. In a matter of seconds, the line was going to slice into my hand like a wire into cheese. I finally said something to Ned, who, taking in the situation at a glance, turned on the engine and slipped it into reverse. The line went slack. My hand was free. Cathy says that in a jam, she'd rather be with Ned than anyone.

People who know Ned only from TV say he seems rather serious—not surprising, given that he's usually talking about earthquakes and revolutions. But he's the funniest of us, the one who can make us laugh so hard we can't breathe, whether he's crooning the worst songs of the seventies ("Sky Pilot," "Billy Don't Be a Hero," "Delilah") as if they were Gershwin ballads; reading faux fortune cookies at Chinese restaurants ("You're a loser"); or playing Scattergories, a game in which contestants guess their teammates' answers to a particular category (Ned, to "Things I Keep in Suitcase," responds, without skipping a beat: "Inflatable Nude"). In his fifties, Ned is still a prankster: pinching swimmers' feet from below, making us laugh in church, then eyeing us sternly and hissing, "Please keep your voices down, this is a sacred space"; pretending to exchange his five-dollar bill for Mark's twenty as the collection plate goes by. At last year's Christmas Eve service, our octogenarian mother, in an attempt to forestall such mischief, insisted on sitting between Ned and his brothers, just as she did a half-century ago. On the tennis court, Ned, who has become something of a fanatic and now joins us for epic doubles matches in any fraternal permutation, is capable at any moment of bringing the game to a halt by breaking into the "Funky Butt," a celebratory dance that involves waving his fanny from side to side while bobbing his arms up and down like an epileptic stork.

Several years ago, Ned suggested to his brothers and several cousins that we join forces to build a kind of time-share vacation house on Cape Cod. Although Harry and Mark couldn't afford to be part of the group, Ned and I and two cousins went ahead. (Harry and Mark would contribute in other ways: poring over the blueprints, weed-whacking the site, donating coffee tables and kayaks.) Ned was an ideal leader, using the organizational and diplomatic skills he'd developed over two decades of reporting to ride herd on—and get along with—a battalion of carpenters, painters, masons, plumbers, and prickly conservation board members. Much of the time, Ned had to oversee the project from halfway around the globe. In Islamabad to report on the assassination of Benazir Bhutto, he arranged a conference call to discuss the placement of the bedroom windows on the architect's proposal. When construction began, the former Frank Lloyd Wright of Lincoln Logs came back to help dig trenches and hammer decking. The boy who was the most visibly unhappy of us as a child is the man most responsible for building a house to which we four brothers will be able to return year after year.

Of the four of us, Mark stayed closest to home. He has worked for twenty-five years at the school for the blind, where, as recycling coordinator, he instituted a prizewinning program. It is a physically demanding job, for which Mark is on his feet all day, collecting and sorting bottles, cans, and paper from each building on campus, then distributing packages and mail. Mark works with a focused intensity that enables him to get twice the work done in half the time. Co-workers tell him he can never quit because it would take three people to replace him. Mark, who has described himself as a blue-collar worker in a white-collar family, still enjoys physical labor. But he sometimes frets that he should have been more ambitious. He loves cooking and at one point spent a year attending culinary school at night with an eye toward becoming a chef. In the end, he stayed with recycling and moonlighted at a friend's barbeque restaurant. After all the upheaval in childhood, Mark is a creature of habit.

Mark hasn't gambled in twenty years, though he is the first to admit that what he calls his "addictive personality" has turned to less-destructive pursuits, like exercise, antiques shopping, and real estate browsing. His two-bedroom home outside Boston is furnished with captain's chests, mahogany tables, and Oriental rugs painstakingly chosen from the auction houses, crafts shows, and flea markets he frequents. His walls are hung with works by a handful of little-known twentieth-century New England artists he's come to admire. Many of them depict images of home: a farmhouse with a plume of smoke curling from its chimney; a front porch lined with wicker chairs; a slice of pie on a china plate. Mark's own home is snug and meticulous: shoes and sneakers aligned at the edge of the rug in the front hall; books in a glassed-in case in the living room; family photos angled on bureaus; towels crisply folded on their racks.

Mark may be the least competitive of the brothers. He wants to do well, but he wants everyone to do well. Golfing, he roots for his opponents to sink their putts even when his own aren't dropping. At auctions, he's more excited when a friend comes away with a find than when he does. Yet whether grilling a steak, bidding on a tiger maple nightstand, or running a marathon, Mark never does anything halfway. Several years back, he cut his foot swimming the first leg of a minitriathlon. Ignoring the pain, he completed the swim, biked ten miles, ran three, and finished a respectable fiftieth out of 250. When he took his sneaker off, his foot was a bloody mess. He ended up in the emergency room, where the doctor gave him five stitches and said he didn't understand how Mark had continued the race.

Commonly described as "the nicest guy I've ever met," Mark may be the most popular of the four brothers. He puts thousands of miles a year on his Pontiac Vibe visiting friends across the Northeast, hosts an annual summer reunion for his friends and their families on the Cape, and gets together with his college buddies for golf weekends in Florida and Vermont. If someone needs a ride to the airport or help lifting a couch, Mark is the first to volunteer. Each fall, he rakes the leaves for the elderly widow who lives next door; each winter he shovels her driveway. When Anne and I moved to Massachusetts, Mark helped us unload; when a half-cord of wood was dumped in our driveway after I hurt my back, Mark stacked it for us. Several years ago, a century-old Norway maple in our front yard was destroyed during a storm and had to be cut down, leaving a large bare spot on the lawn. When Anne and I returned from a vacation, we were amazed to find that Mark had driven out from Boston, graded the lawn, and planted grass seed.

Mark is especially attentive to our parents: driving Dad to the grocery store, helping Mum plant trees in the yard, escorting them to church on Sunday. The day after Dad's back operation, Mark brought a radio to the hospital and sat by his bed, listening to the Red Sox game with him. When Dad had cataract surgery while Mum was on a weeklong Buddhist retreat, Mark used his vacation time to move in with Dad, cook for him, clean for him, and administer his eyedrops four times a day. Several years ago on Cape Cod, the family was walking home through the woods when

I heard a crash. I ran ahead in time to see our father, bleeding from his chin, hobble away. "Be careful, Harry, why are you going so fast?" Mum called after him. As he disappeared down the path, Dad called over his shoulder, "I don't want anyone to see me like this except Mark." At the memorial service for Dad's sister Ellen, it was Mark who helped Dad up the steps to the lectern, where Dad read Psalm 121.

When Mark was younger, he had a series of attractive, accomplished girlfriends to whom he was devoted but whom, in the end, he didn't marry, wondering whether there might be someone even more perfect out there. He'd like to have a family but worries that the older he gets, the less he'll be able to change his ways. His mantel is lined with photos of his brothers' and friends' children. When Mark's nieces and nephews were younger, they knew him as the uncle who was always willing to play with them; now they know him as the uncle who will always listen when they need to talk to a grown-up who isn't their parent. Over the years, Mark and his godson Henry have spent hundreds of hours throwing frisbees, kicking soccer balls, and shooting baskets. Mark attends as many of Henry's games as he can; when he can't, he calls Henry afterward for a recap. Mark has even made the ultimate godfatherly sacrifice and taken Henry to our local amusement park, where the terror-stricken uncle closes his eyes, grits his teeth, and rides the Mind Eraser with his wide-eyed, exultant nephew beside him. Mark, who lacks a younger brother, and Henry, who lacks an older one, fill these roles for each other every time they play pool, race their bikes, or razz each other across the Ping-Pong net.

Several years ago, when Mark saw a mid-size black-and-tan mutt whimpering in a corner of a cage at his local animal shelter, he took the dog home and named her Carly. She had been found on the streets by rescue workers after a South Florida hurricane. I cannot help thinking that Mark, who had survived something of a storm himself, recognized a kindred spirit. (A bumper sticker on his car bears the silhouette of a paw and the words: "WHO RESCUED WHO?") He and Carly were soon inseparable. At work, she rides in his truck, head peering out the window, as he makes his rounds—she has quickly become a favorite among the blind children, who love to bury their faces in her thick fur. Carly still whimpers during thunderstorms and sleeps every night wedged under

Mark's bed, but under his care, she has become more confident. When Mark and I go hiking, Carly runs ahead to explore, but she looks back every so often to make sure her master is still there. And when Mark calls her name, she races toward him, bounding and leaping, performing arabesques of pure joy.

The brother who, because of his age, seemed the most peripheral member of our fraternal foursome growing up is in some ways the center of it. He's the one who knows all of his brothers' phone numbers by heart, and who calls often enough that we can discuss not only the big questions of life, love, and mortality, but also the state of our lawns, the previous night's Bruins game, or the nuances of preparing the perfect grilled cheese sandwich. He's the one who, by example, taught us to say "I love you" at the end of every phone call and to hug every time we say goodbye. Mark's hugs are Olympian clinches in which he squeezes for several seconds, as if, now that he's got us, there's no reason to let go.

Not long ago, I was in Dedham for a funeral. Before the service, I walked around our old neighborhood. The backyard where Dad used to throw the ball so high I thought it would never come down looked barely big enough for a sandbox. The garage from which Harry and I planned to run away was so small that the current owner had to park his SUV on the street. The chestnut tree on Chestnut Street was gone. The jail that once housed Sacco and Vanzetti now housed the retired parents of our boyhood friends in luxury condominiums that started at $600,000: $581,300 more than Mum and Dad paid for our old house in 1958. The jailfield had become part of someone's well-manicured backyard. But the swamp still looked invitingly forbidding, and the only change in the cemetery seemed to be the number of new gravestones.

I have known my wife for thirty years. I have known my closest friends for forty-five. I have known my brothers for almost sixty. We are the only witnesses to one another's rapidly receding pasts, a vanishing world whose giants are disappearing: Soupy Sales, Pumpsie Green, Gump Worsely, Floyd Patterson, Harmon Killebrew, Moe Howard, Haystack Calhoun, Gorilla Monsoon, Fess Parker, Y. A. Tittle, Captain Kangaroo,

Andy Robustelli, Joanie Weston, the Fabulous Moolah. A few years ago, after playing tennis with my brothers and me, a cousin said, "I think I'm beginning to understand your language." It is a language in which only four people are fluent.

In adolescence, as I struggled to carve out my own niche, I saw my brothers and me in terms of our differences. In middle age, I see how alike we are: our frugality, our gluttony, our work ethic, our sportsmanship, our Manichean notions of right and wrong, our love of the outdoors, our fear of being taken for suckers. After all the effort we spent trying to be different, I'm delighted when someone, seeing a photo of the four of us, remarks on how much we resemble one another; when a friend hears Ned's voice on TV and thinks it's me. The two years between Harry and me that once seemed an eternity now seem an instant, as do the six years between Ned and Mark—even if, when asked about my brothers, I reflexively describe them in descending order of birth. I sometimes think of the four of us as a living Venn diagram, each overlapping in various ways with the other three: Ned and Harry share a vigorous social conscience and a love of travel; Mark and I are homebodies who tend to live more cautiously; Harry and I are parents. And so on. Although I know it's not genetically possible, I sometimes feel as if I am composed of one part Harry, one part Ned, one part Mark, and one part myself. Even when I don't know exactly where my brothers are at a given moment, I feel connected to them as surely as if there were an artery—or at least an extra-long, extra-strong strand of drool—that ran from my heart to each of theirs.

* * *

On a Tuesday evening in late May of 2004, I arrived home to find Anne waiting for me at the door. She told me to come upstairs. She had something to tell me out of the children's hearing. Leading me into the guest room and shutting the door, she said, "Ned is alive and not injured." I knew immediately what came next—it was what we worried about whenever Ned was reporting from Iraq—but I couldn't bear to hear the words. I couldn't bear even to think them. Ned had been kidnapped.

I called the number at NBC that Cathy had given Anne and was put through to a man named David, a senior vice president for news. I identified myself as Ned's brother. "Ned has three brothers, right?" he said. I felt unaccountably pleased; Ned must have told him this. Now David passed along what he knew. Ned had arranged to interview Iraqi insurgents in Fallujah. En route, he, his cameraman, his sound man, and their Iraqi driver had been pulled over by two cars full of armed men, who blindfolded them and took them away at gunpoint. NBC was almost certain that the captors were local Iraqis, not al-Qaeda or one of the other militant Islamist groups responsible for the rash of recent suicide bombings and kidnappings. This was good news, relatively speaking. NBC had notified the commander of the U.S. forces at Camp Fallujah, but David urged us not to discuss the situation with anyone outside the family. The network didn't want it on the news lest it "stir things up." David said journalists in Iraq had been kidnapped before and released, unharmed, often the following morning. He didn't want to give us false hope, but everything led him to believe that things would turn out fine.

I called Harry. In some irrational way, I hoped that as the eldest brother, and as a doctor, he could somehow make things right. He couldn't, of course, but the steadiness of his voice was reassuring. It was too late to call Mark, who would be working an early shift the next day and had already turned off his phone and gone to bed, so I left a message on his work phone asking him to call me. After saying good-bye to nine-year-old Henry, who wanted to show me his new yo-yo tricks, and fourteen-year-old Susannah, who knew something was up but not what, I kissed Anne and drove, shivering uncontrollably, to my parents' house, where they were watching the Red Sox game. Mum put her head in her hands. Dad's face reddened and his eyes watered. They had been worried. They hadn't heard from Ned on Sunday, when he always called, and he hadn't been on TV for several days. "Now I know how my parents felt when I was missing," said Dad, who had been MIA behind enemy lines for six weeks during World War II. It was the first time I'd ever heard him bring up the subject on his own.

I stayed another few hours while we stared numbly at the baseball game. What none of us said but all of us were thinking was that anti-American sentiment in Iraq was especially high. It had been only two months since mobs in Fallujah had killed, mutilated, and burned four American security guards and hung two of their charred corpses from a bridge; one month since the Abu Ghraib prisoner abuse scandals, on which Ned had reported; two weeks since a young American business-man had been kidnapped and beheaded by Islamist militants.

That night I lay in bed, unable to sleep. After midnight, I went down-stairs and rummaged through the living room cabinet for a photo of Ned. The first one I came across was of the two of us wearing wetsuits, sticking our bellies out, mugging for the camera. Eventually I found an old shot of him nuzzling his four-month-old godson Henry. I propped it on my bedside table.

The following morning, a chilly, drizzly, late spring day, I returned to Mum and Dad's. Mark arrived at noon. I felt an infinitesimal bit better; being with one of my brothers brought me a step closer to Ned. Mark lit a candle and placed it on the windowsill. He said he would take time off work and stay with Mum and Dad as long as was necessary.

Over the next few days, we lived a strange, hermetic existence in the living room of the retirement home Mum and Dad had moved into the year before. There was nothing we could do but wait for the phone to ring. We wanted the phone to ring because it might be good news. We didn't want the phone to ring because it might be bad news. Whenever it rang, our hearts lurched. Sometimes it was a friend of Mum and Dad's. My parents, trying to sound normal, hung up as quickly and politely as pos-sible. It was usually David at NBC, keeping us posted. Ned and his crew had not been hooded or tied up, and they were being fed. Local sheikhs had vowed to secure their release. NBC had asked the media not to run the story lest it jeopardize negotiations. According to David, all the right people were saying all the right things.

Several times a day, we'd talk with the small circle of people who knew: Harry, Cathy, and Ned's friend Fritz, an NBC colleague who lived near Ned and Cathy in Hong Kong and had worked in Iraq. Occasion-ally, just to do something, Mark and Dad walked to the mailbox or drove to the supermarket for a half-gallon of milk. Mark and Mum made sandwiches, but no one ate much. I felt a constant queasy feeling in my stomach. To pass the time, we'd spend the afternoon watching one of

Mum's Zen-themed foreign films. Each evening, I'd go home to have dinner with Anne and the children, and the hour-long simulacrum of normal life—shooting baskets with Henry, asking Susannah about her algebra quiz—was strangely soothing. Afterward, I'd rush back to Mum and Dad's, where we'd talk and wait for the phone to ring. At ten, I'd go home again and try to sleep.

Each morning, I'd put on one of the NBC T-shirts Ned had given me. I'd drink a cup of Lapsang Souchong, the smoky tea Ned had introduced me to, from the Japanese mug Ned had given me with the 3-D carp on the side. Whenever our dog ran to greet me, I thought of how much Ned loves dogs and they love him; seeing Susannah read on the couch, I thought of how Ned, pretending to be a pinching lobster, used to chase her around the house when she was a toddler; playing Life with Henry, I thought of how Ned used to hide his Monopoly money behind his back, then produce it with a flourish at the last minute. One night, when Mark fell asleep on the couch, Dad said aloud what we both were thinking: there was only one person in the family with a louder snore. I reminded Dad that Ned always thoughtfully provided earplugs for anyone sharing a room with him on vacation.

When I thought of Ned, I couldn't stop seeing him at age five or so, in his robin's-egg-blue pajamas with the padded feet, his blond hair cut short, an impish grin on his face. I reminded myself that Ned was a forty-eight-year-old journalist who had been in dangerous situations before—though none, I knew, as dangerous as this. I pictured Ned and his colleagues sitting on the floor against the wall in a shabby two-room house. I tried not to let my imagination go any further. We agreed that what we wanted and prayed for most was that Ned not feel hopeless. Stray, sad images of Ned in despair—the time he wept in Central Park, the time he was immobilized with anxiety after moving to Duluth—floated through my mind. We worried that Ned might be singled out; that they'd let the others go, one by one, and Ned would be the only one left. I couldn't bear the thought of Ned being alone. We never talked about what could happen if things "didn't go well," as we put it, but we all knew what it would mean. Whenever my mind started to wander in that direction, I'd pray: *Please please let Ned and his crew come home safely. Please help him to be strong.* At times, driving in the car or walking around the house, I'd hear myself say aloud, like a petulant child, "I want my brother."

I craved contact with my other brothers. Spending each day with Mark, talking each night with Harry on the phone, was not only comforting in itself but the next best thing to being with Ned. Harry reminded us that if anyone would do well in this situation, it was Ned; even when we were kids, he had always been fearless. (Mark and I admitted that in the same position we'd probably crumble.) Ned was a risk taker, Harry said, but he always did the right thing in difficult spots. This encouraged us. But we also worried that Ned's stubbornness might get him into trouble.

On Thursday morning, the third day since Ned and his crew had been taken, David called. Negotiations were still under way; there would be another meeting that afternoon. The four men, they had been told, were being kept together, and were being treated humanely. David was hopeful that they might be released in a few days—maybe three, maybe four, maybe sooner. I couldn't help recalling that at first he'd been hopeful it would be over by morning, then it was a day or two, and now it was three or four. And I shook when, for the first time in our conversations, David used the word *hostage*. Dad said he feared that if the situation continued much longer, the marines might attempt a rescue, which would bring its own set of dangers.

At 2:42 on Thursday afternoon, while Mark was out biking and Dad was getting the Camry's oil changed, the phone rang. "Good news," said David. The captors had agreed to release Ned and his crew, although the "handover" wouldn't take place till morning—ten hours from now—because it would be too dangerous at night. David cautioned that it wouldn't be over till the marines had Ned and his crew safely in their hands.

Shortly after midnight, the phone rang. "It's all okay now," said Fritz. "It's over. Ned's safe." I called Mum and Dad and Mark. Cathy and David had already reached them. I called Harry. "Thank God," he said. At 1:30, Ned called Mum and Dad. It was just like Ned to spend most of the twenty-second call telling them how sorry he was to have put them through this.

Late Sunday evening, the phone rang. "*George-aay . . .*" said a familiar voice, saying my name the ridiculous way he—and only he—always does. "It's *Ned-aay* . . ."

When Ned flew home for a visit a week later, we would learn that the experience had been a little more harrowing than we'd known. Their original abductors had treated Ned and his colleagues relatively well. Although they had questioned them on videotape and accused them of being spies, they had given them tea, fed them from the best shish kebab stand in Fallujah (always serving them first, according to Muslim tradition), and even discussed politics and religion with them. They had made Ned and his crew wear the traditional white robes called *dishdashas* and not the orange jumpsuits that had taken on such sinister connotations since Abu Ghraib and the execution of the American businessman. But their relatively benevolent kidnappers had eventually passed them along to more-militant, less-accommodating mujahidin. Four times, Ned and his colleagues were hooded, surrounded by men with AK-47s cocked, and moved to a new location. Several times they were told they would soon be freed, but nothing happened. Ned and his team had no idea where they were or whether anyone even knew they'd been captured. They felt fortunate that they were kept together and that they were able to whisper to one another. They agreed they wouldn't try to escape or resist unless it was clear they were going to be killed. For comfort and support, they held hands. At night, they huddled next to one another and got what sleep they could. We had worried that Ned's instinct to fight back would get him killed. In fact, it sounded as if Ned had been admirably levelheaded: cautioning his fellow captives to be firm but not confrontational, squeezing the hand of a terrified younger colleague to give him strength, acting like an older brother.

On their last night in captivity, a new man came in to interrogate them, a high-ranking Saudi militant. He shouted that there must be no infidels in Iraq. He repeatedly threatened to behead them. "Are you ready to die?" he kept yelling. "You raped our wives and children—now who will weep for you?" Ned was frightened, but he challenged a few of the Saudi's remarks, deciding that if he was going to die anyway, he didn't want to die scared, begging for his life. After several hours of haranguing them, the Saudi left. At dawn, Ned and his colleagues were driven to the outskirts of town and released.

We wouldn't hear this till later, and then only in bits. Ned didn't like talking about it. He reminded us how insignificant his experience had been compared with what soldiers and civilians in Iraq endured every day. We realized how easily things could have turned out differently. On the day Ned was released, two Japanese journalists were killed when insurgents fired a rocket-propelled grenade at their car just south of Baghdad. Over the following three months, nearly one hundred foreigners would be abducted in Iraq. In 2004, twenty-three journalists would die covering the war.

The morning after Ned was released, Mark and I, in the car on our way to the supermarket, talked about how unreal the whole incident now seemed. Ned had been in captivity for four days and three nights, but it had felt like months. Cautiously, we began to discuss some of the fears we hadn't dared mention earlier. "I can't imagine ever being without one of my brothers," Mark finally said. "I can't imagine that we four brothers could ever be three."

*　　*　　*

For several years, my brothers and I, along with my son Henry, have gathered at Harry's house at the end of August for a long weekend of biking. Each day, we take a thirty-mile ride up and down the hills of central Maine. At night, we swim in the new pool, drink beer, eat a lot of vegetables from Harry's garden, and talk trash about the day's ride.

We don't race, but we pedal hard. In the early going, we breeze along in our five-man peloton, joking about Mark's new lime-green bike shorts or discussing such arcane topics as the subtle but vital distinction between *breaking the wind* and *breaking wind*. Gradually, we fan out. Ned, whose taxing work schedule allows him less time for exercise, tends to fall behind on the uphills—and then, just as we're wondering where he is, he'll zoom past us on the downhill in a comically exaggerated tuck position, head down, fanny up, like Lance Armstrong heading down the Col du Tourmalet in the Tour de France. Mark is a companionable rider, dropping back or speeding up to chat with a brother, gee-whizzing at the beauty of the countryside, keeping an eye out for antiques stores and yard sales. Eventually, he'll sail ahead with Henry, who, at fifteen, likes to push the pace. Harry may be the best biker of the brothers, but he takes it easy, making sure no one falls too far behind, calling out when cars approach, acting as a kind of fraternal shepherd, just as he did when we pedaled to elementary school five decades ago. When Ned tires, Harry slows down to keep him company; when we approach a farmhouse where a mean, bike-chasing mutt is known to reside, Harry, knowing I'm frightened of strange dogs, pulls up and rides between me and the house. I cruise along with Harry and Ned for awhile, but when Ned urges us ahead, I take off after Mark and Henry. I can't catch them, which I will later not-so-subtly hint is because my bike has fatter tires. But I keep charge of the map, which not only satisfies my need to feel important but ensures that no one can get very far ahead of me.

As always, our vacation goes too fast. Now, on the last afternoon, our quads are a little sore and our spirits a little dampened, knowing that tomorrow we will disperse in four directions. Mark and Henry, as usual, are in the lead, but as we head into the home stretch, they slow down a bit so Harry, Ned, and I can catch up. For a few miles, we ride together in the late-afternoon sun.

Then we turn onto Harry's road. As we approach the final hill, without saying a word, we pick up the pace. The only sound is the rhythmic chuff of our breathing and the click of shifting gears. Suddenly we're going all out, straining at the pedals, thigh muscles burning, rising from our saddles as we head up the hill. Fanning out across the road, we push hard, fighting to be first. Mark and Henry are a little ahead, but Harry and I are coming on strong and Ned is right behind us. I'm reminded of the opening of *Bonanza*, when the Cartwright brothers ride into view. For a brief moment we're all even. And then suddenly—panting, laughing—we all ease up at once and coast home.

Acknowledgments

Although any errors of fact, emphasis, or interpretation in this book are wholly my own, I have had a great deal of help in getting *Brothers* from my head to the printed page. I am grateful to the following institutions for making their resources available: the Concord Museum; the Forbes Library; the Charles Willard Memorial Library; the Enoch Pratt Free Library; the Booth Research Center of the Historical Society of Harford County; and the Bel Air branch of the Harford County Public Library. I am also indebted to the following people for their generous assistance: Mary Butler of Heritage Battle Creek; Juliette Johnson of the Center for Adventist Research at the James White Library, Andrews University; Garth "Duff" Stoltz, former director of Historic Adventist Village in Battle Creek; and Tiffany Hilton and Betsy Cook of the S. White Dickinson Memorial Library.

Thanks to my old *Life* magazine colleague Sasha Nyary for dogged last-minute research; to Rod Skinner for commenting on drafts of some of these chapters (and for his friendship); to Rob Farnsworth for the four-decades-and-counting conversation; to the Harvard Krokodiloes, my musical band of brothers, for glee and good humor; to Henry Singer for being the honorary fifth Colt brother; and to Mark Patrick O'Donnell for his fraternal example and for his companionship in the Forest of Arden.

For smoothing the way and enabling me to focus my attention on the sentences, I am indebted, once again, to Amanda Urban. For helping me to turn those sentences into this book, thanks to my literary SWAT team at Scribner: Christopher Lin, Mia Crowley-Hald, Carla Jones, Elisa Rivlin, John McGhee, and Kate Lloyd. Special thanks to Nathan Rostron for his judicious editing and to Daniel Burgess for his calm, careful shepherding. Above, all, thanks to Nan Graham for patiently waiting, enthusiastically supporting, and adroitly fine-tuning.

Thanks to my sisters-in-law, Sandy Bell Colt and Cathy Robinson, for not merely tolerating but encouraging Harry, Ned, Mark and me in our fraternal badinage. Thanks to my children, Susannah and Henry, for continuing to teach me what it means to be a sibling and for their example in going the distance whether in writing or running. A shout-out to Biscuit and Bean, guinea pig brothers who provide an ongoing example of how thin the line is between sibling rivalry and sibling love. Thanks to our dog, Typo, who spent much of the five years it took to write this book curled at my feet, perhaps dreaming of his canine brother, Fat Fred.

I am fortunate beyond measure that the best editor with whom I have ever worked happens to be my wife. Anne not only gave successive versions of *Brothers* the benefit of her unblinking editorial eye but unhesitatingly put her own work aside whenever I needed to parse some half-buried incident from my childhood or to share my excitement at a newly-unearthed detail about the Thoreaus' Concord Academy curriculum. I thank her for gracing this book with her attention and for blessing its author with her love.

When I was a child my parents taught my brothers and me to savor words by reading aloud to us. Half a century later they graciously allowed me to read aloud much of this manuscript to them. I will always remember our weekly sandwich-and-editing sessions. I am grateful for their helpful comments, for their willingness to answer questions about our family history, and, even more, for their forbearance, gentle guidance, and love. A few years ago, Mark and I were visiting Harry in Maine. We were discussing a childhood mishap when we suddenly found ourselves talking about how many of our core values we learned from our parents. "How to get through difficulties," Harry said. "The value of hard work," added Mark. "Loyalty," I said. The nouns kept coming: Honesty. Independence. Persistence. Forgiveness. For all these—and for giving me three brothers—I will never be able to thank them enough.

"Children born into the same family remember different things and the same things differently," observes Victoria Glendinning in her biography of Leonard Woolf. Harry, for instance, insists that because his birthday fell at the end of summer, he was never given birthday parties; I recall that precisely *because* his birthday fell at the end of the summer, Harry was given the most carefully planned and best-attended parties. I don't remember Ned chasing me with a knife around the kitchen table when he was twelve, though Ned insists that he did. These days, when a disputed memory surfaces, my brothers and I laugh, but each of us is, no doubt, secretly sure he is right. Although I spoke at length with all my brothers about the events described in this book, *Brothers* is my version of our shared story. My intent is not to define my brothers but to describe my own experience of our fraternal world.

For their generosity—and intestinal fortitude—in allowing me to share my version of our relationships, I owe Harry, Ned, and Mark an unpayable debt. (I'm told that when Ned was asked by someone why he had given his blessing to this book, Ned said, "He's my brother.") Their patience and understanding throughout this process have been remarkable. That they know me so well and continue to love me is a gift for which I will always be grateful.

Selected Bibliography

The biographical facts in *Brothers* are drawn from hundreds of books, essays, papers, journals, and newspaper articles. The following are those sources to which I am especially indebted.

CHAPTER TWO

THE BOOTHS

For the story of the Booths, I relied heavily on three books. *The Mad Booths of Maryland* by Stanley Kimmel, published in 1940, was the first book to treat Edwin and John in the context of their remarkable family, and the first to provide many details about the brothers' early years. Another family biography, less comprehensive but no less absorbing, to which I often turned, was *American Gothic* by Gene Smith. *American Brutus: John Wilkes Booth and the Lincoln Conspiracies* by Michael W. Kauffman, in my opinion the most nuanced and vivid biography of the younger Booth, furnished many essential details. I was also helped by *My Thoughts Be Bloody* by Nora Titone, which focuses on the rivalry between Edwin and John, and *Good Brother, Bad Brother: The Story of Edwin Booth & John Wilkes Booth* by James Cross Giblin, an illustrated biography aimed at younger readers.

Many of the stories I tell about John can be found in *The Unlocked Book: A Memoir of John Wilkes Booth by His Sister Asia Booth Clarke*, which is particularly valuable for its description of their shared childhood and adolescence. (I used a 1996 edition entitled *John Wilkes Booth: A Sister's Memoir*, edited by Terry Alford, which contains an informative biographical essay about Asia.) I was also helped by Asia Booth Clarke's *The Elder and the Younger Booth*, which offers an appreciation of the careers of Edwin and her father. Additional details about the Booth children's early years were drawn from *Sketches of Tudor Hall and the Booth Family* by Ella V. Mahoney, a sympathetic portrait published in 1925 by the woman who bought the Booth home in rural Maryland from Edwin and John's mother. "The House that Booth Built," by Kathryn Hopkins Kavanagh (*Harford Historical Bulletin*, no. 71, Winter 1997), was also of assistance. I am indebted to *Junius Brutus Booth: Theatrical Prometheus* by Stephen M. Archer for several anecdotes about the Booth paterfamilias, and for details on the nineteenth-century theatrical scene.

Many of John Wilkes Booth's letters were destroyed by their recipients in the days following the assassination, when any link to the assassin put one in peril. Those that survived can be found in *Right or Wrong, God Judge Me*, a compilation of Booth's extant writings (letters, diary entries, love poems) edited and annotated by John Rhodehamel and Louise Taper, who also wrote the useful biographical introduction.

For information about John's performances I turned to *Lust for Fame: The Stage Career of John Wilkes Booth*, in which Gordon Samples quotes from or reproduces a trove of reviews, playbills, billboards, and assessments from Booth's fellow actors. Short biographical essays offer context on each segment of John's meteoric rise. In *Yesterdays with Actors*, Kate Reignolds Winslow recalled her theatrical experiences with John ("this sad-faced, handsome, passionate boy"), including the revelation that he occasionally slept covered in oysters. In *Life on the Stage*, her 1901 memoir, actress Clara Morris reminisced about both Edwin and John.

For details on the assassination's aftermath, I am indebted primarily to Michael W. Kauffman's *American Brutus*, but also to *Blood on the Moon: The Assassination of Abraham Lincoln* by Edward Steers Jr.; *John Wilkes Booth: Fact and Fiction of Lincoln's Assassination* by Francis Wilson (Booth's first biographer); *The Life, Crime, and Capture of John Wilkes Booth*, a collection of contemporaneous dispatches by George Alfred Townsend, a reporter for the *New York World*; and *Manhunt: The 12-Day Chase for Lincoln's Killer* by James L. Swanson. (Swanson, along with Daniel R. Weinberg, has also assembled and edited *Lincoln's Assassins: Their Trial and Execution*, a haunting volume of photographs.) For additional information on Booth's post-assassination flight, I made use of the eyewitness testimony of Major M. B. Ruggles, a Confederate officer who encountered Booth and Herold during their failed escape, and Captain Edward P. Doherty, who commanded the 16th New York Cavalry detachment that captured the fugitives. (Interviews with Ruggles and Doherty were conducted by Prentiss Ingraham, a former schoolmate of Booth's, and published as "Pursuit and Death of John Wilkes Booth" in *The Century* magazine, January 1890.) Thomas Jones remarked upon the fleeing Booth's beauty in his 1893 book *J. Wilkes Booth: An Account of His Sojourn in Southern Maryland After the Assassination of Abraham Lincoln, His Passage Across the Potomac and His Death in Virginia.* For you-are-there immediacy, I recommend *The Assassination of President Lincoln and the Trial of the Conspirators,* a facsimile transcript of the trial, compiled and arranged by Benn Pitman and published in 1865. My account of the Confederate attempt to burn down Manhattan on the night the Booth brothers performed *Julius Caesar* is drawn from "The Plot: Full and Minute Particulars, How the Plan Was Conceived, How Its Execution Failed" (*New York Times,* November 27, 1864). The program boy's memories are taken from "This Man Saw Lincoln Shot" by Campbell MacCulloch (*Good Housekeeping,* February 1927).

For details on the life of Edwin Booth, I also consulted *The Last Tragedian* by the actor Otis Skinner, which includes a selection of Booth's correspondence; *Darling of Misfortune,* an early biography by Richard Lockridge (published in 1932); and *Prince of Players* by Eleanor Ruggles. *Life and Art of Edwin Booth,* a tribute to the actor written by his friend, *New York Tribune* theater critic William Winter, and published not long after Booth's death, furnished particulars about the actor's post-1865 career. *Behind the Scenes with Edwin Booth* by Katherine Goodale, a young actress who was part of Edwin's touring company, paints a sympathetic portrait of Booth and of theatrical life in the late nineteenth century. In 1886, a young actor named Edwin Milton Royle toured with Edwin and remembered enough forty-seven years later to write *Edwin Booth As I Knew Him,* including the observation that Booth suffered stage fright everywhere but on the stage. Further material on Edwin's activities during his post-assassination years was culled from "Memories and Letters of Edwin Booth," an account written by his friend William Bispham and published in *The Century* (November and December 1893), as well as from *Edwin Booth: Recollections by His Daughter Edwina Booth Grossman and Letters to Her and to His Friends. Crowding Memories* by Mrs. Thomas Bailey Aldrich, whose husband was a close friend of Edwin's, offers a poignant account of Edwin during the months after the assassination.

SIBLING DIFFERENCE (pp. 29–31)

An excellent introduction to sibling difference and the nonshared environment can be found in *Separate Lives: Why Siblings Are So Different* by Judy Dunn and Robert Plomin, two of the most prominent researchers in the field. See also "Why Are Siblings So Different? The Significance of Differences in Sibling Experiences Within the Family" by Judy Dunn and Robert Plomin (*Family Process*, vol. 30, September 1991), and *Separate Social Worlds of Siblings: The Impact of Nonshared Environment on Development* (edited by E. Mavis Hetherington, David Reiss, and Robert Plomin). Sandra Scarr's provocative quote can be found in an essay she coauthored with Susan Grajek, "Similarities and Differences Among Siblings," and published in *Sibling Relationships: Their Nature and Significance Across the Lifespan*, an early (1981) and influential collection of essays edited by Michael E. Lamb and Brian Sutton-Smith. "Each Sibling Experiences Different Family" by Daniel Goleman (*New York Times*, July 28, 1987) summarizes the research on sibling "micro-environments."

My brief description of the Melville brothers was derived from my reading of *Melville* by Andrew Delbanco; that of the Brown brothers from *Sons of Providence* by Charles Rappleye; that of the Newton brothers from *Revolutionary Suicide* by Huey P. Newton; that of the Capone brothers from *Capone* by Laurence Bergreen.

FAVORITISM (pp. 40–46)

For an overview on the experience of favoritism, I recommend Chapter 7, "The Chosen," in Francine Klagsbrun's *Mixed Feelings: Love, Hate, Rivalry, and Reconciliation Among Brothers and Sisters*; Chapter 8, "Siblings in Conflict: Bonds of Aggression and Rivalry," in Stephen P. Bank and Michael D. Kahn's *The Sibling Bond*; and Chapter 5, "The Golden Child," in Jeffrey Kluger's *The Sibling Effect: What the Bonds Among Brothers and Sisters Reveal About Us*.

My account of the Waughs relies almost entirely on *Fathers and Sons*, a fascinating (and occasionally frightening) family history written by Evelyn's grandson Alexander Waugh. I also made use of *A Little Learning* by Evelyn Waugh, an account of the author's early years; *My Brother Evelyn and Other Portraits* by Alec Waugh; *The Early Years of Alec Waugh*, Alec's chatty, agreeable take on his youth; and *The Best Wine Last*, Alec's breezy summary of his peripatetic adulthood. Louisa Whitman's note to her children can be found in Chapter 16 of Justin Kaplan's *Walt Whitman: A Life*. Favoritism in the Cheever household is discussed in *John Cheever* by Scott Donaldson, and in *Cheever: A Life* by Blake Bailey. The story of the Cheever brothers may be told most revealingly by Cheever himself, in *The Journals of John Cheever* (edited by Robert Gottlieb) and *The Letters of John Cheever* (edited by Benjamin Cheever).

Helen Koch's 1950s study and the Colorado study of favoritism are described in *Separate Lives* by Judy Dunn and Robert Plomin. Katherine Conger's study is mentioned in *The Sibling Effect* by Jeffrey Kluger. The study of thirty elderly mothers was outlined in a press release from Cornell University "Science News," November 20, 1997. Stephen Bank's quote can be found in his essay "Favoritism" in *Practical Concerns About Siblings: Bridging the Research-Practice Gap*, a collection of essays edited by Frances Fuchs Schachter and Richard K. Stone. Schachter's work on "split-parent identification" is described in her essay "Sibling Deidentification and Split-Parent Identification: A Family Tetrad," in *Sibling Relationships*, edited by Michael E. Lamb and Brian Sutton-Smith. Favoritism in the Freud household is discussed in Chapter 8 of *The Sibling Bond* by Stephen P. Bank and Michael D. Kahn. Freud's quote on being the favored child can be found in *The Life and Work of Sigmund Freud* (edited by Ernest Jones) vol. I, p. 5. The Mussolini nursing story is told in the second chapter of *Mussolini*, a biography by R. J. B. Bosworth. Alfred Adler makes the sibling/tree analogy in "Family Influences," Chapter 6 of his book *What Life Should Mean to You*. That both the preferred and nonpreferred child in a family may suffer is the conclusion of "Perceived Parental Favoritism and Suicidal Ideation in Hong Kong Adolescents" (lead author Anton F. De Man), published in *Social Behavior and Personality*, vol. 31, no. 3, 2003.

BIRTH ORDER (pp. 54–67)

Some maintain that birth-order research holds the key to understanding sibling difference. Others insist that it is no more scientific than astrology. The man generally acknowledged to be the first to study—if only in passing—this controversial subject is described in *A Life of Sir Francis Galton* by Nicholas Wright Gillham. Galton's investigation into the effect of birth order on intelligence forms a small part of his book *English Men of Science: Their Nature and Nurture*. Published in 1895, *Primogeniture: A Short History of Its Development in Various Countries and Its Practical Effects* by Evelyn Cecil offers a fascinating early survey of this institutional form of favoritism. Darwin's opinion of primogeniture is quoted by Frank J. Sulloway in Chapter 2 of *Born to Rebel*; the 1974 survey of thirty-nine non-Western societies is mentioned in Chapter 3 of that same book. Although not discussed in this book, *The Pecking Order: Which Siblings Succeed and Why,* by Dalton Conley, offers an interesting analysis of factors that affect sibling fortunes.

Alfred Adler's ideas on birth order can be found in "How Position in Family Constellation Influences Life-Style" (Chapter 25) from volume 7 of *The Collected Clinical Works of Alfred Adler,* and from Chapter 6, "Family Influences" in Adler's *What Life Should Mean to You.* Biographical details are drawn from *The Drive for Self: Alfred Adler and the Founding of Individual Psychology* by Edward Hoffman. The Norwegian IQ study is described in "Research Finds Firstborns Gain the Higher I.Q." by Benedict Carey (*New York Times,* June 22, 2007).

John Adams's warning to his firstborn can be found in Book 1, Chapter 3 of Paul C. Nagel's biography *John Quincy Adams.* Joe Kennedy Jr.'s explanation of an eldest son's responsibilities can be found in Part 1, Chapter 4 of *The Kennedys: An American Drama* by Peter Collier and David Horowitz. The Prince of Wales's advice to the future King George III is taken from the first chapter of *A Royal Affair: George III and His Scandalous Siblings* by Stella Tillyard. James Baldwin's observation on his fraternal duties is taken from the first paragraph of his essay "Autobiographical Notes" in *Notes of a Native Son.* Benjamin Spock's complicated relationship with his siblings is explored in *Dr. Spock: An American Life* by Thomas Maier. The Housman family solar system is charted by Laurence Housman in the first section of his memoir, *My Brother, A. E. Housman.* The story of the Wolff brothers' summer is told by Geoffrey Wolff in "Advice My Brother Never Took" (*New York Times,* August 20, 1989). Each Wolff tells his side of the tale (Geoffrey in "Heavy Lifting" and Tobias in "A Brother's Story") in *Brothers: 26 Stories of Love and Rivalry,* a collection of essays edited by Andrew Blauner. E. B. White's description of his brother's pedagogical gifts is taken from the autobiographical essay that introduces *Letters of E. B. White* (edited by Dorothy Lobrano Guth). Henry Kissinger's letter to his younger brother is quoted in *Kissinger* by Walter Isaacson (Chapter 3). Ben Franklin's account of working for his heavy-handed older brother is taken from his *Autobiography.* Anthony Trollope describes his older brother disciplining him in his *Autobiography.* The Saint-Exupéry brothers' story is from *Saint-Exupéry* by Stacy Schiff. Sam Houston Johnson details the bicycle-buying incident in *My Brother Lyndon.*

Henry James's description of William's sixteen-month head start can be found in his memoir *A Small Boy and Others.* Rupert Everett's boarding-school nickname was mentioned in "Rupert Everett Is Not Having a Midlife Crisis" by Alex Witchel (*New York Times Magazine,* February 22, 2009). Frank Sulloway tells the story of the Cuvier brothers in Chapter 2 of *Born to Rebel.* The quote about John F. Kennedy's freedom to determine his own path can be found in Part 1, Chapter 5 of *The Kennedys* by Peter Collier and David Horowitz. Arthur Miller enthuses abut his escape from orthodontic purgatory in the first chapter of his autobiography, *Timebends*. Richard Ben Cramer tells the story of the DiMaggio brothers in *Joe DiMaggio: The Hero's Life*. The friend who described the young Bobby Kennedy is quoted in Part 2, Chapter 3 of Collier and Horowitz's *The Kennedys*.

Edward M. Kennedy writes of the mellowing effect he had on his father in Chapter 3 of his memoir *True Compass*. The Alice James quote about dwindling parental attention can be found in Jean Strouse's *Alice James*. My brief portrait of Wilky and Bob James is derived from *House of Wits: An Intimate Portrait of the James Family* by Paul Fisher and *Henry James: The Imagination of Genius* by Fred Kaplan.

The Lukas fraternal dramas are described in *Blue Genes*, Christopher Lukas's memoir about his brother. Muslim honor killings are discussed in "The New Berlin Wall" by Peter Schneider (*New York Times Magazine*, December 4, 2005). The analysis of fairy tales by the Brothers Grimm is summarized in the first chapter of *The Sibling* by Brian Sutton-Smith and B. G. Rosenberg.

Philip Roth writes about his father's bequest in Chapter 3 of his memoir, *Patrimony*. Leonard Nimoy's quote about being a second child was taken from "Leonard Nimoy at the Controls," by Aljean Harmetz (*New York Times*, October 30, 1988). Henry James's reaction to his older brother's death is described in Chapter 18 of *The Jameses* by R. W. B. Lewis.

SIBLING NICHES (pp. 67–71)

Frances Schachter's work on deidentification is outlined in her essay "Sibling Deidentification and Split-Parent Identification: A Family Tetrad" in *Sibling Relationships*, edited by Michael E. Lamb and Brian Sutton-Smith. Details about the Kennedy brothers at Choate can be found in *The Fitzgeralds and the Kennedys: An American Saga* by Doris Kearns Goodwin; John's therapy is described by Nigel Hamilton in *JFK: Reckless Youth*. The Wideman brothers' story is told by John Edgar Wideman in *Brothers & Keepers*. That it is an example of sibling deidentification was pointed out by David C. Rowe and Patricia Elam in "Siblings and Mental Illness: Heredity vs. Environment" in *Practical Concerns About Siblings*, edited by Schacter and Stone. For more on the Shackletons, see *Shackleton* by Roland Huntford.

Frank J. Sulloway's work on birth order and creativity is the subject of his book *Born to Rebel*, which also provides a wealth of fascinating sibling stories. Sulloway was profiled in "The Birth of an Idea" by Robert S. Boynton (*The New Yorker*, October 7, 1999).

The Plutarch quote advising brothers against working in the same field can be found in *De Fraterno Amore*. The story of the Hunt brothers is taken largely from *The Greater Journey* by David McCullough. Ezekiel Emanuel's observation about fraternal geographic distribution is from "The Gatekeeper," a profile of Rahm Emanuel by Ryan Lizza (*The New Yorker*, March 2, 2009). My description of the Emanuels also draws from "The Brothers Emanuel" by Elisabeth Bumiller (*New York Times*, June 15, 1997), and "Hug It Out" by Lauren Collins (*The New Yorker*, May 25, 2009).

CHANCE (pp. 74–78)

Francis Galton discussed the role of chance in Chapter 3 of his book *Natural Inheritance*. The young Charles Dickens's reaction to his father's incarceration is described by Peter Ackroyd in Chapter 3 of *Dickens*. The saga of the Adams family is taken primarily from Paul C. Nagel's *John Quincy Adams*; also from David McCullough's *John Adams*. For details on the Roosevelt brothers, see *The Rise of Theodore Roosevelt* by Edmund Morris and *Mornings on Horseback* by David McCullough. The relationship between Prescott Bush Jr. and his younger brother George is explored in *The Bush Tragedy* by Jacob Weisberg and in *The Bushes: Portrait of a Dynasty* by Peter Schweizer and Rochelle Schweizer. J. R. Ackerley writes of his brother's death in *My Father and Myself*; the story is also told in Peter Parker's biography *Ackerley*. My description of Erasmus and Charles Darwin relies chiefly on *Darwin* by Adrian Desmond and James Moore, *The Survival of Charles Darwin* by Ronald W. Clark, and *The Autobiography of Charles Darwin*.

CHAPTER FOUR

THE KELLOGGS

Like everyone who has written about the Kelloggs, I am enormously indebted to Richard W. Schwarz, who turned his doctoral dissertation into an indispensable biography, *John Harvey Kellogg, M.D.*, and to Horace B. Powell, author of *The Original Has This Signature—W. K. Kellogg*. Both are troves of information from which I borrowed heavily. I also relied on *Cornflake Crusade*, Gerald Carson's witty account of the search for the perfect breakfast cereal, and *The New Nuts Among the Berries*, Ronald M. Deutsch's entertaining and enlightening history of food faddists. My portrait of the Kelloggs was enhanced by my reading of *Tales of Battle Creek*, a collection of articles gathered by Berenice Bryant Lowe; *Cerealizing America* by Scott Bruce and Bill Crawford; *Kellogg's Six-Hour Day* by Benjamin Kline Hunnicutt; and *The Battle Creek Sanitarium System: History, Organization, Methods* by J. H. Kellogg. I have also drawn on the collection of unpublished letters by John Harvey Kellogg, Will Kellogg, and their colleagues, at the Center for Adventist Research at the James White Library, Andrews University. For literary dessert, I devoured *The Road to Wellville*, T. Coraghessan Boyle's uproarious fictional take on J. H. Kellogg, the San, and the cereal wars.

RIVALRY (pp. 108–110)

For biographical details on Freud, I turned to Peter Gay's *Freud: A Life for Our Time*. Freud's quote on sibling rivalry can be found in Lecture XIII of *Introductory Lectures on Psychoanalysis*. David Levy's research is described in "Rivalry Between Children in the Same Family," by David M. Levy, *Child Study*, May 1934 (pp. 233–37); and in *Studies in Sibling Rivalry* by David M. Levy (published by the American Orthopsychiatric Association, 1937). I came across Peter Neubauer's quote in the prologue of *Mixed Feelings* by Francine Klagsbrun. The University of Illinois research on the frequency of sibling quarrels is summarized in Chapter 3 of *The Sibling Effect* by Jeffrey Kluger.

RIVALRY: BEGINNINGS (pp. 114–117)

Anna Quindlen told the story about her sons' rivalry in her "Life in the 30's" column (*New York Times*, November 5, 1986). How Robie H. Harris was inspired to write *Mail Harry to the Moon!* is described in "Take My Brother, Please" by Sarah Ellis (*New York Times Book Review*, May 11, 2008). The tale of the Housman siblings quarreling over clouds can be found in the first chapter of *A. E. Housman* by Richard Perceval Graves. Adler recounted the story of the four-year-old who wanted to be as old as his older brother in "How Position in the Family Constellation Influences Life-Style" from volume 7 of *The Collected Clinical Works of Alfred Adler*. The Coleridge brothers' battle over cheese is described in the first chapter of *Coleridge: Early Visions, 1772–1804* by Richard Holmes; the Joyce brothers' battle over the last pancake is from Part 1, Chapter 4 of *James Joyce* by Richard Ellmann; the beggar brothers' battle over bread is from the essay "Cake" in Baudelaire's *Paris Spleen*.

Sibling rivalry in the Eisenhower household is detailed in the first chapter of *Eisenhower: Soldier and President*, the one-volume version of Stephen E. Ambrose's biography. Sibling rivalry saturates every Kennedy biography; I am particularly grateful to *The Fitzgeralds and the Kennedys* by Doris Kearns Goodwin; *The Kennedys at War* by Edward J. Renehan Jr.; *JFK* by Nigel Hamilton (in which Rose Kennedy's quote can be found in Part 2 and the story of JFK's nautical interference on his brother's behalf in Part 4); and *The Kennedys* by Peter Collier and David Horowitz (in which Joe Kennedy Sr.'s quote on winners and losers and a description of the ill-fated bike race can be found, Part 1, Chapter 4).

RIVALRY: THE LATER YEARS (pp. 125–128)

The Clark brothers feud is thoroughly described in Nicholas Fox Weber's *The Clarks of Cooperstown*, as well as in *The Clark Brothers Collect: Impressionist and Early Modern Paintings* by Michael Conforti, James A. Ganz, Neil Harris, Sarah Lees, and Gilbert T. Vincent. Plutarch cites the Charicles and Antiochus squabble in *De Fraterno Amore*. Robert Caro tells the story of Paul and Robert Moses in "Two Brothers," Chapter 26 of *The Power Broker*, his epic biography of Robert Moses. The benign estrangement of Ralph and Herbert Ellison is detailed in *Ralph Ellison* by Arnold Rampersad.

RIVALRY: BENEFITS (pp. 133–139)

Sources for my discussion of sibling conflict in the animal kingdom include: "Early Sibling Rivalry Among Spotted Hyenas" (*New York Times*, May 7, 1991); "Within Nests, Egret Chicks Are Natural Born Killers" by Carol Kaesuk Yoon (*New York Times*, August 6, 1996); "Savage Siblings" by Maria L. Chang (*Science World*, January 10, 1997); and "The Mark of Cain" by Nora Steiner Mealy (*California Wild: The Magazine of the California Academy of Sciences*, Winter 2002). My description of the tension between George and Jeb Bush was gleaned from *The Bushes: Portrait of a Dynasty* by Peter Schweizer and Rochelle Schweizer; *The Family: The Real Story of the Bush Dynasty* by Kitty Kelley; and *The Bush Tragedy* by Jacob Weisberg (in which the story of George W.'s election-night phone call with his father can be found).

John Ed Bradley described the Guy brothers' punting wars in "Hang 'em High" (*Sports Illustrated*, December 21, 2009). Information on the Sutters is from "A Team Unto Itself," by E. M. Swift (*Sports Illustrated*, October 13, 1980) and from *Six Shooters: Hockey's Sutter Brothers* by Dean Spiros. I learned about the

Spinks brothers from "Leon Spinks in Search of Himself and Title" by Michael Katz (*New York Times*, June 8, 1981) and "The Iron Ball and the Bible" by Pat Putnam (*Sports Illustrated*, March 13, 1978). For details on the Quarry brothers, I am grateful to "Staying in the Ring," by Jonathan Mahler (*New York Times Magazine*, December 31, 2006) and to *Hard Luck: The Triumph and Tragedy of "Irish" Jerry Quarry* by Steve Springer and Blake Chavez. (Although I do not cite it in this book, I recommend *Blood Over Water* by David and James Livingston, a candid account of sibling rivalry written by brothers who rowed against each other in the Oxford-Cambridge boat race.)

The faux rivalry between Houdini and Hardeen is recalled in Chapter 5 of *Houdini!!!* by Kenneth Silverman. I learned about their relationship from *The Secret Life of Houdini* by William Kalush and Larry Sloman and *The Life and Many Deaths of Harry Houdini* by Ruth Brandon. For the story of the Dasslers I am entirely indebted to *Sneaker Wars* by Barbara Smit. The Malkovichs' rivalry was examined in "Being Any Number of Versions of the Self He Has Invented," by Lynn Hirschberg (*New York Times Magazine*, April 27, 2003). The story of the Bellow brothers is well told in *Bellow* by James Atlas.

RIVALRY: VIOLENCE, FRATRICIDE, ESTRANGEMENT (pp. 146–151)
The UNH study of sibling violence, "Kid's Stuff: The Nature and Impact of Peer and Sibling Violence on Younger and Older Children," by David Finkelhor, Heather Turner, and Richard Ormrod, was published in *Child Abuse & Neglect*, vol. 30, 2006 (pp. 1401–21). The study was summarized in "Beyond Rivalry, a Hidden World of Sibling Violence," by Katy Butler (*New York Times*, February 28, 2006). The Steinbeck brothers' "primal tug of war" pervades the pages of Nancy Steinbeck's *The Other Side of Eden* (co-written with her husband, John Steinbeck IV). I also benefited from reading *The True Adventures of John Steinbeck, Writer* by Jackson J. Benson, and *Journal of a Novel*, a collection of Steinbeck letters to his editor during the writing of *East of Eden*. For the story of John and Fred Cheever, I relied on Blake Bailey's *Cheever: A Life*, as well as on Scott Donaldson's *John Cheever*, and on two Susan Cheever memoirs, *Home Before Dark* and *Treetops*. *The Journals of John Cheever* and *The Letters of John Cheever* provided further illumination.

My description of the Freud brothers' feud is derived from "Sir Clement Freud and Brother Lucian Freud in Feud as Latter Rejects Knighthood," by Richard Eden (*The Telegraph*, June 28, 2008); "I Am the Forgotten Freud, Says Brother of Sir Clement Freud and Lucian Freud," by Adam Lusher (*The Telegraph*, July 12,

2008); and "Clement Freud Died Without Resolving Feud with His Brother Lucian," by Anita Singh (*The Telegraph*, April 17, 2009). For the Mann brothers' story, I am indebted to Nigel Hamilton's dual biography, *The Brothers Mann*, as well as his essay "A Case of Literary Fratricide: The Brüderzwist Between Heinrich and Thomas Mann," in *Blood Brothers: Siblings as Writers*, a fascinating collection of essays on well-known sibling literary pairs edited by Norman Kiell. I was also helped by *Letters of Heinrich and Thomas Mann, 1900–1949*, edited by Hans Wysling.

Coleridge's observation on his brother's mercurial nature is from the first chapter of *Coleridge: Early Visions, 1772–1804* by Richard Holmes. Alice James's letter about her brother-in-law's death is quoted in the last chapter of *Henry James* by Fred Kaplan.

CHAPTER SIX

THE VAN GOGHS

Wanting to let Vincent and Theo speak for themselves as much as possible, I have relied heavily on the incomparable letters, as published in *The Complete Letters of Vincent van Gogh*. The three-volume Bulfinch Press edition contains Johanna van Gogh-Bonger's biographical sketch of the brothers, among other invaluable supplementary documents. Where I felt the Bulfinch translation was unnecessarily opaque, I have substituted translations from other sources, chiefly *The Letters of Vincent Van Gogh*, translated by Arnold Pomerans, selected and edited by Ronald de Leeuw.

For biographical details I relied mainly on *Vincent van Gogh* by Marc Edo Tralbaut and on *Vincent and Theo van Gogh: A Dual Biography* by Jan Hulsker. For the relationship between Theo and Jo Bonger, I drew from *Brief Happiness: The Correspondence of Theo van Gogh and Jo Bonger*, which has a helpful introduction and commentary by Han van Crimpen. Other books on Van Gogh from which I benefited include Steven Naifeh and Gregory White Smith's monumental *Van Gogh: The Life* (nearly nine hundred pages of text and some five thousand pages of online notes); *The World of van Gogh, 1853–1890* by Robert Wallace; *Vincent van Gogh: A Life* by Philip Callow; *Van Gogh: His Life & His Art* by David Sweetman; *Stranger on the Earth*, a provocative psychological biography by Albert J. Lubin; *The Yellow House: Van Gogh, Gauguin, and Nine Turbulent Weeks in Provence* by Martin Gayford; and *Van Gogh: A Study of His Life and Work* by Frank Elgar. John

Rewald's essay "Theo van Gogh as Art Dealer," from his book *Studies in Post-Impressionism,* was very helpful. So, too, was *Personal Recollections of Vincent van Gogh* by Elizabeth du Quesne van Gogh, in which the sister who scorned him offers an intimate look at the artist's early life. For inspiration but not information, I read *Lust for Life,* Irving Stone's melodramatic fictional take on Van Gogh, as well as Stone's *Dear Theo: The Autobiography of Vincent van Gogh.*

Some of the most detailed and perceptive writing about the Van Goghs can be found in exhibition catalogues and books. I am especially indebted to *Van Gogh and Gauguin: The Studio of the South,* an examination of the life, work, and mutual influence of the painters during their two months in Arles, by Douglas W. Druick and Peter Kort Zegers, and to *Theo van Gogh: Art Dealer, Collector and Brother of Vincent* by Chris Stolwijk and Richard Thomson, which contains informative essays on the life and career of the lesser-known van Gogh. The lavishly illustrated Taschen *Van Gogh* by Rainer Metzger and Ingo F. Walther provided visual stimulation.

BROTHER'S KEEPERS (pp. 193–194)

The story of John Keats nursing his dying brother is told by Robert Gittings in *John Keats.* Mathieu Dreyfus's struggle to free his brother is detailed in *Dreyfus: A Family Affair* by Michael Burns. I found the story of Michael and Brendan Marrocco in "Spirit Intact, Soldier Reclaims His Life" by Lizette Alvarez (*New York Times,* July 2, 2010); Ronald Herrick's kidney donation was described in the Associated Press obituary dated December 30, 2010. The Muir biting incident is taken from the first chapter of *The Story of My Boyhood and Youth* by John Muir. Booker T. Washington tells of his deliverance from flax-shirt agony in the first chapter of his autobiography, *Up From Slavery.*

BROTHER'S KEEPERS (pp. 202–205)

Material on the Bachs is from *Johann Sebastian Bach* by Christoph Wolff; on the Beethovens from *Beethoven: Biography of a Genius* by George R. Marek. The Chaplin brothers' bond is discussed in *Chaplin* by David Robinson; also in *Charles Chaplin: My Autobiography.* John Warhola's role in his younger brother's life was mentioned in "John Warhola, Brother of Andy Warhol, Dies at 85" by William Grimes (*New York Times,* December 28, 2010). Richard Rhodes recounts his harrowing childhood in *A Hole in the World.* The Hagel brothers' heroism is briefly (and modestly) described in *America: Our Next Chapter* by Chuck Hagel. Material on the Whitman brothers is drawn from *Walt Whitman: A Life* by Justin Kaplan, as well as from *Now the Drum of War* by Robert Roper and *Walt Whitman's America* by David S. Reynolds.

SPECIAL NEEDS (pp. 218–220)

Jeanne Safer's quote on being the sibling of a child with special needs is taken from Chapter 7 of her book *The Normal One: Life with a Difficult or Damaged Sibling*. For the story of the Collyer brothers, I am indebted to *Ghosty Men*, in which Franz Lidz digs his way through the Collyer legend. Although I don't refer to them in this book, two memoirs about growing up with a disabled sibling provided provocation and illumination: Jay Neugeboren's *Imagining Robert* and Karl Taro Greenfeld's *Boy Alone*.

TO KEEP OR NOT TO KEEP (pp. 225–232)

The strange case of Herbert and George Silver is taken largely from "Brother Dead for Months . . . in the Next Room" by Bob Joliffe (*Bournemouth Echo*, February 4, 2004). Michael W. Kauffman tells the story of John Atzerodt turning in his brother in *American Brutus*. The Woolf brothers' dinner-table colloquy is recounted in *Sowing*, the first volume of Leonard Woolf's autobiography.

For the story of the Kaczynski brothers, I am especially indebted to "Missing Parts," David Kaczynski's haunting, revealing essay in *Brothers: 26 Stories of Love and Rivalry*, edited by Andrew Blauner. I also leaned heavily on the *New York Times*, particularly "From a Child of Promise to the Unabom Suspect" by Robert D. McFadden (May 26, 1996); "The Tortured Genius of Theodore Kaczynski" by David Johnston and Janny Scott (May 26, 1996); "Heart of Unabom Trial Is Tale of Two Brothers" by William Glaberson (January 5, 1998); and "Making the Death Penalty a Personal Thing" by William Glaberson (October 18, 2004). I was also helped by "I Don't Want to Live Long," an interview with Ted Kaczynski by Stephen J. Dubner (*Time*, October 18, 1999) and by "Harvard and the Making of the Unabomber" by Alston Chase (*The Atlantic*, June, 2000).

For details on the Bulger brothers, I relied most heavily on *Black Mass: The Irish Mob, the FBI, and a Devil's Deal* by Dick Lehr and Gerard O'Neill, the *Boston Globe* reporters who broke the extraordinary story of the Whitey Bulger/FBI alliance. I also made use of *The Brothers Bulger: How They Terrorized and Corrupted Boston for a Quarter Century* by Howie Carr; *Brutal: The Untold Story of My Life Inside Whitey Bulger's Irish Mob* by Kevin Weeks and Phyllis Karas; and *While the Music Lasts: My Life in Politics*, by William M. Bulger. For details of Bulger's 2003 testimony to the House Committee on Government Reform, I turned to "Grilled by US Panel, Bulger Says He Did Not Aid Brother" by Shelley Murphy (*Boston Globe*, June 20, 2003), and on the transcript of his testimony, which can be found in *The Next Step in the Investigation of the Use of Informants by the Department of Justice: The Testimony of William Bulger: Hearing Before the Committee on Government Reform, House of Representatives, One Hundred Eighth Congress, First Session, June 19, 2003, serial No. 108-41* (http://www.gpo.gov/congress/house http://www.house.gov/reform). For details of Whitey's capture, I turned to the comprehensive reporting in the *Boston Globe*, particularly "Bulger Ordered Home" by Peter Schworm and Shelley Murphy (June 24, 2011) and "Ever the Wiseguy, and Sharp as Tack" by Kevin Cullen (June 25, 2011). I was also helped by "F.B.I. Manhunt for Mob Legend Ends After Tip on Companion" by Adam Nagourney and Abby Goodnough (*New York Times,* June 24, 2011). For details on John Bulger, see "John Bulger gets Six Months" by Shelley Murphy (*Boston Globe,* September 4, 2003).

KEEPER OR KEPT (pp. 241–246)

My discussion of the Joyces is drawn primarily from *My Brother's Keeper: James Joyce's Early Years* by Stanislaus Joyce and *James Joyce* by Richard Ellmann; also from *Selected Letters of James Joyce,* edited by Richard Ellmann, and "James and Stanislaus Joyce: A Jungian Speculation," by Jean Kimball, in *Blood Brothers: Siblings as Writers.* Leon Edel's quote on "the martyred siblings of literary history" can be found in Kimball's essay.

CHAPTER EIGHT

THE MARXES

"The Marx Brothers never let facts get in the way of a good story," begins Hector Arce's 1979 biography, *Groucho.* Many of the key stories on the Marx canon come in several variations, depending on who's doing the telling. Both the brothers and their biographers disagree on everything from whether Minnie pulled Groucho from school in the sixth grade or the seventh to whether Gummo was named for his habit of wearing gumshoes (rubbers) or for his habit of sneaking up on people like a gumshoe (detective). Where there is disagreement, I have gone with the source that seems the most trustworthy.

For the biographical framework of the Marx brother's lives, I relied heavily on three books: Hector Arce's pioneering biography, *Groucho;* Stefan Kanfer's comprehensive and astute *Groucho: The Life and Times of Julius Henry Marx*; and Simon Louvish's high-spirited collective biography *Monkey Business: The Lives and Legends of The Marx Brothers*. I also consulted Kyle Chrichton's 1950 biography *The Marx Brothers*, which provides a thorough if not entirely accurate examination of the brothers' early years, and Joe Adamson's *Groucho, Harpo, Chico and Sometimes Zeppo*, a combination biography, filmography, and appreciation that pulls off the often-attempted, rarely achieved feat of writing about the Marxes with Marxian panache.

I also borrowed from *The Marx Bros. Scrapbook*, a collection of photographs and interviews of Groucho, Gummo, Zeppo, and several of the writers and directors who worked on their films. Assembled by Richard J. Anobile, the book provides not only a wealth of stories—some familiar, some not—but also, because the interviews are unedited and unexpurgated, an unfiltered view of Groucho in his later years. (One can see why Groucho, although credited as coauthor, sued—unsuccessfully—to keep this book from being published.) Charlotte Chandler's *Hello, I Must Be Going* is another compendium of invaluable (and, apparently, unedited) interviews with an elderly Groucho and his friends and acolytes. (See also Chandler's March 1974 *Playboy* interview of Groucho.) My account of Groucho's last years relies on Steve Stoliar's *Raised Eyebrows: My Years Inside Groucho's House*, a fly-on-the-wall view of Groucho's chaotic ménage written by a young fan hired to be Groucho's archivist. My description of Harpo and Susan's party for Groucho and his third wife owes everything to Ben Hecht's description of that event in his memoir, *A Child of the Century*.

Several books written (more or less) by the brothers themselves were indispensable. Many of the Harpo stories I cite can be found in *Harpo Speaks!*, an autobiography written with Rowland Barber. I also consulted Groucho's numerous works, including his memoir *Groucho and Me* and *The Groucho Letters: Letters from and to Groucho Marx*. (Groucho's best writing can be found in his letters, in which he was far less circumspect than in his memoirs.)

I also relied heavily on memoirs by Marxian offspring. In *Growing Up with Chico*, Maxine Marx provides an affectionate but clear-eyed look at her father and her uncles; *My Life with Groucho* and *Son of Groucho*, both by Arthur Marx, offer unvarnished views of both father and son. *Love, Groucho: Letters from Groucho Marx to His Daughter Miriam*, edited by Miriam Marx Allen, makes for hilarious, poignant, and occasionally painful reading. I also benefited from Bill Marx's cheery *Son of Harpo Speaks*.

ORIGINS (pp. 284–286)

My discussion of the Rothschilds is drawn from Frederic Morton's witty biography *The Rothschilds*, as well as from *The House of Rothschild: Money's Prophets, 1798–1848*, the first-volume of Niall Ferguson's two-volume biography. For information on the rise of the Lehmann brothers I am grateful to *The Last of the Imperious Rich: Lehman Brothers, 1844–2008* by Peter Chapman. I got my information on the Nicholas brothers from "Fayard Nicholas, Groundbreaking Hoofer, Dies at 91," an Associated Press obituary that ran in the *New York Times* on January 26, 2006. For the Mayos, I owe everything to *The Doctors Mayo* by Helen Clapesattle. Material on the Wrights was mined from *The Wright Brothers: A Biography* by Fred C. Kelly; *Miracle at Kitty Hawk: The Letters of Wilbur & Orville Wright*, edited by Fred C. Kelly; and *Wilbur and Orville* by Fred Howard. I am especially indebted to James Tobin's *To Conquer the Air: The Wright Brothers and the Great Race for Flight*, which not only provides much useful detail but embeds the brothers in the larger history of aviation's early days with a brio that made this reader feel as if he were airborne himself.

CONTRASTS (pp. 298–303, 309–311)

The Howe brothers' story is told in *The Howe Brothers and the American Revolution* by Ira D. Gruber. For the Montgolfier brothers, I relied on their Wikipedia entry. Details on the Disney brothers are from Neal Gabler's *Walt Disney: The Triumph of the American Imagination*. My discussion of the Gershwins borrows from *Gershwin: His Life & Music* by Charles Schwartz; *Fascinating Rhythm: The Collaboration of George and Ira Gershwin* by Deena Rosenberg; and *The Gershwin Years: George and Ira* by Edward Jablonski and Lawrence D. Stewart. For the Grimms, I consulted *The Brothers Grimm* by Jack Zipes, as well as the biographical essay by Maria Tatar in *The Annotated Brothers Grimm* (edited by Tatar). For the Goncourts, I drew on *Pages from the Goncourt Journals* (edited, translated, and with a helpful introduction by Robert Baldick). My description of the James brothers is taken almost entirely from T. J. Stiles's edifying, electrifying *Jesse James: Last Rebel of the Civil War*. John Newman Edwards's description of the brothers is contained in "A Terrible Quintette," his 1873 essay.

FRICTION (pp. 316–320)

Material on the tennis-playing Bryans is from "Togetherness" by Jon Wertheim (*Sports Illustrated*, April 26, 2010) and from "Deuce" by Eric Konigsberg (*New York Times Magazine*, August 30, 2009). My description of the Everlys owes everything to *The Everly Brothers: Walk Right Back* by Roger White.

CHAPTER TEN

THE THOREAUS

For biographical details I relied heavily on Walter Harding's indispensable *The Days of Henry Thoreau*. I also made use of Henry Seidel Canby's idiosyncratic and intuitive *Thoreau*. For sheer intellectual exhilaration, I turned again and again to Robert D. Richardson Jr.'s *Henry Thoreau: A Life of the Mind*; for psychological insight to Richard Lebeaux's two-volume biography, *Young Man Thoreau* and *Thoreau's Seasons*, which offers the most thorough and provocative exploration of John and Henry's complicated bond. I was also helped by Frank B. Sanborn's *Henry David Thoreau*, an informal biography written by a young friend of Thoreau's who was a frequent dinner guest at the Thoreau home during Henry's last years. *Thoreau, The Poet-Naturalist: With Memorial Verses*, an affectionate, idiosyncratic memoir written by Thoreau's neighbor and hiking partner, William Ellery Channing, provides almost as much insight into its author as into its purported subject. I found many details about Thoreau as a young man in "Henry Thoreau as Remembered by a Young Friend," an essay by Edward Emerson, whose childhood was spent largely in Thoreau's company. "Thoreau," an essay by Edward's father, Ralph Waldo Emerson, was also of help. Thoreau's essential flavor comes through most thoroughly, of course, in his own work, especially in the two million words of his journal; I used the two-volume Dover edition. Where I have quoted from his letters, I relied on *The Correspondence of Henry David Thoreau*, edited by Walter Harding and Carl Bode. Where I have quoted from his poems, I used The Library of America's *Thoreau: Collected Essays and Poems*.

My description of the Concord Academy under the Thoreaus owes much to "The Diary of Thoreau's 'Gentle Boy,'" an essay by Clayton Hoagland in *The New England Quarterly* (vol. 28, no. 4, December 1955, pp. 473–89), which examines the journal of Edmund Sewall, a Concord Academy student and the younger brother of Ellen Sewall. My understanding of the Thoreau-Emerson relationship was enriched by *Ralph Waldo Emerson: Days of Encounter* by John McAleer; *Emerson Among the Eccentrics* by Carlos Baker (particularly Chapter 10, "Thoreau"); *Emerson: The Mind on Fire*, another riveting intellectual biography by Robert D. Richardson Jr.; and Robert Sattelmeyer's "Thoreau and Emerson," one of many insightful essays in *The Cambridge Companion to Henry David Thoreau* (edited by Joel Myerson). For details of the Thoreaus' river trip, I am indebted to Linck C. Johnson's historical introduction to *The Illustrated A Week on the Concord and Merrimack Rivers*. Chapters 2 and 3 of David M. Robinson's *Natural Life:*

Thoreau's Worldly Transcendentalism, which discuss John's death and the writing of *A Week*, were also helpful. I consulted the brief discussion of Thoreau in *Louisa May Alcott* by Martha Saxton, as well as the description of Alcott and Thoreau in *American Bloomsbury*, Susan Cheever's portrait of nineteenth-century literary Concord. I also enjoyed the contrarian portrait of Thoreau offered by Robert Sullivan in *The Thoreau You Don't Know*.

SIBLING LOSS (pp. 354–356)

Hallmark's sibling bereavement cards and the childhood sibling-loss study were mentioned in *The Empty Room: Surviving the Loss of a Brother or Sister at Any Age* by Elizabeth DeVita-Raeburn. Information on the Barries comes from *Hide-and-Seek with Angels: A Life of J. M. Barrie* by Lisa Chaney; also from *Margaret Ogilvy*, J. M. Barrie's memoir of his mother. Mary Lincoln's mourning is described by Jean H. Baker in *Mary Todd Lincoln*. I found the Henry James quote about his late brother in the last chapter of *The Jameses* by R. W. B. Lewis.

LOSS: EFFECTS (pp. 367–372)

Erich Lindemann's landmark study, "Symptomatology and Management of Acute Grief," was published in *The American Journal of Psychiatry*, vol. 101, 1944 (pp. 141–48). Albert C. Cain's "Children's Disturbed Reactions to the Death of a Sibling" was published in *The American Journal of Orthopsychiatry*, vol. 34, no. 4, July 1964 (pp. 741–52). The death of Jack Cash is discussed by Johnny Cash in his autobiography, *Cash* (with Patrick Carr), and by Michael Streissguth in *Johnny Cash: The Biography*. My account of Salvador Dali's childhood is derived from *The Persistence of Memory: A Biography of Dali* by Meredith Etherington-Smith and from *The Secret Life of Salvador Dali*, the artist's insouciant autobiography. Joshua Fleck and his blanket are described in "A Singular Pain: When Death Cuts the Bond of Twins" by Neela Banerjee (*New York Times*, March 1, 2007). Arnaz Battle and his tattoo are cited in "Tale of My Tattoo" (*Sports Illustrated*, November 22, 2004). Information on the Presley twins is from *Last Train to Memphis: The Rise of Elvis Presley* by Peter Guralnick. For details on Bill Tilden, I turned to Frank Deford's *Big Bill Tilden*; also *A Terrible Splendor* by Marshall Jon Fisher. Chris Weir's decision to complete his brother's army service is the subject of "A Brother's Unfinished Business" by Lauren Gregory (*Chattanooga Times Free Press*, September 28, 2008). The unconventional Olmsted marriage is discussed by Witold Rybczynski in *A Clearing in the Distance*, his biography of the architect. The effect on Jerry West of his older brother's death is described in *Jerry West: The Life and Legend of a Basketball Icon* by Roland Lazenby; also in "Basketball Was the Easy Part" by Gary Smith (*Sports Illustrated*, October 24, 2011). The story of the Nixon brothers comes from *Richard Nixon: The Shaping of His Character*, a fascinating psychobiography by Fawn M. Brodie, and from *Nixonland*, an exhilarating cultural biography by Rick Perlstein. Art Spiegelman's story is taken from Part II of his graphic novel *Maus: A Survivor's Tale*. John F. Kennedy's "shadow boxing" quote is from Collier and Horowitz, *The Kennedys* (Part 2, Chapter 1). Hitler's sibling losses are discussed in Chapter 10, "Siblings as Survivors: Bonds Beyond the Grave" (which also contains a good general discussion of sibling loss) in *The Sibling Bond* by Bank and Kahn.

LOSS AND CREATIVITY (pp. 375–377)

George H. Pollock discusses the effect on J. M. Barrie of his brother's death in his essay "On Siblings, Childhood Sibling Loss, and Creativity," from *Psychoanalytic Studies of Biography* (edited by George Moraitis and George H. Pollock). The Wordsworth quote ("I shall . . . never be at peace") is from Chapter 12 of *Wordsworth: A Life* by Juliet Barker. The story of Samuel and Henry Clemens is taken from *Mark Twain: A Life* by Ron Powers and *The Autobiography of Mark Twain*. For information on Jack Kerouac, I am indebted to *Kerouac*, Ann Charters's seminal biography; also to *Memory Babe: A Critical Biography of Jack Kerouac* by Gerald Nicosia. For further reading, I recommend two remarkable memoirs about fraternal loss: *Shot in the Heart* by Mikal Gilmore and *In My Brother's Shadow* by Uwe Timm. Thomas Wolfe's short story "The Lost Boy," based on the death of his older brother Grover when Wolfe was four, is no less memorable.

LOSS AND BIRTH ORDER (pp. 385–388)

John F. Kennedy's "It was like being drafted" quote is from Chapter 39 of Goodwin's *The Fitzgeralds and the Kennedys*; the Choate headmaster's quote is from Collier and Horowitz's *The Kennedys* (Part 2, Chapter 1); JFK's quote on the family political hierarchy is from "Social Causes Defined Kennedy Even at the End of a 46-Year Career in the Senate" by John M. Broder (*New York Times*, August 26, 2009). Ted Kennedy's "fallen standard" quote can be found in Collier and Horowitz's *The Kennedys* (Part 4, Chapter 2). The story of the silver cigarette box is from "Ted" by Richard Lacayo (*Time*, September 7, 2009).

GENERAL

Of the numerous books I found helpful but which I did not make direct use of in *Brothers*, I would like to mention a few. I learned about how sibling relationships have changed over the centuries from *Siblings: Brothers & Sisters in American History* by C. Dallett Hemphill and from *We Grew Up Together: Brothers and Sisters in Nineteenth-Century America* by Annette Atkins. *Brothers*, a collection of essays and photographs assembled by the editors of Esquire, provided visual and literary inspiration. Although I limited my scope in *Brothers* to brothers, several books about sisters were useful in helping me formulate my thoughts, especially *Sisters* by Elizabeth Fishel and *You Were Always Mom's Favorite!* by Deborah Tannen.

I have changed the names of three people in this book. Ricky Ratters, Freddie Miller, and Mr. Lammons are pseudonyms.

Index